Waiting for the Millennium

Studies in International Relations
Charles W. Kegley, Jr., and Donald J. Puchala
Series Editors

Waiting for
the Millennium

The United Nations and the
Future of World Order

■

by J. Martin Rochester

University of South Carolina Press

Published in Columbia, South Carolina, by the
University of South Carolina Press

Manufactured in the United States of America

Library of Congress Cataloging-in-Publication Data
Rochester, J. Martin
    Waiting for the millennium : the United Nations and the future of
world order / by J. Martin Rochester.
        p.   cm. — (Studies in international relations)
    Includes bibliographical references and index.
    ISBN 0–87249–882–4 (hardcover : acid-free paper)
        1. United Nations.   2. International relations.   I. Title.
II. Series: Studies in international relations (Columbia, S.C.)
JX1977.R535   1993
    327.1'72–dc20   92–45145

To my brother Stuart,

who was born into this

world with me in 1945,

at the end of one era and

the beginning of another.

War is on its last legs; and a universal peace is as sure as is the prevalence of civilization over barbarism. . . . The question for us is only how soon?

—Ralph Waldo Emerson, 1849

Peace is no new theme.

—George C. Beckwith, *The Peace Manual*, 1868

The mind is slow in unlearning what it has been long in learning.

—Seneca, *Ad Lucilium*, 78, A.D. 50

Things fall apart; the centre cannot hold;
Mere anarchy is loosed upon the world.

—W. B. Yeats, "The Second Coming," 1922

Contents

Editors' Preface

The pace of global change has accelerated greatly in the last decades of the twentieth century, and new problems occurring under novel conditions are challenging the academic study of International Relations. There is today a renaissance in scholarship directed toward enhancing our understanding of world politics, global economics, and foreign policy. To examine the transformed structure of the international system and the expanded agenda of global affairs, researchers are introducing new concepts, theories, and analytic modes. Knowledge is expanding rapidly.

Our goal in this series of books is to record the findings of recent innovative research in International Relations, and make these readily available to a broader readership of professionals and students. Contributors to the series are leading scholars who are expert in particular subfields of the discipline. Their contributions represent the most recent work located at the discipline's research frontiers. Topics, subjects, approaches, methods, and analytical techniques vary from volume to volume in the series, as each book is intended as an original contribution in the broadest sense. Common to all volumes, however, are careful research and the excitement of new discovery.

Waiting for the Millennium: The United Nations and the Future of World Order by J. Martin Rochester is a timely contribution to the current debate over continuity and change in international affairs. Much has been said about the arrival of a "new world order" in the post-Cost War era as the twentieth century draws to a close. However, the shape of this emergent global polity remains uncertain. Recalling Voltaire's remark about the Holy Roman Empire as being "neither holy nor Roman nor an empire," the new world order may well prove to be a misnomer. While some observers have proclaimed the "end of history" or have argued that the Westphalian state system is being so fundamentally transformed that a new "post-international politics" paradigm is called for, others see the contemporary international system as representing simply a return to pre-1945 multipolarity, bearing more than a faint resemblance to the state of the world on the eve of World War I. While some see greater "worldliness," others see the forces of nationalism and regionalism overtaking globalism. And while some take note of "the long peace" and speculate about greater order in international affairs, others worry about a "new world disorder." Indeed, despite the growing visibility of the United Nations since the late 1980s and the growing demands made upon it in peacekeeping and other areas, there remains considerable skepticism among both academics and practitioners regarding the emergence of a new world order and the potential role of the UN as a centerpiece. In the scholarly literature, even with the rise of "the new institutionalism," one finds far greater attention still being given to subglobal multilateralism and regimes than to global organizations.

In this volume Rochester examines what he considers to be the most challenging puzzle of our time: namely, that the need for coordinated problem-solving on a global scale in matters of security, economics, and ecology is greater than at any point in history, precisely at the same moment that central guidance mechanisms appear less feasible than in previous eras due to recent structural changes in the international system. Avoiding the twin traps of "bad idealism" and "bad realism"—in his words, "relying on empirical inquiry rather than merely normative belief or faith"—he carefully explores the constraints and opportunities currently surrounding global institution-building and offers a way out of this paradox that he believes could lead to greater world order through United Nations reform. In parts 1 and 2 the author discusses a variety of theoretical issues related to the dynamics of international institution-building, develops a model of what a desirable and achievable world order might look like, and investigates the extent to which the real world at present conforms to the requirements of the model. In part 3 he lays out the implications of the previous analysis for UN reform, first focusing on the workings of the UN and identifying the major sources of institutional failure, then reviewing past attempts at reform and evaluating recent proposals, and finally offering a set of prescriptions for institutional change. In a concluding chapter Rochester considers global institution-building in the context of longer-term empirical and normative issues. *Waiting for the Millennium* ambitiously attempts to provide a basis for reviving the theory and practice of international organization at a time when global and formal approaches to governance among nations continue to be called into question.

Charles W. Kegley, Jr., and Donald J. Puchala

Preface

I began this project in early 1987, at a time when the United Nations was still being labeled by many as "dangerous" and "irrelevant" and when one could still find common references to the Soviet Union as the "evil empire." The thought of writing a book reflecting on the prospects of the UN and world order struck many of my colleagues at that moment in history as a rather farfetched pursuit.

During the course of the project (1989–1990), an interlude occurred which has variously been called the most revolutionary of the past 50 or 500 years. The last two months of 1989 saw: the dismantling of the Berlin Wall and the collapse of Stalinist regimes in Eastern Europe; the first visit by an Eastern bloc minister to NATO headquarters in Brussels (by Soviet Foreign Minister Shevardnadze, who used his trip also as an occasion to sign a commercial accord with the European Community and to proclaim Moscow's desire to become part of "a common European house"); the Red Army Band and Chorus appearance at an official gala in Washington while leading President Bush and other dignitaries in a stirring rendition of "God Bless America" as a grand finale; and other anecdotal as well as empirical evidence of change. In addition to the movement toward German reunification and the movement of Eastern European states out of the Soviet orbit and toward more open, market-oriented societies, 1989 also witnessed a general worldwide trend toward democratization (the Tiananmen massacre in China aside) and a "breaking out of peace," reflected in the winding down of several regional conflicts in Latin America, Asia, the Middle East, and Africa along with the leveling off of global military spending. The UN suddenly found itself being called upon to play an increasing role in a "new world order," thrust as a peacekeeper into conflicts from Kampuchea to Nicaragua. The UN gained its highest visibility in decades in 1990, as it provided a collective security function in response to the first "post-Cold War crisis" in the Persian Gulf. A book project that in 1987 had invited a degree of criticism as being too far removed from reality subsequently risked being viewed as mundane; the suggestion that the UN had some relevance to international governance concerns somehow seemed less profound in the 1990s than in the 1980s.

Still more startling developments have followed the Gulf War, notably the complete breakup of the Soviet Union. Although I have adjusted my thinking somewhat in reaction to the swirl of events since the late 1980s that few if any students of international relations can claim to have predicted, the basic thrust of my research has remained intact and indeed is more relevant than ever. The future of the UN and world order will be shaped not so much by specific events as by the kinds of larger conditions that are the subject of this book. There continues to be a basis for both optimism and pessimism. If it was premature to pronounce the death of the UN in the 1980s (as many had also done previously), it was likewise premature to become euphoric about the UN's future at the outset of the 1990s; both "bad realism" and "bad idealism," to borrow Giovanni Sartori's phrases, are to be resisted.

I am most grateful for the support of the United States Institute of Peace, the Weldon Spring Fund and the Center for International Studies of the University of Missouri-St. Louis, and the Lentz Peace Research Laboratory. The opinions, findings, and conclusions or recommendations expressed in this work are those of the author and do not reflect the views of the United States Institute of Peace or other funding agencies. Thanks go to Bob Baumann, John Kalinowski, Anita Cleaver, and Mary Hines for their help in the preparation of the manuscript. A special debt of gratitude must go to the members of my family, who had to cope with my mood swings as newspaper headlines over the past couple of years trumpeted shifting East-West and other winds of change in international affairs and made life difficult for anyone attempting to get a firm handle on reality.

Waiting for the Millennium

PART 1

Reviving the Theory and Practice of Global Organization

1

The United Nations and the Global Problematique: From Bad Idealism to Bad Realism

This is a book about international organization, particularly the search for global organization. No doubt many would question the worth and wisdom of doing such a study. As Mark Twain put it, "faith is believin' in what you know ain't true." In the late twentieth century, one would seemingly have to rely upon faith to believe that international organizations—especially those at the global level—deserve to be taken seriously by either practitioners or scholars as *critical* elements of world politics. The history of the United Nations system can be read as the steady erosion of the initial euphoria that accompanied its creation out of the ashes of World War II, with periods of "decline" and "crisis" punctuated by short-term revival and bursts of renewed hope only to be succeeded by another round of failure and ever-compounding cynicism.

This pattern can be traced very easily. While the founders of the UN certainly had doubts about its viability, there was sufficient optimism in 1945 to warrant President Truman's bombastic statement opening the San Francisco Conference expressing the expectation that the delegates were about to create "machinery which will make future peace not only possible, but certain."[1] Truman added at the conclusion of the conference that "I know I speak for every one of you when I say that the United Nations will remain united."[2] Less than a decade later a leading architect of the UN Charter declared that "the UN is in a state of coma, and there isn't much time left to revive it."[3] After successes in the Suez and elsewhere momentarily had resuscitated the UN during the Hammarskjold era, the organization was once again "in crisis" by the 1960s.[4] Following the paralysis of the Vietnam

3

decade the UN experienced a rebirth in the early seventies, based largely on its high-profile intervention in the 1973 Arab-Israeli conflict, leading one of its harshest critics—U.S. Secretary of State Henry Kissinger—to offer guarded praise and optimism about the future role of the organization:

> I must say that the United Nations played a more effective role in this crisis than could have been deduced from my theoretical statements as a professor. . . . It proved to be . . . the most effective way by which the settlement could be achieved. . . . So we believe that the United Nations played a very useful role, and we will take very serious account of that in the solution of other problems.[5]

By the 1980s, UN fortunes had taken another turn, falling precipitously to the point where Americans were labeling the organization "a dangerous place"[6] and even its most fervent supporters lamented it was becoming an "irrelevant" place. In the words of a former UN Secretary-General:

> The fact is plain. The United Nations has fallen upon hard days. It goes through its paces in a workaday routine that is increasingly ignored or condemned and that threatens to become increasingly irrelevant in the real world. . . . To some, its future is at best obscure.[7]

With history as a guide, one should have expected that such prognoses regarding the UN's imminent demise were premature and that the UN was capable of at least partial recovery. Indeed, by the late 1980s there was striking evidence of a revival in the making, manifested by a rediscovery of the organization's peacekeeping capabilities in hotspots in Africa, Asia and the Middle East, related to dramatic improvements in East-West relations and the dissipation of the Cold War. In the early 1990s, UN resolutions supported an economic embargo and authorized the use of armed force by an American-led multinational force to punish Iraq for its invasion of Kuwait (taken under the collective security provisions of the Charter). These resolutions gave the organization more visibility than it had enjoyed in memory and raised the prospect of the UN serving as the centerpiece of a "new world order" in the post-Cold War era. Newspaper headlines and editorials trumpeted the UN's comeback:

> In a wondrous sea-change, the United Nations has silenced
> most of its detractors. A body once scorned as a dithering talk-
> shop has now mobilized impressively to punish Iraq's
> aggressions in the Persian Gulf. Elsewhere, from Afghanistan
> to Namibia, from Cambodia to Central America, the UN has
> also offered a glimpse of . . . hopes for a new world order to
> resolve conflicts by multilateral diplomacy and collective
> security.[8]

After the dust has settled from the Iraqi conflict, it is possible
the UN will emerge with an enhanced status and growth opportunities unequaled in its history. However, this would be too
neat and, many would argue, too sanguine an analysis of the
current state of affairs. After all, in the peace and security area
the UN would appear to have had nowhere to go but upward.
The institution had reached a nadir by the mid-1980s, with one
study finding only 32 percent of "all disputes involving military
operations and fighting" being referred to the UN during that
decade—"the lowest share in the history of the organization."[9]
In the economic arena, the Bretton Woods postwar economic order, the foundation of which has been GATT and related UN
agencies, is widely recognized as having become unravelled and
threatened with collapse, reflected in one writer's observation
that "the case for free trade is currently more in doubt than at
any time since the 1817 publication of Ricardo's *Principles of Political Economy*."[10] In environmental and other more technical issue-areas, the problems are mounting at the same time that
institutional capabilities seem to be diminishing, with the UN attempting to survive a financial crisis that finds the membership
over $500 million in arrears and the administrative staff reduced
by almost 15 percent. Most recently, the UN's prospects once
more have been shaken by the chaotic developments in what
was once the Soviet Union. Whether the UN will be able to
move beyond the past cycle of ups and downs and chart a more
steady course in the future is a question answerable not by judging the fallout from any single episode such as the Iraqi conflict
or the conversion of the USSR into a commonwealth but by in-
quiring into much larger matters having to do with the fundamental requirements for effective global organization.

Just as the future of the UN still seems obscure to many, so
also does the future of international organization as a field of

study, if one defines international organization in conventional terms as referring generally to "a formal arrangement transcending national boundaries that provides for the establishment of institutional machinery to facilitate cooperation among members in the security, economic, social, or related fields."[11] The malaise surrounding the "world of actual international organizations" over the years has been accompanied by the increased disengagement of international organization scholars from the study of those organizations.[12] As two writers characterize the recent relationship between theory and practice in the international organization field, "the leading doctors have become biochemists and have stopped treating and in most cases even seeing patients."[13] Instead of studying multilateral institutions, scholars are studying the institution of multilateralism (as John Ruggie has put it, "institutionalized collective behavior").[14] In other words, the emphasis is on the analysis of "recognized patterns . . . around which expectations converge," which "may or may not be accompanied by explicit organizational arrangements,"[15] i.e. regimes. Regimes constitute widely accepted norms, rules, procedures, or other forms of cooperation—"governing arrangements"[16]—that permit the international community to function and cope with various concerns in the absence of a world government. While this new focus of international organization scholarship is generally felt to represent a healthy maturation of the field away from earlier sterile preoccupation with legal-formal aspects of international affairs toward consideration of broader phenomena, it has rendered the field almost indistinguishable from the rest of the international relations discipline.[17] Moreover, largely unnoticed or unsaid, the deprecation of international *organizations* that is a signature trait of the regime literature reflects a pervasive pessimism toward the prospects of international institution-building that far exceeds earlier skepticism in the postwar era and is perhaps unprecedented in this century.

Such skepticism does not seem entirely justified. If it is obvious that international organizations have experienced serious problems, it is also obvious that it is hard to envision a future for humanity without international organization of some sort. Pollyanish as this statement sounds, it is grounded in what is plainly evident. When one looks beyond present epiphenomena and takes a longer-term perspective, the following simple observations can be made: (1) the trend is unmistakably in the direction of international organizational growth, with one recent study documenting the proliferation of international governmental organizations (IGOs) and counting over 1,000 such entities in the contemporary global system;[18] (2) the "expectation of international organization, the habit of organizing, the taking-for-granted of international bodies . . . are permanent results of the movement" that began almost from scratch a century or so ago;[19] and (3) the United Nations—primitive, flawed, and fragile as it is—represents the latest, most ambitious stage in the historic process of global institution-building.[20]

There are two still simpler observations about the global condition that cannot escape attention today. A few may dispute these facts of international life, but the supporting evidence is overwhelming and does not require lengthy recitation here. On the one hand, notwithstanding a rising tide of transnational activity, elites and attentive publics almost universally remain wedded to the traditional state system culture, with its emphasis on nationalism, national interests, and sovereignty; and it strains human mental capacities to imagine the international organization movement or any other development undermining this condition anytime soon.[21] On the other hand, given technological imperatives that are inexorably producing reduced travel, communications, and other distances between states and concomitantly increased interdependence in terms of "sensitivity" and "vulnerability,"[22] it is equally mindboggling to imagine these same elites and publics—save for the most isolationist-oriented—experiencing in the foreseeable future any diminution in their felt need for improved, more elaborate ways to manage interstate relations. Between these two fundamental realities of the nuclear age lies the potential for unparalleled conflict as well as unparalleled cooperation.

These thoughts, of course, are not new or profound. They have been uttered so often in one manner or another as to border on cliché, which is perhaps why their implications have been so blithely ignored of late and, hence, deserve more careful scrutiny. On the surface at least, one can find as many integrative forces at work in the contemporary international system as disintegrative ones.[23] To the extent that the disintegrative forces currently operating in the international system contribute to a growing sense of chaos and crisis in the international community, they may provide the very impetus needed for forging a consensus among national governments and their constituencies behind the search for new means of international governance. While it is true that "necessities [in themselves] do not create possibilities,"[24] one should also avoid another form of wishful thinking, namely rationalizing that because some change is thought impossible, it is thereby not needed. Determination of what is both necessary and possible with regard to international governance involves complicated empirical and normative judgments that often get blurred. The biggest puzzle of our time is how it is that the need for coordinated problem-solving on a global scale—in matters of security, economics, and ecology—is arguably greater than ever before, at the same moment when the resources committed to global institutions are dwindling and "central guidance" mechanisms seem less feasible in some respects than in previous historical periods.

The purpose of this study is to explore the systematic constraints as well as opportunities surrounding the growth potential of the United Nations as one component of the quest for world order in the late twentieth century, relying on empirical inquiry rather than merely normative belief or faith. As such, the author entertains an *institutionalist* and *globalist* approach to international order, subjecting to investigation the twin propositions that (1) the development of formal intergovernmental organizations is at least as relevant to concerns about order (and, by implication, peaceful change) as the development of less formal modes of interstate cooperation, even though not all organizational arrangements are equally benign in this regard, and (2) any efforts at international institution-building must focus to some extent on the global level, even though many problems can be treated as regional or bilateral in scope and might be usefully addressed through international organizations operating at those levels or having only limited membership participation. These ideas, once part of the orthodoxy of the international organization field, have sounded almost heretical in recent times.

Approaches to World Order:
From Maximalism to Minimalism

The major problematique of the international relations field over the years has been how to minimize conflict and maximize cooperation, thereby maintaining a semblance of order in a decentralized system of sovereign states. A variety of approaches to world order have been suggested — the enlightened management of power (hegemony, balance, or concert), the development of formal rules (international law), the development of formal machinery (international organization), and others. Although these three approaches are not mutually exclusive, they generally have been considered distinct in nature. As noted above, there is some question today whether international organizations are any longer relevant enough to the world order problematique to merit full inclusion in the panoply of approaches worthy of scholarly research. It can be argued, though, that this skepticism goes beyond international organization, extending to international law and, indeed, to the very concept of world order.

Some observers of the contemporary scene have commented:

> Perhaps not since the birth of the modern state system, usually associated with the Peace of Westphalia in 1648, has the image of international law in the political life of the world seemed so tarnished. This is not . . . because there is "less" law or "more" sovereignty, but because the inability of law to satisfy steadily increasing minimal expectations about the requirements of global order . . . create[s] an impression of "failure," deterioration, and disillusionment. Indeed, given the inability of international law to evolve at a pace comparable to that of increasing interdependence, *doing more* can still seem like *achieving less*.[25]

International organization could easily be substituted for international law in the previous sentence. Even if these authors are overstating the case in suggesting that the current cynicism is unparalleled in the roughly 300 years since Westphalia, it would seem unsurpassed at least in this century, since international relations first emerged as an identifiable academic discipline in the period between the two world wars. As David Fromkin states, "The leaders of civilized opinion in every generation since 1914 . . . have believed that there is an urgent need for world politics to be transformed in such a fundamental way that warfare will be abolished and mankind will never have to go back into the trenches and bomb shelters again."[26] Although Fromkin himself exaggerates the degree of consensus that developed after World War I regarding the necessity for radical system transformation —the League and UN were bold experiments, but hardly aimed at altering the status quo—he properly calls attention to what has been a twentieth-century penchant for thinking in larger, world order terms. That is, until now.

The clarion calls for a new world order reverberating at the outset of the 1990s could not conceal a deep-seated incredulity that had taken hold among students of international relations. If the interwar period—during which the idealist school domi- nated international relations thinking, and international organi- zation enjoyed the status of not so much a subfield as the core of the discipline—could be characterized as maximalist in its view of world order possibilities, then the present era—after a pas- sage through realism to neorealism in the post-World War II years, during which time international organization as a distinct subfield was gradually consigned to the periphery and then to virtual oblivion except in name only—can only be labeled mini- malist.[27] In essence, "bad idealism" has been replaced by "bad realism."[28] Many will object to this portrayal of the intellectual odyssey of international relations scholars in the postwar pe- riod. The more common view is that the current state of the field reflects a long overdue convergence of the idealist and realist paradigms, as the intellectual heirs of the realist tradition have generally come to recognize how nonsecurity issues can com- pete for attention with security issues and that order can coexist with anarchy in the international realm, while the descendants of the idealist tradition have generally come to understand how power and interests underlie order and that order can exist in something less than law and organization.[29] It is said that inter- national politics scholars and international organization scholars have met each other halfway, with a single theoretical frame- work able to accommodate the investigation of a whole range of phenomena from military-strategic concerns of a high politics nature to economic and other concerns of a low politics nature, all of which can feature elements of both conflict and cooperation.[30] Writings combining threads of realist and idealist thought into the twin themes of anarchy and order abound.[31]

Why the observation that order can prevail amidst (and cooperation can occur under) anarchy should be treated seemingly as a profound discovery by the current generation of international relations scholars is puzzling, since such assumptions have informed the problematique of the field from the start and were elaborated upon long ago by Arnold Wolfers, Raymond Aron, Morton Kaplan and Nicholas Katzenbach, Inis Claude, and others.[32] What is even more puzzling, however, is how the present synthesis of realism and idealism can be seen as a rather even-handed exchange of concessions made by those representing the two traditions, when in fact realism has gotten much the better of it. There is, after all, no neoidealism to match neorealism.[33] At most, one can speak of neoliberals and those accused of being neorealists (structural realists) but who refuse to be branded as such or to be labeled in any way.[34] There are also neo-Marxists, post-modernist feminists, and assorted other camps, by their own admission far removed from mainstream thought, "speaking the language of exile dissidence in international studies."[35] Although the international relations field has become far too large and diverse to be captured completely by any one school of thought, neorealism seems increasingly to be setting the terms of much scholarly debate despite its many critics.[36] As the authors of a book that led the way in reconciling realist and idealist ideas have recently admitted, "less has been done with the liberal than the realist half of our attempted synthesis."[37] The contemporary study of international relations can rightly be considered minimalist in terms of world order perspectives, inasmuch as those scholars widely viewed as forward thinkers on the leading edge of knowledge production—neorealists and neoliberals alike—tend to harbor more modest expectations about the prospects for progressive change in human affairs than their classical realist and idealist counterparts of yesteryear.[38]

How else can one interpret the disarmingly understated, underwhelming, cautiously worded conclusion reached at the end of a much-publicized 1985 symposium on "Cooperation Under

Anarchy," acknowledging that "[despite anarchy] as the articles in this symposium have shown, cooperation is sometimes attained"[39]? Even with the rise of realism in the late 1940s and 1950s, serious scholarship could still be found in those days asking questions about the feasibility of developing supranational institutions; in the 1960s, asking questions about the dynamics of political integration at regional and other levels; and in the 1970s, asking questions about the implications of transnational and transgovernmental coalition-building within international organizations.[40] Such studies did not necessarily start with rosy premises or yield optimistic conclusions about the prospects for a new world order, but they at least considered it worth the effort to examine relatively elaborate and advanced forms of collaboration across national boundaries. In the past decade, in contrast, the world order problematique commonly found in the major journals and scholarly literature has been reduced to the most elemental, primitive, and truly cynical of all questions, i.e. how is *any* inter-state cooperation possible?

In Robert Jervis's words, "the basic question posed by the recent work is how self-interested actors can cooperate in the face of anarchy and important conflicting interests."[41] Similarly, Robert Axelrod ponders how "cooperation [can] occur in a world of egoists without central authority."[42] Great pain is taken and great satisfaction apparently derived in demonstrating that cooperation can occur in international affairs. Reviewing Robert Keohane's impressive effort in *After Hegemony* to establish why "it would be a mistake to infer . . . that cooperation is impossible without hegemony,"[43] James Rosenau comments, "Genuinely puzzled, Keohane relentlessly pursues this question in chapter after chapter, through the thickets of rational-choice models, along the path of functional explanations, down the road of bounded rationality, and in and around many dead-ends until the diverse pieces of the puzzle fit together."[44]

No doubt Keohane and others would contend that it is not a matter of being more cynical but rather more scholarly in the pursuit of knowledge relevant to world order concerns. The classic problematique continues to preoccupy scholars but the focus has shifted somewhat from controlling violence to the more mundane matter of managing interdependence. New, more sophisticated perspectives and tools are being utilized; as

Jervis notes, "recent analyses have formalized these problems and analyzed them by means of modern social science techniques."[45] The latest approaches—notably game theory, public goods theory, and microeconomic theory comparing the behavior of states with that of profit-maximizing firms in the free market—bring us back to basics, subjecting such terms as cooperation to much tighter conceptualization and employing more rigorous analysis in seeking to uncover the conditions associated with international cooperation. The general view that informs this enterprise is that the grander theorizing which produced a spate of writings on the UN, regional integration, and transnationalism in successive decades earlier in the postwar period made for a series of false starts that could not withstand reality-testing. In short, it is felt that the newer approaches promise to provide more reliable knowledge and, ultimately, more useful advice for policymakers regarding the promotion of cooperation in international affairs.[46]

Still, one is left with a nagging question whether the recent literature takes us much beyond the insights gained from previous work on the dynamics of "why nations collaborate"[47] and, in particular, whether it is capable of providing insights about how states can move from ad hoc cooperation and the striking of bargains to longer-term institution-building—whether it truly has anything to say about world order. The latter requires not merely theorizing about interstate interactions à la Schelling and other pioneering strategic thinkers (microsystemic phenomena)[48] but theorizing about international system change and development (macrosystemic or systemwide phenomena), a focus currently receiving scant attention other than neorealist and neo-Marxist studies of military-economic trends over the historical course of the state system.

For example, the latest game-theoretic approaches treat "the evolution of cooperation" in the context of bilateral and multilateral diplomacy rather than in the context of system development. Although such studies note that the "shadow of the future" (the anticipation of having to play repeated rounds of a game or several different games with the same actor or actors over time) is an important variable that is subject to "willful modification"—states can foster cooperation through strategies which "lengthen" the shadow—few attempts are made to explore the implications for international institution-building at the systemwide (or, for that matter, subsystem) level.[49] One reason is that a key theoretical argument made in this literature—involving another manipulable variable, the number of players—is that cooperation is best achieved through decomposition whereby only the barest number of relevant actors are brought into the bargaining process from issue to issue.[50]

In game-theoretic terms, global institution-building is dismissed from the start as a game of Deadlock as opposed to Prisoners' Dilemma or some other mixed-motive game. Another, more fundamental reason behind the reluctance to think in larger systemic terms is the tendency to equate global institution-building with the structural transformation of the international system from anarchy to world government. Since it is assumed that "any ultimate escape from international anarchy is unlikely,"[51] it appears whimsical to think beyond "cooperation under anarchy" to international system development. However, the development of the international system could conceivably take a number of different paths somewhere between anarchy and world government, possibilities which could be reasonably discussed without any teleological assumptions necessarily embedded in them.

There would appear to be one major exception to the indictment just presented—the heavy attention that neorealists, neoliberals, and others give to the study of regimes. It is not an exaggeration to say that "indeed, 'regimes' seem now to be everywhere!"[52] As noted at the outset, regime analysts are interested in phenomena which go beyond ad hoc inter-state bargaining and involve patterned collective behavior. It is said that regimes help to institutionalize what otherwise would be merely "atomistic reciprocity."[53] Regime studies discuss the learning of consensual knowledge, the use of issue-linkage strategies, and other integrative or aggregative processes. However, other than the theory of hegemonic stability, which is relatively weak in its treatment of institutions, it is hard to find discussions in the regime literature that tend toward a systemwide perspective in dealing with problems of world order.[54]

Robert Keohane, following upon his study of the dynamics of regime-making in the absence of hegemony, perhaps as much as anyone has called for increased attention to international institutions. However, his functional approach "does not distinguish clearly between institutions and organizations, nor indicate the conditions that lead to the international development of the latter."[55] Moreover, even though he, with Joseph Nye, has urged the adoption of "a systemic conception of international relations" that combines the neorealist focus on "structure" with the liberal focus on "process,"[56] the institution-building implied here is as limited as the authors' conception of institutions is broad. In arguing elsewhere against "global unilateralism," Keohane and Nye seem to advocate instead non-global multilateralism, appearing at best ambivalent about systemwide approaches to institution-building in general and organization-building in particular. On the one hand, echoing game-theoretic notions, they note that although "a crazy quilt of international regimes is likely to arise" without universal approaches, "better some roughness around the edges of international regimes than a vacuum at the center. Poorly coordinated coalitions, working effectively on various issues, are in general preferable to universalistic negotiations permanently deadlocked by a diverse membership."[57] They add "only rarely are universal international organizations likely to provide the world with instruments for collective action."[58] On the other hand, "every effort should be made . . . to allow for the eventual universalization of the regimes."[59]

One has to wonder whether the regime literature is yet another fad that will go the way of earlier bodies of international organization theory which had focused heavily on regional integration, transnationalism, and other concerns of passing interest.[60] There is reason to believe that regimes may have more staying power. Unlike previous turns taken in the international organization field over the course of the postwar era which now seem in retrospect to have been knee-jerk responses to specific events of the day—the establishment of the UN, the creation of the European Economic Community, the oil embargo episode and ensuing energy crisis following on the heels of Vietnam— the interest in regimes is the culmination of the accumulated experiences and reflections of a half-century of shattered expectations. Regimes have captured the attention of international organization specialists and much of the international relations discipline not necessarily because of any superior theoretical potency or clarity but perhaps because, after being burned so often in the past, scholars can count on the regime framework as a fairly safe one to bet one's scholarly credentials on insofar as it is sufficiently amorphous to apprehend any number of eventualities within the parameters of the state system.[61]

Unfortunately, the concept of regime is in danger of becoming an "ambiguous symbol"[62] both for scholars seeking to explain international phenomena and for practitioners seeking to prescribe policies. It has become a victim of its popularity. Keohane has urged caution when concepts in international relations gain popularity, especially as a cure for conflict.[63] Noting the problems that befell "balance of power" thinking, he cites Claude's jest that " 'balance of power' is to writers on international relations as 'a pinch of salt' is to cooks, 'stellar southpaw' to baseball writers, and 'dialectical materialism' to Marxist theoreticians."[64] Although unintended by Keohane, the point could apply to regimes today.

If the concept of regime is to become more useful, analysts must deal more explicitly with empirical and normative questions raised by regime analysis. One needs to be more specific about such matters as regime content (what is meant by institutionalization) and regime scope (what part of the international system is covered by it). What degree of acceptance of rules, norms, procedures, and/or organizational machinery, involving how many actors, is the bottom line for a regime to be said to exist in a given issue-area? What are the relationships between the informal and formal elements of a regime, and is there any natural evolution that is observable or preferable? How does one distinguish between regimes as independent variables (devices or settings that bring about the institutionalization of world politics) and as dependent variables (the institutions themselves)? If the number of regimes is increasing, but the average number of actors associated with regimes is decreasing, does this mean we are seeing more or less international institution-building? It is questionable whether regimes have enough empirical and normative meaning that we can make such determinations. If it is hard to do so in the realm of theory, what does that say about the utility of regime analysis in the realm of practice?

To summarize the argument presented thus far, a large segment of the international relations field has lost the capacity to think in world order terms except in the most minimal sense (as piecemeal cooperation), and with it the capacity to think more clearly about what one means by international institutions and institution-building. It is true that, just as political scientists lately have rediscovered institutions as phenomena worth studying and have shown a renewed appreciation of their role in shaping political life at the national level,[65] international relations specialists have begun calling for a "new theory of institutions."[66] However, where the former define institutions in a way that accords prominent treatment to "organizational factors," the latter tend to conceptualize the term more loosely and consciously downplay such factors in the context of regimes. To be sure, the new institutionalists in the international relations field call for including international organizations in their formulations. Oran Young, for example, acknowledges that "relations between the regimes themselves and various explicit organizations are of obvious importance" in pursuing "the promise of institutionalism."[67] Likewise, John Ruggie recognizes that as "international institutions of a formal kind have been left behind" in the wake of the regime literature, there is "the ever-present danger of theory getting out of touch with practice," and hence "it is necessary to link up regimes in some fashion with the formal mechanisms through which real-world actors operate."[68] Regarding the UN's predicament in particular, Ruggie has attempted recently "to begin to rectify the abdication of responsible comment by the academic community," noting that "the academic community can help engender realistic expectations and offer proposals for institutional reform"[69] and adding that, if the "crisis of multilateralism" is to be resolved, "professional students of international organization . . . will have to play their part—which is to rejuvenate the systematic study of the structure and functioning of institutions in the contemporary world system."[70] Still, as critics of the UN have been known to say, there remains much more talk than action on this front, given the token amount of attention international organizations continue to receive in the scholarly literature despite enhanced visibility since the late 1980s.

One can discern a highly guarded, almost anti-globalist and anti-institutionalist posture even on the part of scholars who focus their research on the UN, reflected in a recent study which concluded that "the fact [is] that globalist approaches to world order may have run their course, at least for the present" and that there are "limits to both globalism and intergovernmentalism."[71] That there are limits to international institution-building is obvious; what those limits are is less so.

Toward a New World Order

What follows, then, is an attempt to provide a basis for reviving the theory and practice of the United Nations and, in a broader vein, international organization. The challenge is to overcome the limitations of current international organization perspectives without repeating the mistakes and suffering the dashed expectations associated with earlier approaches. The author will seek to demonstrate how the future of world order is intertwined with international institution-building, and how institution-building is predicated upon some degree of organizationalism and globalism. We will consider how the UN might furnish an element of central guidance compatible with the systemic environment in which it is likely to operate into the next century, i.e. how it might provide a single framework whereby parochialism—ranging from unilateralism to subglobal multilateralism—and pragmatism—including informal as well as formal modes of cooperation—can safely flourish. This study, in other words, is an exercise in "critical theory," which "allows for a . . . choice in favor of a . . . political order different from the prevailing order, but . . . limits the range of choice to alternative orders which are feasible transformations of the existing world."[72] Every effort has been made to inform the analysis with a careful sense of what John Herz called "realistic idealism."[73]

Although this work stems from a set of patently normative concerns, revolving around the search for improved world order, the author is acutely aware that the analysis must be grounded firmly in reality if it is to qualify as more than hortatory in nature. Reality in world politics has become harder to pinpoint lately. In the span of less than a decade, since the mid-1980s, the world has gone from witnessing a U.S. Secretary of Defense (Caspar Weinberger) warning that "we are no longer in the postwar era but a prewar era," to awe over the suddenness with which longstanding blocs collapsed and a new post-Cold War order appeared, to renewed concern over a reversal of trends and even more heightened possibilities for global cataclysm (relating not only to unsettling developments in the Middle East but also to uncertainty in the Balkans and the erstwhile Soviet Union). If it is unreasonable to expect international relationists to develop the capacity to predict specific occurrences — say, "to foretell exactly what events will take place in China [in 1997]" —at the very least one would expect them "to develop skill in showing 'which way the wind is blowing'."[74] For much of the international relations discipline, as with humanity generally, it has been less a case of anticipating "which way the wind is blowing" than being buffeted back and forth, jerking and reeling from the latest happenings, and trying to get one's intellectual bearings.

As the shifting winds over the past decade have reminded, there is a danger of overreacting to headlines of the moment and losing sight of deeper structures and processes.[75] One cannot help recalling Hegel's dictum that "the owl of Minerva always rises at night" —scholars are good at predicting the past, at uncovering truths associated with the tail-end of some phenomenon. While there is a possibility that we will overreact to the recent upheavals in world affairs and attribute larger importance to them than they deserve, especially coming as they have at a time when cosmic visions are being stirred by the impending arrival of a new century and millennium, there is also a chance we will underestimate them and fail to grasp their significance as evidences of a watershed period in the life of the international system. If it is much too premature to declare the epoch we are passing through in the late twentieth century as marking "the end of history"[76] or to equate it historically with the Reformation,[77] it may be just as wrong to dismiss it as merely a déjà vu return to world politics as it looked prior to 1945 or 1914.[78] What is needed is to sort out the various trends and counter-trends and make sense out of a landscape that is not quite as familiar-looking as it used to be.

Although realist thinking and the empiricist tradition associated with it still dominate the study of international relations, other schools of thought (notably post-positivism or post-struc-

turalism) have helped to draw attention to alternative construc-
tions of reality (past and present).[79] Even if one does not accept
the scientific relativism of some of these schools, it is hard to dispute the point that, notwithstanding the many constraints
which seem to limit the menu of choices open to policymakers,
humanity has the general ability to shape what happens, to continue or alter the existing course.

This book hopes to make at least a small contribution in adding to our knowledge and understanding of the parameters of
change in world politics and how the world might be moved.
Although policy often seems to drive scholarship rather than
vice-versa — that is, major research agendas in academia commonly develop in reaction to the swirl of events produced by
those in positions of authority (in a position to make things
happen) — scholars can have some impacts of their own on practitioners in helping "to nudge events in preferred directions."[80]
In John Maynard Keynes's words, "practical men who believe
themselves to be quite exempt from any intellectual influences"
frequently are subtly infected by "some academic scribbler of a
few years back."[81] The impact of one's scribblings is likely to be
greater the clearer the prescriptions that flow from one's analysis.

The starting point, in Part Two, is to examine more closely certain theoretical issues related to the dynamics of international
institution-building so that the problem of United Nations reform can be understood in broader perspective. In Chapter 2, an
attempt is made to define more precisely what is meant by world
order,[82] to develop the outlines of a model of what a desirable
and achievable world order might look like in relation to the
present, and to locate the United Nations in this scheme based
on an analysis of the logic that has given rise to global organization and that continues to sustain it as an element in international governance. The author will offer a vision of what the UN
could become, with the proviso that such a transformation is
contingent upon a concatenation of factors operating in the international system which are hospitable to engineering macro-
level institutional innovation.

Chapter 3 will examine how the real world conforms to the requirements of the model articulated in the previous chapter. Are
the requisite underlying conditions present in the contemporary

international system to support a new stage of international institution-building at the global level? International organizations
are clearly creatures of their environment. An obvious example
of how an international organization is shaped by its environment is the UN itself, which was born out of the maelstrom of
world war, was designed in a manner that mirrored the power
realities of the time, whose success at conflict management has
correlated strongly with the ebb and flow of American-Soviet
tensions, and whose evolution generally has reflected changing
developments in the international system. Contrary to the claim
that the UN is less a microcosm than a distortion of the world
outside its walls, that it is untouched by reality, it has been very
much buffeted by external conditions. Whenever politics within
the UN has been out of synch with politics outside the body, the
organization has been reminded that it cannot move too far
ahead of the system. At the same time, while international organizations may be creatures of their environment, they are not
prisoners. It is well to remember that "structures are not . . .
prior to the human dream itself. . . . Structures are not 'givens'
. . . they are 'mades' . . . made by collective human action and
transformable by collective human action."[83]

In Part Three, in Chapters 4, 5 and 6, the author will discuss
the implications of the theoretical-empirical analysis for UN reform, first delving into the workings of the organization and
what exactly needs repairing, then focusing on various reform
proposals and strategies that have been suggested, and offering
some specific prescriptions that are presented as both meaningful and feasible. Finally, in Part Four, the concluding chapter examines global institution-building in the context of longer-term
empirical and normative concerns.

PART 2

Theory

2
The Logic of Global Institution-Building

World order in the simplest terms refers to the basis upon which humanity has been, or could be, organized politically to govern its affairs.[1] With few exceptions, there is general agreement that the primary structure which currently exists—a decentralized, anarchic system of sovereign nation-states—has remained unchanged in its essential character since it came into being roughly around the time of the Peace of Westphalia, rooted in seventeenth-century European politics and gradually spreading outward across the earth. The Westphalian system, spawned by the bloodbath that was the Thirty Years' War and nourished by a mixture of monarchical and liberal-democratic nationalism, offered a new set of security arrangements built around the territorial state rather than the walled city or universal church.

Within the anarchic state system structure, there is also common recognition that system transformation has occurred. This is where agreement begins to unravel. Using differing criteria, some observers have found system transformation occurring only rarely (Kenneth Waltz, for example, finds only one change over 300 years, the shift from multipolarity to bipolarity in 1945)[2] while others have cited frequent changes (Richard Rosecrance, for example, identifies nine distinct systems between the mid-eighteenth century and the mid-twentieth century).[3] Some have found the degree of transformation relatively modest (for example, from tight or loose bipolarity to bimultipolarity back to multipolarity in the postwar period)[4] while others have noted potentially revolutionary changes (for example, the rise of non-state actors competing with nation-states in a "polyarchic" setting in the contemporary era).[5] Although most evidence points to the international system today being far more complex than the bipolarity commonly attributed to the post-World War II era, it is less clear whether the system merely has returned to the more normal multipolar condition that characterized much of international relations between 1648 and 1945, or whether there are some altogether new elements putting humanity on the threshold of a more profound, radical transformation of the entire fabric of Westphalian political relationships.

In addition to describing historical international systems, scholars have also described theoretically conceivable systems that do not yet have empirical referents (such as Morton Kaplan's unit veto, universal, or hierarchical systems).[6] The various real or hypothetical systems constitute alternative world order models. Rather than thinking of world order in dichotomous (anarchy/nonanarchy) terms, we can plot alternative world order models along an axis containing space between anarchy (decentralization) and nonanarchy (centralization), based on roughly intuitive notions of how much the models tend toward concentration or deconcentration of systemic control capabilities. The axis would pass through variants of a unit veto system, multipolarity and bipolarity, hegemony, a system of specialized IGOs with varying degrees of supranationalism, confederation, and other systems along the way toward nonanarchy in the form of unitary (world) government. Perhaps we need a two-dimensional axis, distinguishing between centralization of power and centralization of authority. It could be argued that hegemony is the functional equivalent of world government (although no hegemon has been able to establish such supremacy unless one counts the empires of Rome and Alexander). The contemporary nation-state system would seem nowhere near nonanarchy, but it is also far from the kind of anarchy posed by a unit veto system or—if nation-states themselves were to disintegrate into smaller, more fragmented entities—by a pre-Westphalian system of feudal relationships.[7] Barry Buzan, contemplating a "spectrum of anarchies," argues that the current international system is midway between high (immature) and low (mature) anarchy.[8] Utilizing our axis, one could go one step further and contemplate a spectrum of nonanarchies.

Different world order models incorporate different approaches to world order as alluded to earlier. (For example, bipolarity and multipolarity, as opposed to hegemony, can involve balance of power or concert of power mechanisms.) To speak of approaches is to imply that there is an element of human control and purposefulness over what kind of world order materializes. Scholars have debated the implications of various world order models for various world order values.[9] The world order problematique has traditionally focused on the maximization of peace, although justice, ecological quality, and other values have been added to the discourse over the years. There remains a divergence of views regarding whether a bipolar or multipolar system is more prone to major violence.[10] There is also controversy over whether greater centralization generally is likely to lead to increased or reduced tensions in the international system; as previously discussed, underlying much of the latest scholarship on interstate cooperation is the notion that the creation of overarching global superstructures is not only unlikely but perhaps undesirable as well, in that such arrangements may be tension-generating or may preclude chances for tension reduction through at least partial agreements.

It should be clear from this excursion into the domain of comparative international systems/alternative world order models that constructing a new science of international cooperation (or a "new theory of institutions") around the axiom that "nations dwell in perpetual anarchy"[11] gives us an incomplete picture of world order possibilities, one that can tell us much about cooperation under anarchy but can tell us little about larger international governance concerns and how the international system might evolve from its present condition to a mature anarchy or, perhaps, even to a higher political order.[12] For that, we need to think of international relations in a more holistic and dynamic fashion.

The Logic of a Global Perspective

In considering what sort of world order is achievable and desirable for the future, I propose thinking of the contemporary international system as a global political system and thinking of system transformation as political development.

THE INTERNATIONAL SYSTEM AS A GLOBAL POLITICAL SYSTEM

Global system refers to a single socio-economic entity covering 510,072,000 km² in which there are regular contacts among groups of human beings found throughout the system. This should not raise eyebrows or hackles. One does not have to carry all the baggage of the spaceship earth metaphor to accept the modest assertion that "we live an an era of interdependence"[13] and that the world as a whole has never been more strategically, economically, and ecologically interrelated, in terms of any corner of the globe being readily susceptible to important impacts stemming from decisions taken elsewhere (ranging from annihilation of the species to lesser impacts).[14] As Robert North and Nazli Choucri state, the "process of globalization—the expansion of human activities and interests (transportation, communications, trade, financial exchange, nuclear targeting around the world)—has become nearly complete."[15]

This does not deny the fact that one can volley bits of data back and forth to make the empirical case for or against growing interdependence, depending on which side of the argument one wishes to take. One study finds that while certain kinds of transactions, such as telephone calls, are increasing more rapidly internationally than domestically, this is less true for other categories, such as mail flows and air travel; in the case of air travel, for example, the authors note:

> Although the number of international travelers leaving the United States in 1980 was almost six hundred times what it was in 1930, the number of domestic air travelers has increased even more rapidly. In fact, [in terms of the foreign component of total air travel] the postwar high for the United States, 11 percent in 1970, was still less . . . than it was in 1930. Neither U.S. nor world air traffic demonstrates any [increased] trend in the ratio of international to domestic travel.[16]

In a different study, two other authors cite other data:

> Several important trends affecting all nations have increased their interdependence in the past two and a half decades. First, the ratio of trade to GDP has increased steadily in nearly all countries with only brief interruptions. . . . Second, international financial markets have expanded rapidly,

outpacing growth in international trade. Between 1965 and
1987, world exports (including services) as a share of output
rose 7 percentage points, to 19 percent, while international
banking activity . . . as a share of output soared from 1 percent
to 17 percent. . . . In 1989, for example, the combined average
daily volume of trade in the foreign exchange markets of Japan,
the United Kingdom, and the United States reached $430
billion (nearly 6 times the volume in 1979).[17]

The interpenetration of national economies in both the developed and developing worlds has been led by multinational corporations. By 1990, "some 500 multinationals and 50,000
affiliates . . . controlled more than 60 percent of foreign trade
and accounted for a like proportion of the value added to industrial production. To a large extent—up to 75 percent—their
transactions replaced conventional exports."[18] In the South, by
way of illustration, "foreign affiliates control 32 percent of production, 32 percent of exports, and 23 percent of the employment of Brazil's manufacturing sector. In Singapore foreign
affiliates control 63 percent of production, 90 percent of exports,
and 55 percent of employment in manufacturing."[19] In the
1980s, "MNCs sponsored 75–80 percent of radio and newspaper
ads in Swahili and English in Kenya."[20] In the North, "overseas
investors can now claim ownership to over one-half of the U.S.
cement, tire, and consumer-electronics industries, 40 percent of
the nation's gold-mining capacity and heavy-truck production,
one-third of the chemical industry, 30 percent of copper mining.
. . . Foreigners own over one-half of the commercial property in
downtown Los Angeles, about 40 percent in Houston, . . . and
20 percent in Denver. . . . The Japanese own six out of the
twelve largest banks in California, and account for . . . more
than 30 percent of the business loans [there]."[21] The American
economy, where foreigners control roughly 7 percent of the
overall business sector, is not nearly as penetrated as the Cana-
dian economy, where foreign firms account for 28 percent of domestic sales, or the French (27 percent) or the British (20
percent).[22]

To speak of a global system also does not deny the fact that interdependence tends to be asymmetrical, that there are distinctive
subsystems preoccupied with local concerns more directly than systemwide concerns, that regionalism may be outpacing globalism in

IGO growth and other respects and that most actors are more regional than global in the normal reach of their activities, that intranational interactions dwarf international transactions, or that discontinuities in various dimensions of system structure can be found. The contemporary international system is certainly complicated, but it is nonetheless global.

Treating the contemporary international system as a *political* system should likewise not be a source of contention. Political system refers to the conceptualization of international relations in generic political science terms as having to do with "who gets what, when and how" in the international arena, with the "how" referring to some sort of governance process that has shape and form to it in an Eastonian sense.[23] It is commonly noted that international governance occurs without international government. "Demands"(related to anything from arms control to zinc mining) get articulated, processed, and disposed of—values get allocated—but through an anarchic rather than central authoritative set of structures, which distinguishes international politics from national politics.[24] Affect, power, salience, and other elements of politics infuse international political processes no less than national political processes, but in the former case they work their effects through a chain of subnational, transnational, transgovernmental, and other relationships mediated mostly by the instrumentality of the nation-state. The outputs of the international political system are not as easily definable as those produced by national political systems; if one does not want to use the term international public policies, one can speak of regimes, which have to do with the collective functioning of different parts of the planet but which operate at different levels in the system.[25] All of this is ongoing, complete with feedback loops. There are winners and losers along the way, satisfied or dissatisfied with certain outputs that have or have not resulted. And of course, in international politics, the resort to violence by the dissatisfied is considered a more endemic if not frequent aspect of political life; the threat of violence—and the resultant "security dilemma"—continues to be a constant shadow hovering over the system, although it is arguably less a part of the political culture than in the past.[26]

George Modelski notes, "The global polity may not be as sharply defined as we might like, because it is still in the process of formation and in the course of being differentiated from other layers of the world system, the regional and national layers in particular. But as an analytic construct it is clear, and empirically we can define the global polity as the sum of institutional complexes . . . power distributions . . . coalitions, and the agenda of global problems."[27] The notion of a global polity squares with Hedley Bull's conceptualization of international politics occurring within an "international society" where the members share common understandings about the fundamental rules governing their interactions. That is, not only do allocation processes occur in something other than totally random, chaotic fashion in the international system, but also underlying the political order are at least a few widely held assumptions about the nature of these processes and what constitutes aberrant behavior. Bull himself argues that international society in the eighteenth and nineteenth centuries was more cohesive and supportive of order than international society in the late twentieth century, although he maintains the concept continues to have relevance.[28]

Centrifugal, tribal forces (the resurgence of Islamic fundamentalism and other long-submerged cultural traditions) are competing with and are offset to an extent by centripetal forces (technology-driven cultural diffusion and homogenization).[29] The rudiments of a common international political culture continue to be discernible. There are two assumptions, in particular, that appear to be at the core of international society today. One, which originated with the Westphalian system, is that national governments acting on behalf of nation-states are the proper respositories of sovereignty, enjoying a monopoly on the legitimate use of force within their borders and having primary responsibility for the protection of their inhabitants vis-à-vis the outside world. The second, which is of more recent vintage, is that international governance is not merely about the maintenance of order. As the state increasingly has come to assume responsibility not only for the physical safety of its citizens but also for their general well-being—with democracies indistinguishable from dictatorships in claiming the right to regulate citizen behavior toward the latter end—world politics has become an arena for pursuing welfare objectives no less than security objectives.[30] The growth of the welfare state[31] has expanded the number and range of issues for which central decisionmakers in

national governments feel responsible. At the same time, technological developments have internationalized many of these
concerns and fostered the intricate web of crossnational relationships, together producing the "complex interdependence" phenomenon about which much has been written.[32] Wolfram
Hanrieder was only half right when he observed several years
ago that "it is not a new type of international politics which is
dissolving the traditional nation-state but a new nation-state
which is dissolving traditional international politics."[33]

It is true that both the national security state and the welfare
state are being threatened. The forces of transnationalism, along
with subnationalism, have seemingly so undermined the integrity of states and put them in competition with nonstate actors in
shaping outcomes in world politics that the editor of a major
work on the origins of the nation-state system confessed at the
end that "perhaps we are writing obituaries for the state."[34]
There is no doubt that nonstate actors such as multinational corporations can have important impacts.[35] It is also the case that,
even if in the life of the Westphalian system "there has not . . .
been any golden age of state control,"[36] the contemporary era is
one in which states seem particularly faced with "loss of control."[37] Some observers have gone so far as to speak of "a global
authority crisis."[38] National governments are expected to combat inflation, yet the success of their policies can be partly dependent on the price of oil on the world market, the ability to
coordinate monetary policy among various central banks as well
as cope with the workings of the Eurodollar and other financial
markets that lie outside official banking channels, and countless
other factors beyond their borders. They are expected to produce policies to deal with environmental problems that transcend their jurisdictional boundaries. And so forth. Further
complicating matters is the ongoing proliferation of microstates,
adding to the belief that "the age of the independent self-suffi-
cient state will [shortly] be at an end."[39] In some respects, statism and nationalism have never been more vibrant; in other
respects, they have never seemed more at risk.

However, whatever autonomy and control states have lost,
they have not yet surrendered their sovereignty. Although the
sovereignty of developed and underdeveloped states alike has
been challenged by the growing complexity of human interac-

tions within and across national boundaries, the nation-state remains at the center of the international anarchy. Whether Charles Kindleberger was correct in his oft-quoted comment that "the state is about through as an economic unit"[40] is open to argument, but one can hardly make a credible case for the view that the state is through as a political unit. The nation-state is still the primary form of political organization, locus of authority, and point of reference in world affairs. While the nation-state system may be competing with a "multicentric actor system" in which "actions and reactions originate with a multiplicity of actors at diverse system levels,"[41] it is still predominantly the interactions of states which shape major developments in world politics and which have the potential to move the international system in one direction or the other.[42]

In subtle ways certain other norms have taken hold and have become somewhat settled features of the international political culture since World War II; most notably, the almost universal renaming of war departments as defense departments within foreign policy establishments, as well as the general elimination of references to civilized nations as opposed to uncivilized nations in treaties (cf. Article 38 of the 1945 International Court of Justice Statute with more recent international legal documents), reflect changed understandings about the acceptability of war and colonialism.

In a sense the phrase "world order" could be considered something of a misnomer as applied to international systems prior to the post-World War II era insofar as those systems were not "truly global."[43] This obviously did not stop earlier generations from thinking globally even if it was within the admittedly parochial context of a predominantly European-centered world. It seems ironic that there has been a retrenchment in world order thinking today precisely at a time when the international system is more clearly global in nature than at any point in history. One might be forgiven for believing that, if comprehensive approaches to world order such as the League of Nations and its successor have failed or worked only marginally in the past, they are even less likely to succeed in the present environment. Compared with 1945, when—in Truman's words—"there were many who doubted that agreement could ever be reached by these fifty countries differing so much in race and religion, in language and culture,"[44] the challenge of global institution-building appears all the more formidable today in a world body politic consisting of over three times as many members representing considerably greater diversity.[45] Still, ignoring problems of international governance at the global level will not make them go away. It is questionable whether technology will ever allow us to revert to a less globalized existence short of some nuclear or other catastrophe. This caveat applies to both lesser actors and major actors, who historically have always defined and pursued their interests in the broadest possible geographical terms. More than ever, realism would seem to dictate that we attempt to frame the world order problematique in global terms. In other words, calling the international system today a global political system seems an empirically accurate statement rather than "globaloney"; arguing that we are better off decomposing problems and treating them in a sub-global fashion may make sense to the extent possible, but one should not confuse prescription with description.

SYSTEM TRANSFORMATION AS POLITICAL DEVELOPMENT

This leads us, then, to think of international system transformation as *political development* of the global system, a notion that might arouse substantial protest on several grounds—that it invites misplaced analogies between domestic and international politics, substitutes a value-laden term (development) for a more straightforward analytical one (transformation), and poses problems for a discipline which has trouble enough agreeing on the criteria for assessing whether any system change has occurred of any magnitude, without also having to assess the direction of change. However, it would not seem to require much of an inferential leap from the assumption that the international system can be treated as a political system to the assumption that such a system is capable of political development. The relevant question is not whether one can contemplate the political development of the international system, but what political development (as opposed to retrogression) means in the context of international politics.

Definitions of political development borrowed from the comparative politics field can provide some help if judiciously applied, at least as a starting point.[46] Alfred Diamant has defined political development as "a process by which a political system acquires an increased capacity to sustain successfully and continuously new types of goals and demands and the creation of new types of organizations."[47] Lucian Pye, commenting on the diverse meanings of the concept, notes three common elements: the development of (1) "a general spirit or attitude of equality"; (2) increased "capacity" of the political system in terms of "sheer magnitude" and "effectiveness and efficiency in the execution of public policy"; and (3) increased "differentiation and specialization of structures" along with their "integration."[48] Pye and others have discussed a number of "development crises" that political systems may encounter—institution-building, community-building, participation, and distribution—either in sequential, gradual fashion (as happened favorably in the West) or simultaneously (as happened unfavorably throughout much of the Third World following decolonialization).[49] In one way or another, political development has to do with a system's capacity to cultivate a political order which combines stability with responsiveness to new demands and, hence, avenues for peaceful change.[50]

The latter definition of political development would seem broadly applicable to all political systems, including the contemporary global system. The connections between stability and responsiveness, or peace and justice (and related values), are just as problematical in international affairs as in national affairs, and probably more so.[51] Not unlike students of comparative politics, Stanley Hoffmann argues that as a general rule "in world affairs, order has to be achieved first" even if it is "established at the cost of justice."[52] However, recognizing that it may not be possible to separate these concerns today, he adds that "it is difficult to conceive of a future international system remaining moderate if the inequality among its members . . . incites recurrent violence."[53] Acknowledging that "there shall be no world order unless some progress is made toward worldwide equity," Hoffmann sees "a growing need for shared powers, joint policies and effective institutions in all the new realms of international politics."[54]

We can carry this generic treatment of politics and political development only so far. There remains the problem of specifying what form institution-building and other aspects of political development might take in a political system that has the special characteristics of the contemporary global polity, which is not a state but a system of states. Political development dilemmas experienced by so many national political systems, difficult as they have been to resolve, seem to pale next to the "nightmare of world order"[55] that is conjured up when one ponders political development in the sphere of international politics. While the uneven level of political development among the states constituting international society is a factor which complicates the political development of the international system,[56] the fundamental constraint is the cult of sovereignty they all uniformly share.

It has been said in regard to the development of nation-states that in the eighteenth century the state preceded the nation, whereas in the nineteenth century the nation preceded the state. Since the rise of nationalism, we have seen how hard it is to create and sustain a state where there is no nation. But this problem is not really relevant to the political development of the contemporary international system. To the extent one can envision the political development of the global polity, one assumes institution-building that falls far short of a world state and community-building that falls far short of a world nation. Although it is debatable how much centralization of the international system is ultimately desirable, few would question that it is premature to try to create world government and that, in any case, there are strict limits on what is possible for the foreseeable future.[57]

The political development of the contemporary international system, defined as the cultivation of a world order which combines stability with adaptability, may be best conceptualized as the progression toward a single pluralistic security-community. As introduced by Karl Deutsch and his associates, the "security-community" concept refers to "a group of people which has become 'integrated' . . . [in that it has achieved] the attainment . . . of a 'sense of community' and of institutions and practices strong enough to assure, for a 'long' time, dependable expectations of 'peaceful change' among its population."[58] In a "pluralistic" security-community, as opposed to the "amalgamated" variety, the latter characteristics develop among political units which retain their formal sovereign independence and separate governments as in the case of the United States and Canada and, some would say, the Western industrialized democracies generally. Pluralistic security-communities are less ambitious political creations than amalgamated ones but may be more durable.

In the Deutsch study, three conditions were found to be important to the successful functioning of pluralistic security-communities: the compatibility of political values held by the members, the capacity of the member governments to respond quickly to each other's needs and actions, and the mutual predictability of behavior.[59] While at present these conditions exist only sparingly at the global level, the same study added that "the outstanding issue leading to the emergence of a pluralistic security-community" in the cases examined "seems to have been the increasing unattractiveness . . . of war among the political units concerned" as war "promised to be both devastating and indecisive."[60] It seems reasonable to argue that constraints on the use of armed force in international relations are likely to increase rather than decrease in the future, certainly among the major actors vis-à-vis each other, and that war—"limited" or otherwise—will become less rather than more attractive system-wide as the nuclear age proceeds into the next century.

Although it is true that historically there has been only a loose correlation between the increasingly destructive potential of war and the commensurate decline in its use, we may be reaching a new threshold of unattractiveness.[61] Empirical studies have found that "major power war" occurred 80 percent of the time in the sixteenth through eighteenth centuries but only one-sixth of the time in the nineteenth and twentieth centuries[62] (scarcely at all between the Napoleonic Wars and World War I, and confined to the two catastrophic but nonetheless relatively short global conflagrations after 1914). Of special note, there has been virtually no instance of direct military confrontation between major powers in the entire post-World War II period (unless one counts the American-Chinese involvement in the Korean War); as neorealist Kenneth Waltz has commented, "Never since the Treaty of Westphalia . . . have great powers enjoyed a longer period of peace than we have known since the Second World War."[63] From both a long-term and more immediate historical perspective, then, it is possible to discern a growing gun-shyness at least among those actors capable of causing the greatest damage to themselves and to the system.

Whether or not the growing unattractiveness of interstate violence in cost-benefit terms will provide the stimulus for a general contraction in war as well as war preparation, resulting in a functioning global security-community, will depend heavily upon interstate interactions acquiring and maintaining the character of mutual responsiveness and predictability alluded to above. The development of a sense of greater predictability of behavior among states requires the increased routinization of international governance processes whereby inputs (demands) enter the international political system, outputs (regimes) emerge, and goods ultimately get allocated. The development of a perception of growing responsiveness of the system entails that such routinization include opportunities for broader participation in the creation and alteration of regimes along with broader sharing of the benefits relative to the costs associated with international cooperation, at least in those issue-areas most salient to members of the system. Broadened access to the decision points in the system and to the goods produced must occur in a manner which stops short of generating inflated participation/distribution expectations and pressures which cannot be realistically handled by the system.

The question remains whether a pluralistic security-community based on predictability and responsiveness can be established in the absence of common political values among the members beyond a commitment to the precepts of the state system culture. The regime literature deals precisely with the problem of achieving greater institutionalization of international politics and provides ample evidence that states with vastly different political values can commit themselves to patterned collective behavior characterized by elements of predictability and responsiveness. However, the kind of institutionalization typically examined is disjointed in nature, covering only parts of the international system; that is, to the extent regimes enhance predictability and responsiveness in the system, establishing rules of the game, they are presumed to do so for only a specified set of states (as few as two players) and in the context of a specified issue-area or nested set of issues (a single game). The logic of regime-making, as it tends to be articulated by scholars and practitioners alike, calls for including in the process only those actors which are "relevant" to the issue in question and/or are "like-minded."[64] Although these observers in the same breath speak of eventually universalizing the process as much as possible, it is not clear how decomposition is to evolve into recomposition so that institutionalization of international politics can occur across sets of actors and issues leading to an expanding security-community.

The notion of decomposition has great theoretical and practical appeal. However, if it is not applied in a larger context, world order will become an oxymoron rather than a meaningful concept. To argue that one can have world order without a globalist worldview amounts to trying to square a circle. It requires one to pretend that the parts of the international system bear no relation to the whole. When one talks of cooperation under anarchy, it must be remembered that anarchy is, after all, a system property. We cannot have it both ways; either there is such a thing as international society, or there isn't. While Ernst Haas rightly cautions against attributing to "the system" a "mystical wholeness,"[65] is it not just as mystical to believe that diffusion processes related to nuclear proliferation, technology transfer, and the like will render goods such as peace and air quality more divisible in the future? Even where policy concerns exist which are not global in scope and do not require global responses, ascertaining relevance and like-mindedness among actors in the contemporary international system would seem to suggest that, in Robert Cox's words, we "look at the problem of world order in the whole" while at the same time we "beware of reifying a world system."[66]

Some sort of central guidance mechanisms are needed to perform the task of "preserving and *extending* the limited consensus that presently exist in the global society [italics mine]."[67] This is not a caveat for making the global polity more hierarchical or for "universal bargaining, issue by issue, deal by deal,"[68] but rather finding ways to cast "the shadow of the future" as wide as possible, providing an established setting within which various groupings of states—ranging from, say, the London Group of nuclear suppliers to the members of the International Atomic Energy Agency, or the Group of Seven to the Group of Seventy-seven—can relate to each other under an umbrella framework. Such a framework would help to routinize and broaden international governance processes by facilitating decisions by the international community as to what type of institutionalization is possible and desirable in any given polity area (in terms of norms, practices, laws, organizations, or other modes of cooperation) as well as what the scope of institutionalization might be (global or sub-global).

The Logic of an Organizational Perspective

Samuel Huntington has noted that "the level of political community a society achieves reflects the relationship between its political institutions and the social forces which comprise it. . . . The more heterogeneous and complex the society, . . . the more the achievement and maintenance of political community become dependent upon the workings of political institutions."[69] As institutionalists argue, institutions are at once a product of their environment, reflecting underlying political-social forces, and also can impact on the environment, providing the boundaries that shape political and social life. There is no reason to believe that institutions are less important to international society than to national societies. According to the functional theory of regimes, institutions in international politics—whether they be formal organizations or the array of other structures which together fall under the rubric of regimes—serve to reduce transaction costs, improve the sharing of reliable information, and lower the sense of risk and uncertainty in the international system. At the global or any other level, these functions theoretically could be performed with or without organizations, with current scholarship suggesting the less organization the better.

However, in considering what if any role international organizations might play as institutions in global society, we need to look more closely not at the functions regimes perform in the abstract but the functions which certain regime structures, such as organizations, perform compared to other structures. It may be that organizations are capable of producing peculiar institutional impacts distinct from other regime elements, or they may produce similar impacts more effectively, or they may simply be reinforcing mechanisms. For example, international law performs some rather specific functions: the allocation of legal competences among states, the regulation of international conflict (by furnishing a common bargaining medium for communicating the nature and extent of disagreements), and the internalization of international political culture, in addition to placement of constraints on state behavior.[70] Little has been said about the "functions of international organization."[71]

The intellectual shift away from an organizational approach to world order seems grounded essentially in two contradictory propositions which can be culled from the international relations literature. One is that international organizations in themselves are of little or no consequence, that overhauling or tinkering with organizational machinery will have no noticeable effects in the absence of changed attitudes on the part of the membership. This is the familiar critique against a preoccupation with formalistic concerns, symbolized by Lord Caradon's oft-invoked dismissal of UN reform efforts: "There is nothing fundamentally wrong with the United Nations—except its members."[72] International organizations, in other words, are thought to be irrelevant or superfluous. Another proposition upon which the case against international organizations rests, though, is that they may be dysfunctional for the international system; this is the argument about the inefficiencies and negative impacts associated with bureaucratization and other features inherent in an organizational culture, particularly in the public sector. International organizations, in other words, tend not so much to be inconsequential but bad. Guided by either or both of these tenets, students of international regimes have chosen to focus attention largely on institutional structures which are non-organizational in nature.

In heeding Robert Keohane's call to avoid "the Mt. Everest syndrome"—that is, studying international organizations for their own sake, "because they are there"—scholars may be overlooking a significant point. The fact that "they are there" in a physical, concrete sense—in a way that norms, rules, practices, and other regime elements are not—makes organizations "live collectivities interacting with their environments"[73] and endows them with particular properties. Any community of any size requires some manner of formal apparatus. As Deutsch and his colleagues acknowledged, "both types of integration [amalgamated and pluralistic] require, at the international level, some kind of organization, even though it may be very loose."[74]

As a society becomes more complex and diverse, there are pressures toward increased formalization of the institutions upon which its viability depends. Informal modes of cooperation suffice less. It is not an accident that as the volume of international interactions has expanded in the twentieth century along with the number and heterogeneity of the actors in the international system, we have witnessed increased reliance on codification of international law, both in developing new rules and in clarifying old ones that previously existed as customary law. Approximately 40,000 international agreements have been concluded in the twentieth century, most of them since 1945.[75] The proliferation of international organizations in this century can be understood in the same terms. The number of IGOs has increased over twentyfold since 1900. Of all IGOs presently in existence some 95 percent were created in the past fifty years.[76] Although IGO growth has been uneven, concentrated particularly among open, technologically advanced states, there is evidence that the web is gradually expanding.[77] The *Yearbook of International Organizations* lists 309 "conventional" IGOs and hundreds more in an "other" category (along with over 4,500 "conventional" NGOs).[78] The growing formalization of the international system is far easier to trace empirically than the growth in shared norms, practices, and other informal dimensions.

International organizations command attention, however, not because they can be easily counted but because they appear to be part of an evolutionary process at work in world politics. John Ruggie has commented that "while numerous descriptions of this 'move to institutions' exist, I know of no good explanation in the literature of why states should have wanted to complicate their lives in this manner." Ruggie attributes the growth of global organizations in particular to the dominance of the United States and its worldview in the postwar period rather than to "instrumental rationality" in the international system, but this is open to debate.[79] Rather than being viewed as experimental, failed responses to war and welfare problems, or as the fading legacy of one state's peculiar propensities and influence during "the American century," international organizations may more cogently be seen as structures which are deeply embedded in historical forces.

Harold Jacobson gives the functionalist account of IGO growth:

> Functionalism argues that mass participation in political life will inexorably increase, that general populations everywhere are primarily interested in increasing their own standard of living, and that mass participation will make economic welfare the dominant concern of governments. Functionalism also argues that technology offers immense possibilities for improving living standards, but that international cooperation is essential to take full advantage of the opportunities provided by technology; states are simply too small.[80]

This may be a compelling explanation of the forces promoting international cooperation, but it fails to explain adequately why international cooperation should necessarily take organizational form as opposed to non-organizational vehicles such as international agreements or periodic conferences. For a fuller understanding of IGO growth, we need to look more carefully at the functional logic of organizations.

Clearly, a key precondition for the historic emergence of IGOs was the emergence of the nation-state system whereby a set of sovereign governments presiding over inhabitants located within relatively well-defined borders replaced the patchwork of quasi-sovereignties found in the feudal era. It took over 150 years after Westphalia for the IGO to be invented, and almost as many years thereafter before it fully caught on and an expansive network could be found worldwide. As Inis Claude has observed:

> The international organization movement [can be seen] . . . as, above all, an effort by states to modernize, remodel, and re-equip the multistate system, adapting it to the changing and increasingly difficult circumstances of the twentieth century. . . . [So] international organization can be interpreted as an attempt to perpetuate the multistate system by making its continued operation tolerable; it is not so much a scheme for creating world government as for making world government unnecessary.[81]

If "the future of international organization is . . . largely dependent on the future of states,"[82] the converse is true as well. Depending upon what continued retooling occurs, states and international organizations may well flourish together or suffer together.

International law and international organization have had a synergistic relationship, with international law helping to create IGOs (although IGOs are increasingly being established as offshoots of existing IGOs rather than owing their existence to treaties) and IGOs helping in turn to create international law (although IGOs are still not the primary producers of international "legislation"). Most treaties are bilateral[83] (e.g. the web of interstate treaties dealing with extradition or use of air space); these "contractual" agreements do not require organizations as vehicles for sponsoring or conducting negotiations, and rarely are concluded through organizations as such. Multilateral treaties are something else. As long as there is a continuing movement toward general "law-making" treaties of a broad multilateral character[84] (e.g. the 1982 Convention on the Law of the Sea or the proposed law of the air treaty dealing with pollution), driven partly by the recognized inefficiency of each state attempting to negotiate separate bilateral pacts with over 150 other states on a myriad of issues, it is predictable that international organizations will take on added rather than declining responsibilities as either indirect facilitators or direct venues in the international bargaining process; it is almost inconceivable that the international political system could produce such outputs in the absence of organizations.

In areas where global bargaining is eschewed and agreements are forged among only a limited group of states on a regional or other basis, in keeping with a decomposition strategy, it is still hard to see how even "minilateral" cooperation can occur in an organizational vacuum. While it is true that international organizations, "because they are there," tend to look for problems to solve and manufacture the need for agreements—where there is international organization, international law is likely to follow— the existence of problems and the need for agreements give rise to organizations in the first place.

IGOs are a long way from becoming the key loci for making the major "decisions that have consequences for the distribution of values in the global political system,"[85] whether these are decisions about the formal rules or about other arrangements governing various areas of international activity. As one empirical study of IGO use shows, "IGOs are used by nations primarily as selective instruments for gaining foreign policy objectives."[86] To the extent that IGOs are involved in international governance processes, though, they can perform several useful functions which relate to the requirements of a security-community. Some organizations will perform these functions more effectively than others. First, aside from facilitating the handling of more demands, organizations permit decisions to be made more openly, in a participatory fashion, with greater opportunities for interest articulation and aggregation, thereby increasing the possibility that the process will be perceived as responsive and the decisions accepted as legitimate regardless of who gets what. As one writing notes, "international organizations . . . are the major venue within which the . . . legitimation struggle over international regimes is carried out today."[87] Second, organizations permit decisions to be made in a regularized, timely, and prescribed manner rather than intermittently, thereby contributing to a greater sense of routinization. Third, they allow for constant communication and information streams and are explicit devices for lengthening the "shadow of the future," with continuous game-playing among the membership a built-in feature, therefore enhancing prospects for the learning of cooperation. Although these attributes make organizations relevant to governance concerns at every level of the international system, they would seem especially important at the global level and may provide a partial rationale for the existence of global IGOs.

Rule-making can occur without organizations more readily than can rule-implementation. Although the bulk of international agreements entered into are not accompanied by the creation of international organizations, the wider the geographical scope of an agreement the more likely that some organizational apparatus will be associated with it, whatever the issue-area in question. Implementing an acid rain agreement between the United States and Canada is unlikely to require the establishment of an organization; implementing such an agreement on a broad multilateral, global scale is likely to if an available body does not already exist.[88]

International cooperation through organizations generally entails greater tangible resource expenditures than other modes of
cooperation. With greater investment in an institution may
come greater commitment. Treaties are somehow easier to aban-
don than the buildings and infrastructure which have been developed around organizations; while relatively few treaties are
broken as a percentage of all treaties,[89] even fewer IGOs disappear once they are born. The durability of IGOs may owe not
only to the material investment they represent, or to the survival
instincts of all bureaucracies, but also to their symbolic importance to their memberships and the psychic investment the latter have at stake in the organizations. It is not just a case of few
IGOs dying; a sampling of individual IGO histories also shows
few members leaving over time. In the UN system the few recorded withdrawals from the UN and such specialized agencies
as WHO, FAO, UNESCO, and ILO in almost all instances have
been followed by resumption of membership. International organizations may satisfy certain subtle needs, such as the need
for a larger sense of community and a feeling that there is at least
a modicum of order rather than total chaos. Particularly at the
global level, a latent function which international organization
perhaps performs is that—in the guise of the UN system—it is
the most visible sign of humanity groping for world order, offering a faint glimmer of the stirrings of a single security-community in the making.[90]

Globalism, Institutionalism, and the United Nations

It is, of course, problematical whether such a public order will
ever materialize. The problem confronting the future development of the international system may not be a lack of organizations but a lack of organization. The "dizzying pace" of IGO
proliferation, which already poses enormous obstacles to rational control and coordination by states,[91] is likely to continue
even as scholars ignore the existence of organizations and in-
veigh against their necessity. How these organizations will relate to each other and to the larger regimes they are
encapsulated in will determine whatever progress occurs in the

quest toward world order. Many regimes will operate without organizations, although the larger their "membership" the more likely some organizational component will be present. There is much to be said for pragmatism, flexibility, and pluralism in governing arrangements; the decentralized nature of the international system ensures that these qualities will never be lacking. However, it is questionable whether the willy-nilly manner in which international governance processes are evolving (characterized by some as functional eclecticism)[92] can be expected to promote the kind of predictability and responsiveness associated with a security-community. If world politics is to become more institutionalized—if the world is to be made safe for parochialism in all its permutations, including unilateralism, bilateralism, minilateralism, and multilateralism—then we will need to think more self-consciously about concepts of international governance and institution-building and consider how some degree of central guidance might be injected into the global political system.

Unless one is prepared to make an argument for U.S. hegemony, an increasingly tenuous proposition, the United Nations is the one available mechanism which is even remotely in a position to impart a measure of central guidance to the international system. If it is to do so, however, it will have to become more proactive and less reactive in its organizational behavior. Conceived primarily as a conflict manager, the UN over the years has been viewed mainly in terms of how well or how poorly it has succeeded at collective security, peacekeeping, and peaceful settlement. The UN Charter, as well as practicality, has dictated that the conflict management mission be carried out with the UN as the forum of last (or late) resort, to be utilized after local or regional efforts have failed. There has been relatively little attention given to the UN as a manager of cooperation, a mission which, if developed more fully beyond the modest rule-making and implementation role it has played to date, would render the UN the forum of first (or early) resort in many instances.

As a cooperation manager, the UN could serve as a conduit through which regime-making efforts pass and international waters are tested to determine those issue-areas in which a basis for international cooperation exists, what organizational or non-

organizational form such cooperation might take, and the maximum number of states to be included. In its capacity as a regime
processing center, the UN would be a place where emerging
problems (for example, ozone layer deterioration, debt relief,
drug trafficking) could be identified, monitored, and proposed
for consideration on the global agenda; where bargaining could
occur which would indicate the degree of consensus ("consensual knowledge") mobilizable in support of international action;
and where signals ultimately would be provided as to whether
global solutions are possible or whether regime-making should
be pursued at some lower level in the system. Decomposition
strategies would not be precluded, but would not drive the process. Periodic review of regimes could be built into the process
to determine how they are working, what improvements might
be made, and whether participation can be expanded without
diluting the robustness of existing cooperation. Regimes would
be something more than theoretical constructs invented by academics, as they often seem.

In some ways the UN already engages in these activities
through its various organs and specialized agencies, although
not in any systematic fashion. The UN cannot be the lone gate-
keeper for international cooperation—such a responsibility
would totally overload the institution—but it can play a more active and pivotal part in expanding the capacity of the international system to respond to new demands and in helping to
define the outer limits of collaboration for the international community. Depending on how a cooperation management role is
operationalized (for example, relying on non-voting, relatively
non-confrontational decisionmaking procedures), the UN's
reach need not exceed its grasp, with expectations, frustrations,
and disillusionment held in check.

The dilemma posed by UN reform is that those proposals
which appear feasible also seem trivial, while those which might
truly matter seem the least feasible. One could choose a strategy
of merely tinkering with the present institutional machinery—
focusing on reforms mainly of a managerial and administrative
nature, such as achieving better coordination among the specialized agencies, streamlining debate and other procedures in the
General Assembly, developing more sophisticated program
budgeting, planning, and evaluation techniques along with

more stringent requirements for personnel recruitment and promotion in the Secretariat, and upgrading the Security Council's capabilities through the creation of standing panels of mediators and fact-finders. Then, however, one stands accused of engaging in a wasteful expenditure of time, money, and intellectual effort given the benefits that are likely to accrue from these seemingly innocuous changes. Although some proposals relating to matters like the professionalization of the international civil service and reorganization of the specialized agencies can be quite controversial, any UN reform exercise which is limited largely to nuts and bolts changes will be perceived as such, merely confirming the image of international organizations as being relatively insignificant and unworthy of serious attention in world politics. On the other hand, if one takes the position that only a total rethinking and overhauling of the UN's structure is a worthwhile exercise—focusing on substantial revision of the basic political arrangements embodied in the Charter, or starting over from scratch—then one, too, can be charged with irrelevancy but for overreaching rather than underreaching. Somewhere between tinkering and rethinking there may be opportunities for engineering change in a manner that is both realistic and meaningful.

I have attempted here to sketch in general terms the need for a changed conception of the UN, calling for UN reform without spelling out in any detail exactly what needs fixing and what the repairs might look like. Suffice it to say, there is a substantial gap between the present institution and the one envisioned as the centerpiece of a global security-community. Organizational design will be taken up later, and occupies much of this book. First, we need to give further thought to the matter of organizational setting. As one writer stated in the early 1970s, "[although] it has become banal to assert that the successes or failures of international organizations stem not so much from their formal-legal covenants as from changing configurations and distributions of power, systemic issues and forces, and the attitudes and resources of member states," there is "little . . . known at a general level about the interrelationships between universal . . . organizations and their varying systemic contexts."[93] Little attempt has been made to pursue this line of research in recent years, given the prevailing antipathy of the

scholarly establishment toward universal and formal approaches to international cooperation. We have seen how large-
scale historical forces have provided generalized impetus for
global organization. However, these forces in themselves were
not enough to create major new institutional forms like the
League and UN in the twentieth century. A catalyst was required, namely a *systemwide crisis* (world war) combined with
the existence of a *critical mass of actors disposed toward and capable
of moving the system* in an innovative direction. The kind of significant institutional change entertained in this chapter may materialize as part of a gradual, unfolding process but—judging
from the past dynamics of international institution-building—
may require a push from specific actors responding to a specific
crisis, insofar as crisis provides the best opportunity for the inertia of existing arrangements to be overcome and for the learning of new behaviors to occur.

It would appear, at least on the surface, that certain elements
may be present in the international system which offer a win-
dow of opportunity for institutional change. As one analysis put
it at the very outset of the 1990s:

> We see the next few years as a watershed—a significant
> turning point in post-World War II political, economic, and
> security relations. It is a uniquely promising moment in
> history, when Western Europe is moving toward unity; Japan
> has attained great economic power and is seeking appropriate
> world responsibilities; the Soviet Union, several nations in
> Eastern Europe, and China are [attempting] . . . economic and
> political reforms; and many developing countries have emerged
> as pace-setters in political and economic reform. In short, we
> have relative peace and many shared political and economic
> goals. . . . Moreover, this remarkable moment in history is
> formed by a fast-moving, multi-dimensional technological
> revolution which has heightened the increasing
> interdependence of nations.[94]

Not unexpectedly, the decade thus far has shown that economic and social change within and across societies does not
come easily or smoothly and without setbacks. Internally, Marxist societies undergoing reform have experienced varying degrees of political convulsion. Internationally, the much
ballyhooed "breaking out of peace" in the late 1980s[95] was shat-

tered by Iraq's invasion of Kuwait in August 1990 and the subsequent dispatch of over 500,000 American and allied troops. Even before the Gulf War, more ominous conditions were juxtaposed against the newly promising developments on the world scene. These included the $1.2 trillion debt bomb aggravating already volatile conditions in much of the South; the specter of rising neomercantilism in the North; the challenge in both the North and South of sustaining economic growth compatible with ecological stewardship of the planet; the threat of nuclear, biological, and chemical weapons proliferation among states; and the proliferation of other, in some respects more complicated, security problems not fitting neatly into the Westphalian mold, such as international terrorism, drug trafficking, and ethnic strife. This mélange of ingredients is a critical part of the systemic context that sets the parameters for global institution-building today, defining both the possibilities and limits.

The future of the UN can be captured in three possible scenarios. One scenario is that the organization will decline further and maybe disappear as the League did. A second is that it will be supported enough by the membership to at least muddle through. The third is that it will experience organizational growth and be an engine for the political development of the international system, contributing to "the development of long-term viability for the states . . . in the system."[96] The second scenario seems more realistic than the first. Short of a system-wide war, which in the nuclear age would be "the last crisis," the UN is not likely to suffer the fate of the League; there is evidence, based on their recent behavior (including public statements and sudden infusions of cash to arrest financial hemorrhaging), that several important members have concluded that the decline of the organization has gone far enough. As for the third scenario, it will depend upon whether the "crisis of multilateralism" becomes perceived and felt more deeply, whether the major actors are willing and able to have the UN do more than muddle through, and whether other aspects of the international environment are conducive to institution-building. We turn now to a closer examination of the contemporary international system, focusing on various system properties which relate to organizational growth and assessing the prospects of international political development.

3

The Contemporary
International System:
Crisis, Power, Will, and
the Potential for
Institutional Innovation

Is There A Growing Systemic Crisis?

The ecopolitics school argues that technological changes ultimately shape human socio-political structures and values. It also
claims that today growing technology-based interdependence
and its attendant problems are creating pressures putting mankind on the brink of rethinking how governments and peoples
relate to each other. In Dennis Pirages's words: "The forces of
ecological and technological change . . . are driving potentially
revolutionary shifts in the structure of relations among nations
and in the values that guide human behavior."[1] However, even
if there is a compelling logic dictating a reformation in international governance arrangements, the question must be asked, as
Stanley Hoffmann has put it, "will the need forge a way?"[2]
Whether individuals and societies in the contemporary international system are prepared to find their way toward a new world
order, and how distant they are willing to go, will primarily be
contingent upon just how urgent the need for change is perceived, whether problems are approaching crisis proportions
and are being experienced at the systemic level.[3]

As one author explains, the relationship between adversity
and innovation is a complicated one:

> Adversity does . . . produce innovation, but most often it is
> grudging innovation. . . . The response to adversity tends to

> move along the continuum of intellectual adjustment from the
> specific to the general, from incremental adjustments that occur
> at the edge of consciousness to systematic reassessments of
> principles. . . . Reappraisal of general principles occurs only in
> the face of great pressure. Discontinuity is minimized thus:
> operational tactics change before strategy; specific programs
> before policy postulates; postulates before beliefs about the
> environment in general; and beliefs about today's international
> situation before the underlying images of the nature of world
> politics itself.[4]

How far along this path of adversity and adjustment have we
come? Does the current situation truly qualify as a systemic crisis as such? Is this a time of sufficient adversity as to constitute a
"Grotian moment"[5] capable of provoking a change in the general principles and underlying images upon which the fabric of
world order is based?

A world in crisis is not a new theme, and has been part of our
vernacular for so long in the postwar era that it is easy to dismiss
as a tired and hollow notion. The implications of nuclear weapons and the unprecedented "interdependence of doom" they
created had been cogently analyzed by John Herz and others in
the 1950s. As for the potentially doomsdayish implications of
nonmilitary aspects of interdependence, the first wave of apoc-
alyptic, neo-Malthusian warnings was touched off by the formation of the Club of Rome in 1968 and the publication of *The Limits
to Growth*, guided by an "overriding conviction that the major
problems facing mankind are of such complexity and are so interrelated that traditional institutions and policies are no longer
able to cope with them."[6] The Club of Rome caveat, warning of
a destructive link between population and economic growth on
the one hand and renewable and nonrenewable resource management on the other, was echoed in the late 1970s in the U.S.
by the Carter administration. *The Global 2000 Report to the President* opened with the observation that "the world in 2000 will be
more crowded, more polluted, less stable ecologically, and more
vulnerable to disruption than the world we live in now" unless
"the nations of the world act decisively to alter current trends."[7]
In 1980 the report of the Independent Commission on International Development Issues (the Brandt Commission), focusing
particularly on Third World economic conditions, argued the cri-

sis was already here: "The crisis through which international relations and the world economy are now passing presents great dangers, and they appear to be growing more serious."[8] More recently, the UN-sponsored Brundtland Commission issued a study with a similar ring, although emphasizing the environmental context of economic decisions and calling for a worldwide movement in support of "sustainable development."[9]

The litany of sermons sounding the alarm about Armageddon has desensitized many to the existence of crisis, especially since there has been no concrete, palpable manifestation—no single event or series of events to galvanize concern equivalent to the great depression sandwiched between two world wars experienced in successive decades by an older generation. Instead, what appear to be geographically and temporally isolated disasters have occurred, such as Chernobyl, the Sahel famine, the oil embargo and subsequent gas lines, the savings and loan debacle in the U.S., and other episodes which produced some rumblings of discontent and anxiety and an ill-defined malaise.

Whether the world is in crisis is partly a question of fact and partly a question of perception. The general improvement in living conditions in the industrialized nations since the industrial revolution, along with the subsequent communications revolution which brought the imagery if not the benefits of the good life to the rest of the world, have created a widespread revolution of rising expectations among mass publics that elites everywhere are struggling to meet under increasing pressures. Herman Kahn, Julian Simon, and other critics of limits-to-growth thinking have argued that, if one takes a long-term historical perspective, humanity is doing better even if it may be feeling worse. Simon points out, for example, that female life expectancy in France increased from under thirty years in the 1740s to seventy-five years by the 1960s, and the infant mortality rate was still 200 per thousand in much of Europe as late as 1900 compared with the present norm of ten to fifteen per thousand, and that similar progress is gradually being repeated elsewhere in the world today.[10] Kahn and his associates see the current era as a transitional one from a world where "200 years ago almost everywhere human beings were comparatively few, poor, and at the mercy of the forces of nature to one 200 years ahead where, barring bad luck and/or bad management, almost every-

where they will be numerous, rich, and in control of the forces of nature."[11]

Of course, planetary management is precisely what is at issue in this study. There is empirical evidence of poor management lately, of humanity not only feeling worse but doing worse as well, and of problems becoming less isolated or episodic and more structural in nature:

> The last two decades have been filled with anomalies . . .
> indicative of an international system under stress.
> Economically, this period has seen two energy crisis cycles
> . . . , a major world food shortage that many thought would
> lead to global starvation, two very deep global recessions, a
> protracted global debt problem, and a collapse of world stock
> markets. In the decade prior to 1973, the annual real growth
> rate of the industrial economies was about 5 percent. Since
> then it has been in the vicinity of 2 percent. The less developed
> countries saw their vigorous growth rate of 6 percent of the
> previous decade drop to less than 2 percent in the . . . 1980s.[12]

These data covering recent experience in the last two decades would seem more relevant to our inquiry than the data gleaned from a longitudinal analysis of over two centuries. Although cumulative historical experience shapes individual and national consciousness, the time frame which typically informs reflection and action is not so much one's sense of the sweep of history or long-term future as one's sense of the immediate past, the present, and the impending near-term.[13] Compared with the early postwar period, the international system today seems to be stalling as an engine of progress across several regions and cultures. Elsewhere, the author has conducted an extensive analysis of trends in three broad issue-areas since the late 1960s—economic well-being (examining data on GNP and GNP per capita growth rates), quality of life (examining data on life expectancy, infant mortality rates, daily calorie supply per capita, and other such indicators), and ecological balance (examining air quality levels and other environmental characteristics)—and found that matters have on balance been getting worse systemwide across all major groupings of states despite some rays of progress found in some places on some specific dimensions.[14]

As adversity rises, people and societies become increasingly disposed toward change. Today there would seem to be a general bias in the direction of change in the international system at large, given the fact that all categories of states are witnessing evidence of growing malfunctioning of their economic-social-ecological systems. States are being buffeted by forces from without and from within which are undermining the ability of national governments to engage in purposive, goal-directed behavior and to achieve objectives. References to a global authority crisis and loss of control were made earlier. A core premise of this study is that, in conjunction with traditional security concerns that will not go away (the specter of atomic-bacteriological-chemical weapons proliferation and the like), the growing complexity of other, nonsecurity concerns confronting national governments can be expected to sustain pressures for a reexamination of systemwide governance arrangements that can only occur in the context of the United Nations. If the "pillars of the Westphalian temple" are eroding, might they be replaced with a new institutional foundation?[15]

Small changes generally are preferred to big changes, so that one's first inclination is to look for correctives closest to home, internally within one's borders rather than externally in the international realm, and regionally rather than globally. Even if the international system is primed for change, as seems to be the case, states will have to be convinced that the failings of international governance structures are at the root of current problems — or that, whatever the explanation, the overhauling of these structures offers a way out — before the suggested kind of innovative macro-level institution-building can materialize. Assuming one values international institution-building, things may have to get still worse before they can get better. Considering the nature of the high-case and base-case scenarios presented by the World Bank and other bodies in projecting trends in the 1990s, the future prognosis for most countries is at best guarded.[16]

As matters worsen, the paradox is that there is the opportunity not only for increased international institution-building but also massive conflagration. Indeed, a point can be reached at which crisis becomes immobilizing and destructive rather than releasing creative energies; as one writer puts it, "when the risks become too many or unbearable our ability to assess and cope often breaks down."[17] Whether the institution-building path is followed will depend not merely on the degree of stimulation furnished by crisis but on other variables as well.

Large-scale social change, unless glacial and unconscious as with the agricultural and industrial revolutions, requires an agent or set of agents. Historically in the international political system, certain national leaderships have taken the initiative in socializing the other members of the system to accept new concepts and norms (such as diplomatic immunity, territorial waters, and other sovereignty-based notions which found their way into international law from the seventeenth century on) along with new institutional forms (such as global IGOs). Although some have suggested that such "modernizing" elites today are to be found in the guise of nongovernmental and transnational social movements,[18] the latter are still no match for governments presiding, however tenuously, over nation-states. We now need to turn to questions of power and will as additional elements in the equation of system change.

Is There the Power to Move the System?

Since this study deals with the problem of *engineering* change in the international system, the focus here is not on what Oran Young calls spontaneous orders, those institutionalized arrangements relating to the governance of a society that emerge without being the product of any human design. The alternatives to spontaneous orders are imposed orders, dictated by a dominant power or set of powers, and negotiated orders, which are "characterized by conscious efforts to agree on their major provisions, explicit consent on the part of individual participants, and formal expression of the results."[19]

The distinction between imposed and negotiated orders can be somewhat overdrawn. Those who have advanced the theory of hegemonic stability have pointed out that even when order in the international system is achieved through a concentration of power possessed by a hegemonic state, the exercise of power ordinarily entails not merely the capacity to coerce other states through a stick approach but also the capacity to cajole, entice, and earn respect; as one hegemony theorist states, "it is possible to lead without arm-twisting, to act responsibly without pushing and shoving other countries."[20] In other words, even hegemony-based order tends not to be wholly imposed. While some have contended that the smaller and weaker the states in the international system the more order that is likely (i.e. "wars are due to the accumulation of the critical mass of power"),[21] history does not provide convincing evidence to support the proposition. International institution-building has been associated not with the absence or weakness of national power but with the existence of some constellation of power, whether hegemonic or otherwise, helping to drive the international system. In Robert Gilpin's words, "the distribution of power among states constitutes the principal form of control in every international system."[22]

However, power alone does not confer a global leadership role. One must also have the willingness to invest one's resources in steering the system. This is seen most clearly in the case of the U.S., whose internationalist orientation at the turn of the century fell far short of the power position it occupied in the world. Thomas Bailey describes the emergence of the U.S. as a global power:

> By 1890 we were the number two white nation in population, still trying to catch up to the Russians. We had bounded into first place in total manufacturing, including top rank in iron and steel—the standard indices of military potential. In addition, we held either first or second place in railroads, telegraphs, telephones, merchant marine, and in the production of cattle, coal, gold, copper, lead, petroleum, cotton, corn, wheat, and rye. The armies and navies were not there, but we had the means of creating them when we needed them—and did.[23]

Despite growing power capabilities the U.S. remained relatively aloof from efforts to engage the international system in institution-building after World War I, when the British displayed the will but lacked the strength. As Charles Kindleberger remarks in regard to the failed search for interwar leadership of the international economic order, "the United Kingdom could not; the United States (with or without the help of France) would not."[24]

This was to be contrasted with the U.S. conversion from isolationism to internationalism after World War II. Bergsten summarizes the now widely held conclusion that "history shows that an effective international system requires a custodian [in the form of either individual or collective leadership] which [feels there is enough at stake that it] is willing to internalize systemic costs."[25] Whether one chooses to view such leadership in Hobbesian terms as a would-be Leviathan or in nobler terms as a subsidizer of order as a public good, it is a critical variable in international institution-building.

It follows, then—assuming we are now living in a post-hegemonic world in the nuclear age[26]—that any attempt to promote the development of the contemporary international system toward a more mature anarchy or still higher political order through United Nations reform will need the imprimatur of a combination of states that have sufficiently compatible issue-positions, shared salience levels, and joint power capabilities as to constitute a dominant coalition willing to be able to lead the other members to behave in accordance with the new principles.[27] The very problems which recently have afflicted the U.S. and other states and which seemingly have created in the system a stronger inclination to countenance change have at the same time sapped the power of many actors which might be candidates for a custodial role. In order to judge whether there is a critical mass of actors in a position to guide systemic change, and who they might be, we need to examine briefly the configuration of power in the contemporary international system before exploring more extensively the matter of will.[28]

Much has been said about the diffusion of power in international politics, notably the decline of the U.S. and USSR.[29] It is not just a case of the end of hegemony or superpower duopoly, with bipolarity giving way to multipolarity in the form of five power centers—the United States, the Russian Federation (with or without the Commonwealth), the European Community, Japan, and China.[30] Power seemingly has become so issue-specific—resources are so lacking in fungibility[31]—that it is hard to identify any clear stratification pattern. If the end of bipolarity makes it more cumbersome to forge a dominant coalition in support of action at the global level, however, the enhanced fluidity of alignments can help grease coalition-building. Can any countries acting in concert find the wherewithal to bring the remaining members of the international community in line behind global institution-building? If it is true that the U.S. "has become a hegemon in decay," is it necessarily the case that "it is set on a course that points to an ignominious end"? And if it is also true that "we have passed the high-water mark of [Russian] power and influence in the world," is a similar ending in store for the USSR's successor state?[32] What of other possible aspirants for a stewardship role? Is there no concentration of power left in the system?

Three sets of variables would seem to bear on the capacity to effect substantial UN reform. These are the degree of concentration of military capability, economic capability, and demographic capability.[33] A rationale for focusing on these variables, along with a look at how they are presently distributed in the international system, follows below.

THE MILITARY DIMENSION

The historical link between military power (war-making ability) and systemic order has been undermined. The point is not that military resources are now irrelevant or useless, only that they are just one element of power, with a different and in many respects diminished utility today compared with the past. To the extent military strength continues to have importance, it lies predominantly in the threatened rather than actual use of force. Certainly those states with sizeable military arsenals that can be projected well beyond their borders—actors which traditionally have been labeled "great powers"—now find it far more awkward to employ those resources against lesser actors (despite the availability of "low intensity" options) and find it practically impossible altogether to employ them against each other in any rational cost-benefit sense.[34] Although the successful application of force by the U.S. to thwart Iraq's 1990 aggression against Kuwait suggests that military resources have not lost their historical luster, one could argue that the victors were the beneficiaries of an unusually propitious combination of circumstances (ranging from easily negotiable terrain to almost universal condemnation of a state which, in attempting to annex a fellow UN member, had violated a fundamental tenet observed religiously since World War II) and that in any event such politically and economically enervating operations cannot be undertaken with any regularity.

Having said this, it is nonetheless virtually inconceivable that the formation and maintenance of a global security-community can occur without a measure of coercive potential residing somewhere in the community. The most highly developed political systems must carry out police functions as one basis, if not the prime basis, for societal order. Hence, military power, though not figured to be directly involved in the process of UN reform, will nonetheless linger over it, just as it continues to lurk in the background of international politics.

The huge nuclear arsenals possessed by the United States and the Commonwealth of Independent States (the erstwhile USSR), in particular, are the shadow that hovers over the entire international system and in a sense grants these entities ultimate control over "the fate of the earth."[35] Notwithstanding the membership of the United Kingdom, France, China, and India in the nuclear club as well as at least twenty other states reported on the brink of joining,[36] the U.S. and the Commonwealth still together account for 97 percent of the global stockpile of almost 55,000 nuclear weapons.[37] Although the 1991 START treaty negotiated between the U.S. and the USSR has set in motion a substantial reduction in the strategic weapons held by the two sides, well over half of their arsenals are untouched by the agreement. (Although there has been some question about the status of the agreement and about central control over nuclear weapons in the new Commonwealth, as well as uncertainty over the long-term viability of the Commonwealth itself, it appears that dominant command over strategic nuclear arsenals is still being exercised from Moscow. The Russian Federation alone houses some 75 percent of Soviet ground-based strategic nuclear missiles, half of the strategic bombers, and all nuclear-armed submarine bases.)

Looking at more conventional measures of military power, while no one state now equals the commanding position enjoyed by the U.S. early in the postwar period—when it accounted for well over half of all military spending in the world— there has hardly been a leveling of military resources. Just six actors (the U.S., the former USSR, France, Germany, Britain, and China) are responsible for 75 percent of military spending worldwide, down somewhat from their 85 percent share in 1960 but still representing a large concentration of resources; if one adds Japan, which has very recently joined the top rank of spenders, seven states claim more than three-quarters of global arms expenditures.[38] A lesser but also substantial pattern of concentration can be found in regard to armed forces levels. The U.S. in combination with the former USSR (currently sorting out military relations under the Commonwealth arrangement) and China still control over one-third of all military manpower on the globe.[39] If one adds India, the only other state with a standing army of substantially more than a million troops, the four actors possess over 40 percent of all men under arms; and if one adds to this foursome the remaining four top-spending countries, the octet constitutes a virtual majority proprietorship over the policing agents in the world body politic.[40]

THE ECONOMIC DIMENSION

Economic capabilities likewise are important to making a security-community work, in terms of providing the resources to fund peacekeeping and other conflict resolution machinery and to address an increased demand load. Economic power rather than military power can be expected to constitute the main medium through which any UN reform process itself comes to pass. Successful UN reform will require appeals to mutual state interests based not on the fear of being subjected to negative sanctions but the fear of missing out on positive benefits. Economic leverage in the form of the power to confer concrete rewards as a means to induce support for institutional change will be critical. In a more immediate sense, economic resources are needed to alleviate the UN budget crisis that finds the UN proper experiencing a shortfall of over $500 million in member arrearages.

If one takes gross national product—that "most fungible of resources"[41]—as a summary measure of economic power, the trend line shows the U.S. share of the planetary product falling sharply from 40 percent in 1950 to 26 percent in 1960, and continuing to decline to 23 percent in 1970 and 22 percent by 1980.[42] With the postwar recovery of the Japanese and Western Euro-

pean economies and their ascendancy to competitive status with
the U.S.,[43] along with the rise of OPEC, NICs and other actors in
the Third World, American economic hegemony centered
around the Bretton Woods system has been replaced with attempted leadership through the Group of Seven major industrialized democracies (the U.S., Japan, Germany, France, Britain,
Italy, and Canada), using annual summits and periodic consul-
tations as vehicles for steering the economic behavior of OECD
countries and in turn the international system at large. The capacity of the U.S. to provide leadership has been weakened by
the triple deficits the American economy has suffered recently.[44]
In the late 1980s and early 1990s, Japan jockeyed for position
with the U.S. as the world's leading foreign aid donor, while
Germany flirted with being the chief exporter.

One would do well, though, to place the waning of U.S. economic power in proper perspective. Bruce Russett points out
that, while the overwhelming superiority once enjoyed by the
United States in 1945 on military as well as economic indicators
has dwindled, such a degree of hegemony was extraordinary by
historical standards and could not possibly last for long. He
adds that American power has not completely dissipated, noting that "despite slippage since filling the void [left by the decline of Britain as a 'hegemon'] immediately after World War II,
the United States retains [on most military and economic indica-
tors] a degree of dominance reached by the United Kingdom at
no point, and one that compares favorably with the U.S. position in 1938."[45] There is still a considerable degree of economic
clout retained by the U.S. By the late 1980s, the U.S. share of the
planetary product had stabilized and in fact had increased somewhat to 26 percent,[46] its $5 trillion economy double the size of its
nearest competitor. Based on other indicators as well,[47] the bottom line is that there seems no imminent prospect of the U.S.
"being overtaken and pushed into second class status by a new
global leader."[48]

If one adds the GNPs of just a handful of states to that of the
U.S., one finds a panoply of economic power today which compares well with the power distribution of the immediate postwar
period. As of 1991, the ten largest countries in the world in GNP
terms—the members of the Group of Seven, the USSR, China,
and Brazil (India ranked 11th)—accounted for 70 percent of the

planetary product. The OECD membership alone possessed almost half of the global GNP, as did the triumvirate of the U.S., Japan, and the USSR. In 1980 it took a minimum of four states to amass 50 percent of the world GNP, so that one could argue that economic power actually has become more concentrated of late.[49] Although the dissolution of the USSR now throws this proposition into question, it has been noted that "Russia [alone] maintains 90 percent of Soviet oil, nearly 80 percent of the natural gas, 62 percent of electricity, 70 percent of gold production, and 70 percent of the trained workers for the overall union," suggesting "Russia, then, will not need its empire to become an impressive state in its own right."[50] As with military power, the glass of economic power in the international system could be viewed as at least half full, or half empty, depending upon one's frame of reference.

THE DEMOGRAPHIC DIMENSION

Historically a relatively large population has been a necessary, though not sufficient, condition associated with sizable military and economic capabilities and great power status in the international system. However, the relevance of the demographic variable to global institution-building goes beyond its relationship to material capabilities and touches that intersection of political order where the element of power blends into the element of legitimacy. In the long run, a stable security-community will be founded primarily not upon the threat of punishment (coercive impulses) or even the calculation of mutual self-interests (utilitarian impulses) but upon what Deutsch labeled "habits of compliance,"[51] i.e. internalization of the norms of the society as being fair and reasonable (identitive impulses).

The closer that international governance arrangements come to reflecting an intersubjective image of fairness and reasonableness, the more workable they are likely to be.[52] The implementation of UN reform proposals is thus likely to be enhanced to the extent that they can claim the appearance of sensitivity to the need to have broad constituencies represented and can garner the support of the major population bases (majorities) within these constituencies. Although democracy is not on the march everywhere in the contemporary world,[53] it is a concept generally understood and publicly subscribed to almost as universally as sovereignty, and it remains a potent symbol usable by those who would seek to capture the high ground in a conflict over the future shape of world order.[54] The importance of rhetoric should not be dismissed, "The critical element in political maneuver for advantage is the creation of meaning. . . . The strategic need is to immobilize opposition and mobilize support. While coercion and intimidation help to check resistance in all political systems, the key tactic must always be the evocation of meanings that legitimize favored courses of action."[55]

To be truly effective, rhetoric must have some correspondence to reality. There are clearly vast disparities among states in terms of population size, ranging from megastates such as China and India, which together represent nearly 40 percent of the earth's population, to microstates found among those thirty-eight UN members with populations below a million.[56] Two-thirds of the countries constituting the international community are individually less populous than the state of Ohio in the U.S. In these circumstances, it is admittedly hazardous to attempt to develop international governance arrangements that embody democratic norms of representation, especially given the continued attachment in IGOs to the one-state–one-vote principle based on the bedrock international legal precept of the sovereign equality of all states. Even in those cases where IGOs allow weighted voting (for example, the World Bank and IMF) or give a privileged status to a few states on certain nonplenary bodies (for example, the UN Security Council), the criteria used tend to reflect traditional power considerations or other factors, such as budget contributions, rather than merely population size.[57] Nonetheless, it is hard to think about international governance structures without considering population factors at least to some extent. If anything, the ministate phenomenon has occasioned renewed interest in demographic factors as they bear on international governance and has created some pressures against the kind of rigid state-centric egalitarianism embodied in one-state–one-vote formulas. A look at the distribution of "demographic capability," and how this relates to the distribution of military and economic capabilities just discussed, might suggest some fertile possibilities for UN reform as well as special problems.

The population bomb is still ticking. Although by 1990 the global annual population growth rate had declined to 1.7 percent,
the current world population is projected to increase to 6.1 billion by 2000, with 90 percent of the growth contributed by the
Third World.[58] As Pirages cautions, "the dramatically different
demographic futures of industrializing and industrially mature
countries may very well portend growing friction between them
in a much more contentious international system."[59] Despite
volatile world population growth dynamics in the postwar era,
an analysis of trends shows that regional shares of global population have not changed drastically. South Asia accounted for 28
percent of the world total in 1950, compared with 32 percent in
the late 1980s; East Asia accounted for 23 percent in 1950 and 26
percent in the late 1980s; Africa's share increased from 9 percent
to 12 percent in that time; Latin America's, from 6 percent to 8
percent; Oceania's share declined from 4 percent to 1 percent;
North America's share also fell, from 7 percent to 5 percent, as
did the Soviet share; the biggest decline was recorded by Europe, whose share dropped from 16 percent to 10 percent.[60] According to projections cited in the Brundtland Report, this
picture is likely to persist in its basic contours into the foreseeable future, granted the longer term outlook is less benign for
the developed world.[61] Of course, some large countries that are
now pigeonholed as belonging to the South may in time prosper
enough to think of themselves as economically if not geographically part of the North, thereby shifting the axis of global population in the direction of developed countries.

In a sense, defining demographic reality in regional terms is
somewhat misplaced. As realists would contend, the major actors in international relations are not regions but countries. In
1960, just four states—China, India, the U.S., and USSR—
represented nearly a majority of the world's population (49.4
percent), a fact that still held true in 1975 (48.3 percent) and in
the late 1980s (47.4 percent).[62] Even with the disintegration of
the USSR, Russia accounts for 150 million people, in addition to
being the largest state in geographic size.[63] One could make a
persuasive normative argument that if these four states by
themselves or in combination with a handful of other states
somehow were to form a dominant coalition in the UN, it would
be no worse from a democratic theory standpoint than the

present situation; it is now hypothetically possible for a two-thirds majority (needed under the Charter for "important" questions) to be formed in the General Assembly by a coalition of states representing less than 10 percent of the world's population (although it is true that the first, second, and third worlds viewed as blocs in the 1980s did possess the number of seats and votes roughly proportionate to their aggregate populations).

The aim here is not to make a normative point but an empirical one, namely that as blocs continue to loosen, if a dominant coalition along the lines suggested above were to throw its demographic weight behind UN reform, giving due respect to national sovereignty, it would go far toward defusing any debate over whether power or legitimacy should have primacy in world order engineering.[64] The two desiderata would mesh rather than being in conflict. This would particularly be the case if such a coalition were to be enlarged to include a broad cross section of constituencies along the lines of, say, the GLOBUS project, which created a "political world model" out of twenty-five states "representing examples of industrialized and developing countries, Western and non-Western, noncommunist and communist-ruled" and accounting for "75 percent of the world's population, 80 percent of its income, and 85 percent of its armaments."[65] The author is not interested in identifying a specific set of states as candidates to move the international system, only in demonstrating that it seems within the realm of possibility to harness together a critical mass of power in support of UN reform which relates to coercive, utilitarian, and identitive bases of community-building. The ultimate power of the latter coalition would be the power not to browbeat the remaining members of the system into submission but to ignore them.

To sum up, those who harbor visions of a world order more highly developed than the present one cannot afford to ignore the element of power. As Bergsten states, "history has shown that the greatest dangers to international stability often arise from those actors whose real power is inadequately reflected in . . . involvement in the relevant sets of international arrangements."[66] Cox and Jacobson note that "any significant future growth or task expansion of international organization is likely to be through" an "oligarchic model."[67]

At the same time, a global security-community cannot rest upon a permanent power elite. Cox and Jacobson acknowledge that the "problem ahead is how . . . the oligarchic model—which will reinforce the existing distribution and stratification of power and wealth—can be squared with the rising demands of the poor."[68] I have suggested that, within limits, the wider the dominant coalition the more it will stand a chance of successfully initiating institutional change. In time, "there is no reason to believe that the oligarchic model cannot be transformed in new ways toward a broader diffusion of influence."[69] In other words, an "imposed" order might evolve into something different.

It is true that large coalitions in international politics are difficult to energize and have a way of eventually breaking down. One is reminded both of Robert Keohane's analysis of the free rider and high transaction cost problems associated with forging cooperation among a large number of actors as well as William Riker's size principle—that alliances tend to stay intact only so long as they contain an aggregation of power representing a minimal winning coalition.[70] No one is suggesting that mobilizing and sustaining a dominant coalition in support of UN reform will be easy. The main problem to be addressed, however, is not the existence of a power vacuum—there remains a concentration of power in the international system even with the fragmentation that has occurred—but a "leadership vacuum."[71]

Is There the Will to Move the System?

If one thinks of United Nations reform in game-theory terms as a competition in which the outcome cannot be determined by a single player and is produced instead by bargaining between the players, then how the contest is likely to be played out will depend upon not only the actors' "relative abilities to escalate threats or offer inducements" but also the "expected utilities which the . . . actors assign to . . . outcomes."[72] In other words, the final result of any UN reform exercise will depend on not only the relative power of the actors involved but also on their relative will to use those resources toward certain ends—i.e., the issue-positions they take on the range of possible outcomes (extending from do nothing to radical change) and the salience they attach to each of these outcomes.

A central assumption of realist and neorealist thought is that all states — regardless of the personal idiosyncracies of their leadership and no matter their form of government or other attributes — can be conceptualized as rational actors whose foreign policy behavior tends to be driven by calculations of national interests in an anarchic system, and that states will "attempt to change the international system as the expected benefits of so doing exceed the costs."[73] Others question the simplicity of the rational actor model and stress that one often needs to look well within the state for explanations of foreign policy behavior, at bureaucratic politics and other domestic factors and how they interact with the international system.[74] Rational actor assumptions have especially been called into question by those who see states increasingly faced with loss of control. As a general proposition, one would expect that the more clearly some concern impinges on broad, core national values, the more applicable the rational actor model, since (1) the more likely there will be sufficiently high salience attached to the problem as to attract the attention and involvement of the highest-level central decision makers (those most inclined by their institutional role to define the national interest according to realist expectations) and (2) the greater decision latitude likely to be given the latter by elites and publics within the society to act in the name of the state (i.e. the more successfully will leaders be able to manipulate their domestic environment invoking national interest symbolism).

It is practically a given that any state will prefer surrendering as little sovereignty as possible to an international organization, especially one that deals with high politics concerns.[75] Beyond this generalization, though, what else can be said about the behaviors states might display in a hypothetical game of UN reform? Of special interest here is the behavior of those states which, if a dominant coalition in support of UN reform is to materialize, will likely have to throw their power behind such an effort. We will be in a better position to assess the current possibilities for UN reform after a careful consideration of the underlying forces at work shaping the UN policy of key actors and a determination of the degree to which there are potentially compatible issue-positions and shared salience levels liable to facilitate the bargaining process, as evidenced by official statements, voting records, and other indicators of country orientation.

THE VIEW FROM WASHINGTON

Hedley Bull, reacting to the spate of writings on the decline of American hegemony, once wrote: "The problem America presents for us is not, as so many Americans appear to think, the relative decline of its power, but the decline of its capacity for sound judgment and leadership."[76] Bull was alluding to the element of will. The United Nations from the start, as a microcosm of the global political system, has been a testing ground for America's claim to world leadership. Let us trace the evolution of American foreign policy behavior toward the UN and examine the current calculus.

In many respects the U.S. view of the UN over the years has evolved in a manner consistent with rational actor model explanations of foreign policy behavior. In its very creation, the UN represented a vehicle whereby the U.S., as the single most powerful state emerging out of World War II, could attempt to maintain the status quo and possibly further enhance its position. No doubt U.S. leaders in San Francisco, rejecting an isolationist-oriented "return to normalcy," also saw themselves as global visionaries hoping to establish a new world order which would prevent another holocaust of the magnitude their generation had just experienced. But this vision would not be achieved at the expense of American national interests. The U.S., along with the other four major victors, was to be accorded a special status within the organization, notably through the exclusivity of permanent membership and veto rights on the Security Council.[77]

As the capstone of Franklin Roosevelt's "Grand Design" for the postwar period, featuring a strong internationalist role for the U.S., the UN's founding was a blend of moralism and realism. As Inis Claude states, with a bow also to the impact of domestic politics, "The proposals of the American government necessarily represented a mixture of ideas of national interest and conceptions of the essential principles of international organization, with provisions included primarily to avoid the danger of provoking the Senate to veto American membership in the United Nations."[78] On the one hand, Claude notes:

> Emphasis upon the hegemonic position of the Big Five should not be allowed to obscure the 'democratic' aspect of the San Francisco Conference. . . . In the final result, the United Nations Charter was to a surprising extent a 'hammered-out' document, the product of the most extensively multilateral debate ever held for the shaping of the broad outlines of the world political system, and the reflection of the best ideas on international organization and the best compromises on points of national conflict that the statesmen of fifty nations could produce.[79]

At the same time, ultimately the deliberations led to "the adoption of a Charter which was fundamentally based upon principles advocated by the United States."[80] Not surprisingly, the U.S. left San Francisco as the chief champion of the UN, embracing the new institution it had just fathered.

Through the first two decades of the UN's existence, when the American-led Western bloc could count on majority control of the General Assembly as well as dominance of the specialized agencies, the U.S. was highly supportive of the organization despite the frequent ineffectiveness of the institutional machinery owing to Cold War politics and other problems. The main development which began to turn the U.S. against the UN was the decolonialization process, a movement set in motion initially under American pressure based not only on moral principles and the growing indefensibility of colonialism but also American self-interest in gaining fuller access to economies that were still incorporated in European empires. After the mid-1960s, with the influx of new nations into the UN and the emergence of a more militant Third World bloc, American control of the General Assembly and other organs declined, and with it American backing for and interest in the organization as an instrument of foreign policy.[81] Whereas in the 1940s and 1950s the U.S. found itself voting with the General Assembly majority over 70 percent of the time, in the 1970s American agreement with the majority declined to below 40 percent at the same time Soviet agreement with the majority was on the rise. American disenchantment with the UN increased in response to what was perceived as a growing tyranny of the majority, reflected in General Assembly passage of resolutions attacking Zionism as racism and calling for a redistribution of wealth from the North to the South through creation of a "New International Economic Order." By the end of the Nixon administration, the UN was being seen more and more as "a dangerous place."[82]

The steady deterioration of American support for the UN was punctuated briefly by the arrival of the Carter administration, which attempted to redefine American interests away from a preoccupation with Cold War conflict and toward a wider set of concerns. At the outset of his presidency, Carter suggested a new order was emerging: "A rapidly changing world . . . requires U.S. foreign policy to be based on a wider framework of international cooperation. Our policy during the [postwar] period was guided by two principles: a belief that Soviet expansion must be contained, and the corresponding belief in the importance of an almost exclusive alliance among non-Communist nations on both sides of the Atlantic. . . . That system could not last forever unchanged."[83] Carter's Assistant Secretary of State for International Organization Affairs, Charles Maynes, summarized the administration's view of the world and the UN:

> [The Carter administration recognizes] a need in world affairs to debate multilaterally the great issues of the day. . . . That's why we are committed to serious global debate, and worldwide consciousness raising, regarding such issues as human rights and improving worldwide economic cooperation between rich and poor nations. Except through global debate . . . we can't do these things. And there is no other place to engage countries in this type of debate than in some of the global U.N. forums.[84]

Although the president was far ahead of Congress in his attraction toward the UN, there was sufficient interest among legislators in exploring new possibilities that an amendment to the Foreign Relations Authorization Act for Fiscal Year 1978 (the Baker-McGovern Amendment) contained a bipartisan mandate calling on the Carter administration "to make a major effort toward reforming and restructuring the U.N. system."[85] However, the international and domestic political environments were not conducive to such an exercise, with neither the Soviet leadership under Leonid Brezhnev nor many American elites and publics quite ready to share Carter's vision.

U.S. voting agreement with UN General Assembly majorities fell below 15 percent as Soviet agreement rose to almost 80 percent in the early 1980s,[86] when the Reagan administration raised American condemnation of the UN to a new level. The administration began to withhold certain assessed payments to UN bodies in violation of Charter obligations, withdrew from UNESCO, failed to comply with a World Court ruling over U.S. mining of Nicaraguan harbors and reversed a thirty-nine year commitment to the compulsory jurisdiction of the court honored by seven previous administrations, and took other actions which together added up to a policy viewed in many quarters as "global unilateralism." The Deputy U.S. Ambassador to the UN went so far as to suggest the UN get out of the U.S. or the U.S. get out of the UN.[87] Executive Branch hostility toward the UN was matched in the Congress, which passed the Kassebaum-Solomon Amendment to the Foreign Relations Authorization Act in August 1985, authorizing the president to pay no more than 20 percent (rather than the obligated 25 percent) of the total assessed budgets of UN agencies until UN budgetary procedures were changed to permit a weighted majority formula giving more power to the major donors.

Jeanne Kirkpatrick, Reagan's UN ambassador, lamented the lack of American influence in the UN, noting the U.S. had "none at all" and was "essentially impotent."[88] However, she argued that this stemmed not from a lack of power but from a lack of willingness to exercise power in the organization, and urged that "we need to communicate to nations that their votes, their attitudes and their actions inside the UN system inevitably must have consequences for their relations with the United States outside the UN system."[89] Although Kirkpatrick's stance was extremely confrontational toward the UN, it concomitantly held out the possibility of imparting a renewed salience to the role of the UN in American foreign policy:

> To an extent greater than often realized, what occurs at the
> United Nations involves central issues of world politics and

frequently touches upon vital U.S. national goals and interests.
. . . Annual reviews of UN voting patterns and practices
provide . . . a systematic basis for assessing the . . . decisions
of UN members on the salient questions of our time that come
before the UN General Assembly and Security Council. . . .
Often . . . only casual, intermittent, and inadequate efforts
have been made to integrate U.S. policies and relations [inside
and outside the UN]. . . . The United States [needs to] make
clear to others that we take a serious interest in decisions in
these areas and are no longer willing to shrug off UN
interactions as without importance.[90]

As the Reagan administration progressed into its second
term, a dampening of Third World militant rhetoric due to the
developing countries' failure to achieve NIEO goals and their
worsening economic plight, along with increased criticism by
UN members of Soviet bloc actions in such places as Afghanistan and Kampuchea, seemed to promise a more positive UN
environment from the American perspective. U.S. hardline tac-
tics, including continued threats to withhold dues payments to
the UN and to tie foreign aid support for various states to their
voting records in the General Assembly and other UN bodies,
appeared to be bearing fruit. In autumn 1985, during the 40th
General Assembly, the U.S. position prevailed in seven out of
ten key votes on issues Washington had identified as most critical and for which it had lobbied hardest.[91] During the 42nd
General Assembly in 1987, the U.S. position coincided with the
majority over 60 percent of the time (taking into account not
only roll-call votes but decisions reached by consensus).[92] By
1988, the so-called Group of Eighteen intergovernmental experts
commissioned by the UN to address complaints over budgetary
procedures and organizational inefficiency had issued recommendations which the Reagan administration acknowledged
were "unprecedented and sweeping" and which were essentially accepted by the General Assembly.[93] Congress indicated a
willingness to restore full U.S. funding to the UN pending a
presidential determination that three conditions associated with
the Group of Eighteen reform process had been met: implementation of the newly approved consensus-based budget reform
procedures (which gave the U.S. and other major donors what
amounted to veto power); implementation of a 15 percent reduc-

tion in UN Secretariat professional staff; and "progress in reaching a 50 percent limitation for nationals of any member state seconded to the UN Secretariat"[94] (a requirement aimed particularly at curbing the Soviet practice of allowing their nationals to occupy UN posts only on temporary, fixed-term appointments).

Progress was being made on all three fronts as President Reagan neared completion of his tenure in office, as testified to by Kirkpatrick's successor, Vernon Walters, who urged that "we must treat [the UN] as a serious institution" and who warned that "we cannot continue to neglect our financial commitments to the United Nations and then expect that our opinions, policies, and positions will carry . . . weight in the world body."[95] Changed Soviet behavior toward the West and toward the UN further reinforced the inclination to rethink UN policy. President Reagan himself, in his last address to the UN General Assembly, intimated the potentially far-reaching implications of the shifting winds in East-West relations, "A change that is cause for shaking the head in wonder is upon us [and offers] . . . the prospect of a new age of world peace. . . . The United Nations has an opportunity to live and breathe and work as never before."[96] The basis had seemingly been laid for a more serious and more supportive U.S. role in the UN.

While much of American foreign policy behavior toward the UN in the postwar era can be readily understood in terms of a rational actor model, U.S. behavior of late—the failure to follow up developments in the late 1980s and to seize the opportunity to reshape the UN in a manner which could both serve American interests and reinvigorate the organization—requires a more complex explanation. One might well argue that American policy toward the UN recently has been driven primarily by factors having nothing to do with the UN and, indeed, tangential to foreign policy considerations altogether. By "policy, " I mean the overall, broad conception of the UN, and not the momentary, expedient usage of the organization as dramatically occurred in the wake of Iraq's invasion of Kuwait in 1990.

As the Reagan administration in the late eighties was articulating a policy of linkage whereby American financial support for the UN was to be contingent upon UN budgetary and other changes, U.S. support became tied more to the vagaries of American domestic budgetary politics than to UN politics. As a function of large federal government deficits and the enactment of the 1985 Gramm-Rudman mandatory deficit reduction plan (requiring across-the-board cuts if annual deficit reduction targets were not met), the retrenchment in American funding of the UN proceeded with a momentum of its own irrespective of any monitoring of how UN reform squared with American national interests as defined in the Kassebaum-Solomon Amendment. The U.S. contribution to the UN in 1986 was $100 million, $110 million short of the $210 million owed based on assessed obligations. In 1987 the U.S. shortfall was $93 million. The U.S. payments bore no relation to the Kassebaum-Solomon Amendment, which had called for the U.S. to fund only 20 percent of the UN budget until reforms were instituted. The U.S. was paying barely half of its dues, funding 12–13 percent of the UN budget—despite the fact that the UN had come close to implementing the consensus-based budget reforms, had achieved a 15 percent cut in the Secretariat staff, and had largely responded to the package of American demands. The General Assembly probably would have implemented the new budget procedures during the 42nd session in 1987, had many Third World members not felt betrayed by Washington's failure to restore full funding in return for the concessions it had extracted; as it was, even though the budget was determined by recorded vote rather than consensus, the large majority supporting the resolution was "closer to a consensus approval of the budget than at any previous time in the UN's history."[97] The month before George Bush was elected to succeed Ronald Reagan in 1988, the U.S. Assistant Secretary of State for International Organization Affairs conceded that, notwithstanding "general agreement that the U.S. should pay its assessed obligations to international organizations," even if the UN were to meet every American demand in total, "U.S. budget constraints prevent us from doing that in FY1988 and 1989."[98] Even after the 43rd General Assembly's adoption of the biennial UN budget by consensus in December of 1988, a major milestone, the U.S. continued to default on its financial obligations.

Early in the Bush administration, U.S. policy toward the UN was held hostage to the "no new taxes" commitment inherited from the Reagan era that limited the options available for addressing the deficit problem. It was clear from public statements that the Bush White House desired at the outset to respond positively to the latest UN initiatives, realizing that continued American delinquency in dues payments risked undermining the hard-fought gains achieved by the U.S., but was unwilling to push for full funding as long as Congress tied it to a tax increase.[99] Congress could have exempted the UN from cuts, but there was still some ambivalence toward the organization left over from the UN bashing of the previous era and a general reluctance to save international programs at the expense of domestic ones.[100] The UN had no natural domestic constituency or client group to push its case.

In short, on the eve of the Iraqi conflict, American foreign policy toward the UN was being pulled along aimlessly in a direction which few supported on its merits, resulting in the U.S. owing the UN as of 1990 some $500 million in total arrears—80 percent of all members' arrearages—and still adding to that sum in annual withholdings. It was true that, notwithstanding Washington's increased utilization of the UN to assist regional conflict resolution efforts in Africa and elsewhere, genuine policy disagreements persisted within both the executive and legislative branches regarding the value of the UN as a vehicle for pursuing American interests and that these differences contributed to the lack of a decisive, coherent governmental response to events. Ostensibly higher foreign policy priorities that enjoyed more uniform support than UN funding, such as increased foreign aid to Eastern European states undergoing political transformation, also went begging in the domestic political climate of the U.S. However, the overt hostility which once characterized Washington's view of the UN had largely dissipated. Hostility had been replaced with indifference. What was preventing a more constructive role for the U.S. in the process of UN reform was not so much a negative American position toward the UN and the prospect of reform as the low salience accorded it relative to other competing concerns.

Then came Saddam Hussein's folly. With the 1990-1991 Gulf War, the UN found itself suddenly thrust into the limelight as the U.S. became dependent on the world body for much of its political strategy in responding to Iraq's aggression against Kuwait. With James Baker serving as Security Council President in November of 1990—the first time in UN history that an American secretary of state presided over a Council meeting—the UN passed a resolution (678) authorizing military action under Chapter VII; this was only the second time in its history, apart from the Korean War in 1950, that the Council had acted in such a fashion, and was unprecedented in that collective security action here was taken with the participation of all permanent Council members. (In the case of the Korean War, the U.S. was designated as the Unified Command under UN auspices when the Soviets were absent from Council proceedings; the 1990 vote, which technically did not establish a Unified Command under Council direction, drew Soviet support and Chinese abstention.) At the same time that the Gulf crisis gave the UN a higher profile in Washington, another development in the fall of 1990 held out further possibilities for a new U.S.-UN relationship. In the course of the domestic battle over the FY 1991 federal budget, President Bush rescinded his no new taxes pledge and Gramm-Rudman effectively was replaced by a new set of budgetary routines (designating domestic, defense, and international program spending as separate self-contained categories each with its own ceiling shielded from encroachment by the others). Congress in November appropriated full funding to cover U.S. assessed contributions to the UN budget for the fiscal year while also appropriating funds for partial payment of accumulated American arrearages in 1991 and authorizing a total payment of arrearages phased in over five years.[101] UN funding and other debates were then put on hold during the 1992 presidential election season.

Whether the latest American attention and commitment to the UN will be sustained as the Gulf War fades into memory is open to question. If the U.S. is to treat the UN as "a serious institution" and is to resume leadership in the organization, the world body will somehow have to register higher visibility in the agenda-setting process in Washington beyond one-shot affairs such as the Gulf War.[102] The domestic base of support for the UN has improved considerably, to the point where the American public seems flexible were elites to make a strong case for a greater UN role in U.S. foreign policy. Although in the mid-1980s it was argued that "internationalist impulses have pretty well exhausted themselves in mainstream American life,"[103] such impulses have always contended with isolationist tendencies and have often overtaken the latter in response to changed circumstances; just as strong public sentiment emerged in the early 1980s behind a stronger defense budget in support of global unilateralism, it is not unthinkable that public sentiment could be harnessed in the 1990s in support of a return to global multilateralism.

It is instructive to examine public opinion polls taken in the U.S. even before the Gulf crisis had impacted public perceptions of the UN. A Roper Poll conducted in 1989 showed that for the first time since 1975 the UN received a positive job rating (with more Americans viewing the organization as doing a good job than a bad job); an overwhelming percentage backed full American payment of UN dues, with 60 percent favoring always making such payments and not tying them to institutional reforms; a three to one margin existed in support of using the UN in regional conflicts rather than relying on direct American intervention; a majority favored increasing American financial support to the UN to enhance its effectiveness in peacekeeping as well as the areas of environmental protection, world food production, disease prevention, and disaster relief (though there was less support for an expanded UN role in managing the global economy); a two to one margin favored "increased participation in the UN" as opposed to decreased involvement.

A 1991 poll revealed 88 percent of those surveyed supporting a standing UN peacekeeping force and 60 percent going so far as to endorse the proposition that "UN resolutions should have the force of law and should rule over the actions and laws of individual countries, including the U.S., where necessary to fulfill essential United Nations functions."[104]

While American public opinion remains volatile, and can be swayed by events such as the latest Third World attempts to give the PLO membership in UN agencies, there has always been a general reservoir of public support for the organization at the conceptual level even when the UN has been perceived at its worst in terms of actual performance. A survey of American attitudes toward the UN in the mid-seventies revealed that even though "support for cooperating fully with the United Nations dropped from 72 percent in 1968 . . . to 46 percent [in 1976]" and "the public's rating of the United Nations' performance [had] declined to a thirty-year low point," nonetheless "almost three-quarters of Americans felt we should remain a member."[105] The best guarantee that the most egregious anti-U.S. behavior in the UN can be held in check in the future, and public support maintained, is through Washington signalling to the UN membership that it intends to take the organization seriously. In any event, there is no ingrained public animosity toward the UN posing a constraint under which the American foreign policy establishment must labor in considering a renewed commitment to the world organization.

With regard to financial constraints, the U.S. cannot hope to consolidate the recent budgetary and other UN reforms unless it is prepared at a minimum to restore full funding to the organization on a regular basis and to pay all arrearages in keeping with its Charter obligations. This scenario is not unrealistic, even under present recessionary conditions and continuing deficit problems. The U.S. already has begun moving in this direction, albeit with some foot-dragging. A resumption of American leadership in the UN can be purchased cheaply, especially when opportunity costs are factored in. The UN, after all, is a small ticket item in the federal budget. The biennial regular budget of the UN proper (UNO), as distinct from the specialized agencies, is now on the order of $2 billion. Of the $1 billion annual total (which is smaller than the annual budget of the New York City Police Department) the assessed contribution of the U.S., based on the 25 percent share it is obligated to pay, amounts to some $250 million—roughly one-third the cost of one B-2 Stealth bomber.[106] Even if one takes into account all American financial contributions (assessed and voluntary) not only to UNO but to the entire UN system, the annual figure barely exceeds $500 million—less than the operating budget of an average American state university system. Indeed, the entire annual appropriation for all forty-six IGOs covered under the State Department's international organization account—of which the UN receives one-third—is well under $1 billion.[107] In terms of ability to pay, as a percentage of U.S. GNP the American expenditures on the UN system declined from .010 percent in 1971 to .0065 percent by 1988, with no improvement since, suggesting ample room for upgrading the UN allocation.[108] The U.S. spent more each week to maintain its forces in the Persian Gulf during the Gulf War than it owed in arrearages to the UN.

One might argue that cost comparisons with police departments, state university systems, weapons systems and the like are irrelevant since the dollars spent on the UN are so miniscule as to suggest strongly that what is at the root of American reluctance to increase its financial support is not economics at all but politics. It is true that much American foreign policy behavior toward the UN, such as the Kassebaum-Solomon Amendment, has been motivated not so much by concern over the weight of economic burdens or perceived waste and inefficiency in the UN system as the desire to gain greater control over the UN agenda through increased control over the organization's budget. Yet precisely when the U.S. is on the brink of achieving such control, it seems bent on squandering the opportunity. Again, there is no questioning that U.S. funding support has been caught up in domestic budgetary dynamics seemingly oblivious to political fallout in American foreign policy. Certainly financial arguments have become part of the official explanation for American delinquency and stinginess and are not wholly disingenuous. However, with UN funding now somewhat extricated from the Gramm-Rudman straightjacket, one might reasonably expect the UN to be in line for favorable treatment insofar as the monies involved are small and hardly budget-busting. It must be added that the more benefits the U.S. hopes to obtain from UN reform, the more it will have to go beyond merely paying its current UN assessments and, in conjunction with other major donors, offer added inducements to the UN membership, such as helping to relieve debt burdens.

Collective goods theory, as applied to international politics, postulates that if an actor has a large enough stake in some collective good (for example, an ecologically and otherwise safe systemic order) it may well be rational behavior for that actor to incur a disproportionate cost of producing the good despite other actors essentially benefitting as free riders.[109] Insofar as the U.S. remains the preeminent global actor, still leading on most indicators of systemic involvement,[110] it would seem to have the single greatest stake of any country in world order, in promoting the organization of human affairs in a manner which maximizes the possibilities for routinizing international transactions systemwide. Although some have argued that it may be wise and even imperative for the U.S. to cut back its global commitments,[111] there is little evidence that the U.S. is becoming less globally oriented in the definition of its interests.[112]

The choices may no longer be global multilateralism versus global unilateralism but global multilateralism versus isolationism (or "disengagement").[113] Subglobal multilateralism or "minilateralism," exemplified by the Group of Seven, may be feasible but has its limitations; as Assistant U.S. Secretary of State Richard Williamson commented following the annual economic summit of the Group of Seven in 1988, "it was not by accident . . . that the most recent economic summit looked to many of these [UN] organizations for leadership and critical followup on problems requiring a multilateral solution."[114] It might be possible to support selectively certain specialized agencies without necessarily supporting the UN proper, but these distinctions are not easily operationalized since politically "the technical agencies [tend in the U.S. to be] caught up in questions about the New York-based United Nations"[115] and functionally "the actions of individual UN agencies affect the operation of the entire system."[116] All of this points to an abiding American interest in the future shape of the UN.

What sort of reforms might be acceptable to the U.S.? We can judge the utilities the U.S. might assign to a variety of outcomes, based on past and present public positions taken toward UN reform. The U.S. over the years has shied away from major reform requiring Charter amendment.[117] Washington has also been resistant to the kind of dramatically expansive role for the UN envisioned in the 1986 Soviet proposal for a "comprehensive security system," although the resistance to the latter owed less to any inherent objection against strengthening the UN than to the vague nature of the proposal and suspicions about the sponsor's motives. Led by American opposition, a large number of UN members have withheld their support for the proposal.[118] While opposing the notion of a comprehensive security system, the Bush administration has gone on record as acknowledging the need for "a policy that treated the UN system comprehensively" based on the recognition that there is "the great and growing need for the work of the UN system."[119] Bush's Assistant Secretary of State for International Organization Affairs has suggested the concept of "the unitary UN," having in mind a holistic approach to the UN that would stress improved coordination and would permit greater central guidance in problem solving but in a manner consistent with the U.S. desire to maintain a degree of pluralism within the UN system as well as zero real growth in the overall UN budget.[120] Though modest in its vision of organizational growth, the unitary UN concept nonetheless is grounded in globalist and institutionalist assumptions and appears almost antithetical to reliance on strategies of decomposition.

Beyond administrative reform, the U.S. of course would like to see political reform. The call for greater efficiency and rationalization of activities in the UN system reflects real U.S. dissatisfaction with the administrative machinery but admittedly also masks a larger concern over the political machinery and the felt need for reform of decision-making procedures. Rather than mount a frontal assault on the main political arrangements, such as attempting to promote a shift toward weighted voting in the General Assembly — which would require Charter amendment, consume enormous political capital, and call into question other established practices including American veto privileges on the Security Council — the U.S. has adopted a more subtle strategy of seeking to alter fundamentally how business is done in UN bodies by focusing on reform of budgetary procedures. In the UNO and elsewhere in the UN system the American aim is in effect to achieve veto power over organizational budgets, and thereby over agendas, under the guise of implementing consensus procedures whereby the U.S. is assured of membership on relatively small but nominally representative screening committees whose unanimous approval is needed in setting spending parameters to be subsequently voted on by plenary bodies. The relevant model here is the process induced by the Group of Eighteen, which calls for the thirty-six-member Committee for Program and Coordination to reach unanimous agreement on the recommended ceilings and broad programmatic priorities of the UN budget before the budget can be submitted to the General Assembly for its final approval. The CPC emphasis on consensus, formal equality of participation, and representativeness — as opposed to explicit American veto rights, weighted voting, and major donor dominance — seems to reflect a conscious attempt to avoid charges of heavy-handedness, and also reflects American willingness to settle for a form of lowest-common-denominator decisionmaking and the role of spoiler, putting Washington in a position at least to block expenditures it disapproves of even if its ability to push its own agenda is more limited. The U.S. has been quite open about this reform strategy,[121] and as noted earlier has succeeded in gaining general acceptance of the Group of Eighteen proposals, helped by the fact that criticism of UN budgetary processes is not confined to the U.S. but is widespread among the UN membership.[122]

As President Carter remarked in his ill-fated 1978 Report to Congress on the Reform and Restructuring of the United Nations System, "an active and imaginative leadership by the U.S. can do much to strengthen the UN."[123] Whether UN reform proceeds along the lines advocated by the U.S. will depend upon a host of factors operating in the international environment as well as the American domestic political environment. The relaxation of East-West tensions, should it continue, offers an obvious opportunity for greater cooperation and institution-building at the global level, holding out the possibility that the American view of UN reform might be reconcilable with that of former adversaries. It is true that George Bush's own waxing about a new world order belies a continued American tendency to position itself outside the mainstream, in regard to such issues as the law of the sea treaty, a comprehensive nuclear test ban, and many other matters. It is true as well that the reduced military threat may produce a peace dividend in the U.S. that will be siphoned off by pressing domestic needs—including infrastructure repair, health care, and further deficit reduction— rather than used for foreign policy ends, although whether American society turns inward and whether problems at home are pursued to the exclusion of those abroad will depend heavily upon how priorities are defined and balanced by governmental leaders in the Bush and post-Bush era. It is too soon to tell how all this will play out in the administration of George Bush's newly elected successor, Bill Clinton, although there is little in Clinton's record to suggest he is any less an internationalist than Bush.

There was a passage in the Carter report which perhaps has more relevance today than then:

Although the Charter itself provides for formal amendment as a procedure, this has not been a principal method of change in the life of the United Nations. The amendment procedure is a slow one and becomes practicable only when there is a sufficient convergence of interests among Member states with respect to the proposed change. Indeed, the great strength of the Charter—like our own Constitution—lies precisely in the fact that it has not created a static institution but has permitted evolutionary change. . . . Even today the possibilities for improving the functioning of the organization within the existing constitutional framework are extensive. Far-reaching reforms involving Charter revision may well have to await the development of a much greater community of interests in the United Nations. Despite this, we would be prepared to participate in a Charter review conference if a substantial majority of the Member states came to believe that the outcome of such a conference was likely to be productive.[124]

There may well be an emergent "community of interests" in the contemporary international system which could provide a basis for significant UN reform, whether through Charter amendment or some other route. One could argue its activation only awaits fuller American involvement in the organization. The reason for dwelling on the view from Washington is not that the foreign policy behavior of other key actors is less important, but that they have been far more inclined recently to support the UN financially and otherwise and do not pose the same obstacle to reform as American hostility and indifference have. The view from Moscow has been a more positive one.

THE VIEW FROM MOSCOW

While Mikhail Gorbachev still presided over an entity called the Soviet Union, one observer summed up the historical record of Soviet involvement in international organizations by noting "the Soviet Union's attitude to international organizations has long been ambivalent."[125] This ambivalence could be seen in the writings of perhaps the leading Soviet authority on international law and organization in the postwar period, Professor G. I. Tunkin. Expressing the traditional, limited Soviet view of IGOs, Tunkin wrote bluntly: "International organizations are created by states; they are brought into being by states, but [their] . . .

actions are not in any way . . . to be equated to the actions of states."[126] At the same time IGOs were seen as having a necessary historic role: "The nature of contemporary international organizations is to a very great extent determined by the existence of states belonging to different socio-economic systems. . . . That is why peaceful coexistence is now the basic condition of the development of general international organization."[127] Among other things, Gorbachev offered a new conceptualization of international organizations, particularly global IGOs. Whether Gorbachev's view of the UN will be adopted by his successors remains to be seen. It is admittedly difficult to assess the view from Moscow at the present moment when members of the post-Gorbachev, post-Soviet Commonwealth individually and collectively are preoccupied with coping with their own political and economic crises and defining their interrelationships vis-à-vis each other. Nonetheless, looking beyond the moment, it is reasonable to focus on the Russian Federation as the would-be inheritor of the USSR's great-power mantle—certainly its seat on the UN Security Council—and to consider how its policy toward the UN is likely to evolve. Before reaching any conclusions, it is useful to examine changes in Soviet behavior in the UN over time, preceding and during the Gorbachev era.

Despite an unhappy and abbreviated membership experience with the League of Nations, the Soviet Union opted to join the United Nations as a charter member. Although Tunkin suggested the UN enjoyed a certain primacy in Soviet formal-legal international relations—"the Charter is above all other treaties concluded by the members of the UN"[128]—the Soviet commitment to the institution was low throughout most of the postwar period, even after Washington became more isolated than Moscow in the General Assembly.[129]

Soviet foreign policy behavior toward the UN conformed well to the rational actor model. The Soviet decision to join the institution in 1945 derived from similar calculations that informed the American decision, although Soviets approached the collaboration from a more defensive posture. From the start, given the minority status of communist state representation in the UN, the Soviets were wary of the organization being used against them. The veto power over nonprocedural matters on the Security Council, favored by each of the Big Five, was of special importance to Moscow as a protective device against possible majority-mandated actions. During the first few decades Soviet behavior was characterized by Western critics as obstructionist, with the USSR employing the veto 105 times between 1945 and 1970 to block Security Council action, in contrast to the absence of any veto usage by the U.S. over that period.[130] Early Soviet isolation on the Security Council was mirrored in the General Assembly, where the USSR's agreement score with the majority was only 34 percent in the 1940s and barely 50 percent in the 1950s.[131] Soviet antipathy toward the organization was reinforced by the UN role in Korea (where UN action against communist North Korea was made possible by the Soviet boycott of Security Council meetings in protest against the non-seating of the People's Republic of China), in the Congo (where Secretary-General Hammarskjold took action resulting in the death of the communist leader Patrice Lumumba), and in several other conflicts. Soviet cynicism was reflected in the 1960 *troika* reform proposal presented by Nikita Khrushchev (advocating a weakened, hydra-headed Secretary-General), the subsequent Article 19 crisis sparked by the Soviet refusal to pay for the Congo peacekeeping mission despite the Security Council having authorized it initially, and Moscow's insistence on permitting Soviet nationals to serve in the Secretariat only on a seconded, short-term basis (often operating along with members of the Soviet UN mission as not-so-secret state intelligence agents).[132]

In 1965 the Soviets "witnessed the first American defeat on an issue that was crucial to that superpower"[133] (the failure to have the USSR's General Assembly voting rights suspended as punishment for its financial arrearages in accordance with Article 19) and Soviet agreement with the majority started to exceed that of the U.S.[134] Still, the Russians continued to hold a jaundiced view of the UN and remained reluctant participants other than using the body as an instrument for orchestrating propaganda attacks against the West as the enemy of the Third World. The Soviet Union did support strong UN actions on certain occasions when regional conflicts threatened to escalate into superpower military confrontation, such as the creation of peacekeeping forces in the Suez in 1973 (UNEF II) and in Lebanon in 1978 (UNIFIL), only to renege later on its financial commitments. Despite reversing roles with the U.S. on the Security

Council after 1970—the U.S. vetoed five times as many resolutions as the USSR between 1970 and 1986—and seeing its percentage agreement with the General Assembly majority reach an all-time high of almost 80 percent in the 1981–1985 period (sixty-five points better than the U.S.),[135] Moscow shared Washington's concern about Third World demands for increased UN spending on various projects and the possible repercussions stemming from an uncontrollable "tyranny of the majority," especially as membership criticism mounted over the Soviet role in Afghanistan and Kampuchea. The Soviets were as wary of Charter reform as the Americans and were content to let the organization do no more than subsist.

Hence, as Mikhail Gorbachev assumed power in the Kremlin in March of 1985, he inherited a Soviet view of the UN which was at best indifferent to the institution and somewhat fearful of it, based on many of the same misgivings that had developed in the American mind. If a rational actor model provided a good explanation of Soviet policy toward the UN in the pre-Gorbachev era, it also fit well with the new-look Soviet policy that evolved subsequently.

The words which emanated from the Kremlin during the Gorbachev era had a Carter-like resonance to them. Witness Gorbachev's report to the 27th Congress of the Communist Party of the USSR in 1986: "The real dialectics of present day development lies in a combination of competition and confrontation between the two systems [capitalism and communism], with a growing trend toward interdependence among the states of the world community. In just this way . . . a contradictory but interdependent, and in many ways an integral, world is taking shape."[136] He elaborated on this theme in a 1987 writing:

> The exacerbation of global problems is also a characteristic of today's world. They cannot be resolved without the combined efforts of all states and nations. Exploration of epidemics, poverty and backwardness—all these are realities of the age that call for international . . . cooperation.[137]

Likewise, Soviet Foreign Minister Eduard Shevardnadze stated at a Foreign Ministry conference in July of 1988 that "the confrontation between the two systems can no longer be looked upon as the dominant tendency of the current epoch" and that in its place was "the growing tendency towards the mutual interdependence of states in world society."[138] Shevardnadze again, in his September 1988 address to the 43rd UN General Assembly: "The dividing lines of the bipolar world are receding. The biosphere recognizes no division into blocs, alliances, or systems."[139] Before the same body three months later, Gorbachev repeated his call for a new realism: "Behind differences in social structure . . . [and] values stand interests. There is no getting away from that, but neither is there any getting away from the need to find a balance of interests with an international framework."[140] Although such statements were read by some as having a stale quality to them, recalling previous declarations of "peaceful coexistence," there were indications Gorbachev was attempting to distance himself from his predecessors in that "all references to peaceful coexistence as 'a specific form of class struggle'—that first appeared under Khrushchev—were removed from the Party programme at the 27th Party Congress in February 1986."[141]

The new Soviet view of the world was accompanied by a new view of the United Nations in particular.[142] It was the UN that was to be the central international framework Gorbachev had in mind, as expressed in his much-publicized article published shortly after the opening of the 42nd UN General Assembly Meeting in September 1987:

> Objective processes are making our complex and diverse world
> increasingly interrelated and interdependent. And it
> increasingly needs a mechanism which is capable of discussing
> its common problems in a responsible fashion and at a
> representative level. . . . The United Nations Organization is
> called upon to be such a mechanism by its underlying idea and
> its origin.[143]

This was in contrast to what had been the prevailing sentiment, confessed to by the deputy head of the Moscow Institute of the USA and Canada in a fresh show of candor: "We have become accustomed—there is no point in hiding it—to the fact that as short a time as just five years ago hardly anyone read about what was going on in the United Nations . . . it was so boring. People were fed up with it."[144] The UN suddenly seemed not only to take on added salience in Soviet foreign policy but also was seen as "a friendly place."[145]

It would have been easy to dismiss Soviet words as pious and hollow were it not for the fact that they were matched by actions representing a dramatic shift in foreign policy behavior. In addition to their UN-mediated troop withdrawal from Afghanistan, support for peacekeeping efforts in southern Africa, southeast Asia and Latin America, and hands-off posture in regard to the political upheavals in Eastern Europe, the Soviets

in 1986 joined the rest of the Security Council in voting to renew the UNIFIL mandate in Lebanon rather than abstain as in the past and even agreed to help finance the 5,700 man force;

in 1987 indicated an interest in becoming a member of the General Agreement on Tariffs and Trade (GATT);[146]

in 1988 agreed to meet the American demand that no more than half of the nationals of any state could be employed at the upper levels of the UN Secretariat on fixed-term appointments;

in 1989 departed from its traditional support for Arab-bloc attempts to remove Israel from the General Assembly by abstaining on a vote challenging the Israeli delegation's credentials (explaining that "the Soviet Union will seek to participate in all international organizations, and it recognizes that this should be applied to all countries");[147]

by the end of 1989 had paid virtually all of its UN arrearages, totalling over $200 million, making good on Gorbachev's 1987 pledge to "actively cooperate in overcoming the budget difficulties that have arisen in the UNO";[148]

in 1990 upgraded its representation at the UN by appointing a Deputy Foreign Minister as its head delegate;

in 1990–1991 joined with the U.S. and the UN as a whole to facilitate collective security action against its former client Iraq;

and had gone on record as advocating a series of proposals for enhancing the status and capabilities of the UN which could only be described as "remarkable . . . not so much [in] the novelty of such ideas" but in the identity of the state "putting them forward."[149]

The turnabout in Soviet behavior could not be attributed to any moral imperative or religious conversion or domestic political pressure but followed logically from Gorbachev's redefinition of Soviet national interests as requiring international stability in order to buy time for an overhaul of the Soviet economy. Although Gorbachev said that "in a word, a strong and healthy economy is what will bring success in our peace policy,"[150] it was the converse which seemed the motive force behind Soviet behavior, i.e. peace was needed to provide an opportunity to achieve the primary goal of economic modernization. The "new thinking" in foreign policy (*novoye myshleniye*) was a natural complement to *perestroika* and *glasnost*.[151] This logic, along with some subsidiary considerations, explained the sudden Soviet fascination with the UN.

Soviet proposals supporting a strengthening of UN peaceful settlement and peacekeeping machinery recognized the potential utility of the organization as a vehicle for promoting a more peaceful international environment. The Soviets also undoubtedly wished to project a more progressive image and to repair their international reputation tarnished by such episodes as Afghanistan, Kampuchea, and Chernobyl. In addition, insofar as the proposals tended to reinforce the Soviet Union's elite position in the UN, they were calculated to reaffirm the USSR's great-power status at a time when Moscow's prestige was suffering from the loss of control in Eastern Europe, abandonment of client states elsewhere, and still more serious problems internally. It was understood that, were the UN to play a bigger role in world politics, the Soviets were well-equipped to take advantage of the situation. More so than the U.S., they had a substantial bureaucracy with considerable expertise in the workings of the UN (even though as of 1990 they only belonged to eleven of the sixteen specialized agencies).[152]

What specific UN reforms were proposed? The proposals for "the creation of a comprehensive system of international security"—found in two main documents, Gorbachev's September 17, 1987, article in *Pravda* and *Izvestia* and his December 7, 1988, address before the 43rd UN General Assembly[153]—were

first advanced at the 27th Party Congress in 1986 and presented
to the 41st UN General Assembly later that year. As noted previously, Gorbachev was never able to garner support for the
proposals from the U.S. or the bulk of the UN membership despite their attracting considerable attention.[154] Although the initial set of proposals looked, in the words of one observer,
"suspiciously like the reformulation of only too familiar offers
made at various times in the past—even down to proposals on
economic non-aggression dusted off from the Foreign Ministry
files for 1930-1931,"[155] they were refined to the point where they
contained more striking ideas which were far removed from the
Soviet past and far out in front of what many UN members were
prepared to accept.

Among the reforms suggested by the USSR were:

increased compulsory jurisdiction for the World Court;

creation of a tribunal to investigate acts of international ter-
rorism;

increased regulatory power for the International Atomic Energy Agency;

annual meetings of the Security Council at the Foreign Minister level prior to the opening of the General Assembly;

a more active role for the Secretary-General, entitled to "maximum support";

improvement of UN capabilities in the peace and security
area, including more use of independent fact-finding and observer missions, a revival of the Military Staff Committee
(consisting of the Chiefs of Staff of the permanent members of
the Security Council), and creation of mechanisms for "extensive international verification of compliance" with arms control agreements;

establishment of a world consultative council composed of intellectuals with international reputations;

"stricter compliance with decisions of a binding character";

and institutionalization of the "principle of governments' annual report about their conservationist activity and about ecological accidents."

The Soviets proceeded to articulate broader themes which appeared responsive to American concerns about the need for depoliticization, greater efficiency, and improved functioning of a unitary UN amidst pluralism. The Deputy Head of the Soviet UN mission called for "deideologization" and "action to overcome the false politicization of the activities of the UN and its specialized agencies"; "increased professionalization" and "the freeing of the United Nations from . . . fruitless polemics"; "the combining of unified political goals with the multiplicity of procedural . . . decisions and the flexible search for forms of international interaction in each specific case"; "rationalization of the work of international organizations, elimination of duplication and overlapping, concentration on priority issues, and the achievement of effective management of international organizations as a whole"; and "action to . . . make optimal use of the material and financial resources available to the UN."[156]

Admittedly, many of the statements pouring forth from Moscow were largely hortatory in nature and lacking in concreteness (such as the call for greater use of peaceful settlement machinery), some were ritualized incantations (such as the call for removing politics from the technical agencies), others bordered on utopianism (such as the eventual abolition of all weapons of mass destruction), still others defied credibility (such as the claim in the human rights area that "it is essential to develop constructive dialogue with all groups of states in order to . . . give effect to generally accepted international standards . . . and to spur the activities of the relevant international monitoring machinery"),[157] and several fitted more neatly into the conventional Soviet mold (such as the call for a "new international economic order"). In short, the proposal package was a potpourri of thoughts, some more serious than others but on the whole representing a sea-change in Soviet attitudes.

As the Gorbachev era was nearing its end, the Soviets clearly seemed open to a wide number of possibilities and in an accommodative mood. The Soviet commitment to the UN sounded almost boundless. The First Deputy Chairman of the Supreme Soviet stated that, "we are firmly convinced that a new system of international security cannot be built *without* the UN and *outside* the UN" and that "the humanization of international relations is impossible to achieve without humanizing the internal

life of every member country of the international community."[158] Speaking before the "first gathering of the United Nations General Assembly in the post-Cold War era" (one week
after the UN adopted a peace plan for Kampuchea), the Soviet
Deputy Foreign Minister echoed George Bush in urging the UN
to "get down to creative work on shaping a new world order."[159] As Brian Urquhart, a long-time UN observer, commented at the time, "in listening to all this one sometimes feels
like pinching oneself, but there is no question that the international climate has become clement in a way that it has not been
since 1945."[160]

The climate has become more unsettling with the December 8,
1991 demise of the Soviet Union and the instability within and
among the Commonwealth of Independent States that has followed. The Commonwealth is essentially a paper entity whose
future is clouded at best. However, even if Russia and the other
republics are not in a position to devote their full energies to
constructive international institution-building, they at least are
not likely to be obstructionist.

The Russian Federation undoubtedly will emerge as the dominant actor. Although the continuity of the Gorbachev policy toward the UN remains uncertain under Boris Yeltsin or other
successors, there is reason to believe that the same rational actor
calculations which drove Gorbachev to alter Soviet behavior—
particularly the need for a calm international environment to
provide time to repair a ravaged economy—will continue to inform policy formulation in Moscow. Jerry Hough had argued
that Soviet behavior in the 1980s was being driven by factors
larger than a single individual and would continue to evolve
with or without Gorbachev; Hough's thesis was that Gorbachev
reflected mainstream Soviet thinking and was merely trying to
direct and use the "major forces of contemporary Russian history."[161] Similarly, Robert Legvold argued that the change in
foreign policy wrought by Gorbachev was the most far-reaching
since the Bolshevik Revolution in terms of how Moscow viewed
the outside world, and was unlikely to be wholly undone even if
Gorbachev fell from power.[162] (One should not exaggerate Gorbachev's impact on American foreign policy either; it is worth
noting that the U.S. defense budget started shrinking in 1985,
before Gorbachev's arrival on the scene.)

In addition to the changed UN attitudes of the Russians, Urquhart has noted "on top of this the countries of the Third World, after all the rhetoric and radicalism of the 1970s and early 1980s, have become pragmatic, unideological, cooperative, mature and constructively self-critical."[163] Even if the latter observation seems a somewhat exaggerated characterization of the Third World's current posture in the UN, there has been a marked decline in the level of rhetoric heard in the General Assembly debates of late, a fact which can contribute another piece to the puzzle of UN reform. In the words of the former Soviet ambassador to the UN, "the efforts to enhance the role and authority of the United Nations and to make the process irreversible call for the collective will of all Member states and a pooling of their individual efforts."[164] UN reform may not require the blessing of "all Member states," but it will require considerably more than the imprimatur of Moscow along with Washington. As discussed earlier in the chapter, other actors will have to be enlisted in the campaign.

THE VIEW FROM OTHER CAPITALS

The foreign policy behavior exhibited by Western industrialized states in the UN during the postwar period would appear consistent with rational actor model expectations. For the most part, the NATO allies, Japan (once it entered the organization in 1956), and other members of the Western bloc were content to follow the American lead in the UN as long as the U.S. was willing to commit the necessary resources to provide leadership in the international system generally and the world economy in particular, including paying at least 25 percent of the UN budget. This did not mean automatic agreement—there were any number of conflicts with U.S. positions, such as the discord experienced during the Suez and Congo episodes in 1956 and 1960–1964—but rather an overall tendency to vote with the U.S. on decolonialization and other issues which Washington considered important.[165] One analyst of UN roll-call voting, in an early study of political questions debated during the first nine sessions of the General Assembly, found that the U.S. was able to command a majority in the Assembly whenever it chose "to exert strong influence."[166] In a subsequent study, in 1971, the same author noted that despite some erosion in American dominance, "the United States is still, by all informed estimates, the most influential single member of the United Nations and its views are a very important determinant of what goes on there."[167] By the late 1980s, even though the U.S. had long since surrendered control over the General Assembly and regularly found itself at odds with the Scandinavian and Oceanic states and several other OECD members, Washington was still able to realize agreement with its NATO allies as well as Japan almost two-thirds of the time on roll-call votes, with the highest coincidence registered with the United Kingdom, West Germany, and France.[168] However, increasingly in recent years, as Japan and other Western states have become economically competitive with the U.S. and Washington has wavered in its commitment of resources in support of global multilateralism, these states have had to wrestle with their own independent decisions regarding continued support for the UN and the extent to which they were prepared to assume a greater burden of organizational leadership. As discussed below, almost without exception they have reaffirmed their commitment to the UN in financial and other terms, while hoping to prod the U.S. to resume the role of a reliable chief donor.

The behavior of the Warsaw Pact countries in the UN was more readily predictable during the course of the postwar period than the behavior of OECD states or any other group of states, owing to their satellite relationship with Moscow. Within the Eastern European bloc, voting agreement with the USSR in the General Assembly had been close to 100 percent over several decades—the bloc rejecting three out of every four resolutions voted on in the early years and approving four out of every five during the 1980s—although some members, notably Romania, on occasion adopted a maverick stance.[169] One can discern a degree of independent thinking developing even before the Gorbachev era, exemplified by the decision of Poland and Hungary to join the World Bank and International Monetary Fund in the early 1980s. Following upon the upheavals in Eastern Europe in the late 1980s, the Council on Mutual Economic Assistance (COMECON) dissolved in 1991 as did the Warsaw Pact.

With the demise of the Soviet bloc, the Eastern Europeans like their Western European counterparts can be expected to weigh their foreign policy options with greater discretion both inside and outside the UN. Whether a function of inertia, rational choice or other factors, the entire Warsaw Pact membership consistently has supported the Soviet proposal for a comprehensive security system. The bloc's erstwhile members have now all either joined the Bretton Woods institutions or are pursuing membership, meaning that in some ways central guidance in the economic sphere is becoming more fully possible, and in other ways more problematical.

As for the Third World, the less developed countries have behaved in a rational fashion in the UN insofar as they have attempted to overcome differences within and between regional caucusing groups in order to forge a unified nonaligned coalition capable of translating numerical superiority in General Assembly seating into the promotion of mutual interests such as a New International Economic Order. Having failed to achieve NIEO and other goals, scoring little more than symbolic victories during the 1970s and experiencing worsening economic problems in the 1980s, the LDCs as a group have lowered their sights somewhat and have attempted to cut whatever deals they could. Continued frustration could revive militancy among Southern states, although the solidarity of the Third World bloc is being subjected to complicated strains related both to the growing disparity in wealth between various segments of its membership as well as the growing irrelevance of the nonalignment concept as the East-West axis of conflict becomes less and less pronounced. Consensus decision making in the General Assembly as a whole has been on the increase, with nearly 70 percent of decisions taken unanimously during the 45th session in 1990.[170]

There have always been cross-cutting cleavages in the General Assembly as a function of multiple axes of conflict, for example a persistent tendency for East and West to join against Third World efforts to push for Charter revision. The possibilities for manufacturing coalitions across different camps on various issues, such as UN reform, are likely to be especially fertile in the future as the integrity of the major postwar blocs becomes harder to maintain. One need only reflect upon the recent call emanating from Moscow for "the construction of a common European house" and "a common European economic space,"[171] as well as the Cairns group of nine developing countries and five industrialized countries pushing a common agenda on agricultural exports at the 1990 Uruguay Round negotiations. Although new rigidities may well replace the old, there is an element of common ground that can support widescale bridge-building, namely the fact that an assortment of states across geographical, ideological, and other divides are experiencing some malfunctioning of their societies rendering them open to exploring institutional innovation at the systemic level. Commenting on the general disposition of the international system toward change, Henry Kissinger has stated: "Rarely have so many elements of international relations been so fluid simultaneously. The occasion to build a more stable and more hopeful international order occurs no more than once in a century."[172]

Other than the former superpowers, what specific countries can be identified as potential candidates to help constitute the critical mass needed to move the system, based not only on their military, economic or demographic weight but also their manifest disposition to play a leadership role in international institutions? In searching for countries which might contribute to filling the leadership vacuum, it is instructive to look among those states which have demonstrated a particularly strong international organization orientation as measured by number of IGO memberships. In constructing a ranking of the top twenty-six states in terms of IGO affiliations, Jacobson and his colleagues offer the observation that "what is most impressive about the list . . . and the participation of states in IGOs more generally . . . is the extent to which the web has become global."[173] In addition to most members of the European Community as well as Japan, one finds on the list traditionally strong multilateralist states such as Canada and the Scandinavian countries and also a number of states in the Third World increasingly referred to as "middle powers," including India, Brazil, Egypt, and Mexico. Although the list does not distinguish between participation in global as opposed to regional or limited membership IGOs, there is a correlation between the two; the ranking can be taken as an indicator of propensity to commit resources to the pursuit of international collaboration through multilateral institutions.

The People's Republic of China is conspicuously absent from the list, owing both to its delayed entry into the UN in 1971 and China's historical Middle Kingdom inward-looking syndrome. Despite posing as a champion of Third World concerns throughout the postwar era, during its first decade in the UN the PRC was relatively inactive in the General Assembly, regularly was recorded as not participating in Security Council votes (particularly regarding peacekeeping operations), and as of 1980 had ratified only six out of 190 UN treaties while belonging to only five IGOs in the UN system.[174] While China's low profile in the UN was consistent with its attempts to cultivate an image as a true anti-imperialist state devoid of superpower ambitions, its behavior went well beyond merely resisting the use of the veto privilege and other great power trappings. Samuel Kim summed up the PRC's first decade of UN membership, noting:

> China has shown no desire or willingness to assume a leadership role in the United Nations. Except in the Security Council, where the presidency rotates on a monthly basis . . . the PRC has consciously and deliberately avoided occupying any leadership role. None of the PRC delegates has ever served as chairman of any committee or subsidiary body of the General Assembly. In the Asian group meeting, China declines chairmanship even by the rotational system. China's support of the Third World countries generally takes the form of a partisan spectator who cheers, moralizes, and votes when necessary, rather than an active, not to say leading, player in the game of global politics. . . . China almost never sponsors a draft resolution on her own initiative, the most conspicuous exception being the draft resolution to adopt Chinese among the working languages of the General Assembly. . . . The PRC's behavior in the General Assembly may well be recorded in the annals of UN history as a classic case of a major power commanding respect and influence without really trying.[175]

Under Deng Xiaoping's leadership following Mao Zedong's death in 1976, Beijing launched a modernization drive hoping to take advantage of expanding contacts with the West and an open door policy vis-à-vis the world economy. China began to develop an increased presence in the UN during the 1980s, becoming more vocal in Security Council and General Assembly sessions (for example, vetoing Kurt Waldheim's nomination for a second term as Secretary-General in 1981), joining most of the specialized agencies including the World Bank and IMF, and supporting all UN peacekeeping operations (even applying in 1988 for membership in the UN Special Committee on Peace-keeping Operations).[176] China joined the General Assembly consensus supporting the Group of Eighteen recommendations but has abstained on the comprehensive security system pro-posals. On the matter of Charter review, China over the years has been alone among the Big Five in taking a revisionist stance in support of Third World concerns, although Chinese support has been "more symbolic than substantive, more generalized than specific."[177] While recent domestic political problems raise questions about the future direction of the Chinese leadership in foreign policy and other matters, there is reason to believe China will continue on a multilateralist course, given its grow-ing IGO memberships, the payment of all its arrearages to the UN regular budget, and other indicators.

Japan, an obvious choice for a large global leadership role, "appears to be paying increasingly serious attention to interna-tional organizational affairs":

> It is certainly the case that the Japanese financial role in the
> international system has grown steadily during the last decade.
> Japan is now the third largest contributor . . . to the UN's
> regular budget, its assessed share having grown from 2.19% in
> 1956 . . . to 10.32% [by] 1983. If contributions to voluntary
> funds are taken into account, Japan is the second largest
> contributor to the UN system. Moreover, its contributions to
> the multilateral agencies have been increasing. Japan recently
> raised its contributions to the World Bank's IDA, increased its
> subscription to the World Bank generally, increased its
> contributions to UNICEF as well as to various refugee agencies.
> . . . Most recently, Japan announced a . . . plan to recycle $30
> billion of its current account surplus to the developing world,
> with about 60 percent of these funds earmarked for multilateral
> institutions. At the same time Japanese private institutions
> have also been making sizeable loans to the World Bank and
> other international agencies.[178]

Japan played an important part in creating the Group of Eigh-teen reform process and building consensus in support of the recommendations, although it has been virtually alone with the

U.S. in casting its vote against Moscow's most recent UN reform initiatives rather than merely abstaining. It has been argued that Japan lacks not only military prowess and other material assets but also "the ideological appeal to be a twentieth-century super-power,"[179] a reference to the culturally rooted racist and impe-rialist reputation attributed to the Japanese. In trying to dispel such historical images, Tokyo has attempted as much as possible to avoid controversy in the UN, pursuing a policy of "being friendly with everybody."[180] Whether Japan exercises greater multilateral leadership in the future, including adopting a more assertive posture and agreeing to participate in peacekeeping, is more a question of will than power, with the evidence pointing in the direction of Japan becoming an increasingly energetic if still reluctant globally-oriented actor.

In addition to Japan, other members of the Group of Seven major industrialized capitalist states have sought to move the UN reform process along and at recent G-7 economic summits and in other forums have endeavored to bring the U.S. more fully back into the UN fold. By the end of the Gorbachev era, Canada had shifted its vote in favor of the comprehensive secu-rity system proposals and the United Kingdom and France, erst-while opponents, had joined Italy and Germany among the ranks of the abstainers. The role of Germany, in particular, as a key agent in support of global institution-building will hinge upon how it copes with its own national unification and regional integration processes. European Community members in recent years have voted identically in the UN General Assembly ap-proximately 50 percent of the time. Samuel Huntington con-tends that, if the European Community were to achieve greater political cohesion, it would not only have collective resources to be "the preeminent power of the 21st century," but—in contrast to Japan—"it is also possible to conceive of a European ideolog-ical appeal comparable to the American one. . . . The baton of world leadership that passed westward across the Atlantic in the early twentieth century could move back eastward a hun-dred years later."[181] Although the Europeans clearly have their own imperialist history to live down, European states both in-side and outside the Community have evidenced far-reaching internationalism in certain areas, particularly in the environmental field, where they have assumed a leadership role at recent UNEP conferences in London, Helsinki, and the Hague.

Puchala and Coate, in their assessment of "the state of the United Nations," note that "numerous middle powers are now looking for ways to assert themselves in the context of the UN's leadership void," citing in particular Brazil, Egypt, Indonesia, and Nigeria in the South.[182] Along with India, Algeria, and Mexico—among the top countries in IGO memberships—and Argentina, Pakistan, Iran, Saudi Arabia, and Venezuela—among the twenty-five countries constituting the conglomeration of global power represented in the GLOBUS world political model alluded to earlier[183]—these Third World states can add an important demographic and cross-cultural ingredient legitimizing the efforts of an emergent critical mass of actors to develop an improved world order, if their leadership capacities are not excessively stifled by their own serious internal problems. All of the above-mentioned LDCs (excepting Pakistan) have voted in the past in favor of Moscow's call for a comprehensive approach to strengthening international peace and security, associating themselves with the cause of UN reform.

One would be remiss not to add that other kinds of actors, notably global IGO executive heads and secretariats, have more than a casual interest in the subject of UN reform along with some capacity to serve as catalysts for change (as well as forces for conservatism). Still, notwithstanding the assets many such nonstate actors possess, their potential importance in the reform process pales in comparison with "the crucial importance of the governments of states [which] control the resources necessary for action."[184]

Toward a Prominent Solution

Inis Claude has written that

> small states can be expected in very important respects to
> dominate the activity of most international organizations. The
> fundamental reason for this is that small states are more
> interested than great powers in international organizations,
> both in the sense that they have greater need for what those

organizations can give them and in the sense that they are more energetically concerned to exercise control—they work harder at the job. Being significantly dependent upon international agencies for assistance, status, and voice in world affairs, small states tend to treat them as vehicles for their self-assertion. . . . Great powers, dominant in the extra-organizational international environment, tend to treat organizations less seriously, surrendering control over them to small states—and making them less important in the process. . . . There is no indication that the major states of the world are likely to exercise their latent capacity for taking charge of most international organizations.[185]

Claude raises here the critical matter of salience. Are we forced to conclude that, even with the evolving convergence of viewpoints providing generalized systemic support for the revival of multilateralism, it is questionable whether UN governance issues will reach a level of sufficiently high visibility and importance in the capitals of "major states" for the latter to invest their resources to engage the rest of the international community in a serious bargaining exercise over institutional reform? It is true that lesser states are ostensibly more dependent on the UN, especially as a vehicle for regional and extra-regional diplomatic contacts and activities in lieu of the prohibitively expensive alternative of maintaining a global network of bilateral ambassadorial exchanges.[186] In an empirical study of IGO use, James McCormick and Young Kihl conclude that "developing states . . . tend to be selective in their employment of IGOs and seek the greatest payoff when they use them—primarily through the global and high politics IGOs."[187]

However, aside from understating the impact major states have on IGO outputs, Claude may also be understating the importance attached to IGOs by such states, including the countries comprising the Geneva Group which pay over 70 percent of the UN budget while having only 5 percent of the votes in the General Assembly. There is a basis for believing the UN may elicit growing salience from the major actors in the future, with their degree of interest contingent upon the extent to which a restructuring of decision making processes in their favor is viewed as possible. This is so for reasons noted earlier and suggested by Claude himself: as international organizations go, so goes the state system in which the major states have the largest stake. Lynn Miller puts it most plainly when he says, after all, "it is *their* system" for the most part.[188] Even though the stakes have become diffused, and no one actor may have a singularly vested interest in promoting global order as much as in the past, there would appear enough at stake for some subset of states to provide the collective good represented by international institution-building. While national governments may be oblivious to any growing crisis in the human condition, more concrete events, namely the UN's financial crisis as well as the systemic upheavals relating to the demise of the bipolar order, are in fact serving as a stimulus for renewed interest in UN reform. It is possible that the winding down of the East-West geopolitical struggle that has been played out in Latin America, Asia, Africa, and the Middle East over the past half-century will have the effect of focusing the attention of the major players away from the global level, consigning non-Eurasian concerns to benign or not-so-benign neglect, although there is little evidence to support this proposition thus far.[189]

Is there, then, a "prominent solution" to the UN reform "game," an outcome which might be widely acceptable and also have potentially wide impact in terms of institution-building?[190] A prominent solution might well consist of the following general elements: (1) the full restoration of U.S. funding to the UN and payment of arrearages, along with the Geneva Group and other major states utilizing a post-Cold War international peace dividend to provide debt relief or other incentives to persuade the bulk of the UN membership to accept a followership role in institutional reform;[191] (2) an upgrading of the organizational status of those states accepting a greater leadership role, joining the Big Five as part of an enlarged critical mass capable of and willing to move the system;[192] and (3) the full implementation and elaboration of the Group of Eighteen reform package, which combines administrative and political retooling and offers a framework for facilitating a concert of powers approach suitable to the contemporary era, one that permits "some 'power steering' in multilateral agencies, through more sophisticated decision-making devices as well as . . . 'coalitions of the willing' — groups of like-minded countries acting responsibly *under a larger multilateral umbrella* [italics mine]."[193]

As the drama of international institution-building continues to unfold, all signs at present point toward the possibility of a not-so-dramatic but nonetheless hopeful denouement, what Richard Gardner calls "practical internationalism"—a blending of "bilateral, regional, 'plurilateral' and global approaches" to problem solving.[194] This grayish prospect is in need of an animating vision, one that might activate the "latent capacity" of major states to "take charge." Such a vision could be supplied by the model laid out in the previous chapter of an international political development process with the UN situated at the core as a cooperation manager performing the function of a regime-processing center. The author agrees with Oran Young that despite the fact "it is exceedingly difficult to bring about planned or guided changes in complex institutions," "[not] all efforts are doomed to failure."[195] The preceding analysis of the contemporary international system has suggested that conditions are theoretically conducive to the construction of a new order. We now need to explore further how theory can be translated into practice.

PART 3

Practice

4

An Overview of the United Nations System: What Needs Repair?

Is the Problem the Designs of the Members, Or the Design of the Organization?

The aphorism "if it ain't broke, don't fix it" does not apply to the United Nations. That the UN has not worked well and that changes of some sort are needed is an observation which finds few dissenters among serious students or practitioners of international organization.[1] There is disagreement, however, over the potency of formal-legal, as opposed to contextual, explanations of and solutions to UN malfunctioning. In the discussion of the logic of institutionalism in chapter 2, the author quoted Lord Caradon's deprecation of formal-legal critiques of the UN's failure to live up to the expectations that attended its creation in 1945: "There is nothing fundamentally wrong with the United Nations—except its members."[2] Lord Caradon is not alone in his analysis of the UN's troubles. Many individuals closely associated with the UN over time have cautioned against expecting too much from institutional reform. Former Secretary-General Trygve Lie once commented, "The United Nations is what the Member governments want it to be, neither better nor worse."[3] Seymour Finger, a veteran UN watcher, has stated similarly that "my own experience at fifteen sessions of the General Assembly and numerous ECOSOC sessions leads me to conclude that government attitudes are the crucial factor rather than procedural and administrative arrangements."[4] A UN study group charged explicitly with undertaking a reform effort in the 1970s acknowledged in its report that "we wish to emphasize at the outset that no amount of restructuring can re-

place the political will of the Member States to discharge their obligations [under the Charter]."[5]

In one sense these statements border on tautology. With few
exceptions, the organization can do only what its members allow it to do. Much of this study up to now has been taken up
precisely with an exploration of member state characteristics
and other aspects of the UN's organizational environment.
However, characteristics of the organization itself should not be
ignored. Organizational attributes matter, if only because what
its members are willing to utilize the organization for—what
outputs emerge—depends on how power and other relationships are built into the structure of the institution. Institutionalists have pointed out how institutional arrangements have
consequences, and how institutional rearrangement also has
consequences, though not always entirely foreseen or intended.
One can contemplate in eighteenth-century America the Cara-
dons of the day dismissing the call for a constitutional convention with the words: "There is nothing wrong with the United
States under the Articles of Confederation—except its members." Few would argue the U.S. Constitution was superfluous
to the effective functioning and development of the fledgling
American society. While attitudes are obviously critical to the
functioning of collectivities, the nature of the structures themselves can be considered a separate, intervening variable. Attitudinal change may be a prerequisite for organizational change.
But organizational change can also be a catalyst for attitudinal
change.

This study looks at the United Nations and its various organs
(UNO) along with the specialized agencies which together constitute the UN system. If one wishes to properly evaluate and
prescribe remedies for what ails some individual, one must do a
careful diagnosis of the problems that require treatment. Thus
far, I have considered the subject of UN institutional reform
only in very general terms, in the way a doctor might do a pre-
liminary screening of vital signs or inquiry of a patient's mood
prior to launching into a full-scale physical exam. I have examined the world body politic more than the world body itself. We
will now probe more deeply. Before engaging in specific aspects
of organizational design and offering specific prescriptions for
UN reform, it is necessary to analyze the UN's organizational

structure and behavior and what weaknesses have been most evident, particularly as this relates to its serving as an engine for the growth of a global security-community. Following this overview, the next chapter will survey the history of UN reform efforts in the form of critical reports and studies aimed at addressing weaknesses, to see what if any lessons can be learned from these experiences, and will focus on some recent proposals.

The UN Charter: A Backward- and Forward-Looking Constitution

While in many respects there has been enormous (some might say cancerous) growth in the UN system through the proliferation of programs, committees, commissions, councils, agencies and other organizational forms, the basic underlying structural foundation of the system ordained in the UN Charter has remained largely intact. The UN Charter as a treaty can trace its lineage as far back as the agreement concluded between the city-states of Lagash and Umma around 3100 B.C., written in the Sumerian language on a stone monument, the oldest record of formal cooperation between societies. The Charter itself in some ways seems written in stone insofar as it has gone virtually unamended, although organizational evolution has occurred nonetheless. The UN as an organization can trace its roots from the Delian League of ancient Greece, and in modern times from the Concert of Europe and the Hague conference system in the nineteenth century through the League of Nations in the early twentieth century—all experiments in multilateral *institution-building* innervated mostly by a formalized concert of great powers approach to world order as an alternative to cruder balance of power or hegemonic invisible hand mechanisms.

The UN represented a new, higher level of institutionalization that went well beyond its predecessors. Unlike the Concert of Europe (which, aside from its geographical limits, was not really an organization), the Hague system (which had a physical apparatus in the form of a Permanent Court of Arbitration but was not a comprehensive organization), and the League (which did

possess machinery to deal with a full range of war/peace and
economic/social concerns but whose mandate in the former area
was only to obligate disputants to wait three months before
turning from peaceful settlement to war, and whose mandate in
the latter area was even more limited),[6] the United Nations—
"mankind's most ambitious international structure,"[7] at least on
paper—sought to outlaw armed aggression totally through explicit enforcement machinery and sought to attack economic
and other problems through an expanded network of institutions unprecedented in their scope and reach.

The establishment of a set of organs whose ostensible mission
was not only war prevention but also economic and related problem-solving could be attributed to a variety of factors, including
habit (the inclination to replicate and build on the League foundation), politics (the felt need by the great-power architects of the organization to offer lesser states a trade-off for the special
institutional privileges accorded the former), and perhaps even
thoughtful analysis (the recognition of the relationship between
physical violence and structural violence). As noted in the earlier
discussion of the American view of the UN, the founders con-
cocted an organization formed by a mix of motives, blending at
least one part idealism with several parts realism. It was not conceived as a pie-in-the-sky institution. The plan was ambitious; naive it was not, certainly not as naive as the pious Kellogg-Briand
Pact of the interwar period with its wholly hollow contents. In assessing what went wrong and what problems continue to plague
the organization, I will focus first on the performance of the UN
machinery in the peace and security field and will then examine
the other parts of the system.

The UN as a Promoter of Peace

THE STRUCTURAL FOUNDATION

No amount of data drawn from participant observation or
subsequent analysis can reveal for certain the thinking that went
into the creation of the UN between its genesis at the Moscow
Conference in October 1943 and its Charter coming into force
two years later in October 1945. Nonetheless, there is every rea-

son to believe that among the uppermost considerations in the minds of many elites representing their brethren of the World War II generation was the desire, stated at the very outset of the preamble to the United Nations Charter, "to save succeeding generations from the scourge of war." This primary concern was reiterated in the first line of the first article of the first chapter of the Charter with the stated goal "to maintain international peace and security." Even for the supreme cynic, it should not be hard to imagine the leadership of the day in the U.S. and elsewhere being genuinely moved by the devastation caused by World War II, which claimed over 60 million lives and touched almost every family in the thirty participating states as well as peoples in other corners of the world not directly parties to the conflict. With World War I within living memory of the same generation, this was a crucible experience on a scale beyond any previous human calamity before or since. While one could cite other historical catastrophes that were quantitatively comparable or even more striking in their destructiveness (for example, the total annihilation of Carthage in the Third Punic War, the death of one-third of the Germanic population during the Thirty Years War, the death of roughly 25 million victims of the Bubonic Plague between 1347 and 1350 resulting in the extinction of one-third to one-half of all of Europe, the death of 30 million Chinese during the T'ai P'ing rebellion between 1850 and 1864, and the influenza pandemic that took 22 million lives in 1917–1918 adding to the wages of war), much of humanity could be blissfully ignorant or unconcerned about such episodes and the larger prospect of species extermination in a way they could not be after Hiroshima.

It is also not hard to imagine the leadership of these states that had just emerged victorious from the war and had assumed the burden of designing the new organization as defining the problem of world order in terms consistent with their interests and rationalizing their architectural plan as the product of noble, altruistic impulses serving the whole of humanity. Still, the self-serving framework of the edifice could be seen by any worldly schoolchildren who bothered to read the Charter or make the trip to New York. The chief framers of the Charter, mindful of the need to imbue the organization with as much legitimacy as possible, took care to mention the General Assembly plenary body first under the principal organs identified in Chapter III and to elaborate its functions and other features in Chapter IV before any other organ. However, it was understood that the Security Council would be where the main action would occur; it was given in Chapter V "primary responsibility for the maintenance of international peace and security" (Article 24) and, toward that end, the rare power to make certain decisions binding on the entire UN membership. It was also understood that a select few would dominate the Council, namely the Big Five members of the winning wartime coalition, who were accorded permanent seats and veto power.

Not wanting to overburden the organization, or inflate its importance, the authors of the Charter specified in Chapter VI that the UN was to be used selectively and sparingly in conflict resolution, with disputants directed "first of all [to] seek a solution" by themselves or through "regional agencies" and only then, having failed, to "refer it to the Security Council" (Articles 33 and 37). Chapter VII of the Charter proscribed the use of armed force in relations between states except under three conditions: in individual or collective self-defense, through an alliance, against an armed attack (Article 51); in the service of the UN as part of a collective security operation (Article 42); or as part of a regional security organization with the approval of the Security Council (Article 53). (In an admitted flight from reality, the Charter even went so far as to prohibit the "threat of force.") The main implication of the veto provision was that five states were effectively exempted from the judgment of the organization as to whether their behavior constituted aggression, or for that matter constituted any other serious breach of the Charter. Although technically a Council member was supposed to refrain from voting in cases where it was a party to a dispute, the veto provision extended to determinations of whether a situation could be labeled as such.

The logic of a "concert of great powers" approach to international order was hardly grounded in moral precepts or scientific analysis. The accepted wisdom—few states were in a position to question it—was that, based on the League experience in which several major actors were absent from the organization at one time or another, the UN's best shot at success required the full participation of the great powers, with the veto privilege the price of cooptation and commitment. It was not unreasonable to assume in 1945 that the organization stood a chance of at least preventing aggression by a revisionist-minded Germany or other "enemy state" (Article 53) as well as by lesser powers, as long as the leading Council members shared an interest in the status quo. As for aggression by the U.S., Britain, France, China or the USSR, sitting as they were on top of the world, they presumably could afford to be exemplars of non-aggression. There was certainly more realism evident in developing the UN's collective security mandate than had been the case with the League, whose Covenant provided for a Permanent Military, Naval and Air Commission to facilitate "reduction of armaments" (Article 8) but provided only vague "guarantees against aggression" (Articles 10, 11, and 16). The founders of the UN recognized the need to construct enforcement machinery that could be activated should pacific settlement fail and the peace be violated. Hence, the peaceful settlement provisions enunciated in Chapter VI of the Charter calling for the use of mediation, arbitration, and other such procedures were supported by collective security provisions in Chapter VII calling for specific economic and military sanctions against aggressors (Articles 41–45) and establishing a Military Staff Committee composed of "the Chiefs of Staff of the permanent members . . . responsible for the strategic direction of any armed forces placed at the disposal of the Security Council" (Article 47).

Alas, the onset of the Cold War rendered all these assumptions and efforts highly problematic. The Big Five concert framework was left to operate as best it could in a world that had moved quickly toward a bipolar balance of power structure. The essential features of the Council have remained unchanged over five decades, notwithstanding the 1965 Charter amendment expanding the body's nonpermanent membership from six to ten states, the subsequent General Assembly resolution producing a distribution formula for the rotating seats (five allocated to Asia and Africa, two to Latin America, one to Eastern Europe and two to Western Europe and other states), the displacement of the Republic of China by the People's Republic as the occupant of the Chinese seat, and some other constitutional-statutory developments. Efforts to amend the Charter to modify the veto power or to make other significant changes have been deterred not only by the expectation that the Big Five would use their veto power over Charter amendments to block any such proposals but also by a general unreadiness of the UN membership to engage in the kind of fundamental rethinking of organizational arrangements such changes would entail.

In assessing how the UN has performed since 1945 in the peace and security field, it is worth quoting a diplomat who, commenting on the flurry of conflict resolution activity undertaken by the organization in the late 1980s and early 1990s, remarked at the time that "the UN plumbing has been in place for many years even though nothing was flowing through the pipes."[8] While substantial structures had been created, they were never fully operational despite some retrofitting done during the course of the postwar era. At the same time, the volume of outputs generated during the postwar era was uneven, marked by profuse failure but at least a trickle of successes.

UN performance in the peace and security field is hard to assess, since it depends upon the criteria employed, which can include the relative amount of usage (the number of disputes submitted to the organization as a percentage of all disputes in the international system), the capacity to take action (the number of peacekeeping missions and other responses attempted in conflict situations), the relative degree of success in conflict management or resolution (as a percentage of all conflicts or as a percentage of all conflicts handled), and other measures. Aside from operationalization difficulties as to what constitutes a dispute and what constitutes action or success, there is much that can be distorted or overlooked in evaluating the UN record.[9] Actions can range from mere entreaties embodied in Security Council resolutions (for example, Resolution 598 in 1987 calling for an armistice during the Iran-Iraq War) to full-scale operations (such as the UNIIMOG observer mission subsequently organized to police the ceasefire). There is no way to know how many wars have been averted as a result of the surrogate for violence or safety valve function often attributed to the UN. It is problematical to demonstrate empirically Oran Young's argument made some time ago that during periods of crisis the UN "has some effect in setting the general atmosphere and climate of opinion in which bargaining among the principals [takes] place."[10] Likewise, it is hard to capture in statistical terms the role of the UN in presiding over one of the largest transformations in human history—the coming to independence of some 1 billion people and 100 new states after 1945, a relatively peaceful revolution, all things considered. Still, one does not have to do a systematic analysis to conclude that, measured against the Charter's blanket proscription regarding the threat or use of offensive armed force against any member of the international community, the record has come up short.

Those who have bothered to do systematic analyses have found that over its lifetime the UN has compiled a mixed record on various dimensions. Haas found that between 1945 and the early 1980s, almost half of all interstate disputes he identified were referred to the UN; of those referred to it, the UN helped to manage if not settle roughly half.[11] Wilkenfeld and Brecher found that between 1945 and 1975, the organization became involved in more than half of all international crises and was effective at crisis abatement in one-third of those cases, with effectiveness increasing as the situation became more serious and more violent.[12] Another study on which this author collaborated found that the UN has tended to receive more salient disputes than the League did.[13] Consistent with the Charter conception of the UN as a forum of last, or late, resort, the UN has attracted its share of seriously escalated conflicts, which can be taken as an indicator of success but also as an invitation to failure.

Although initially the UN acted in the war/peace area as had been envisioned (with the Security Council averaging over 130 meetings annually between 1946 and 1948), what successes occurred during the UN's first decades, in terms of not only attracting business but also taking energetic action of some consequence, owed partly to institutional usage not fully comprehended by the Charter.[14] This was certainly true of the three most visible episodes in the UN's early history. The collective security operation during the Korean War was made possible by the Soviet Union's boycott of Security Council meetings in protest of the exclusion of the Communist Chinese, and by the acceptance of the convention that, in Council voting, abstention or nonparticipation by a permanent member was not equivalent to a veto. The 6,000-person UN Emergency Force (UNEF I) inserted into the Suez crisis in 1956 was authorized by the General Assembly under the Uniting for Peace Resolution in circumvention of British and French vetos on the Security Council and in seeming incompatibility with the Charter. The 20,000-person UN Operation in the Congo (ONUC) formed in 1960 was largely the creation of Secretary-General Hammarskjold, whose actions went well beyond the power of initiative implied in Article 99. Although these cases showed the adaptability of the organization, they did little to strengthen it. None were to become models of organizational behavior to be emulated in future crises.

The innovation of peacekeeping, whereby the UN undertook to furnish a neutral military presence or observer mission representing a degree of involvement beyond peaceful settlement but short of collective security (so-called "Chapter VI and one half"), evolved without the organization formally taking notice of it despite some attempts to institutionalize the practice, such as the guidelines contained in the Secretary-General's report two years after the creation of UNEF I.[15] Alan James has pointed out that peacekeeping actually predated the UN; he counted 75 cases between 1920 and 1990, including many in the interwar period.[16] Notwithstanding several such operations in the immediate postwar period—UNSCOB established in 1947 to monitor violations along the Greek border, UNTSO created in 1948 to supervise the Arab-Israeli truce, and UNMOGIP formed in 1949 to monitor the Kashmir ceasefire between India and Pakistan, these missions ranging in size from 20 to 700 persons— peacekeeping did not enter the UN vernacular and conceptual scheme until well after Suez, and has never received expression in the Charter.

The gravitation of the peace and security function away from the Security Council and toward other organs (manifested by the Security Council meeting only five times in 1959)—a rearranging of the pipes—was short-lived. As the postwar era progressed, UN peacekeeping and other activities were increasingly constrained by the structural paralysis built into the Security Council, held hostage to the American-Soviet tacit agreement that the Council should be reinstated as the locus of decision making and to the willingness of the U.S. and the Soviet Union to refrain from their use of the veto.[17] The UN spigot could be turned on and off only by the two superpowers, depending upon their level of cooperation. No peacekeeping missions were created between 1965 and 1973, the UN climate poisoned by the fallout from the Vietnam War and the Article 17 financial crisis following the Congo operation. The UN Force in Cyprus (UNFICYP) was established in 1964 only through reliance on voluntary contributions rather than on Charter-mandated assessments. There were stirrings of activity during the detente era of the 1970s, with the Security Council in 1973–1974 authorizing the UNEF II and UN Disengagement Observer Force (UNDOF) operations to help disengage the Israelis from the Egyptians and Syrians following the fourth Arab-Israeli war, and in 1978 authorizing the UN Interim Force in Lebanon (UNIFIL) to facilitate Israeli withdrawal from Lebanon, each with over 1,000 troops. Although each received the Council's blessing, financing issues remained unresolved as the Soviets and others rejected the principle of mandatory assessments.

While the UN's overall postwar record showed some measure of accomplishment in the peace and security field despite periodic "plumbing" stoppages, the situation had become more serious by the late 1980s as UN activity had practically dried up in the wake of the American-Soviet Cold War revival. No new peacekeeping operations were mounted between 1979 and 1988, although UNIFIL and a few other extant operations were continued. Other actions were attempted, such as Secretary-General Waldheim's rare invocation of Article 99 in 1979–1980 in an effort to mediate an end to the Iranian hostage crisis, along with the initiatives taken by his successor to defuse the Iran-Iraq war and other regional conflicts. UNIFIL—which had been approved after only a few minutes of debate (the Soviets abstaining), which matched the size of UNEF I, and which persisted despite its interim title and rather dismal results—was a reminder that the UN's capacity to take and sustain substantial action was not to be equated necessarily with successful organizational performance.[18]

The UN's performance had declined to the point where serious scholarly work could be found in the 1980s entitled "Is There a Role for the United Nations in Conflict Resolution?"[19] The common view prevailing through most of the decade, even

among the UN faithful, was expressed in one 1987 study that
characterized "the current situation of the United Nations [as]
one of deep crisis" and attributed this to the fact that "the world
has changed since 1945," leaving the UN behind.[20] In particular,
in the peace and security area

> the most commonplace conflicts now fall beyond the primary
> scope of action envisioned in the security provisions of the UN
> Charter. They include: civil wars; wars between a superpower
> and a Third World regime (fought directly or through proxies);
> terrorist campaigns; attacks upon the civil authorities by
> powerful outlaw groups, such as narcotics gangs; and so on.
> . . . The result is that the UN tends to be marginal to the
> prevention, containment and resolution of most modern day
> conflict.[21]

The world seemed to change again rather quickly and dramatically within one year after the above study was published, as
observers witnessed not merely another thaw in the Cold War
but the melting away of the entire bipolar era. Ronald Reagan's
remark before the UN General Assembly in 1988, that "a change
that is cause for shaking the head in wonder is upon us,"[22] captured the feelings of much of humanity, intellectuals and non-
intellectuals alike. The problem was that the situation was so
fluid that one had to wonder when the next sea-change might
occur. The UN, meanwhile, was suddenly awash in demands
for its conflict resolution services. Four peacekeeping missions
were authorized in 1988, with others to follow, as the UN assumed a central role in the "breaking out of peace" phenomenon that cut across various regional conflicts (including a
number of civil wars). With the breakout of war in the Gulf in
1990 (pitting inter alia the Council's permanent membership
against a secondary power), the UN performed a collective security function much as the Charter had envisaged. There was
also activity on the antiterrorism front (including resolutions
and conventions aimed at narcoterrorism). It appeared the UN
was still relevant to the times, maybe more relevant than ever.
Writings no longer asked whether the UN had a role to play but
what that role might be and how it might best be facilitated.[23]

One should not rush to judgment on such matters, given the failure of one of the 1988 peacekeeping missions and the uncertainty surrounding the other UN involvements of late. The 1988 Good Offices Mission in Afghanistan (UNGOMAP), through the dispatch of 50 military observers, did help facilitate the withdrawal of 100,000 Soviet troops but was terminated out of inability to cope with the ancillary issues relating to the power struggle between the Afghan government and the Mujahedeen rebels, leaving the Secretary-General to search for a settlement. The contribution of over 300 UN observers forming the Iran-Iraq Military Observer Group (UNIIMOG), sent in 1988 to supervise the ceasefire between the two states, remains to be fully weighed, given the absence of a final settlement regarding sovereignty over the Shatt al-Arab waterway. Two other peacekeeping missions authorized in 1988—the UN Angola Verification Mission (UNAVEM) and the UN Transition Assistance Group (UNTAG)—can be considered successes up to now, although these also evidence a fragile quality. Approximately 70 UNAVEM observers monitored the withdrawal of Cuban and South African troops from Angola. The much larger UNTAG mission (approximately 7,500 military and civilian personnel drawn from 109 countries), managed to supervise elections in Namibia in 1989 and to bring that country to independence in 1990. Since 1989, the UN Security Council and the Secretary-General in conjunction with the Association of South East Asian Nations have labored to fashion a settlement of the Kampuchea conflict, with some progress made in completing the removal of Vietnamese troops and forging a new government of national reconciliation. The 1991 accord that created a UN Transitional Authority to monitor the ceasefire and conduct elections, however, left lingering issues. Similarly, the tentative agreement reached in 1988 between Morocco and POLISARIO insurgents over the status of Western Sahara, under the auspices of the UN and the Organization of African Unity, called for a cease-fire and referendum yet to be fully implemented; the UN mission sent to assist the process (MINURSA) has experienced great difficulty in getting the parties to cooperate. The ultimate success of the

UN Observer Group (ONUCA) created in 1989 to monitor the
cease-fire between the Contras and Sandinistas in the Nicaraguan civil war (arranged with the help of the Organization of
American States), along with that of the follow-up UN mission
sent to monitor the election of a new Nicaraguan government
(ONUVEN), remains in doubt as political and economic instability prevails. The 15,000 peacekeepers dispatched to Yugoslavia
in 1992 (UNPROFOR) from the start found themselves in harm's
way, facing a highly volatile situation. UNFICYP continues to
function (the recent good offices efforts of the Secretary-General
to get agreement on a single federal Cypriot state not yet bearing
fruit), as do UNTSO, UNMOGIP, UNIFIL, and UNDOF—their
longevity testifying to both the stubbornness of the conflicts and
the latters' amenability in some measure to conflict management
if not conflict resolution.

While the UN role in the Gulf War has been widely viewed as
a victory for collective security, its historical importance will depend upon whether it proves to be an isolated case or to have set
a precedent that can be duplicated and routinized to some degree in the future. In some respects the utilization of the UN to
combat Iraqi aggression was an institutional advancement over
the Korean War collective security operation insofar as it took
advantage of the full array of economic and military sanctions
alluded to in Chapter VII and occurred with the full participation of the permanent members of the Security Council (China
abstaining on key resolutions, thereby giving its tacit approval).
In other respects, the Gulf War case marked an institutional setback compared to Korea insofar as the military force that was
mobilized (Desert Storm) was not technically a UN force—there
was no Unified Command designated by the Council—but
rather was an American-led multinational force organized in the
first instance under the self-defense provisions of Article 51 and
only secondarily supported by Council resolutions taken under
the collective security provisions of Chapter VII. Although the
allied coalition suffered relatively few casualties (under 200
killed in action) despite predictions of Vietnam War-level losses
on the American side, it is conceivable that fewer risks might
have been incurred and war perhaps averted altogether if somehow it had been possible to confront Iraq with the specter of a
military force that was more plainly a UN army (complete with

the powerful symbolism of blue-helmeted troops serving under a UN flag and an Arab or non-American general sharing at least nominal command). Even though over 500 UN soldiers have been killed in action since 1945, military forces functioning under the UN banner have tended to have a greater protective aura of neutrality around them than other combatants. In the end it was the political cover provided by the UN, in tandem with superior firepower, that won the day for the coalition.

The Gulf War offered a model not only for punishing aggression but also for organizing the subsequent peace. Security Council resolution 687, passed in April 1991, established the UN Iraq-Kuwait Observer Mission (UNIKOM), consisting of over 1,000 military observers and support troops from thirty-six countries (including all the Big Five) under the command of the Secretary-General and charged with policing a demilitarized zone extending into Iraq and Kuwait. UNIKOM was to be financed by the assessed contributions of UN member states to a special account along with voluntary contributions, with costs estimated at $123 million for twelve months (compared to the $50 billion price tag of the entire Desert Storm operation, borne by the U.S. and a handful of states). Resolution 687 also created a special commission to supervise other aspects of the cease-fire agreement, including elimination of Iraq's chemical and nuclear weapons capabilities and certain classes of ballistic missiles. The UN role did not stop there, as the organization also became involved in developing a formula for providing a safe haven (a substate) for Kurdish rebels within Iraq following their attempted rebellion against the Hussein regime.

It is too soon to say whether all of this signals a new world order or at least a new UN. Aside from the as yet uncertain outcomes of specific conflicts, there are larger questions to be confronted. The UN's recent activism has a familiar cast to it, dependent as it has been on past correlates of success, namely the relaxation of East-West tensions, begging the question of whether those tensions will continue to subside and allow opportunities for organizational involvement in conflict situations. But the UN's recent activism also evidences some new elements and raises questions regarding the possibilities for task expansion and organizational growth. The traditional categories of interstate war and civil war and of peaceful settlement, peacekeeping, and collective security do not do justice to the range of situations in which the UN has involved itself and the range of functions it has been called upon to perform since the late 1980s. As two writers note:

> At times the UN has mediated in an effort to find a formula for a cease-fire and peace talks (Afghanistan, Gulf War); at other times it has only been an observer in those talks (Namibia). . . . In Namibia it had to contribute, during a transitional period, to nation-building. In Nicaragua, the UN had to monitor elections for the first time in a sovereign country. In other cases, the stationing of peacekeeping forces became part of the settlement, with a steadily increasing set of functions, including monitoring cease-fires, the withdrawal of foreign troops, and the disarmament and demobilization of irregular forces, as well as supervising the repatriation and integration of former guerrillas, refugees, and prisoners of war, and non-interference in internal affairs, arms supplies, electoral processes, referenda, and economic reconstruction.[24]

These writers add that "recent UN involvement has led to a . . . complex structure of ad hoc cooperation among the Security Council, the Secretary-General, the General Assembly, . . . UN agencies, and . . . regional and global actors."[25]

Clearly, there is little to support the argument that the UN is marginal to most modern day conflict. The Charter was actually quite visionary in taking a broad view of the problem of global violence and the varied, murky forms it might assume in the postwar era (including "force without war," "low intensity conflict," "peaceful engagement," and "national liberation struggles"); the term "war" is mentioned only once, in the preamble. But the original "plumbing", which at best has worked erratically, can stand some reinspection and repair if the organization hopes to cope with the current deluge of demands and to produce a more sustainable flow of activity. The problem to be fixed is not the disuse of the UN. The purpose of improvements should not be to increase the number of conflicts with which the UN is busied but (1) to reduce the number of conflicts in the international system, particularly militarized disputes (those that are characterized by the threatened or actual use of armed force), and (2) to develop effective mechanisms for managing and resolving those that arise. The first desideratum must await the cultivation of habits of cooperation; while waiting for the latter to materialize, the second desideratum entails some routinization of conflict termination processes. Rather than relying so heavily on ad hoc arrangements, there is the need and the opportunity at present to achieve greater institutionalization of the UN role in the peace and security area, granted each situation has its own unique features calling for a degree of flexible response.

Regional organizations remain an alternative to the UN as vehicles for handling conflicts, but the historical record shows that since 1945 regional IGOs have tended to be reserved for "far less intense" disputes,[26] and in recent years especially have complemented rather than substituted for global institutional responses to local conflicts. Peacekeeping (in its various guises) and collective security are far more impressive modes of UN action than peaceful settlement, but are also far more taxing. Although it may be unrealistic as a rule to expect the UN to be used in the early stages of a dispute, it may be possible—in synch with regional security organizations—to develop a capability to intervene early enough with good offices and related techniques so as to obviate any need for peacekeeping or collective security responses. The recent creation of the UN Office of Research and Collection of Information, designed to facilitate fact-finding by the Secretary-General as part of an early warning system of crisis avoidance, is a step in the right direction, although ORCI was conceived more as a "global watch" structure for international problem solving and policy making than as a structure for defusing specific disputes. Another structural matter to be addressed is the growing tendency when disputes come before the Security Council for Council meetings to be taken up with the presentations made by dozens of states not members of the Council or parties to the conflict, in effect utilizing the forum as a variant of the General Assembly's Political and Security Committee; what is gained in opening up the Council meetings to full-scale debate among many participants has to be weighed against the inevitable shift of Council members toward even greater reliance than previously on informal, closed-door settings as a basis for deliberations.

It is a sign of the times that even adjudication, the most ambitious and least utilized mode of peaceful settlement at the global level, has attracted somewhat increased attention recently.[27] After seeing its caseload decline from twenty-nine contentious cases submitted during the 1950s to five during the 1980s— rendering a total of fifty-one judgments (along with twenty-one advisory opinions) between 1945 and 1990—the International Court of Justice found itself at the outset of the 1990s with eight cases on its docket and with some momentum generated by the use of the court by states as varied as the U.S. and Canada, Mali and Burkina Faso, and El Salvador and Honduras. As one observer noted, this was "not exactly a thundering herd, but a sign of something new leading perhaps to the more frequent and effective use of the Court."[28] The newness consisted particularly in the employment of the chambers procedure of the Court, exemplified by the smaller panel of ICJ judges hearing the *Gulf of Maine* dispute between the U.S. and Canada (in addition to one judge from each side). Although this is suggestive of how creative institutional retooling can reinvigorate institutions, the Court obviously has a long way to go before it can be considered a major cog in the peace and security machinery and something more than "the highest legal aspiration of civilized man."[29] Aside from the fact that as of 1990 only forty-six states had signed the Optional Clause of the ICJ Statute, agreeing to give the Court compulsory jurisdiction in certain kinds of cases, the Court suffers from the fundamental problem that in disputes involving vital interests states are unwilling to entrust a third party with ultimate decision-making competence, while in disputes over lesser matters it is normally simpler and cheaper (even with the chambers innovation) to settle out of court.

In the case of those conflicts escalating to the point that Chapter VI solutions are unavailing and more strenuous action is necessitated, it would behoove the UN to have in place certain guidelines and standard operating procedures for recruiting, training, equipping, and financing the various types of missions that now fall under the rubric of peacekeeping. The Senior Planning and Monitoring Group created in 1990 to help the Secretary-General administer the sundry peacekeeping operations under his supervision needs further elaboration. Despite some improvements made recently in reorganizing the UN Department of Political Affairs, peacekeeping and peace-making/ mediation functions remain segmented under separate institutional roofs and are in need of better articulation with emergency relief and other related activities. The UNGOMAP and MINURSA experiences, and particularly the Yugoslav case, demonstrate the dangers UN missions are exposed to when they are inserted into hostilities prematurely before adequate progress has occurred on the diplomatic front. There is a problem also with peacekeeping expenses usually treated separately from the UN budget and based on different assessment scales, adding to the haphazard functioning of the organization in the peace and security field. The UN Special Committee for Peacekeeping, which since 1965 has endeavored unsuccessfully to produce a set of guidelines governing the management of peacekeeping operations, may now be in a better position to carry out its task given China's recent acceptance of committee membership, the generally improved international climate, and the fact that the issues are getting harder to avoid (with the money spent annually on peacekeeping since 1989 approaching or exceeding the regular UN budget).[30]

The Gulf War collective security operation, although in many respects a highly efficient enterprise, came close to collapse at various points due to a variety of problems having to do with uncertainty over the imposition and monitoring of nonmilitary sanctions, the extent of the Security Council mandate authorizing military sanctions, the troop command structure, intelligence coordination and other aspects of the multinational force, and the procedures for arriving at and implementing the terms of a cease-fire. Because the operation was not a UN force as such meant that financing could not be done readily through a UN account based on assessments or voluntary contributions. The absence of accepted burden-sharing arrangements in turn required the U.S. to go hat-in-hand from country to country, thereby undermining American domestic political support for military sanctions and contributing to the close vote in Congress supporting the use of armed force.[31] Some of the problems were unavoidable, but others could have been provided for and anticipated.[32] The punishment inflicted on Iraq figures to deter the most blatant kinds of interstate aggression in the near term at least. However, if the lessons of the Gulf War experience are to become part of the memory bank of would-be aggressors and have an enduring effect—if the expectation of collective security is to become a reality—attention needs to be given to promoting greater institutional readiness in the form of clearer understandings surrounding the application of economic sanctions, a standby military force with a regularized chain of command supported by a reserve fund, and other ingredients for successful collective security.

The Kurdish question, left as a loose end from the Gulf War, along with Namibia, Nicaragua, and some other recent UN involvements have posed further opportunities and problems. Again, these cases represent new territory for the UN to enter in terms of more complex tasks assigned to it that fall between the cracks of peaceful settlement, peacekeeping, and collective security. Although the notion of creating a semi-sovereign Kurdish substate under UN supervision within Iraqi territory (or a like Palestinian entity as proposed within Israel) seems a throwback to the old mandate and trusteeship systems in the colonial era, and although the UN involvement in Namibia and Nicaragua recalls the UN's Congo civil war intervention, what is novel here is the major role being thrust upon the UN as an agent of not only nation-building but also democratization. Institutional capabilities in this area are lacking and need to be developed. One study labels the Namibia case as "a classic example of institutional overlap and confusion," citing the assorted attempts at one time or another to use standing and ad hoc committees of the General Assembly, the Security Council, the Secretary-General's office, the ICJ, and other instrumentalities.[33]

While the possibilities such situations present for organizational growth are intriguing, the UN risks becoming seriously overextended and tarnished with failure. Notwithstanding the trend toward democratization, stable democracies have proven extremely difficult to establish through any means in the postwar era. To say the UN is being called upon to provide "technical assistance for democracy"[34] does not begin to describe the enormity of the challenge and the potentially explosive issues to be addressed. In arranging for and monitoring free elections, the UN role is complicated by the ever-present danger of alienating the Russians and Chinese from other permanent members of the Security Council on human rights issues and by the weak membership consensus generally behind definitions of democracy. Although Western-style principles and operational measures have begun to take hold,[35] the controversial nature of the criteria to be employed is reflected in the recent efforts of the Third World states to pack the Economic and Social Council's Human Rights Commission with additional Third World seats over American objections. It is hard to see how the UN can take effective action as an agent of democratization in the absence of solid institutional underpinnings in the human rights field and, for that matter, in the general realm of economic and social problem solving.

The "Other UN"

THE UN AS A GLOBAL POLICY SYSTEM

Although summary judgments about the value and effectiveness of the UN in the minds of publics and elites tend to be based on the organization's performance in the peace and security field, over three-fourths of its regular budget is expended on activities in economic, social and technical areas—the "other UN."[36] As Maurice Bertrand indicates, peacekeeping aside, "the distribution of the total resources . . . in the [UN's] program budget . . . shows that the UN is mainly an economic and social organization with heavy emphasis on humanitarian and operational activities in the field of development. In fact, 75 percent of the UN's resources are used in these fields. Political and legal activities represent less than 6 percent. The remaining 20 percent is used for the support of the forum of discussion and negotiation and for general administration."[37] Peacekeeping operations, at least until recently, have represented "7.6 percent of the total amount of resources available to the UN."[38] When one adds the work of the specialized agencies in the UN system, the equation becomes all the more weighted toward functional (welfare-oriented) concerns. The performance of the "other UN" has always been the subject of considerable criticism, but has elicited particularly negative reactions lately when juxtaposed against the newfound UN vibrancy in the war/peace area. Based on extensive interviews with UN Secretariat officials and diplomats, Donald Puchala and Roger Coate found that "the [recent] enthusiasm and optimism of the peacekeepers differs markedly from the frustration and pessimism of the international developers."[39]

The pessimism is understandable given the stagnating conditions found throughout much of the developing world over the past decade and the seeming inability of the UN to make a dent in the problems despite the presence of a vast institutional apparatus, the convening of numerous conferences and special sessions of the General Assembly, and substantial outlays of technical and other assistance. Just as in the case of the peace and security field, however, the UN record in the economic and social sector can be difficult to assess and must be put in proper perspective. First, one must identify and measure economic and social indicators of progress in the global system relating not just to development but welfare concerns generally; second, one must try to ascertain how much credit or blame to attribute to the UN for progress or lack thereof. Successes—where they can be found—need to be distinguished from failures, and the factors associated with each isolated. Harold Lasswell and some colleagues at one time proposed the creation of "a global monitoring system" for "appraising the effects of government on human dignity," operated by a private transnational network of policy scientists; appraisal was defined as "the assessment of institutional performance in terms of policy processes and actual outcomes as compared to avowed goals and the fundamental values associated with human dignity."[40] One can conceivably monitor and determine how much attainment of human values is occurring in the global system. In addition to the studies referred to in chapter 3, a number of other scholars have gathered systematic data on the human condition, along with governmental, nongovernmental, and intergovernmental bodies (the annual Amnesty International and Freedom House reports, the UN's initiation in 1990 of periodic Human Development Reports based on a Human Development Index, etc.).[41] But assessing in Lasswellian terms the institutional performance of an IGO such as the UN (as apart from the performance of governmental actors) begs the question of whether the UN can be considered a true system for making and carrying out "policy."

Certainly, instances of successful global problem solving traceable to the UN system can be found. The successes tend to be in areas where widely shared but narrowly defined mutual interests are clearly at stake (such as the routinization of international mail and air traffic transaction flows) more so than in areas where interests are more divisible and less circumscribed (such as economic development). Although the governments of developed states might accept the argument that economic development of poor countries can benefit rich countries in terms of expanding purchasing power and potential export markets, "international development" is generally viewed as a misnomer, standing for national development of a subset of states and, hence, a redistribution of wealth. While the number of pieces of mail sent and the number of passenger-miles flown by scheduled airlines across national boundaries without incident increases annually (approximately 8 billion and 700 billion respectively in 1990), such unilinear progress is not evidenced in the tracing of per capita GNP, numbers of malnourished persons, and the like (although there have been steady gains in life expectancy and certain other quality of life indicators worldwide at least until recently).

The World Health Organization's smallpox eradication program, credited with marking "the first time that a human malady has ever been totally eliminated,"[42] would seem to represent the ultimate UN success story, even though the benefits were known to be quite unevenly distributed among member states and flowed in the direction of the least powerful actors. The program was started in 1959; a special WHO budget with increased funding, along with a ten-year target date for completion of the project, was established in 1967; global eradication was declared by the WHO Assembly in 1980; and by 1985, all smallpox vaccinations had been eliminated in member countries.[43] It was made possible by not only the common recognition of the magnitude and nature of the problem but also (1) the availability of a technological solution that was relatively easy and cheap to apply (a simple vaccine providing long-term immunization),[44] (2) sufficient convergence of interests to support a UN response (developed countries such as the U.S. could achieve savings of up to $150 million yearly with no longer having to mount ongoing national vaccination programs as a precaution against the importation of the disease), and (3) the design of effective strategies and actions for delivering preventive medicine services relevant to the problem (through WHO procedures for detecting and quarantining smallpox cases and instituting mass vaccinations against the disease).

One might conclude simply that the UN system functions reasonably well when there is a convergence of interests (at least non-polarization) and/or a quick fix surrounding a clearly defined problem, and less so when there is not—with structural factors, again, deemed irrelevant or marginal to institutional performance. However, one has to wonder how much more effective the system would be if there were better machinery for engaging the international community in the kind of policy processes to which Lasswell alluded. The smallpox case gives the appearance of a policy process at work in the UN, complete with the language of "strategies," "targets," "programmes," and "impact statements"; so do such designations as "Development Decades" (the 1990s being the fourth), "The International Drinking Water Supply and Sanitation Decade" (during the 1980s), "International Women's Year" (1975), and "The Year of the Child" (1991). For the most part, however, this is more appearance than reality.

Marvin Soroos and others speak of the UN system as a vehicle for creating "global policy," defined as "joint responses to common problems that . . . national governments work out with one another" which are "products of the international community as a whole."[45] As one reads the global policy literature and delves into the workings of the UN system, one finds that "public policy" in the international realm amounts to little more than cooperation or at best regime making—a post-hoc label for whatever mélange of norms, rules, procedures and other patterned behaviors happens to emerge in a given problem area, as opposed to a more rigorous enterprise involving purposive collective decision making resulting in a chosen set of general guides to action to be applied to specific situations as they arise.[46]

If cooperative problem-solving among the members of a society can often be difficult, policy making and implementation as a relatively structured mode of cooperation is an even more demanding process:

> It is hard enough to design public policies . . . that look good on paper. It is harder still to formulate them in words and

slogans that resonate pleasingly in the ears of political leaders and the constituencies to which they are responsive. And it is excruciatingly hard to implement them in a way that pleases anyone at all, including the supposed beneficiaries or clients.[47]

While it is true that in national political systems, including the most highly developed ones, "very often policy is the sum of a congeries of separate or only vaguely related actions,"[48] such characterizations would seem to apply a fortiori to the international system.

Indeed, it might be argued that global policy is a contradiction in terms, that it is impossible to engage in policy making, implementation, and related operations in a global context or for that matter in any international context. Eugene Meehan points out that policy cannot be understood except in relation to "an identifiable actor with some capacity to produce change."[49] In other words, policy does not exist in a political system apart from some identifiable central guidance apparatus (a government or the functional equivalent) through which the policy process can occur in its various stages: agenda setting, formulation of proposals, decision adoption and legitimization, implementation, evaluation, and termination.[50] Some such apparatus presumably is just as essential if one treats policy as not so much a political as an intellectual exercise—involving the discovery of some condition calling for action, the specification of goals and objectives, the development of a menu of options, the performance of a cost-benefit analysis of the alternatives, and so forth. Having no central government, the international system has no apparent apparatus for performing the various political-intellectual routines associated with the formation and conduct of public policy relevant to the international community as a whole.

Still, as suggested above, there are at least quasi-policy processes discernible in UN assembly halls and corridors that perhaps could be more fully developed. To do so requires dealing with a number of institutional features that limit the UN's problem-solving capabilities from both a political and rational standpoint, namely, that do not allow the UN to realize its potential to facilitate agreement on problems worthy of global attention and to act effectively where such agreement exists.

STRUCTURAL PROBLEMS AND PERFORMANCE FAILURES

A global policy process can be conceptualized as starting when one actor or set of actors seeks to have a particular demand acted upon by the international system as a whole, whether it is a coordinated international response to one's concern about smallpox or AIDS, or drug trafficking or some other matter. In any political system, few concerns are so obvious, unambiguous, and universally felt that they force their way onto the agenda by the sheer weight of the evidence testifying to their importance; and equally few have obvious remedies immediately evident to all. The essence of the policy process in any political system is to convince others that, first, one's demand is not so much a self-serving value to be maximized as it is a critical public policy problem to be attacked and, second, one's preferred policy outcome is the best societal solution.

Is there a global agenda as such? If so, how do actors gain access to the agenda-setting process, and who gets access? Demands for global policy can originate from a variety of sources, including individual national governments, blocs of states, subnational and transnational interest groups, and officials of intergovernmental and nongovernmental organizations. If many national political systems like the U.S. are considered porous in terms of having multiple access points (executive agencies, courts, and so forth) whereby actors can supply inputs into the policy process, the international system is even more so. At least in national systems the access points are bound together within a single institutional framework through which policy must move. In the international system no such matrix exists, with numerous access points having only random connectedness. The chief structures that receive and process global policy demands—the "primary arenas in which global policies are made"[51]—are the various UN organs, subsidiary bodies, and specialized agencies, with their disparate memberships and uneven ties with each other. The disjointedness of the UN system often makes it hard for observers as well as participants to decipher any logic as to which IGOs take up which issues and, at the opposite end of the policy process, how the outputs produced by one IGO relate to those produced by others, especially where several international bodies have overlapping responsibility for a given issue-area as in the case of economic development. With the proliferation of international bodies at the global and also regional levels, adding to the venues for interest articulation and aggregation, the entire system is overloaded as it becomes increasingly difficult to keep track of what issues are on the global agenda or are somewhere else in the policy process.

The flaws in the system begin with the UN General Assembly, the plenary body endowed from the start with the competence to address a domain of issues that was as wide as its powers were narrow—Article 10 permitting it to "discuss any questions or any matters within the scope of the Charter" except as restricted by the Security Council's prerogatives, and the pursuant articles granting it mainly the ability to "initiate studies" and "make recommendations" only. Although the framers of the Charter gave more serious attention to the design of the General Assembly than the framers of the Covenant had given to the League Assembly—international norms had progressed to the point where great powers felt the need to worry somewhat about plenary bodies as agencies of empowerment—the Assembly's role was ill-defined. It was not envisioned as a parliament with legislative functions or even as a forum for parliamentary diplomacy so much as, at one level, a place for discussion of the great issues of the day and, at another level, "the supervisor of organizational housekeeping arrangements and activities in economic and social fields."[52] The Charter made the General Assembly the clearinghouse and locus of accountability through which almost all reports, if not decisions, dealing with nonsecurity matters had to pass.

The Assembly's provisional agenda, drafted during the summer prior to the annual session, is assured of crowdedness given the rules requiring inclusion of the annual reports of various UN organs, unfinished business from the previous year, and "all items proposed by any member of the UN." Despite the General Committee's putative responsibility for organizing the business of the Assembly, there is relatively little discretion exercised as to what issues merit a special place among the more than 100 items that typically end up constituting the formal agenda in a regular Assembly session. What passes for agenda-setting, then, is driven by bureaucratic routines and a politics of inclusion.

Agenda items are parcelled out to Assembly standing committees distinguished only by name and number rather than by
their membership, area of competence, or other normal policy-
relevant criteria: the First (Political and Security), Special Political, Second (Economic and Financial), Third (Social, Humanitarian, and Cultural), Fourth (Trusteeship), Fifth (Administrative and Budgetary), and Sixth (Legal). Like much of the UN
structure, the committee structure seems frozen in time, with no
changes instituted since the Special Political Committee was
added in 1948, at first as an ad hoc body to discuss the Palestine
question and subsequently given permanent status. Perhaps no
other structural feature of the UN system provides a more telling commentary on the lack of progress made in global community-building than the committee system, in which each of the
main committees remains a committee of the whole duplicating
the membership of the General Assembly and essentially making the Assembly superfluous as a deliberative plenary body.
This is in contrast to the U.S. Senate, where less than half the
states are typically represented on a given committee yet where
the pattern is such that if 60 to 80 percent of the committee vote
for a bill the bill is passed on the floor of the Senate 90 percent of
the time, and if over 80 percent support the bill its passage by
the plenary body is a virtual certainty.[53]

Aside from the redundant relationship between the General
Assembly and its main committees, the sheer size of each committee undermines the logic of using such bodies as vehicles
for distributing workloads and expediting the Assembly's business. The General Assembly committees might not have been
altogether unwieldy in size in 1945, when the original UN membership numbered 51. By comparison, U.S. congressional committees have averaged 45 members in recent years. However,
the size of Assembly committees is more open to question today
with the UN membership having more than tripled, with the
delegations of many newer states being strained beyond their
capacities, and with no real subcommittee structure in place. (As
of 1990, the UN membership had stabilized at 159, the same total
as in the mid-eighties. The addition of Liechtenstein and Namibia in 1990 was offset by the reduction of two seats caused by the
mergers of the two Germanys and the two Yemens. The Assembly's 46th annual session in 1991 saw the membership total

rise to 166 with the admission of the two Koreas, the newly independent Baltic republics, and two Pacific island nations, followed in 1992 by the entrance of thirteen more states including San Marino and former Soviet and Yugoslav republics.) Notwithstanding the vote by 75 percent of the Swiss electorate in a 1986 referendum rejecting Switzerland's proposed application for UN membership, joining the UN has become a prima facie signature of sovereignty for political units claiming statehood. The ranks of the General Assembly are likely to continue to swell over time as the ministate phenomenon would appear to be a more powerful force than any merger mania in the foreseeable future. The pressures, then, would seem to be in the direction of altering the committee system in some fashion, and with it the general framework in which the Assembly conducts its affairs. At the same time, if states up to now have insisted on representation on each committee even though most resolutions sent to and passed in the Assembly are only advisory, one might expect them to cherish that arrangement all the more should any reforms aim to endow the Assembly with greater decision-making competence.

The future of the committee structure will depend partly upon the future shape of the relationship between the General Assembly and other parts of the UN system. Not only are there no clear institutional roles performed by the Second Committee as opposed to the Third Committee and by the entire committee system as opposed to the plenary body, but the same indictment holds for the General Assembly relative to the Economic and Social Council. In considering the requirements for sound public policy, Meehan states the obvious when he says "the case for preferring intelligent direction of action to blind foraging is overwhelming."[54] Yet "blind foraging" is not far from the truth as an apt description of the processes one finds in the General Assembly, reflected in the comment of one observer who notes: "Like a herd of grazing cattle, that moves as it chews, head down, the Assembly gets through its day . . . without any particular drive, yet not without a certain vaguely diffused sense of purpose."[55]

ECOSOC was envisioned in 1945 as the linchpin for "international economic and social cooperation," helping to provide general policy direction and coordination for the various programs and operations of the UN in these areas as well as the

work of the specialized agencies (Articles 57 and 62–64). It was
ECOSOC through which most of these entities were to report to
the General Assembly and whose recommendations were to be
relied upon by the latter as a basis for taking action. ECOSOC's
original composition provided for in the Charter—only eighteen
members, six of which were to be elected for three-year terms
and the rest for shorter terms (Article 61)—reflected its design as
a vehicle whereby the great powers could manipulate the
agenda and maintain a degree of steerage over economic-social
issues, complementing the more exclusive and manifest control
they assigned themselves in the peace and security field
through the Security Council. As ECOSOC expanded in size
and grew beyond the control of the U.S. and the major industrialized economies, mirroring the upsizing and power shift in
the General Assembly, the major players lost interest in it. The
fact that the permanent members of the Security Council did not
use their veto power to block the 1965 Charter amendment en-
larging ECOSOC to twenty-seven seats (and additionally giving
all members staggered three-year terms) can be attributed to either their willingness to tolerate what appeared at the time to be
a relatively minor incremental change or, alternatively, to their
disengagement from ECOSOC already by the 1960s as they had
become disillusioned over their capacity to ride herd over economic-social problem-solving through the UN. The doubling of
ECOSOC membership to fifty-four in 1973 transpired with little
debate.

ECOSOC's failure as the institutional key to managing the
economic-social agenda can be blamed on a host of factors, some
of which are more amenable to manipulation and change than
others. These include:

1. the sheer size of the organizational network it is charged
with overseeing, including its own functional and regional
economic commissions, the assorted units that have been created by the General Assembly which fall in the interstices between the Secretariat and the specialized agencies (UNICEF,
UNHCR, UNCTAD, UNEP, UNDP, inter alia), and various
special committees and subsidiary bodies attached to different organs and agencies within the UN system, many of
which have their own governing bodies and secretariats;

2. the sheer range and complexity of the issues, often involving core values of states and also often riding on the decisions and behaviors of private, nonstate actors;

3. poor scheduling routines (the convening of two lengthy general sessions annually, making for unwieldy, unfocused discussions);

4. the caliber of governmental representation in ECOSOC proceedings (the participation of junior-level delegates rather than ambassadorial or ministerial-level officials);

5. the developing countries' preference for using the General Assembly's Second or Third Committee, UNCTAD, and other forums despite ECOSOC's gradual enlargement;

6. the preference of developed countries, particularly the major actors, for conducting business in smaller forums (notably the Group of Seven, which has become in some respects a de facto substitute for ECOSOC, although situated outside the UN and hence not positioned as well to give coherence or legitimacy to direction of the world economy);

7. the resistance of the specialized agencies to anything that threatens agency autonomy.

Given ECOSOC's failure to serve as a political linchpin for economic and social cooperation, it has fallen primarily to the UN Secretariat to try to provide at least managerial coordination. The Secretariat was meant to be the main administrative arm of the UN, an executor and implementor rather than initiator of policy, although the fact that the great powers bothered to give themselves a veto over the nomination of the head of the Secretariat suggests they recognized the potential for power or mischief that resided there. The Charter says virtually nothing about the nature of the Secretariat, other than that it "shall comprise a Secretary-General and such staff as the Organization may require" (Article 97), leaving it to the Secretary-General to define the staffing requirements subject to the oversight of the Assembly that elected him. Even the term of the Secretary-General is unspecified in the Charter; the first General Assembly in 1946 had to determine the length, deciding on a five-year renewable term (in contrast to the ten-year term of the League Secretary-General). Just as the Charter, beyond Article 99, is mum regarding the role of the Secretary-General in the peace and security area, it is practically as silent on the role of the Secretary-General in other areas, requiring only an annual report to the General Assembly. In an effort to sharpen the UN's sense of purpose and to get a handle on priorities, the UN membership since the early 1970s has called upon the Secretary-General to prepare a Medium-Term Plan, currently based on a six-year planning cycle linked to three biennial program budgets. Although this exercise affords the Secretary-General the opportunity to identify problems considered most pressing from an international community perspective, to bring these to the attention of the policy-making bodies, and to tie these to the allocation of resources, his powers in this regard are limited (more so than, say, those possessed by European Community Commissioners). The Secretary-General and his staff at most can provide "intellectual leadership."[56] Even this is undermined by the politicization of the UN Secretariat and the ineffectiveness of the UN's intergovernmental policy-making machinery in establishing priorities as well as the weak links between the UN political-administrative apparatus and counterpart structures in the specialized agencies.

The UN system structure practically assures rampant bureaucratic politics, balkanization, and inter-agency competition, given the highly decentralized framework governing the relationship between the special-purpose organizations and the UN proper, with the specialized agencies having their own separate charters, memberships, budgets, headquarters, and bureaucracies, and linked to UNO only through agreements reached with ECOSOC (Article 63). The sixteen specialized agencies that at present are related to the UN by special agreement share a symmetry of structure, each having a plenary body that is the nominal supreme authority, a smaller council or board of directors instrumental in setting agendas and furnishing oversight, and a secretariat run by an executive head. They also share an underlying principle, namely, the degree to which key member states will seek to use their financial clout, knowledge, and other resources to shape organizational agendas and outcomes will depend upon the importance they attach to the work of the agency. Within this general mold, there is considerable variation. While the amount of variation is such as to confound anyone looking for cohesion in the system, it also permits one to view the agencies as laboratories suggesting alternative models for international governance.

There is no need here to describe the individual structures in any detail; a quick comparative review reminds one of the great diversity that is both a strength of the system and an obstacle that any UN reform effort must confront. In some cases the plenary body meets annually (for example, ILO's International Labor Conference, WHO's World Health Assembly, the Board of Governors of both the World Bank and IMF), in others biennially (for example, FAO's and UNESCO's Conference) or triennially (for example, ICAO's Assembly), and in others every five to eight years (for example, UPU's Universal Postal Congress and ITU's Plenipotentiary Conference). There is no correlation between the irregularity of plenary meetings and the size and power of the more exclusive bodies entrusted with seeing to the continuity of the organization.

The executive boards vary in size from the twenty-two Executive Directors of the World Bank and IMF, to the thirty-odd members of ICAO's Council and WHO's Executive Board (the latter chosen as individuals rather than as member state appointees), to the forty or so members of the ITU's Administrative Council and FAO's Council, to the over fifty members of ILO's Governing Body (reflecting ILO's unique provision for national delegations to include tripartite representation drawn from governmental, employer, and worker sectors). Although it is true "there is a general tendency for organs with more inclusive membership to seek the prerogatives assigned to those with less inclusive membership,"[57] some executive boards have retained more power than others (notably those of the World Bank and IMF). Most accord special treatment to a select subset of actors (for example, IMF's weighted voting system, based on financial assessments, giving the U.S., EC members, and Japan control over 80 percent of Executive Board votes; the provision in ILO's constitution requiring that the ten member states "of chief industrial importance" be represented on the Governing Body; the provision in ICAO's constitution requiring adequate Council representation for nations "of major importance in air transport"; and the dominance of IMCO's Council by states with the largest international shipping interests). Some IGO secretariats (for example, WHO) are more decentralized than others, one (ITU) is in effect multiheaded, and executive heads in some cases (such as WMO) are better positioned to exercise power than in others (although this can depend as much on personality as on institutional characteristics). Most agencies rely on regular assessments or voluntary contributions, but at least one (WIPO) derives significant income from an independent revenue source in the form of patent and license registration fees.[58]

In UNO alone, one writer notes "the power to initiate and in effect authorize program activities is shared among a rather large number of intergovernmental organs. . . . Since all the many activities approved cannot be adequately carried out with the resources allocated to them, there is a good deal of uncertainty as to which of them will in fact be pursued and with what degree of diligence."[59] As another puts it, "under existing arrangements . . . the program track and the budget track never intersect in such a way as to provide for the meaningful examination of program goals and program capabilities *at the same time and in the same place.*"[60] Neither the Committee for Program and Coordination (CPC), the thirty-six member intergovernmental subsidiary of ECOSOC charged with reviewing the overall medium-term budget and establishing programmatic priorities, nor the Advisory Committee on Administrative and Budgetary Questions (ACABQ) charged with supplementing the work of CPC by focusing more on budget and finance matters than on substantive policy concerns, nor the Advisory Committee on Coordination (ACC) made up of the executive heads of the specialized agencies and chaired by the UN Secretary-General have succeeded up to now in providing greater rationalization of the policy process, although the Group of Eighteen report has given impetus to focusing on construction of UN system budgets— shaped through these three entities channeling recommendations to the General Assembly's Fifth Committee—as the chief engine for defining and pursuing system-wide priorities.[61]

Focusing on economic development, Coate and Puchala note that the failure of the UN system to produce any consensus in this area has resulted in a delay in launching the Fourth Development Decade and in "a prevailing 'ad hocism' ":

Agencies are moving in directions that interest their executive heads and governing boards, as with UNESCO's literacy efforts or the UNDP's "multi-bi" schemes that encourage the use of multilateral mechanisms to coordinate bilateral activities. Programs are launched when donors make funds available for projects of particular interest to themselves, as with U.S. funds for WHO's AIDS efforts. Member governments are riding policy hobby horses such as "privatization" and "zero-growth budgets," where they seek to globalize national values regardless of whether these are actually pertinent to fostering enhanced well-being among the poor peoples of the world.[62]

Coate and Puchala argue that the seeming drift of the UN system is a function of the changing political landscape, particularly the shifting of blocs and the absence of strong political leadership capable of building coalitions within and between the developed and developing worlds. This brings us back, though, to the structural deficiencies of the UN that make it hard to arouse such leadership and to energize the "latent capacity [of major states] for taking charge."

The existence of multiple paths for providing inputs into the global political system would be nonproblematic, and in fact would be healthy in terms of broadening a sense of participation (akin to the use of the courts as alternative avenues for participation by minority groups denied access to other branches of the American political system), if there were some clearer connection between agenda-setting and other phases of what can be loosely called the global policy process. However, the politics of agenda-setting tends to be divorced from the rest of the process. In the UN General Assembly, in particular, several issues such as the Palestinian refugee question can stay on the formal agenda for decades without significant action, while others such as desertification and deforestation move on and off almost serendipitously. Some problems do manage to occupy the agenda more firmly than others and to become endowed with sufficient visibility that major efforts at policy formulation are undertaken, usually through a labyrinthine process involving plenary body authorization of an expert study group or commission, the subsequent organization of a diplomatic conference based on the latter's report and preceded by a special preparatory session as a first-cut negotiating exercise, eventually culminating in action plans, conventions, or other outputs. This has been the general routine associated with the series of world conferences sponsored by the UN over the past two decades on the law of the sea, the environment, population, and other topics. Such efforts do not assure policy adoption as such; they may or may not yield outcomes that deserve to be called regimes.

In those IGOs which deal with highly technical matters placing a premium on expertise possessed by relatively few states, or which have weighted voting formulas or other arrangements that allow power realities to be reflected more accurately, there is a closer fit between the capacity to control agendas and the capacity to engage members in serious policy formulation likely to lead to the adoption of decisions having policy impacts. One factor that especially complicates efforts to achieve greater interagency and intersectoral articulation in the UN system is precisely the fact that the specialized agencies tend to have their own distinctive institutional cultures which are not easily reconcilable vis-à-vis each other and UNO (for example, the unabashedly elitist, market-oriented style of decision making in the IMF and World Bank, compared with FAO and some other parts of the system). States such as the U.S. wish to see greater efficiency achieved in the UN system as a whole through better coordination, but not at the cost of possibly undermining institutions they view as relatively efficient at present. Hence, the U.S. and Western states generally have been inclined to maintain the separateness of the Bretton Woods institutions from the rest of the UN system rather than pushing for integration even though some linkages have developed with UNDP, UNEP, and other bodies.[63] The capacity of the Bretton Woods institutions to translate words into actions is enhanced by the composition of their executive boards, which are dominated by the prime donor states, who are represented by ministerial-level officials; ministerial-level representation alone does not necessarily produce results, though, as can be seen in the case of the World Food Council. Pressures in the UN system are currently pulling between elitism and egalitarianism; in the case of ILO, for example, a constitutional amendment approved in 1986 that would remove the provision for allocating ten seats on the Governing Body specifically to "members of chief industrial importance" has yet to gain the necessary ratifications to take effect.[64]

Of course, what constitutes "adoption" of formulated proposals in the global policy process is problematical. In any issue-area, some policy outputs qua regimes can be found that "vary with respect to explicitness, adherence, and stability."[65] Some are more global in scope than others, and some incorporate more formal instruments than others, although the matter of *what* rules, norms, tacit understandings, and/or organizational machinery have been accepted by *whom* tends to be sketchy. So also is the question of when, if at all, policy/regime change or termination has occurred.

In regard to the rule-making function of the specialized agencies, such decisions tend to be treated either as referenda requiring subsequent ratification by member states (in the case of conventions) or as legal instruments directly binding on the entire membership subject to a variety of qualifiers found in different organizations (in the case of regulations).[66] For example, once conventions are adopted by a majority of the WHO Assembly, all members must submit these to their respective ratifying bodies within eighteen months and must report to WHO the result, including reasons for nonacceptance; International Health Regulations and other regulatory codes adopted by the WHO Assembly are viewed as directly binding on all members except those expressly indicating rejection within a specified time frame. Standards adopted by the ICAO Council as Annexes to the ICAO Convention are ordinarily binding on all members unless one can demonstrate it is not possible to comply. Revisions of the UPU Constitution require the ratification of two-thirds of the membership, while revisions of postal regulations are automatically binding on all members upon a simple majority vote of the UPU Congress, with noncompliance necessitating withdrawal from the organization.

The reality, then, is that even those IGOs which approach universality and are empowered to take regulatory action binding on the entire membership allow for selective noncompliance through unilateral reservations or other devices. Furthermore, global policy outputs in the form of treaties are often arrived at in decidedly subglobal settings—the Montreal Protocol on Substances that Deplete the Ozone Layer emerged from a twenty-four-nation meeting in Stockholm in 1982, a thirty-four-nation meeting in Vienna in 1985, and a fifty-five-nation meeting in

Montreal in 1987—and are often adopted by a decidedly subglobal number of states—the latter protocol entered into force in
1989 upon its ratification by less than one dozen governments. It
is open to question what constitutes global policy adoption
when, in the case of environmental policy for example, "UNEP
has been pushing for its global treaty conventions, like that on
hazardous wastes, to enter into force with as few as twenty ratifications in order to 'get them on the books.' "[67] Is the threshold
of global policy adoption reached when the international political system has obtained the requisite number of ratifications, or
the *right* number of ratifications, namely, the blessing of those
states whose cooperation is most critical for the successful implementation of the policy? What constitutes the adoption of
new customary law or norms by the international community is
more elusive still.

Nothing has bred more cynicism toward the UN than the pa-
rade of resolutions and decisions adopted by the UN General
Assembly that go unimplemented or, if implemented, have miniscule impacts. The number of resolutions passed has steadily
risen over the years, from an average of 117 annually in 1946–
1950 to 343 in 1981–1985 to 375 in 1985–1990.[68] There has been a
distinct trend toward decision making based on consensus
rather than voting procedures. Whereas 78 percent of all resolutions were adopted by vote in 1950, 65 percent were adopted by
consensus forty years later.[69] The shift toward reliance on consensus procedures for a majority of decisions taken is a long-
term trend that was already in evidence by the mid-1970s, well
before the improved international climate of the late 1980s. Even
on roll-call votes, "by 1986, resolutions were adopted by an average of 127 votes in favor and 5.2 against, with 25.7 abstentions
or absences . . . translating into an average approval rate of 80
percent of all member states, the highest ever in UN annals."[70]
Approval approaching unanimity provides the ultimate legitimation for some policy, but it may or may not translate into con-
sequential action. Resort to consensus means some decisions
may never be taken, while those that are taken—by calculating
the lowest common denominator among over 150 states—may
be so amorphous as to not be worth the effort expended, particularly when in the final analysis most decisions are not legally
binding on any member.

Although consensus decision making supports global institution-building insofar as it contributes to a less threatening and confrontational atmosphere, it also undermines it insofar as it relieves any pressure to come up with voting formulas that might enable institutions to be taken more seriously. No amount of informal adjustment of UN General Assembly decision-making procedures can compensate for the absurdity of the Assembly's formal arrangements that permit a two-thirds majority to be constructed by a coalition of states paying less than 2 percent of the organization's assessed budget, that give the residents of one state (Liechtenstein) more than 39,000 times the influence of those of another state (China), and that defy almost any reasonable criteria.[71] While the Assembly voting formula is not unlike that found in many plenary bodies in the UN system, in these other cases the feared tyranny of the majority is tempered by other organizational arrangements (more irregular plenary meetings giving play to more exclusive councils, etc.). The prospect of getting agreement on a new governance scheme that would dampen populist impulses in the General Assembly is presumed dubious, yet the continued drift of the UN in the development field might make a growing number of LDCs open to a grand bargain that would replace the illusion of control over the decision-making process with greater concrete payoffs.

Given the many shortcomings of the global policy process relating to agenda-setting and policy formulation and adoption, it is not surprising that policy implementation and evaluation suffer as well. The UN architects could not have fully anticipated the administrative needs of an organization that now consumes 2,200 tons of paper and sponsors 5,000 meetings annually and employs 25,000 individuals to carry out its work. The UN Secretariat has become synonymous with inefficiency, waste, and duplication, attributable partly to structural defects and partly to poor personnel policies. Although the Charter framers intended for Secretariat employment to be based as much as possible on principles of merit and professionalism (norms which happened to favor those states possessing the most well-trained human resources), they invited the intrusion of politics by recognizing that for an "international" civil service to be truly international, "due regard [had to] be paid to the importance of recruiting the staff on as wide a geographical basis as possible" (Article 101).

From the beginning the most senior posts as a general rule were reserved for occupants belonging to and approved by the permanent members of the Security Council, a model of personnel recruitment not lost on the general membership, which authorized the General Assembly to institute an explicit formula for allocating Secretariat posts based on budgetary contributions and population along with "desirable ranges" for each member country and region.[72] Roughly 3,000 Secretariat positions are considered professional or upper-level in nature and are still subject to geographical distribution, with some one-third of these filled by individuals on fixed-term, seconded appointments, although this figure may drop as ideological and other rationales behind secondment are undermined.[73] The politicization of the UN bureaucracy has contributed to a lack of confidence in the Secretariat's program monitoring and evaluation capabilities, with the problems going far beyond the normal tensions between the policy-making community and the analytical community that one finds in national political systems.

Regarding structural problems that hamper implementation and evaluation, it has been estimated that, in addition to some 150 different decision-making bodies in the UN system dealing with economic and social concerns, there are some 600 sub-programs responsible for economic-social research and policy analysis.[74] Despite efforts to integrate this network through the Department of International Economic and Social Activities (DIESA) and the Office of Program Planning, Budget and Finance within the UN Secretariat as well as the Joint Inspection Unit (JIU), ACC and other mechanisms, a clear chain of command and management structure is still lacking.[75] The coordination problem is really several problems, involving relationships at the global, headquarters level between the UN Secretariat, other UNO administrative bodies, and the specialized agencies, and relationships at the field level, between regional and country programs. If anything, the UN system over time has been characterized by growing fragmentation, decentralization, and redundancy more so than integration and streamlining, although the recent reduction of the more than two dozen Under-Secretaries-General and Assistant Secretaries-General down to eight deputies reporting directly to the UN Secretary-General is a step in the right direction. Coordinating bodies themselves continue to proliferate, exemplified by the plan for an Environmental Coordination Board headed by the executive director of UNEP, which would bring together officials from all agencies with environmentally related missions, overlapping somewhat with ACC.[76]

The experience of the UN Development Program is an object lesson in the coordinating challenges posed by the UN system. UNDP at one time was envisioned as a logical "central coordinating organization" in the development field,[77] but this role has been undermined by collusion between various agency executive heads and donor states that has resulted in UNDP now controlling less than half of all technical assistance funds channeled through the system. Using a team concept, the UNDP resident representative in a given country is supposed to coordinate FAO, WHO, and other agency development activity in that country; but "when coordination succeeds at this level" it is often "for serendipitous reasons, such as the particular competence of the on-site UNDP representatives, or because of the compatible personalities of particular clusters of field representatives from different agencies."[78]

Efforts to improve inter-agency coordination among both secretariats and intergovernmental bodies, and to infuse the entire global policy process with greater rationalization, are complicated by the fact that states do not entirely conform to the rational, unitary actor model that most accounts of IGO behaviors presuppose. Robert Cox and Harold Jacobson have noted the role of "country subsystems" in defining national interests in international organizations.[79] Different ministries within a country may pursue competing agendas in the UN system or may have competing views on implementation strategies, with intranational bureaucratic politics interacting with bureaucratic politics on the international plane as government departments and UN agencies with similar missions forge special relationships. In some cases individual nation-state delegates in UN forums are put in the position of having to define their nation's interests when they have few instructions of any kind from home. "Loose cannon" bureaucracies and individuals are more commonly associated with LDCs than with developed states, whose more elaborate and established policy machinery allows central decision makers to ride herd better, but there is slippage of central control in any system.[80] The vast number of issues and organizations encompassed by the global policy enterprise taxes the capacity of any actors to direct policy processes from above, making "global policy" an oxymoron in the eyes of many. Some observers have suggested, in fact, that "coordination" of the UN system may be hopeless and that those concerned about greater coherence among the parts of the system should settle for "cooperation."[81]

Avoiding Formalities: The Problems of Governance Without Government

The Westphalian state system continues the search for governance without government. The main decisions bearing on the allocation of values in the international political system are not made at the formal institutional center, in the United Nations, but elsewhere. Those decisions that are made through the UN and that might be labeled global policy tend to be in reality hardly global and hardly policy but at least may be the stuff of "international regimes." The formal machinery for producing these outputs reflects a continued attachment to the Westphalian culture—most institutional arrangements respect the sovereign equality of all states—although precedents for abandoning Westphalian principles have been set, as in some cases equality is compromised by weighted voting or other exclusivity provisions while sovereignty is compromised by the capacity of majorities to take decisions putatively binding on all states regardless of their consent. Political decentralization is closely related to managerial decentralization. Absent the existence of more intelligible and routinized ways of allocating values in the international system, a security community has not yet developed, although the system continues to attempt to develop mechanisms (in some cases regimes) to deal with the security dilemma and other problems stemming from the design of the Westphalian order.

Of course, Grotius and the Peace of Westphalia notwithstanding, the Westphalian system was never the product of human design as such in the way the United Nations was. The UN called for buildings, which required the services of architects. The nature of the activities the buildings were to house posed the ultimate challenge for human engineering. There was at least a plan in 1945. What institutional development has occurred since has been more a matter of evolution than design. The UN experience has shown that when formal institutional features are not conducive to the functioning of organizations and to the production of hoped-for outcomes, to some extent it is possible to avoid investing the time and effort necessary to change the structures by *circumventing* them either through disregarding the dysfunctional elements (desuetude, as exemplified by acceptance of the practice that abstention in Security Council proceedings does not constitute a veto-blocking action) or through stretching them within the rules (as exemplified by the invention of peacekeeping to supplement peaceful settlement and collective security, and by the shift toward consensus decision making in the General Assembly).

When change via circumvention occurs, it represents organizational adaptation that is not the result of any conscious redesign effort informed by a study group or mandated by a political body. Such adaptation can allow an organization to survive, but as a basis for organizational growth it can take an organization only so far. If the UN is to overcome its many weaknesses, the flaws inherent in its formal structure will have to be addressed. This will require deliberate institutional reform, something that has met with little success up to now.

5

The Problem of United Nations Reform: Between Tinkering And Rethinking

In the case of the UN, "institutional reform" can have different meanings depending upon the extent of the changes envisioned (for example, changes requiring Charter revision as opposed to those that can be implemented outside the Charter), the nature of the problem or mission areas in which changes are proposed (for example, economic or social areas as opposed to the peace and security area), and the identity of the actors advancing reform proposals. Some advocates (such as the World Federalists, members of United Nations Association affiliates, and most officials in the UN bureaucracy itself) wish essentially to see a more effective institution with enhanced problem-solving capabilities in peacekeeping, arms control, economic development, resource management, environmental protection, and other domains. Their primary value is the improvement of the general human condition, although they also have a personal stake in any change that elevates the status of the UN and thereby vindicates their view of the world and their resource claims. Others (national governments) want some type of reform either because they are only marginally satisfied with the present arrangements and believe their interests can be better served by further institutional development along the lines it has taken over the past forty-five years (as in the case of developing countries) or because they feel uncomfortable with present arrangements and want to reverse the trends in institutional development (as in the case of some major powers).

Whatever the extent of the reform process, the problem areas in which it is undertaken, and the constellation of interests involved, any attempt at UN reform faces formidable obstacles.

Ronald Meltzer, commenting about the problem of institutional reform in political systems generally, notes that "institutional reform is a highly complex task. It requires not only the identification of suitable instruments to meet desired outcomes, but also the accommodation of various viewpoints about organizational goals and priorities."[1]

Most people would agree that reform should be conceived as contributing to rather than hindering the development of a global security-community, although practitioners would state such a goal in more mundane terms than theoreticians and might disagree somewhat on the specific objectives subsumed by such a lofty aim. The question becomes: given the institutional weaknesses that need fixing, what might the repairs look like? What manner of reform is desirable and feasible? It is obvious what is to be avoided—excessive centralization or excessive decentralization. The former would not work politically even if it made rational sense from an administrative-managerial standpoint; the latter would not work rationally insofar as it could aggravate already recognized inefficiencies and problems of coordination in the UN system and would ultimately then fail the political test as well.

The paths open to UN reform were suggested earlier by the author. In terms of the scope of change, the choices lie between tinkering and rethinking, between mere nuts-and-bolts changes (which would not energize serious involvement in institution-building and would amount to rearranging the deck chairs on the *Titanic*) and a sweeping rewriting of the Charter (which would seem too titanic an endeavor). The characteristics of the institution, as well as the requirements of a security-community, dictate that the reform process not be confined to improving UN performance in the peace and security field but include also the operation of the organization in economic, social, and technical fields.

An added difficulty that the challenge of UN reform currently encounters is the legacy of many past failed institutional reform exercises. As a result, there is a good deal of ennui to be overcome. Some have noticed "restructuring fatigue" that has set in among many delegation and staff members, with the resultant attitude that it may be preferable at this moment in time "to 'muddle through' with existing machinery rather than to try to

make drastic changes."[2] Certainly UN reform has not failed for
lack of in-house studies and reports — represented most recently
by the Group of Eighteen exercise begun in the mid-1980s (initiated by developed countries led by Japan) and by the General
Assembly special session on reform and restructuring of the UN
system in the economic and social fields held in the spring of
1991 (initiated by a resolution sponsored by the Group of Seventy-seven). Nor has UN reform failed for lack of external analyses. It is a measure of the unmet challenge of UN reform and
the felt need for improvement that so much of the membership
persists in keeping the matter on the agenda, tired or not. Offsetting the fatigue factor is the stimulus of a new international
environment suggesting fresh possibilities as well as unprecedented perils.

The author realizes there is a déjà vu quality to all this. It may
be instructive to examine briefly the history of UN reform, on
the assumption that George Santayana's statement ("those who
cannot remember the past are condemned to repeat it") has
more validity than Crane Brinton's ("while those who do not
know history are bound to repeat it, those who know it are
bound to repeat it as well").[3] The discussion of past UN reform
efforts that follows is accompanied by an evaluation of some recent reform proposals.

The History of UN Reform

Not only is the UN in disrepair, but the UN reform process
itself could stand improvement, as the history of UN reform
reads much like a broken record. The author is interested here in
only those reform efforts officially mandated and undertaken by
the UN, such as the Group of Eighteen and the 1991 Special Session cases. The reform proposals floated by individual member
states (for example, the Soviet proposal for a comprehensive security system presented in the late 1980s, or the various ideas
proposed by the United States in the Carter Report related to the
Baker-McGovern Amendment of the 1970s) and those suggested
by academic and other nongovernmental sources will be treated
later.

As UN self-reform endeavors, the Group of Eighteen and 1991 Special Session exercises have many antecedents going almost back to the very beginnings of the organization. UN reform has been an ongoing task.[4] It has been on the General Assembly agenda as a formal item for decades. The Special Committee on the Charter of the UN and on the Strengthening of the Organization has been in existence since December 1975, and still reports regularly to the General Assembly on its progress or lack thereof. Likewise, the 1975 Report of the Group of Experts on the Structure of the United Nations System (the Group of Twenty-five), entitled *A New United Nations Structure for Global Economic Cooperation,* continues to be discussed in UN bodies. Many reform proposals have been debated, relatively few have been adopted, and still fewer have been implemented fully, whether constitutional in nature (involving Charter amendment) or statutory (involving extraconstitutional changes).

The UN Charter has been especially resistant to tampering. It has been amended only four times (Articles 23, 27, 61, and 109)—all relating to the enlargement of Security Council membership in 1965 and the enlargement of ECOSOC membership in 1965 and 1973 brought on by the growth in UN membership. Several obvious anachronisms continue to survive the passage of time, some (such as the identity of the five permanent members of the Security Council listed in Article 23) of greater consequence than others (such as the Article 53 reference to "enemy state" participants in World War II).

The paucity of amendments can be attributed to a variety of factors. One is sheer inertia, which might explain the failure to expunge certain dated elements such as the "enemy state" reference (although the Soviet Union continued to rely on that provision throughout much of the postwar era to give a legal justification for military intervention in Eastern Europe). Another is the onerous nature of the formal amendment process, requiring adoption by either a two-thirds majority of the General Assembly or two-thirds of the participants in a General Conference, followed by ratification by two-thirds of the UN membership including all the permanent members of the Security Council (Articles 108 and 109). The main explanation for the dearth of amendments is the fact that key members whose approval is needed have been ill-disposed toward Charter reform as a mode of institutional change, not wishing to revisit the original debates that took place in San Francisco. Even the Carter administration, supportive as it was of global institution-building, barely was willing to associate itself with Charter reform. The standard U.S. view through much of the postwar period was captured in the comments of the State Department Legal Advisor in the Ford administration, speaking before the Sixth Committee of the General Assembly in 1975:

> We continue to view the question of Charter review with both skepticism and concern. . . . Impediments to greater effectiveness of this organization do not lie in any restrictions or limitations imposed by the Charter. . . . Our doubts about this Charter review exercise are based on a concern that the UN will lose even that degree of consensus which we now share. . . . The reopening of questions on matters to which we have all finally agreed . . . is hardly likely to widen areas of agreement among us. It is more likely to lead to a hardening of positions.[5]

The general attitudes toward Charter reform harbored by the U.S. and other actors were mentioned in chapter 3, where it was noted that resistance continues even though recent developments point to a possible softening of postures. The UN experience with both Charter and non-Charter reform is recounted below.

REFORM EFFORTS IN THE PEACE AND SECURITY FIELD

Efforts to improve the functioning of the UN in the peace and security field have occurred in the context of both broad organizational reform exercises as well as more narrowly focused exercises explicitly dealing with problems of war and peace. Some of these efforts have generated proposals requiring Charter revision and others have not. As early as 1948–1950, the Interim Committee (the precursor of the General Assembly's standing Special Political Committee) undertook a systematic study of ways in which the institution could facilitate dispute settlement. It forwarded several recommendations to the General Assembly, including the creation of a panel of experts to staff a commission for inquiry and conciliation (suggested by the U.S. and

China and approved by the Assembly).[6] This began a pattern of endless, almost ritualistic debate characterized by reiteration of problems and proposed solutions resulting in token implementation of reforms at best.

One of the first focused attempts to deal with peace and security matters was the creation of the Special Committee on Peacekeeping Operations in 1965,[7] coinciding with the acceptance of the Charter amendment expanding the size of the Security Council. The committee, consisting of thirty-three members, was charged with reviewing UN peacekeeping activities and developing recommendations dealing with financial and other aspects. In 1968 the committee established a smaller working group to study military observer missions and to formulate guidelines relating to staffing, training, and funding. In the 1970s, various proposals were considered, such as those advanced by the United Kingdom and Canada urging a revitalization of the Military Staff Committee, with the latter to include the permanent members of the Security Council and the chief contributors to peacekeeping operations and to have clearer lines of responsibility vis-à-vis the Council and Secretary-General in authorizing and defining missions, obtaining financing, and determining the size, makeup, and command of UN forces.[8] The committee has continued to meet and report to the General Assembly annually, with little to show for its efforts. It has been plagued over the years primarily by superpower disagreement and Third World equivocation, although China's recent acceptance of membership along with other signs of progress offer hope for more fruitful deliberations.

A broader reform movement began in 1970 with the formation of the Twenty-Fifth Anniversary Committee, stimulated by Colombia's request to include on the agenda of the 1969 General Assembly session an item entitled "Need to consider suggestions regarding the review of the Charter of the United Nations."[9] The committee invited reform proposals but saw its efforts frustrated by members of an East-West coalition (notably the U.S., U.K., and USSR) who were concerned about their ability to control the reform process. Proposals surfaced at succeeding General Assembly sessions but were defeated until, on the same day, December 17, 1974, the Assembly voted to create an Ad Hoc Committee on the Charter and to authorize the Secretary-General to appoint a Group of Experts to produce proposals for restructuring the economic-social sector of the UN system.[10] The Ad Hoc Committee, established over American and Soviet objections, consisted of forty-two members and was charged with considering any proposals aimed at improving the effectiveness of the organization in carrying out the purposes stated in the Charter. Following upon an agenda item that had been introduced into the General Assembly by Romania in 1972, entitled "Strengthening of the role of the United Nations with regard to the maintenance and consolidation of international peace and security, the development of cooperation among all nations and the promotion of the rules of international law in relations between States," the Assembly in 1975 replaced the Ad Hoc Committee with the Special Committee on the Charter of the United Nations and on the Strengthening of the Role of the Organization.[11] Enlarged to forty-seven members, the Special Committee was given a mandate to identify and examine those proposals for improving the UN "which have awakened special interest" among the members and to forward those to the General Assembly for possible action. The committee was expected to consider proposals pertaining to a wide range of activities and to broad structural features of the organization, involving both Charter and non-Charter changes, with special reference to the role of the organization in the maintenance of peace.

Although the effect of reconstituting the committee was to focus particular attention on peace and security concerns, the security concerns had to compete with the larger issues falling within the committee's purview. The first session of the Special Committee, held in 1976, consisted mainly of a review of an "analytical study of Governments' views with respect to aspects of UN functioning" that had been prepared by the Secretary-General. The committee reported to the General Assembly later that year, providing a summary of the Secretary-General's study and requesting an extension of at least one more year to complete its work. At its next session in 1977, the committee discussed a wide number of topics, including the size of the Security Council and the veto power enjoyed by permanent members, the economic rights and duties of states under the Charter, the criteria for admitting new states into the UN, the conversion of the Trusteeship Council into a Council for Human Rights, the financial plight of the organization, the decline in usage of the World Court, ways of improving peaceful settlement procedures, and ways of improving peacekeeping capabilities.

The first actual committee vote was not taken until the end of the 1977 session; the deliberations proceeded on the basis of consensus up to that time. The vote was on the matter of formally identifying those proposals worthy of special attention at the next committee session, through annexing two papers to the committee report to be submitted to the General Assembly. Thirty members of the committee voted in support of annexing the papers (mostly Third World states), eight voted against (including the U.S. and USSR), with the remaining abstaining. One of the papers, drafted by sixteen developing countries, called for a greatly enlarged role for the General Assembly as well as greater participation of LDCs on the Security Council, both nonstarters from the perspective of the superpowers. The committee report that was submitted to the General Assembly contained no specific recommendations for action but requested a further extension of its mandate.

The committee's 1978 session, following the submission of more than twenty working papers by various governments, concentrated on two sets of issues, the peaceful settlement of disputes and the rationalization of work and procedures of the UN. Among the proposals discussed in the peaceful settlement area were establishment of a permanent commission to perform mediation and conciliation services under the authority of the General Assembly or Security Council, nonuse of the veto by Security Council members in cases involving peaceful settlement of disputes and threats to the peace, establishment of a standing committee available for fact-finding, and enhancement of the role of the World Court. The committee members were attempting to add new wrinkles to old prescriptions, aware that the Charter already limited the use of the veto under Chapter VI, that the 1975 Report of the Secretary-General to the General Assembly on the Peaceful Settlement of International Disputes had pointed out the availability and disuse of already existing UN bodies such as a Panel for Inquiry and Conciliation, a Peace Observation Commission, and a Register of Experts for Fact-Finding (all the products of previous reform efforts), and that rehabilitation of the Court had been the subject of repeated

study and discussion. Once again the committee report offered
no action items for the General Assembly to consider, reflecting
a similar earlier division of views. The Third World members
tended to call for more radical overhauling requiring Charter revision and upgrading of the Assembly at the expense of the
Council, while the established powers favored less wide-ranging reform.

The energies of the committee, however, were becoming increasingly directed toward peaceful settlement. At its 1980 session in the Philippines, the committee drafted the Manila
Declaration on the Peaceful Settlement of Disputes; adopted by
the General Assembly in 1982, it was heralded as a major accomplishment demonstrating the feasibility of consensus-based reform, even though it did little more than reaffirm the Charter
principles regarding the nonuse of armed force and seemed to
duplicate a treaty being drafted by another newly created body,
the thirty-five member Special Committee on Non-Use of Force.

The General Assembly has continued to reconvene annually
and review the reports of the Special Committee on the Charter
of the United Nations and on the Strengthening of the Role of
the Organization. Most recently the committee has drafted a
Declaration on the Prevention and Removal of Disputes and Situations Which May Threaten International Peace and Security
and on the Role of the United Nations in this Field. It has prepared a Handbook on the Peaceful Settlement of Disputes Between States, and has engaged in further discussion of various
proposals aired over the course of the past two decades, including many found in the 1982 Palme Report authored by the Independent Commission on Disarmament and Security Issues.[12]
The Palme Report contained some novel ideas as well as ideas
recycled from the 1970s and earlier decades. Although the Report's recommendations relating to disarmament issues received
little response, mainly because the U.S. and other major actors
objected to the link posited between disarmament and transfer
of resources for economic development purposes, the proposals
for institutional reform in the peace and security area attracted
considerable attention, especially after UN conflict management
services became more in demand in the late 1980s.

Among the ideas contained in the Palme Report and discussed since in the General Assembly's First Committee and in

other forums are: the creation of a standing panel of mediators; an upgrade of the information-gathering capabilities of the Secretary-General's office, utilizing computers, satellite technology and other means to monitor conflict situations in order to prevent or curtail hostilities; more regularized meetings of the Security Council, attended by foreign ministers reviewing periodic reports from the Secretary-General; the creation of a peacekeeping reserve fund along with standby forces drawn from national military units specifically earmarked and trained for UN peacekeeping missions; reactivation of the Military Staff Committee; and the establishment of a global arms registry furnishing a comprehensive public record of all global arms transfers and military expenditures (the latter notion discussed at the 1978 UN Special Session on Disarmament and more recently at the 1991 Group of Seven London summit).

Most of these proposals remain under consideration and were given new life in January 1992 when the first ever summit meeting of the heads of government of the fifteen Security Council members took place. The summit authorized newly appointed Secretary-General Boutros Boutros-Ghali to prepare recommendations "on how to strengthen the UN capacity for preventive diplomacy, for peacemaking and for peacekeeping." Some institutional innovation has occurred, such as the reorganization of the Department of Political Affairs as part of a general streamlining of the Secretariat. Under this arrangement there are two Under-Secretaries-General for Political Affairs, one responsible for the Security Council and General Assembly and peacemaking in selected regions and the other focusing on Africa and Asia, with yet another Under-Secretary in the peace and security field also reporting directly to the Secretary-General (but oddly heading a completely separate Office for Peacekeeping Operations).[13] In the final analysis there has been relatively little institutional reform achieved in the peace and security field despite the fact that suggested reforms can be accommodated without amending the Charter. Looking back over the history of UN reform in this area, progress in the past has been hampered by the rambling nature of the dialogue and the surfeit of recommendations generated by bodies with overlapping mandates (resulting in disarmament and other tangential issues intruding into discussions of peaceful settlement, peacekeeping and collective security), this in turn being a function of the underlying disagreement between different blocs of states over the proper locus of responsibility for peace and security matters. The Gulf War and its aftermath served to provide a sharper focus to reform efforts and have weakened the Third World claim that the great powers through the Security Council are incapable of playing the role prescribed for them by the Charter. Greater progress may now be forthcoming, although ad hoc-ism continues to prevail over institutionalization. The bulk of the UN membership remains reluctant to reaffirm the primacy of the Security Council as it is presently constructed, and the Council's permanent members themselves have yet to agree on the logical next step in building on the Gulf War experience. There is still the sense that many proposed reforms are of a band-aid variety not worth the investment of effort while others are more serious responses with potentially far-reaching effects that may go too far.

REFORM EFFORTS IN THE ECONOMIC AND SOCIAL FIELD

Other than the expansion of ECOSOC, virtually no UN reform efforts undertaken in the economic-social field have resulted in recommendations entailing Charter revision. Some efforts have been designed primarily to call attention to the nature and magnitude of certain problems and have only incidentally treated institutional reform questions, such as the 1969 Pearson Commission Report and 1980 Brandt Commission Report on world poverty and the 1987 Brundtland Commission Report on environment and development concerns.[14] Those efforts aimed explicitly at institutional reform have included some dealing with rather broad structural issues, such as the 1975 Group of Twenty-five Report, others dealing with more narrow personnel and administrative concerns, such as the periodic reports of the International Civil Service Commission and the Joint Inspection Unit, and others dealing with a combination of these, such as the Group of Eighteen Report.

The Committee of Eight and the Committee on the Reorganization of the Secretariat[15] which examined the overall structure of the UN Secretariat were some early attempts at minor reform. This was followed in 1969 by Sir Robert Jackson's *A Study of the Capacity of the UN Development System*[16] that urged a substantial overhaul of the economic development machinery. Even with the merger of the Expanded Program for Technical Assistance and the Special Fund into UNDP after 1966, the Jackson Report found the system inordinately cumbersome and likened it to "some prehistoric monster." The report recommended that all operational activities of the UN in the development field be co-ordinated through UNDP, with country-centered projects involving several UN agencies coordinated by a UNDP "resident representative." While many elements of the Jackson Report were adopted and implemented, the system remained a target of criticism because of its lack of the kind of coordination envisioned by the study.

Both the Special Committee on the Charter of the United Nations and on the Strengthening of the Role of the Organization and the Group of Experts on the Structure of the United Nations System (the Group of Twenty-five), keystones of the 1970s institutional reform movement, considered the need to impart greater rationalization to the workings of the UN through such devices as streamlining (a reduction in the number of agenda items, volume of reports, and subsidiary organs). The Group of Twenty-five took as its focus the functioning of the UN in the economic-social realm, based on the 1974 General Assembly resolution that requested the Secretary-General to appoint "a small group of high-level experts" to prepare "a study containing proposals on structural changes within the United Nations system so as to make it fully capable of dealing with problems of international economic cooperation in a comprehensive manner."[17] The analysis that was undertaken ultimately did encompass virtually the entire UN system ranging from the operational activities in the technical assistance area treated by the Jackson Report, to the central intergovernmental decision-making machinery in the General Assembly and ECOSOC, to intersectoral coordination among the specialized agencies, to hiring and firing practices in the UN Secretariat.

The Group of Twenty-five project benefitted at the outset from widespread dissatisfaction with the status quo felt by both developed and developing states, since "by the late 1960s it had become apparent that the confusion and overlap within the United Nations made the whole economic development problem-solving system unwieldy both for rational allocation of UN resources and for useability on the part of less developed countries."[18] However, this initial generalized support for reform was undercut by the fact that most governments in the North viewed the restructuring effort as merely an exercise in upgrading the efficiency of the organization while most in the South were more interested in the overarching substantive economic issues. The North hoped the South would accept the notion that it should be interested in improved efficiency for its own sake; the South hoped the North would enter into global negotiations to alter fundamental international economic relationships as a quid pro quo for Third World acceptance of Northern-inspired institutional reforms. Kenneth Dadzie of Ghana, who was to become heavily involved in the restructuring process, bluntly tied the process to NIEO politics with his statement that "structural change could not replace, but must proceed pari passu with, the elaboration of policies . . . aimed at realization of the new international economic order."[19]

The Group of Twenty-five transmitted its report to the General Assembly in May 1975, for discussion in the upcoming Seventh Special Session. The report[20] contained conclusions and recommendations pertaining to both the policy-making and administrative apparatus for planning, coordinating, and implementing economic-social activities. Among the specific recommendations of the report were the following:

> 1. ECOSOC should be revitalized along the lines conceived in the Charter, restructured so that it might serve as the central hub of the system for establishment of priorities and policy formulation and implementation in the economic-social field;
>
> 2. ECOSOC's calendar should be revised to allow more frequent subject-oriented sets of short sessions and more timely review of program budgets and medium-term plans, and its agenda synchronized with that of the General Assembly on a biennial basis;
>
> 3. small negotiating or consultative groups, composed of ten to thirty members and meant to be broadly representative, should be set up around specific key issues identified by ECOSOC, possibly meeting up to two years in advance in an

effort to achieve consensus after which recommendations would be submitted to ECOSOC and ultimately the relevant committees of the General Assembly;

4. the General Assembly committees should be given a more clearly defined division of labor, with the Second Committee renamed the Committee on Development and International Economic Cooperation and the Third Committee renamed the Committee on Social Problems, Human Rights, and Humanitarian Activities;

5. the myriad ad hoc global conferences on food, population and other problems should be replaced by the General Assembly convening special sessions on selected topics in a more organized fashion;

6. there should be greater senior, ministerial-level involvement in ECOSOC and General Assembly proceedings at various states in the policy process;

7. some ECOSOC subsidiary bodies should be eliminated, with provision made at ECOSOC meetings for accommodating participation by those states and blocs deprived of representation;

8. a new post of Director-General for Development and International Economic Cooperation should be created, with this individual chairing a new inter-agency Advisory Committee on Economic Cooperation and Development (a supplement to ACC) and assisting the Secretary-General as his "second in command" in overseeing the integrated development and implementation of global policies systemwide;

9. a new UN Development Authority should be established to consolidate all technical assistance-related funds, to be headed by a deputy to the new Director-General and supervised by an Operations Board composed of members drawn from both developed and less developed countries;

10. the research and analytical capabilities of the UN Secretariat should be enhanced so as to provide an early warning system in the economic sphere;

11. budget cycles should be harmonized throughout the system, and CPC strengthened in a way that would enable it to

assist ECOSOC in furnishing centralized policy direction regarding programming and budgeting;

12. ECOSOC's regional commissions should be encouraged to play a greater role in formulating and executing regional and subregional projects, in close articulation with the global policy apparatus.

The report had a certain technocratic flavor to it and did not really touch the basic governing arrangements under the Charter. The document was the product of respected minds from academia and government representing twenty-five countries, fifteen of which were Southern.[21] Still, the recommendations drew considerable criticism from Third World countries, who were dissatisfied not only with the report's failure to address their substantive economic concerns but also with the political implications they read into the restructuring provisions. In particular, the suggestion of small consultative groups struck Third World states as a Western subterfuge for fragmenting and weakening their General Assembly majority coalition while the proposed revival of ECOSOC was viewed as a Western ploy to undermine UNCTAD, their preferred specialized forum for debate on economic issues. There was the distinct suspicion that Western interest in the report was motivated more by a desire to reduce budgetary contributions than by a desire to achieve greater efficiency per se. Moreover, the proposed reorganization scheme upset various countries that over time had managed to gain influence in certain bureaucracies which were now threatened with possible downgrading, retrenchment, or extinction.

Because the Group of Experts Report was felt to be somewhat biased toward the Western position on restructuring, a new group was created by the Seventh Special Session in 1975—the Ad Hoc Committee on the Restructuring of the Economic and Social Sectors of the UN System, chaired by Kenneth Dadzie—to continue the work of the Group of Twenty-five and to try to resolve the conflicts arising out of the latter's proposals. Out of its deliberations over the next year a "consolidated text" emerged from the Dadzie Committee in June 1976, and went through various revisions that resulted in a final report submitted to the General Assembly in December 1977. This report, adopted through General Assembly resolution 32/197 (the so-called restructuring resolution) on December 30, 1977, consisted of a set of restructuring guidelines which essentially incorporated the bulk of the Group of Twenty-five recommendations but in diluted and vaguely worded fashion, especially those proposals pertaining to ECOSOC's role vis-à-vis the General Assembly and UNCTAD (for example, the consultative group idea was accepted but only on an "experimental" basis).

The implementation of the Group of Twenty-five/Dadzie Committee reforms continues to be the subject of debate in the UN. Most reforms remain to be implemented; those that have been acted upon—for example, the appointment of a Director-General for economic matters and the shift toward a biennial basis for organizing the work of ECOSOC—have not noticeably improved the functioning of the organization, as pointed out by a recent JIU report.[22] While the environment has changed dramatically since the 1970s, as the shrill rhetoric of the NIEO debate has been toned down in the face of Northern stonewalling and Southern regrouping, the battle lines still remain drawn in the 1990s over structural issues similar to the past.

The Group of Eighteen exercise that began in 1985 was intended to deal with some of the unfinished business from the Group of Twenty-five project and to cover some new ground. The growing UN financial crisis during the 1980s, mounting frustration over the administrative weaknesses of the organization (as expressed in a highly critical 1985 JIU report),[23] and a reassertion of Northern influence formed the backdrop for the Group of Eighteen reform movement. Based on a Japanese initiative, the General Assembly in December 1985 passed a resolution authorizing an eighteen-member Group of High-Level Intergovernmental Experts whose task was to conduct a "thorough review of the administrative and financial matters of the United Nations with a view to identifying measures for further improving the efficiency of its administrative and financial functioning."[24]

Several prior studies had been conducted focusing specifically on managerial and financial issues. A fourteen-member Ad Hoc Committee of Experts to Examine the Finances of the UN and the Specialized Agencies was organized in 1965, in the midst of the Article 17 crisis, but produced few results other than contributing to the establishment of the Joint Inspection Unit in 1967 and the renaming of the Committee on Coordination as the Committee on Program and Coordination in 1966, and also laying the groundwork for the biennial budget cycle.[25] A seventeen-member Committee of Governmental Experts to Evaluate the Present Structure of the Secretariat in the Administrative, Finance and Personnel Areas, created in 1980, had less success.[26] The Joint Inspection Unit had issued, to no avail, a report on personnel problems as early as 1971. Typical of JIU's efforts that drew lukewarm responses was a 1984 "Staff Costs" report which criticized UN staff expansion, salary increases, and faulty program evaluation only to be ignored at the time by both intergovernmental bodies as well as the Secretary-General and ACC, although these criticisms were to receive stronger expression in the Group of Eighteen Report.[27] The 1969 JIU study on "Programming and Budgets in the UN Family of Organizations" did eventuate in the institution of medium-term planning linked to biennial budgeting.[28]

The Group of Eighteen examined such issues in a broader context, considering not only staffing, travel expenses, and other managerial questions associated with the operation of the UN Secretariat but also the relationship among the intergovernmental structures affecting the setting of priorities and making of programmatic and budgetary decisions. There was the familiar refrain about the need to streamline and rationalize the work routines of the organization and to find a more constructive role for ECOSOC. There were also fresh proposals of a "spectacular" nature.[29] Over seventy recommendations were contained in the report submitted to the General Assembly in August 1986.[30]

In the managerial area, referring to the Secretariat as "complex, fragmented, and top-heavy," the report called for numerous changes that included a dramatic 15 percent reduction in regular budget posts over three years, with a 25 percent cut at the Under- and Assistant-Secretary-General level; a 20 percent reduction in official travel along with decreased staff entitlements; greater use of competitive examinations for hiring professional staff at the P-1 through P-3 levels as well as special exams given at the P-4 and P-5 levels, with staff members eligible for permanent appointments after three years, all designed to depoliticize and raise the quality of personnel recruitment under the leadership of the Secretary-General; a reorganization of Secretariat departments, particularly those responsible for program monitoring and evaluation; and a reduction in the number of conferences, meetings, and resolutions. In the area of overall planning, programming, budgeting, and evaluation, the report laid out three options for moving toward a more coherent, consensus-based process governing the preparation and adoption of program budgets, although no specific recommendation was offered. As regards the role of ECOSOC and its relation to other intergovernmental machinery in the economic-social field, the report urged that the General Assembly appoint an intergovernmental body to undertake an "in-depth study" that would essentially reexamine the concerns covered by the Group of Twenty-five. Most of the report's recommendations were approved in a General Assembly resolution sponsored by nineteen states, including all the permanent members of the Security Council, and adopted by consensus in December 1986.[31]

The latter resolution (41/213) endorsed the major proposals pertaining to staff reductions and streamlining of the Secretariat. It also settled on a set of reforms surrounding the budget process, and designated ECOSOC to perform the study of UN structures in the economic-social field. Implementation of the reforms has been uneven.[32] While substantial staff cuts and budgetary belt-tightening have been achieved,[33] the kind of quality control exercised by the Secretary-General over a merit-based personnel recruitment and promotion system that was envisioned by the Group of Eighteen has yet to take hold; although the proposed reforms were supposed to increase efficiency through fostering greater technical expertise and esprit de corps in the Secretariat, organizational retrenchment has resulted in lower morale and has undermined the Secretary-General's ability to build a first-class international civil service.[34] Some departmental reorganization has occurred, for example the consolidation of several functions in a new Office of Program Planning, Budget and Finance. In place of forty-eight USGs and ASGs, almost all of whom had immediate contact with the SG, eight deputies are to report directly to the Secretary-General under the reforms instituted by Boutros-Ghali following his appointment in 1992. In addition to the two USGs attached to the Department of Political Affairs and a third head-

ing Peacekeeping Operations, others are in charge of Economic
Development, Administration and Management, Emergency
Relief, Legal Affairs, and Public Information.[35] The budget process reforms embodied in resolution 41/213 and pushed especially by the major donor states gave the Committee on Program
and Coordination (whose size was increased from twenty-one to
thirty-six members) an enhanced role in decision making, em-
powering CPC to identify programmatic priorities and to determine funding ceilings through consensus before submitting the
budget to the General Assembly Fifth Committee and plenary
body for final approval. Although the 43rd General Assembly in
1988 for the first time approved the budget without a vote, and
agreement was reached on offsetting budget add-ons with parallel savings, the procedures are still only fragilely in place and
have not yet produced an orderly planning-programming-budgeting-evaluation system, partially because of the failure to
bring about larger structural reform. The in-depth study of intergovernmental structures in the economic-social field assigned
to ECOSOC was in turn given over in 1987 to a Special Commission, which a year later produced a report reaching no agreed
upon conclusions and leaving the whole restructuring exercise
in limbo.[36]

Two General Assembly special sessions held in the 1990s offer
a postscript to the Group of Eighteen round of reform. The Eighteenth Special Session in the spring of 1990 dealt with the structure of the world economy and economic conditions in the Third
World rather than with international organizational structures
having to do with economic-social cooperation. The terms of reference were drastically different from the emphasis on the New
International Economic Order that had characterized special session discussions a decade earlier; "topics which used to be infre-
quently mentioned were . . . [in 1990] main themes in almost
every speech," including "domestic policies of developing
countries, human rights observance, democratization . . . , accountability of national elites, reduction of military expenditures
. . . , environmentally sound management, . . . and the role of
the private sector."[37] Although the United States and other
Western countries succeeded in redefining the nature of the
North-South debate, it remained to be seen how long the South
would be content to couch the debate in those terms without

debt relief and other concessions from the North in the short run and without some economic progress to show for it in the longer run. The thirty-eight-point Declaration on International Economic Cooperation that resulted from the 1990 Special Session consisted of vague developing country commitments to adopt free market and other domestic reforms along with equally vague developed country commitments to approach a target of .7 percent of their GNPs devoted to development assistance and to take other steps to help alleviate Third World poverty.

In jeopardy at present is not only the capacity of the U.S. and other wealthy states to continue to frame the North-South debate and command legitimacy for their views but also the capacity of these states to continue to move UN budget reform and related institutional reform in the direction contemplated by the Western-initiated Group of Eighteen process. The Nineteenth Special Session, convened in the spring of 1991 at the behest of the Group of Seventy-seven, shifted the focus back to institutional restructuring in the economic-social field in an attempt to follow up the abortive effort made by the Special Commission. While some developing countries expressed interest in the use of small consultative groups bringing together a subset of Southern states with the Group of Seven or some comparable subset of Northern states (as opposed to reliance on UNCTAD or the near-universalization of ECOSOC), and while some developed countries (notably the Nordic group) offered new proposals for revitalizing ECOSOC, the session failed to achieve sufficient consensus to advance the Group of Eighteen process forward and ended with only a few very minor procedural changes accepted.

Major UN structural reform in support of international economic-social cooperation continues to founder over the search for a formula that concomitantly protects the interests of the dominant members of the organization and is acceptable to the rest. There is the need for the parties to bridge the conceptual gap over whether reform is about efficiency or governance. The Group of Eighteen project was useful in suggesting how these concerns could be merged and how the organization could be made more effective at managing political disagreements and not just managing the store. A constructive role was played also by a diverse coalition of thirty states (including the Group of

Seven, the USSR, and many LDCs) whose campaign for Secretariat reorganization in the fall of 1991 was instrumental in enacting the 1992 reforms.[38] Given the recent narrowing of differences and the incentives various groups of states have to cooperate further, it should be possible to keep the reform process on track. If the wheels of reform, seemingly forever spinning, can be greased by the fashioning of creative solutions to the restructuring puzzle, it could usher in a new chapter in UN institutional change.

A Potpourri of Proposals

Over the years numerous reform proposals in both the peace and security and economic-social fields have been advanced externally, apart from UN in-house proceedings, the product of either independent governmental studies or academic and other nongovernmental studies.[39] External sources at times have heavily influenced the in-house reform efforts. For example, a number of proposals contained in the U.S. State Department study in the mid-1970s, refined and submitted to Congress as President Carter's Report on the Reform and Restructuring of the United Nations System,[40] not surprisingly found their way into the UN Charter Committee and Dadzie Committee deliberations during that era. Similarly, the series of studies sponsored by the United Nations Association-USA in the 1980s became intertwined with the Group of Eighteen reform movement.[41] Published proposals have run the gamut from the quite radical (maximalist) to the quite prosaic (minimalist).[42]

The Carter Report, mandated by the Baker-McGovern Amendment (as alluded to in chapter 3), was generally modest and cautious in its recommendations. Only one proposal in the entire report—"the adoption of a procedure which would permit private parties to have indirect access to the World Court on questions of international law"—required amending the UN Charter or ICJ Statute. The report reiterated the need to achieve greater efficiency in the UN system, seconding the recommendations already endorsed by the Dadzie Committee and the General Assembly advocating "the development of an enhanced planning, programming, budgeting and evaluation capability in the UN Secretariat; improved central management and leadership in the UN Secretariat; better policy analysis, research and data-gathering capability in the Secretariat on international economic and social issues; and increased efficiency and effectiveness in development assistance programs." In the personnel area, the report merely expressed U.S. willingness "with other interested countries to take common steps toward ensuring promotion of the best qualified staff." On financing, the report acknowledged the merits of developing "autonomous sources of revenue for the international community" although only "as a long-term goal" and "as long as we and the other nations retain adequate control of the budget." On human rights, it proposed the creation of a new senior post of UN High Commissioner for Human Rights but stopped short of advocating the conversion of the Trusteeship Council into a Human Rights Council, which would have entailed Charter revision. In the peace and security area, other than the ICJ proposal, the report essentially repeated several items that had appeared in a 1971 document emanating from the Nixon White House,[43] supporting "the creation of a UN Peacekeeping Reserve composed of national contingents trained in peacekeeping functions," "a Special Peacekeeping Fund to help cover the initial costs of peacekeeping operations," U.S. pledges of "airlift services and communications technology" to assist peacekeeping efforts, and "annual private meetings at the Foreign Minister level" to "review the state of world peace and security." After much analysis of possible alterations in the constitutional features of the Security Council and General Assembly, the report only suggested "the offer to very small new states of some form of associate member status" and promised to "employ our efforts toward defining voluntary but common standards to curtail the use of the veto in the Security Council and reduce the necessity of invoking it" and to "give substantially greater weight in our national policy to decisions . . . arrived at [by consensus]."

The Carter Report, in short, was emblematic of the failure of UN reform, with so many of its recommendations skirting the edges of institutional change and having been aired previously by various parties inside and outside the UN only to be echoed again subsequently. These may be ideas, however, whose time finally has come, ready to be fleshed out with greater specifity and implemented—or perhaps they are ideas whose time has passed, ready to be skipped over in favor of reforms that go further in testing the boundaries of institutional development. New ideas are coming from several quarters, some relating to peace and security concerns and given momentum by the Gulf War episode, others relating to the "other UN" and given momentum by the Group of Eighteen experience, though all struggling against "restructuring fatigue."

In addition to ongoing U.S. State Department review crystallizing recently around the concept of a unitary UN, yet another executive-legislative branch reform exercise has been initiated in Washington in the form of the sixteen-member U.S. Commission on Improving the Effectiveness of the United Nations, which was authorized by Congress in 1987 but did not hold its first meeting until June of 1992.[44] Even with its current problems, the leadership that succeeded Gorbachev continues to make reference to the plan for a comprehensive system of international security built around the UN. As discussed in chapter 3, Moscow has associated itself with some of the reforms Washington has subscribed to in the past (including more regularized Security Council meetings at the ministerial level, strengthening of peacekeeping machinery, and increased professionalization of the UN Secretariat)—in some respects taking positions stronger than the U.S.—and has articulated even bolder if still sketchy notions (such as revival of the Council's Military Staff Committee and increased compulsory jurisdiction for the World Court). Japan has proposed adding to the Security Council six new permanent seats without veto power (for itself, Germany, India, Brazil, Nigeria, and Egypt).[45]

The Center for War/Peace Studies in New York has stepped up its campaign for a "binding triad" arrangement capable of turning the General Assembly into more of a legislative body.[46] Scholars and practitioners have elaborated upon previous suggestions for improving UN capabilities to anticipate and defuse crises through better fact-finding machinery and other means, exemplified by Brian Urquhart's proposal for a double-barreled organization of peacekeeping forces, the first consisting of "tripwire" personnel stationed in "awkward places" to report on tension escalation and the second consisting of a standby force supported by "a universal training code" and "an international legal basis on which they can be used."[47] The leaders of Argentina, Greece, India, Mexico, Sweden, and Tanzania have put forward a plan for an International Arms Control Verification System, while the concept of a global arms registry operating through the UN has been brought closer to reality by the endorsement given at the 1991 London economic summit meeting of the Group of Seven (joined by the then Soviet Union, invited as an observer). The World Institute for Development Economics Research, part of the UN University, has suggested the institution of annual meetings between the "Group of Five" (U.S., U.K., France, Germany, and Japan) and the "Group of Non-Five," or "Group of Seven (Ten)" and "Group of Non-Seven (Non-Ten)," with membership in the nonelite group based primarily on elections in the various world regions and with the meetings paving the way for an "Interim World Economic Council."[48] The Group of Fifteen developing states (representing 30 percent of the world's population) that first met in Malaysia in June 1990, around the time of the Group of Seven summit in Houston, has proposed itself as a Third World bargaining agent with the G-7.[49] The governments of France, Norway, and the Netherlands co-sponsored a conference in March 1989, attended by high-ranking officials from two dozen countries representing a cross-section of East-West and North-South elements (though minus the U.S., U.K., USSR, and China), which produced The Hague Declaration calling for the existence of a UN environmental urgency with powers to make non-consensus-based binding decisions. With the retirement of Javier Perez de Cuellar and his replacement by Boutros-Ghali, special attention has been given lately to the Secretary-General's mode of selection (whether such blatantly political criteria as underlaid the recent "it's Africa's turn" campaign strengthen or weaken the office), desired qualities (whether management skills should be emphasized more than diplomatic ones), and term of office (whether a single seven-year term would make for greater effectiveness).[50] There is still debate over whether the UN's problems are primarily managerial or structural in nature, but as noted the gap is being bridged.

Intriguing combinations of institutional reforms are being countenanced by intriguing combinations of states. Some proposals are more far-reaching and farfetched than others. A few recent proposals, nonstate in their authorship, will be examined below that cover the reform spectrum from minimalist to maximalist views. The reform spectrum here refers to the range of UN reform proposals articulated. By definition, all of these are more ambitious than the views harbored by individuals who dismiss institutional reform of any magnitude either because they feel that the UN is beyond hope or that the problems run far deeper than institutional defects.[51]

MINIMALISM: TAKING LOW POLITICS TO A NEW LEVEL

At one extreme is the approach taken by Yves Beigbeder, a personnel administration specialist with experience in FAO, WHO and other UN agencies, who confines his analysis and recommendations essentially to administrative fine-tuning of the existing machinery and focuses on such bodies as the International Civil Service Commission.[52] His premise is that "structural reform plans are spectacular, but are not very realistic. Instead of changing the basic institutions by the dissolution or division of existing ones, a more realistic goal is to improve the operational management of the organizations."[53]

His suggestions for management improvement read like the findings of an efficiency expert. To cite just a few recommendations, he urges that "external consultants and internal management services should carry out periodical management reviews"; "internal auditors should be well qualified on recruitment and re-trained periodically"; "governing bodies should monitor more closely external auditors' reports"; "JIU should liase with the internal management services of the organizations"; "ICSC members should be appointed only if they have the required qualifications in personnel management"; "ICSC should promote more staff training in management, supervisory skills, information and communications systems at all managerial levels."[54] The most daring reorganization idea, though not a novel one, is that "ACABQ and CPC should become one committee."

Beigbeder cannot be faulted for giving attention to managerial concerns. They are part of the UN reform equation, and are easy to overlook. However, if no account of restructuring can substitute for the political will of member states to honor their Charter obligations, no amount of manipulation of managerial elements can substitute for flawed structures. Beigbeder errs in treating managerial reform mostly as an apolitical task and in minimizing the importance of reforms that go beyond mismanagement problems, as when he suggests that it was management failure as much as programmatic disagreements that accounted for American criticism of and withdrawal from UNESCO. It is hard to understand how countries such as the United States would find a more efficient UNESCO seeking to promote a New World Information Order preferable to a less efficient one.[55]

The history of UN reform, which has seen considerable efforts made to improve the administrative functioning of the organization (manifested by the creation of JIU, introduction of medium-term planning and budgeting, and other innovations), demonstrates that it is not realistic to expect nuts-and-bolts changes alone—divorced from the larger structures in which they are embedded—to reshape the institution in significant ways. Such reforms may be implementable but have marginal utility. In posing a false dichotomy between the relative merits of radical constitutional change and more measured modifications in the day to day operations of the UN system, Beigbeder forecloses consideration of intermediate possibilities.

MAXIMALISM: TAKING HIGH POLITICS TO A NEW LEVEL

At the other end of the reform spectrum, one finds the brainstorming proposals of Marc Nerfin, a former staff member of the UN Secretariat and head of the International Foundation for Development Alternatives, who combines World Federalism and New Left thinking. The gist of his argument is contained in the following statement: "the UN is much more than 159 Member States: it is a project which, as the only embryo of a planetary organization, belongs to all of us, members of the human species living on this only one earth."[56] He contemplates a tripartite Assembly based only partially on representation of territorial units: a Prince Chamber, in which national governments would be represented and security issues would predominate; a Merchant Chamber, in which major economic actors would be represented, including state entities, Bretton Woods institutions, and other IGOs in the economic field, and multinational corporations and private bodies; and a Citizen Chamber, representing grassroots associations, with equal participation by men and women.

As noted previously, Rosenau and others have called attention to the emergence of a "multicentric actor system" alongside the Westphalian state-centric system.[57] The state system has even accorded recognition to this phenomenon, the League of Nations Covenant (Article 25) explicitly making reference to the Red Cross, the UN Charter (Article 71) providing for ECOSOC to enter into consultative relationships with nongovernmental organizations, and the ILO Constitution mandating tripartite representation in the ILO's governing bodies. NGOs have had significant involvement in shaping regimes in a number of areas, including human rights—Amnesty International has been so extensively relied on for accurate monitoring of human rights violations that it has been considered "almost an arm of the UN"[58]—and even the laws of war—the International Red Cross was the prime drafting agent of the 1949 Geneva Conventions and the 1977 Geneva Protocols. However, Nerfin sees nonstate actors in a much more revolutionary light, with the NGOs of the future competing with official centers of power in global political processes far more than their contemporary counterparts. Aside from failing to take into account how any national governments could be expected to support enhanced, practically coequal status for nonstate actors in a multipurpose global decision-making structure, Nerfin neglects to consider how states such as the U.S. would react to the World Bank, IMF, and GATT being folded into the same forum with UNCTAD with the decision rules left unspecified. The writer additionally glosses over the matter of how political-security and economic concerns can be neatly compartmentalized and how the strong central guidance thrust of the plan is compatible with the equally strong emphasis on individual and local autonomy. Finally, he is oblivious to the history of UN reform and the resistance of the membership to Charter amendment much less wholesale institutional metamorphosis. Nerfin's ideas are earthshaking to say the least, so ethereal as to require perhaps another millennium before they stand a chance of acceptance.

In rejecting the Westphalian state-centric model altogether, Nerfin makes the binding triad proposal developed by Richard Hudson of the Center for War/Peace Studies appear conservative by comparison.[59] The latter proposal calls for significant Charter revision, albeit limited to two articles, that would empower the General Assembly to make binding decisions upon approval of three concurrent majorities, one based on the current one state-one vote formula, another based on a formula weighted by a state's contribution to the regular UN budget, and a third proportioned by national population. Hudson argues that there is too much concentration of power at the nation-state level and that more decision-making competence must be transferred to both the global level (not only with the conversion of the General Assembly into a legislature but also ultimately with the creation of a UN Bank and Treasury with its own currency as well as other global institutions) and lower, subnational levels.

The Hudson proposal has received little serious attention. It has been criticized for its sheer impracticality in terms of everything from technical difficulties that would be encountered in having to perform the necessary calculations in a political arena to the utopian nature of the recommendations generally. The criticism that coalition-building and lobbying would be problematical due to the difficulty of calculating voting outcomes based on different voting combinations can be handled fairly easily by resort to computer technology. The utopian charge cannot be handled as easily. If it is true that, as Inis Claude states, "the history of international organization is the story of efforts to achieve progressive emancipation from the tradition-based rule of equality and unanimity,"[60] the binding triad in some ways seems to suggest an at least semi-credible, eventual denouement to the drama.[61] Although there has been movement away from voting toward de facto use of consensus procedures in the UN General Assembly, it is questionable how workable such procedures can be in their present form as the main basis for reaching decisions in such a large body. The sticking point with the binding triad proposal is not so much its attack on the principles of equality and unanimity, which have already lost a good bit of their sacred quality in international organizational practice (and are being undermined further today by the shrinking size of many states and the growing size of the interstate system), as its assault on the principle of voluntary compliance in international affairs. Even in regard to the latter, though, there has been some attrition as the de jure principle of binding majoritarianism has been accepted and observed by states in certain circumscribed areas within regional as well as global organizations.

Where the binding triad proposal most goes astray is in its attempt to impose binding majoritarianism upon the entire governance structure of the UN, with the General Assembly having blanket authority to legislate across any and all issue-areas subject only to a few safeguards provided primarily by the World Court. A more thinkable possibility would be be to limit binding majoritarianism to carefully specified types of decisions with flexible allowances for reservations or other qualified compliance instruments. For years, UN members accepted such a principle as applying to regular budgetary matters, until American and Soviet violations gradually eroded the integrity of the rule. The Kassebaum Amendment, focusing on budgetary decision making in the UN, envisioned the U.S. willing to live with binding majoritarianism tied to a weighted voting formula based on financial contributions. Even though this was viewed by many as unacceptable to Third World states, the widely endorsed Group of Eighteen reforms stressing CPC consensus among major donors and other committee members before submitting the budget for majority approval in the General Assembly in effect is more protective of American interests insofar as it gives the U.S. an absolute budgetary veto power it would not otherwise have. The point is that, in pursuit of political development of the international system, it may be possible to fashion a less blunt but nonetheless powerful instrument than the binding triad, which while more grounded in state-centrism than the Nerfin proposals still raises the specter of supranational government and all too squarely challenges Westphalian ways.

Claude reminds that majority rule—whether a simple majority, extraordinary majority, or a binding triad-like concurrent majority—"works only when the minority has . . . confidence in the ultimate reasonableness of the majority" and "the majority recognize[s] the rights of the minority."[62] He sums up the crux of the problem in noting that "by and large, neither majorities nor minorities in the United Nations are spiritually fit to play their roles in a majoritarian system" and will not be until "a genuine community has emerged."[63] The question is whether some system of decision making less spiritually demanding and less jarring to the Westphalian culture than the binding triad can be devised that might help nurture a growing sense of community. Utopian as even this may sound, it is no more so than the thought of parliamentary diplomacy based on formalized rules of order and voting procedures must have appeared to observers of international relations in an earlier time.

SPLITTING THE DIFFERENCE: LOW POLITICS AS HIGH POLITICS

Among UN reform studies falling in the middle are three that were published in 1987, at a time when American references to the "evil empire" were still plentiful and the consummation of American-Soviet rapprochement had not yet produced the birth of the post-Cold War era. Hence, these studies were victims of unfortunate timing, colored by Cold War assumptions which were in the process of becoming dated to a degree few could have foreseen. One such assumption was that (the Palme Commission and other efforts notwithstanding) problems in the peace and security field were relatively intractable and that, to the extent UN reform was worthwhile pursuing, it was the economic-social realm that held far greater promise. In the latter realm all three writings were actually quite bullish on the possibilities for institutional change, the authors leaning toward the maximalist persuasion even as they hedged their conclusions against the backdrop of the ongoing East-West and North-South conflicts.

One study was done by Maurice Bertrand, a former JIU member and member of the Group of Eighteen panel of experts, as a research paper for the UNA-USA's UN Management and Decision-Making Project.[64] In his 1985 JIU report, which was more a personal than institutional statement, Bertrand had laid out many of the ideas that were to appear in the 1987 paper; the earlier document called for greater centralization of the inter-governmental and inter-secretariat machinery in the UN system, bringing UNO and the specialized agencies together under one roof to coordinate policy, although also stressing greater regionalization of activities at the operational level.[65] The UNA paper begins with the conventional wisdom of the day, that "because improvement of the UN's efficiency in the economic and social fields is a more likely prospect than improvement in the field of peace and security, it is the only *practical* way to create a better climate for international and peaceful cooperation."[66] Bertrand develops the outlines of a reorganization scheme based upon "a transposition to the world level of the model of the European Community."[67]

Bertrand takes as the major structural flaw in the UN system the absence of "a center able to fulfill the functions of synthesis, identification, and distribution of work to other bodies,"[68] i.e., the lack of institutional machinery able to provide policy guidance both politically and intellectually. Politically, there is a special need for a structure that can harmonize different agendas and overcome the duplicative, often cross-purposed functioning of the Second Committee, UNCTAD, and ECOSOC. Intellectually, there is the need for a structure that can pull together bodies of technical experts in an interdisciplinary fashion and overcome the narrow sectoralism fostered by the disjointed, rivalrous relationships among the specialized agencies and other parts of the system.

The political dimension of the problem is to be resolved by the creation of a council modeled after the EEC's Council of Ministers. Bertrand argues that the "main institutional difference between the European Community and the UN system is that the European Community has a 'center' of decisions and negotiations in which member states are represented at a credible level of responsibility."[69] He proposes that the member states on a new UN Council be represented at the ministerial level as frequently as possible, and regularly at the ambassadorial level. It is understood that the likelihood of direct high-level participation is dependent upon the perceived likelihood of meaningful action taking place, which is correlated with the size of the setting. The body would be relatively small, with "major countries" (perhaps those with a GNP greater than 2.5 percent of the World Product or a population more than 100 million) each having a seat, and "smaller countries" represented on a regional basis. He suggests this could be accomplished by rescinding two Charter amendments and returning ECOSOC to its original size.

The intellectual dimension of the problem is to be resolved through the creation of a commission modeled after the EEC Commission, "a group of competent people" whose main task would be "to identify problems, analyze their many aspects and differing interpretations, and, through discussion and negotiation among member states, try to develop the possibility for convergence and common ground."[70] The Commission, chaired by the UN Secretary-General or the Director-General, would supplant the present ACC, its members being the executive heads of the main agencies but coming under the authority of the UN's central organs (each nominated by the Council and confirmed by the General Assembly) and thereby better positioned to take a global view. The Commission would perform an enhanced global watch function ("consideration should be given to the possibility of developing a centralized economic and social information system and of putting the most modern electronic equipment at the disposal of the Commission to supply it with all the data it would need"),[71] and would prepare a consolidated systemwide budget to be approved by the Council before given more detailed treatment by the executive boards of individual agencies. The competence enjoyed by the General Assembly under Article 17 of the UN Charter (giving it a right to "examine the administrative budget of the specialized agencies with a view to making recommendations") should be extended to the Council and the Commission, while "the constitution[s] of the agencies should be modified in order to transfer budgetary powers to these central organs."[72]

In many respects, these ideas are not all that pathbreaking, echoing long-standing pleas for restructuring made by the Group of Twenty-five. Others have also invoked the European Community model as a conceivable exemplar for the UN.[73] Still, Bertrand adds some distinctive touches involving major institutional changes in the economic-social sphere, necessitating revision of the UN Charter as well as the constitutions of the specialized agencies.

The proposal admittedly invites criticism on several counts. He understates the problem of getting the bulk of the UN membership to accept regional representation on a truncated Council without an appropriate quid pro quo; although the principle of regional representation on various UN bodies is well established, the issues of what constitutes a region and who should be designated regional spokespersons become more controversial the more importance with which a body is endowed, and become more open to question as the traditional blocs and caucusing groups are somewhat reshaped. Although high-level Council representation would appear to translate into instant salience for global issues, the early experience of ECOSOC when ministerial-level meetings were held suggests this would not be an automatic outcome; as two observers have remarked, problems "did not become intractable because ministers were not present" but rather "the ministers did not come because . . . problems seemed to be intractable."[74] Bertrand is vague about the relationship between the Council and the General Assembly, and about the decision-making procedures on the Council. The EEC Council of Ministers operates formally on the basis of weighted voting tied to binding majoritarianism on most issues falling under the Treaty of Rome, but informally acts through consensus on issues of any significance; Bertrand's analysis leads one to ask whether the EEC could continue to function in this manner if it even remotely approached the size of the UN, were it for example to double or triple in membership as some envision. With regard to the Commission, Bertrand recognizes his prescriptions here may be harder to implement than those pertaining to the Council, given the degree of autonomy that would be lost by the specialized agencies and the complete reordering of the UN system that would have to occur, although he counts on the lure of super-sophisticated global watch gadgetry and the compelling need for "intellectual leadership" to sway minds.[75] Yet "minor technical agencies" dealing with telecommunications and the like as well as "all technical cooperation programs"[76] would be given only secondary representation on the Commission under his scheme, akin to the smaller countries on the Council, with UNCTAD's executive head elevated to membership and selected through the same procedures as the heads of the Bretton Woods institutions—a recipe for potentially volatile technopolitics.

Bertrand was a senior consultant associated with the UNA-USA's UN Management and Decision-Making Project, and his hand can be seen clearly in the core set of reform recommendations contained in the project's "Successor Vision" report.[77] Relying heavily on Bertrand's analysis as a foundation, the report assumes that reform in the welfare field ("human security" as opposed to international security) deserves primary attention ("where UN peace and security mechanisms are concerned, major structural changes will not yield the sort of results anticipated in the realm of social, economic, and humanitarian affairs").[78] The report generally avoids discussion of major changes in the UN's main political organs ("voting procedures and composition of the General Assembly and the Security Council . . . are not promising candidates for reform efforts" insofar as they "reflect finely balanced considerations and are deeply rooted"),[79] and treats many problems as being no less intellectual than political in nature and solvable through some combination of expert research and analysis, timely identification, and mobilization of consensus ("the very process of producing credible [scientific] information will itself help to foster political will to act on the information").[80]

The "Successor Vision" report, however, does range more widely than the Bertrand paper and is somewhat more attuned to possible roadblocks in the reform process. The report touches upon the peace and security field, but recommends nothing more than better consultation between the Secretary-General and the heads of regional organizations and greater use of multilateral inspection teams capable of monitoring and verifying arms control agreements.[81] In regard to "the other UN," the report most notably recommends:

1. the creation of a Ministerial Board within ECOSOC of no more than twenty-five members, which would feature a core permanent membership composed of the largest states joined by smaller states participating on a temporary basis through rotating regional representation, would a la the EEC model attract as delegates senior-level governmental officials from relevant ministries depending upon the particular issues under discussion at a given moment, would seek to "forge communities of interests" through "ad hoc working groups of the most affected countries" whose tentative agreements would be communicated to the Board as a whole for its imprimatur, would reach such decisions by consensus, and would report its recommendations to ECOSOC and the Assembly;

2. the elimination of the Second and Third Committees of the General Assembly and the expansion of ECOSOC into a plenary body meeting once a year concurrently with the Assembly;

3. establishment of a fifteen to eighteen member UN Commission (preceded by an interim, experimental five-person advisory commission), operating along the lines suggested by Bertrand except that the Bretton Woods agencies would retain a special status with their directors chosen as at present;

4. replacement of the existing governing boards of UNDP and other technical cooperation programs with a single Development Assistance Board;

5. creation of a Bureau of Global Watch as part of a reorganization of DIESA and the UN Secretariat, presided over by a Secretary-General elected for a single seven-year term, assisted by deputies whose tenure would coincide with his.[82]

There is much to commend the UNA plan. Its diagnosis of the UN's problems and its proffered solutions cut to the heart of the failings of the UN as a vehicle for global policy making and implementation. As discussed in the previous chapter, there is a need to develop better political-intellectual routines for engaging the international system in economic-social problem solving; cooperation that can bring greater expertise to bear on various problems, and harness it to stronger political forces, not only enhances the system's capability for rational action to remedy specific ills but also enhances the prospects for larger institution-building and community-building. The UNA report seeks to bring the Group of Twenty-five/Group of Eighteen process to closure through a delicate, judicious compromise of elements that include a greater degree of central guidance without sacrificing the virtues of decomposition strategies and non-hierarchical decision making. The "successor vision" comes off as visionary yet pragmatic. The report carefully distances itself from the supranational pretensions of the EEC model, the latter receiving only one minor passing reference in a 100-page document.[83] It argues the UN should be content to attract "the support of a balanced majority of its members," relying heavily on "coalitions of the like-minded" and "the most affected parties," "flexible forum and process," and "dialogue vs. parliamentary decision."[84]

The UNA proposal is almost too artful. The West is to be coopted by the special status accorded the Bretton Woods institutions and the promise of greater efficiency, the Third World is to be coopted by the universalization of ECOSOC, and everyone is to be relieved over the obviation of massive Charter rewriting. However, the fact that, at least in the initial stages of implementation, only one Charter amendment would be required (the enlargement of ECOSOC) belies the true scale of change being contemplated. Stripped of its appeal for the application of human reason to global problem solving, the report in the end boils down mostly to the quest for power steering of global policy. In shunning any Charter reform having to do with the main political organs, the report merely shifts the battle over power steering to other organs where it is to be played out in ways that are unclear. In particular, how would ECOSOC as a plenary body differ functionally from the Second and Third Committees it is to substitute for? If one removes the Second and Third Committees from the General Assembly, will the plenary Assembly still not take up economic and social matters? If a plenary ECOSOC is seen in fact as a surrogate for the Assembly on such matters, what does this leave for the Assembly to discuss?[85] Combined with the UNA emphasis on the role of the General Assembly as a place for dialogue rather than decisions, the Assembly is envisioned as little more than a giant schmoozing society, relegated to being even more of a talk shop than it is at present.

A more logical alternative would seem to be the conversion of ECOSOC into the Ministerial Board in keeping with the intent of the Charter framers, along with a merger of the Second and Third Committees of the General Assembly. This may or may not be palatable to the bulk of the membership. In altering ECOSOC in this fashion, it is not as if one is tampering with an institution that the majority of states now highly value. The Ministerial Board will be viewed as an elite entity no matter whether it is housed within ECOSOC or is free-standing, so that either way its acceptance may require a more substantial set of tradeoffs. This alternative at least preserves the status of the General Assembly and avoids spinning off more awkward relationships between organs than already exist. It also puts the not-so-hidden agenda of power steering more openly on the table.

While there has been much lament in Western quarters about the increased politicization of the specialized agencies, there is inevitably a politics to problem solving even in the most technical of fields. In issue-areas defined as high-politics in nature, the kill-the-messenger syndrome often prevails. Some of the issues cited by the UNA report as "appropriate subjects for global watch"[86]—global biosphere, international debt, disease control, international narcotics trafficking, cross-border population movements—can beget bargaining closer to high politics than low politics. If science is to be allowed to play a greater role in international problem solving, political concerns will have to be confronted more squarely through the invention of ways to facilitate the learning and use of "consensual knowledge."[87] The UNA proposal only partially comes to grips with this question.

A study by David Steele treats the UN in a more holistic manner.[88] He examines UN reform from the perspective of three different time frames—short-run reforms that can be implemented without Charter revision, longer-term Charter reform, and ultimately "a theoretically different basis for the UN." He gives more serious attention to security concerns than the UNA study,[89] although the bulk of the work deals with other matters. In the short-term, his suggestions include the creation of a Commission on the Security Council that would perform fact-finding and other services and reduce the burdens on an overloaded Secretary-General; introduction of weighted voting (tilted toward major donors) on certain subsidiary organs such as CPC, in return for an enhanced role for LDCs on the Security Council; and creation of a Commission that would take over some of the functions of ECOSOC. In the longer-term he envisions a smaller ECOSOC, operating similar to the EEC Council of Ministers, with the power to approve all agency heads and budgets; weighted voting in the General Assembly; and some modification in the use of the Security Council veto. In the still more distant future, he sees the General Assembly as a legislature based on direct election of national delegates akin to the European Parliament. Putting aside his musings about the UN one day becoming a supranational entity, Steele perhaps offers a more realistic vision than the previous writing discussed.

Like the authors of the UNA study, Steele is clearly in favor of greater integration and centralization of the UN system, with the Director-General for Development, for example, becoming "responsible . . . for ensuring high-level coordination and policy planning for all agencies in the area of development" through better use of CPC, ACC, and regular meetings of agency governing bodies "to exercise his powers of coordination, supported by his own office staff and that of the DIESA."[90] However, he argues that if these and any other changes are to come to pass, even in the short run, it is impossible to avoid coming to terms with larger governance issues, particularly those surrounding the General Assembly and its relationship to the Security Council, ECOSOC, and the specialized agencies:

> A solution to the problem of the legitimacy of the decisions of the General Assembly will pave the way for all the reforms of the system which will lead to its greater relevancy and more efficient operation. The question of perceived imbalances of power is the priority issue and it is clear that institutional reform cannot be tackled piecemeal.[91]

Steele sees "power balancing" as the essence of the reform puzzle: "Despite the dissatisfaction with the voting systems in the General Assembly and ECOSOC by the industrialized countries, the existing, albeit very precarious, balances [between East and West, North and South] must either be preserved or replaced deliberately with . . . structures having an equal balance of power and chance of longevity."[92] He adds: "Any new alignment has to provide a much greater influence of the North/East to give it a stake in a stronger and more efficient UN system."[93] Writing in the 1980s, Steele could not foresee that the "North/East" quadrant of his schematic would pose much less of a quandary for power balancing in the 1990s. Still, his point is well-taken that to achieve power steering in the UN system there is a need for some degree of power balancing, or at least broad-based agreement on "major political trade-offs," with "initial reform efforts concentrated on putting together a balanced and phased package."[94]

The Perfect is the Enemy of the Good

UN reform will not make a perfect institution out of an imperfect one. However, it can contribute to a far better institution. The two criteria that any set of UN reform proposals must address are: feasibility (are they politically capable of implementation?) and meaningfulness (are they worth expending any political effort in terms of there being a likelihood that once implemented they will make a noticeable constructive difference in the functioning of the institution?). The difficulty of reconciling these two desiderata is confirmed by the history of UN reform. The historical pattern has been that institutional change has occurred more through evolution than design, that to the extent deliberate reform has been attempted it has taken the form of tinkering, and that such reform has proven hardly worth the effort.

At the end of his 1990 essay on strengthening UN economic-social programs, published by the Academic Council on the UN System, Jacques Fomerand expresses the understandable skepticism that continues to be the dominant attitude toward global institutional reform even among those who take the UN most seriously, even in an era of UN revival. He considers "large-scale change an unlikely scenario." He sees

> instead, the persistence of an on-going process of remedial
> adjustments. In this respect, the very mild form of reporting to
> ECOSOC now required from the specialized agencies
> illustrates, once again, the prevalence of this dominant pattern
> [in the reform process] of 'disjointed incrementalism.' In all
> probability the system will continue to evolve as it has since its
> inception. One should not, therefore, be exceedingly surprised
> if, in a not too distant future, this approach triggered a
> renewed flurry of 'utopies de l'organigramme'.[95]

At the risk of being branded a utopian futurist, I would only call the reader's attention to the fact that this sort of thinking contains a certain self-fulfilling prophecy based on a faulty syllogism: The only deliberate UN institutional reform that is at all possible is piecemeal, minor reform; such reform is virtually inconsequential in its effects, except insofar as it contributes to cumulative change that cannot be planned; no real reform is possible. It is possible to break out of this circular argument if one understands that the view of history upon which it is based is unduly narrow and deterministic. After all, the creation of the UN itself testifies to the fact that, at certain moments in time, not insignificant, conscious international institutional development is politically possible. Just as realist thinking cannot fully account for the beginnings of the nation-state system,[96] it hardly can be said to have predicted or postdicted the establishment of the UN.

Oran Young's reference to "negotiated orders" as one avenue for change in institutional arrangements was alluded to earlier. Young speaks of "institutional bargaining" as consisting of

> efforts on the part of autonomous actors to reach agreement among themselves on the terms of constitutional contracts or interlocking sets of rights and rules that are expected to govern their subsequential interactions. Occasionally, these contracts take the form of broad, framework agreements encompassing the basic order or ordering principles of an entire social system.[97]

He cites "San Francisco in 1945" as belonging to "this class of comprehensive or framework agreements." Could the present moment perhaps represent an occasion for forging the next framework agreement in the life of the international system, or at least reworking if not rethinking the one entered into in San Francisco? In order to answer this question, the author now needs to spell out the elements of a grand bargain that conceivably might constitute a prominent solution to the UN reform game.

6

Prescriptions

Let us briefly retrace the ground traversed in the preceding pages. Against the backdrop of prevailing antiglobalist and anti-institutionalist (more specifically, anti-organizationalist) thinking commonly found among students of international relations, a case can be made for not only the increased need of global institution-building but also for its increased possibility. I have equated the growth of world order with the political development of the international system, which has been conceptualized as the progression toward a single pluralistic security-community. This in turn, requires interstate interactions acquiring and maintaining qualities of mutual responsiveness and predictability, ultimately entailing broadening and increased routinization of international governance processes whereby values (goods) get allocated in the system (that is, whereby regimes or "international public policies" get produced). Such a scenario cannot materialize without some manner of global organization capable of furnishing a degree of central guidance.

The United Nations and its affiliated agencies appear at this time to be the prime, arguably only, candidate for the job. Indeed, the UN can be understood as the resultant of large-scale, long-term technological and other forces contributing to the establishment of the "habit of international organization" in the nineteenth century and the creation of global organization in the twentieth century. Whether this historical pattern of growing formalization and universalization of international politics continues, and can be given an accelerated push, will depend upon several factors. The past dynamics of international institution-building suggests that major innovation in the development of the international system, in terms of new macro-level governance arrangements ("framework agreements") resulting from human design, tends to be associated with the existence of a systemwide crisis combined with the existence of a critical mass of actors disposed toward and capable of moving the system.

The contemporary international system that forms the organizational environment of the UN is like a great double-edged sword having various properties which pose both constraints as well as opportunities for enhanced institution-building at the global level. In some respects, central guidance through global organization is more problematical than ever, given the multitude of nation-state actors now found in the international system claiming a seat at the global bargaining table and the increasingly convoluted relationships evolving between their governments and a host of nonstate actors enmeshed in complex interdependence. At the same time, a potentially catalytic systemic crisis exists insofar as groups of people representing a wide cross-section of societies are experiencing mounting problems and frustrations in meeting their needs and aspirations, leaving them open to change. The dramatic upheavals in the international system since the late 1980s are themselves forcing a widespread reexamination of many of the assumptions which colored world politics over the past almost half-century. While power recently has become more diffused—American hegemony in the economic sphere and superpower bipolarity in the military sphere have been replaced by multipolarity and the diminished fungibility of resources—there still remains a considerable concentration of power sufficient to constitute a dominant coalition of actors (national governments) capable of moving the system. What has been lost in power concentration has been more than offset by the reduced rigidity of alignments and increased convergence of interests allowing more creative possibilities for an enlightened concert of power approach to international governance. Shared issue-positions in support of global institution-building on the part of elites are on the rise, as are salience levels pressured by the aforementioned crisis of problem-solving, bringing will closer in line with power. There are present in the contemporary international system, then, the prerequisites for innovation in macro-level governance arrangements, with conditions on balance being conducive to significant institutional change in the UN—not merely of an evolutionary nature but in the way of deliberate reform.

The UN suffers from numerous defects in both its administrative-managerial structures and major decision-making structures that are widely recognized to the point where they have become the subject of almost ritualistic criticism. It is not merely a matter of getting the trains to run on time but also determining where it is they should be going. The impetus for change provided by the general dissatisfaction with current UN arrangements and consensus behind the need for improvement, buttressed by the collapse of the familiar postwar order, contends with restructuring fatigue fostered by years of reform failure. (One must add as another countervailing factor the complications presented by what might be called the attention deficit phenomenon, namely, the tendency for concrete, immediate events—such as the Gulf War and the Gorbachev coup and counter-coup, two August surprises on the eve of the 1990 and 1991 opening of the UN General Assembly—to divert the energies of the international community from larger matters.) The challenge of UN reform today is to seize the moment, to see if a package of proposals can be devised that makes sense—is feasible and meaningful—in the context of an emergent international system that more than one national leader has labeled "the new world order" and others have characterized as "the new world disorder."[1]

What prescriptions follow from all this? Although any UN reform project is inescapably a political bargaining exercise, the search for a prominent solution may be helped along by getting the participants to think in terms of a strategic planning exercise of the type periodically engaged in by corporate and other large organizations for purposes of forced self-reflection. A strategic plan by its nature contains an overall vision/mission statement and then proceeds to connect this to goals, objectives, instruments/strategies, and implementation processes.

Missions, Goals, Objectives

There is the need first to reach a common understanding of the proper mission of the United Nations. There have been shifting views in recent years as to whether the organization should be (and can be) primarily looked to and relied upon to address war-peace concerns as opposed to other concerns. Harold Jacobson notes that "historically, the first goal of early IGOs was to promote economic growth," manifested by the creation in 1815 of the Central Commission for the Navigation of the Rhine, "the first modern international governmental organization."[2] However, as Inis Claude has noted, "the organizing movement of the twentieth century can be interpreted as a reaction to the increasingly terrible consequences of armed conflict,"[3] that is, as fundamentally tied to the problem of war; elsewhere Claude has written likewise that "international organization . . . represents a trend toward the systematic development of an enterprising quest for political means of making the world safe for human habitation."[4] How high-politics, peace and security concerns relate to low-politics, functional, welfare concerns, and what might be the proper place of the UN in these respective areas, has become somewhat muddled as the conceptual distinctions themselves have become blurred.

Lip service continues to be paid to the need for institutional organizations such as the UN to address both sets of issues, based on the link between physical and structural violence (alternatively phrased as "collective security" and "cooperative security,"[5] or "peacekeeping" and "peace-building,"[6] and the like). However, where once it was a given that the second set of issues offered the greater growth potential for the UN—based on the assumption shared by functionalists and nonfunctionalists alike that an international organization's ease and effectiveness in forging collaboration was likely to be inversely related to its degree of involvement in matters touching the core interests of states—this bit of conventional wisdom has now been turned on its head. In a stunning role reversal at odds with both the theory of international organization and the practice of the UN historically (especially throughout much of the 1980s), the tractability of problems, the utility of the UN, and the prospects for institutional reform in the 1990s are being deemed greater in the war-peace area than in other areas, notably in the field of economic development. Two observers have summed up this situation in commenting that "the UN has become a Janus-like system of two faces—the UN of peace and security, relatively purposeful and effective, to which influential governments pay

active and growing attention; and the UN of economic and social affairs, halting, hortatory, and often ignored by powers
great and small."[7] This is the prevailing mindset despite recent
UN setbacks in the Yugoslavian conflict and elsewhere.

It is the very broadening of the concept of national security,
increasingly being defined as encompassing economic, environmental, and other dimensions, that is converting many erstwhile low-politics (or, more accurately in the case of economics,
middle-politics) issues into issues with higher stakes and higher
politicization.[8] It is not so much that traditional war-peace concerns have now become easier to tackle than previously, granted
the current environment provides the UN with special opportunities for an enhanced conflict management role; rather that
other concerns, relating to what can be construed as cooperation
management, in some respects have become more difficult.
Again, though, one must be mindful of the pitfalls of overreacting to the latest developments, either exaggerating the promise
of the UN in the war-peace area or dismissing it in the economic,
social and technical realm. If it was premature to write off the
UN in the former domain at the start of the 1980s, it seems premature as well to do so in the latter domain at the start of the
1990s.

It may be true that more than ever there is no "sheltered area
of concordant interests" in which "we are vouchsafed the privilege of warming up the motors of institutional collaboration . . .
getting off to an easy start and building up momentum for crash-
ing the barriers of conflicting interests that interpose between us
and the ideal of world order."[9] Yet the basic logic of functional-
ism still would appear to have considerable validity. That is, national governments are most sensitive to the potential negative
impacts of entering into new international institutional arrangements, and least likely to contemplate future constraints on their
behavior much less surrendering a degree of sovereign control,
in those issue-areas that are perceived to bear most directly on
the state's physical integrity and survival. States can be expected
to remain more open to international institution-building and
the development of routinized governance processes for reaching agreements on sharing cancer research data than on controlling armaments, even if the climate for confidence-building in
military-strategic matters is improving. Notwithstanding the im-

pressive demonstration of collective security possibilities provided by the Gulf War experience, Iraq was not the only UN member that felt discomforted by the prospect of a newly energized Security Council of questionable representativeness (or any amount of representativeness) prepared to take intervention to new lengths in the name of world order. While the war-peace area may hold unprecedented potential for global institution-building, it remains a far more delicate thread upon which to hang the UN's future than the functional one.

There are many ways in which one can think about missions, goals, and objectives in the context of the UN. Many years ago Wolfram Hanrieder spoke of three "task systems" associated with IGOs: collective security, peaceful change, and peaceful settlement.[10] Oran Young around the same time suggested several conceivable UN "roles", including: "a device for regulating relationships of power in the international system," "an effector of agreements among the major powers," "an instrument for the accomplishment of political change," "a creator of norms and a source of collective legitimization," and "a contributor to the development of long-term viability for the states in the system."[11] Jacobson has posited a generic "taxonomy of functions" which IGOs such as the UN perform: informational, normative, rule-creating, rule-supervisory, and operational.[12] More recently, Peter Fromuth, a contributor to the UNA Successor Vision project, has articulated five "purposes" the UN can serve, areas in which it enjoys a "comparative advantage over other international actors": peacekeeper and crisis manager, humanitarian agent, global watch organization, development catalyst, and global economic forum.[13] The times may change, and also the vernacular used to describe what it is the UN does or should do. However, in the end one is left with the proposition that the UN's mission is primarily to promote order and that order cannot be had without a measure of justice, that stable peace cannot occur without expectations of peaceful change.

Regarding the maintenance of order, can the UN be anything more than a court of last or late resort in war-peace matters? The UN is positioned to serve as a screening mechanism for facilitating decisions by the international community as to the indivisibility of peace when disputes arise which are characterized by threatened or actual violence. The goal of the UN should be to help prevent situations on the brink of localized, civil violence from escalating to interstate war and to help prevent any dyadic or regional interstate conflicts from escalating to systemic war. Obviously, not all violent conflicts on the planet have equal potential to spill over onto the international much less global plane. The civil war that began in Yugoslavia in 1991 did not threaten, for example, Canadian-Yugoslav relations, where the probability for war remained close to zero. Although the more a conflict approaches the systemic level, the more likely it will trigger some sort of UN response, the extent to which the UN becomes involved in a given dispute and the specific management role it assumes relative to the role played by other actors such as regional IGOs is something to be worked out in each case. Institution-building in this area should focus on improving the capacity of the international community to reach such decisions in an expeditious and effective manner and, where a UN role is called for, on providing peaceful settlement, peacekeeping, collective security and related services in a similarly expeditious, effective manner that can deter or defuse the resort to violence.

Again, there are no doubt limits on how far the international community is willing to go to enhance the UN's war prevention and war termination capabilities. Regional forums continue to provide a first line of defense, exemplified by the 1991 accord reached by the foreign ministers of the thirty-five-nation Conference on Security and Cooperation in Europe, which established hot lines and a ten-day crisis resolution routine for settling potentially explosive interstate disputes; under this arrangement, thirteen states can call an immediate meeting within two or three days to discuss "major disruptions endangering peace, security or stability." It would be helpful to develop regularized lines of communication between such regional forums and the UN and to articulate these relationships more clearly. The UN will remain peculiarly suited to dealing with certain kinds of situations and problems that transcend regional boundaries. The enhancement of UN capabilities in the war-peace area may require changes in existing organizational structures or possibly new organizational machinery. For example, if a UN arms registry were to be established, it might require a new agency to be created for monitoring purposes. The very process of the international community through the UN engaging in an analysis of how states can reasonably develop a system of shared, accurate, and trustworthy data on armaments, and what kind of organizational or non-organizational mode of collaboration would be appropriate, can itself be a constructive exercise in the movement toward a security-community.

What of the "other UN" and the promotion of peaceful change? Conceivably, the link between the UN proper (UNO) and the specialized agencies could be severed, leaving UNO to concentrate on war-peace problems and leaving the latter entities with complete autonomy to combat their narrower concerns in their own way. Such an approach is not without merit, supported by functionalist theory. As Fred Bergsten writes: "Functional specificity works better for a variety of reasons. The issues are smaller and better defined, and hence more manageable. Like-minded officials are thrown together. There can be less blackmail over setting agendas. Perhaps most important, issue-area linkage and politicization—both of which usually deter functional progress—are better avoided."[14] John Ruggie also has suggested the benefits of moving away from thinking in terms of multipurpose organizations (or even organizations altogether) and instead considering different institutional designs appropriate to different issue-areas.[15] However, aside from the radical rethinking of the UN system a divorce of the specialized agencies would entail, such an arrangement seems unrealistic also in view of the interconnectedness of many functional issues with each other and with traditional security issues. As Bergsten is forced to acknowledge, given "increased interdependence among the whole array of functional issues," "it is impossible to keep separate the major international economic, and even security, issues."[16] Only an overarching, comprehensive, full-service global organization can cope with the functional eclecticism problem alluded to earlier and can provide central guidance in support of security-community-building.

Robert Keohane and Joseph Nye have suggested that although IGOs are not "incipient world governments," they can be conceptualized as "institutionalized policy networks, within which transgovernmental policy coordination and coalition-building" can occur.[17] Under present arrangements, these networks do not work very effectively at facilitating either coordination or coalition-building. Organization theory posits that "under conditions of high heterogeneity and instability [as characterizes the contemporary international environment], organizational performance is enhanced by . . . functional divisions of labor, which are linked together by specific integrative mechanisms."[18] As Bertrand and others have pointed out, the UN fails as a "linking-pin organization"; "the position of a linking-pin organization is seldom based entirely on formal authority but rests largely on its ability to manipulate network characteristics by mobilizing coalitions around specific issues or controlling the bargaining process."[19]

Meehan offers another perspective, arguing that if policies "are to serve as guides to real world actions and be subject to criticism and improvement," there must be an "intellectual apparatus" which includes "both the empirical or scientific knowledge needed to determine and modify the . . . available alternative future states of the world from which a choice is made and the ethical or normative knowledge needed to choose one of those future states rather than the others."[20] There must also be a political apparatus capable of mobilizing scientific and value consensus—consensual knowledge—behind some policy and thereby moving the political system to act. Might international regime-making processes better approximate routines "for directing human actions in . . . reasoned, corrigible ways,"[21] so that what comes out more clearly resembles policy? In short, can the world improve upon functional eclecticism?

As an alternative to functional eclecticism, another model of global organization might be considered which I would label "dirigible pluralism," whose main defining feature is subsystem autonomy within a central guidance system built around the UN. Partly inspired by the work of Bertrand and others associated with UNA reform studies during the eighties, I envision the UN here as a regime-processing center or, more ambitiously, as a fulcrum for "global policy."[22] Just as in the war-peace area, in other areas as well not all concerns are global in scope or require organizational solutions. One might reason that it is precisely the task of global policy to sort these matters out. The UN proper, as distinct from the specialized agencies, is uniquely situated to furnish the necessary filtering apparatus for engaging the international system in policy-relevant political-intellectual routines at the systemwide level, permitting a determination of how much globalism and institutionalism is optimal for the system. In other words, rather than our starting with a priori anti-institutionalist and antiglobalist presumptions regarding the parameters of international problem solving, the UN should be viewed as a general facilitator of decisions by the international community as to what type of regime instrument is possible and desirable in a given problem area (in terms of norms, rules, organizations, programs, or other outputs) as well as what the regime scope might be (global or subglobal). Present references to "the nuclear proliferation regime" or "the monetary regime" have the air of impressive accomplishments engineered by the international system in response to common problems. They would be all the more impressive if they could more rightly claim to be the fruits of policy—conscious, deliberate, goal-directed acts of creation and remaking that stretch the bounds of intelligent collaboration to the fullest extent imaginable. Such an image of the UN is consistent with current calls for "practical internationalism," yet at the same time offers a more expansive vision as a basis for framing the debate over institutional reform.

Dirigible pluralism is characterized by three basic operating principles. First, the model envisions an enhanced capacity of the international system as a whole to respond to problems confronting humanity, without foreclosing or limiting local and regional efforts. Global and subglobal approaches would not be mutually exclusive or competitive but would have a synergistic relationship, with global-level agencies stimulating subglobal activities (as in the case of the Regional Seas program sponsored by UNEP and the series of bilateral, regional, and inter-regional code of conduct agreements generated by the UN Commission on Transnational Corporations) and subglobal projects providing laboratory settings for experiments in international collaboration which if successful might be applied elsewhere in the system (along the lines of the function often attributed to the political subdivisions in the U.S. and other federal systems, and exemplified by the role of the UN Economic Commission for Europe in developing road signal standards that have been instituted worldwide).[23] With a few exceptions such as the UNEP example, global and subglobal approaches at present tend to be viewed as separate rather than interrelated, reinforcing layers of problem-solving activity. This condition might be remedied if

the UN were to more self-consciously build subglobal components into its programs, serve as a clearinghouse for information
on subglobal collaborative undertakings, and provide better
mechanisms for encouraging bandwagoning where subglobal
cooperation has the potential to be enlarged to the global level
(as with certain limited membership IGOs or multilateral treaties).

Second, the model points to increased rationalization of international governance processes but without sacrificing the benefits of flexibility. On the input side of the equation, agenda-
setting, formulation and adoption phases of global policy-
making would be brought more into synch, while on the output
side the system would furnish better feedback as to which policy
instruments work more effectively than others. UN organizational routines need to be developed so as to permit more demands to be converted into public policy enjoying widespread
legitimacy and so as to maximize cooperative learning, although
the resulting shared experience may well suggest the less organization the better in certain problem areas. In particular, it
should be possible to take better advantage of global policy opportunities presented in those situations where there is already
existent or emerging knowledge and value consensus surrounding specific problems and solutions (in the case of, say, AIDS or
ozone layer deterioration).[24] If knowledge is to be viewed as
authoritative and is to be acted upon by the international
community—if "epistemic communities" are to contribute to
problem solving—it would help to have an established multinational research operation in the UN reliable for its technical expertise and objectivity, linked not only to other IGO and NGO
scientific networks but also to political machinery capable of
raising salience levels among governments and their constituencies sufficiently to focus the energies of the system on the problem at hand.[25] Instructive here are the ideas contained in the
1987 UNA Successor Vision study, which proposed the creation
of a UN Bureau of Global Watch that would regularly monitor
and report on evolving "human security" concerns, in the service of a Ministerial Board composed of national cabinet-level
ministers meeting periodically to discuss issues within their substantive domain (although resisting comparisons with the EEC
model).

The third operating principle is that any efforts to improve global policy processes must take into account the polyarchic characteristics of the international system. This means inter alia ensuring as much as possible that various interests are broadly represented in any new arrangements at the global level; utilizing primarily non-command, consensus-based decision-making procedures that minimize threats to sovereignty; exploring creative ways through treaty reservations, IGO associate memberships, and other devices to promote at least partial but explicit commitments to global policy endeavors; and reducing overlap and duplication in the system while avoiding overcentralization (notably developing better control and accountability mechanisms over the specialized agencies without destroying their independent capacities for problem solving and tension reduction within their limited sphere of concern).

Drawing on "lessons learned in global environmental governance," Peter Sand has suggested some specific ways in which the difficulties inherent in global bargaining can be at least partially alleviated. He stresses incorporating into regime-making processes asymmetrical standards ("selective incentives, differential obligations, and regionalization") as a way to "beat the bottomline rule" (the lowest common denominator problem), and fast tracks ("provisional treaty application, soft-law options, and delegated law-making") as a way to "beat the slowest-boat rule" (the problem of delayed ratification and taking effect of agreements). He argues regime-implementation can be aided by "alert diffusion, epistemic networks" and other means as "alternatives to supranational regulation" and by "local remedies and environmental audits" as "alternatives to intergovernmental litigation."[26] Richard Benedick draws similar lessons in his case study of the 1987 Montreal Protocol on Substances that Deplete the Ozone Layer, whose negotiation he argues "was only possible through an intimate collaboration between scientists and policymakers."[27] The scientific component was based on "continually evolving theories of atmospheric processes, on state-of-the-art computer models simulating the results of intricate chemical and physical reactions . . . and on satellite-, land-, and rocket-based monitoring of remote gases measured in parts per trillion."[28] The policy-making component related to UNEP's role as a catalyst for promoting cosmopolitan research teams and for convening the conference itself; to the existence of the 1985 Vienna Convention as an umbrella agreement providing a basis for more specific protocols; to provisions mandating the protocol to take effect upon ratification by eleven states accounting for at least two-thirds of CFC consumption worldwide while allowing differential compliance on the part of signatories (with developing countries permitted to postpone compliance for ten years); and to the use of flexible procedures for making modifications in the protocol without having to undertake complete renegotiation and reratification (permitting the initial target of a 50 percent reduction in CFC production by 1998 to be changed to a complete ban by 2000).[29]

Can these lessons be applied in a broader context? Kaufmann and Schrijver raise the possibility of the UN promulgating a "Charter for Development" that would provide a comprehensive framework for international development cooperation but with a high degree of adaptability. Although somewhat whimsical, it is worth considering as suggestive of what some of the elements of "dirigible pluralism" might look like:

> A 'Charter for Development' should be as clear and brief as possible, providing a framework for specific undertakings in the context of the competent specialized agencies and UN organs. The specific undertakings could be adopted in the form of protocols to the original framework or 'mother' treaty, as in the case of the Ozone Layer Convention. . . . The protocols should be of a binding nature and could be called 'development contracts.' Areas to be covered could include: (a) the amount of development aid; (b) special measures for least developed countries; (c) additional measures for the liberalization of trade for the benefit of (sub-groups of) developing countries, beyond GATT commitments; (d) special measures for the protection of the environment . . . ; (e) debt rescheduling; (f) standards for the treatment of foreign investments.
>
> Such an approach would enable development-oriented industrialized nations to move a step ahead of the others and would provide opportunities for a more differentiated approach. For example, a group of industrialized nations can decide to enter into a special relationship with a certain group of developing countries, along the lines of the Scandinavian concept for a

so-called mini-NIEO in Southern Africa. The approach could also be differentiated according to certain sectors; e.g., a global contract could be concluded for the shipping sector, . . . or the trade in textiles and clothing as an alternative to the Multi-Fibre Agreement. . . . More structured cooperation between the United Nations and the specialized agencies and a new approach of a Charter for Development, supplemented by development contracts, would enable international development cooperation to be placed on a firmer . . . footing [and based on] . . . both the political will of donor states as well as the needs of developing countries or specific sectors.[30]

These same authors also contemplate a "General Agreement on the Global Environment," into which might be fitted as-sorted regional and global environmental regimes dealing with various environmental dimensions (ozone layer deterioration, greenhouse warming, toxic waste disposal, deforestation, de-sertification, etc.) through various cooperative modes, including organizations (notably UNEP and its fifty-eight member Gov-erning Council, Earthwatch monitoring system, and Nairobi-based secretariat), treaties (with some 140 environmental agreements registered with UNEP), and "softer legal instru-ments such as guidelines or principles of conduct."[31]

The concept of a comprehensive agreement for the environ-ment was put to a first test in Rio de Janeiro in June 1992, at the UN Conference on Environment and Development, informally called Earth Summit. The Rio Conference proceeded from the assumption that there were limits to the extent one could de-compose problems geographically—the meeting was expected to be attended by heads of state from virtually every country (unlike the 1972 UN Conference on the Human Environment in Stockholm)—and sectorally—the meeting sought to produce a framework for action sensitive to the linkages between a wide range of concerns in the ecological issue-area as well as linkages between the latter and the economic development issue-area. In his 1991 Statement to the Second Session of the Preparatory Committee for the Rio Conference, the secretary-general of the conference, Maurice Strong, identified six desired outcomes:

an Earth Charter, a general declaration of principles connect-ing environmental and development concerns;

an "Agenda 21" action plan setting priorities to be addressed in the remainder of the century;

commitment of resources for purposes of implementation;

universal access to environmentally sound technologies through regional development banks helping to create in each region a "sustainable development and technology support system";

strengthening of UNEP and other existing UN institutions in the environmental field;

signing of specific conventions on climate change and biodiversity.[32]

Strong noted related "processes underway at both the expert and intergovernmental levels," including the UNEP/WMO Intergovernmental Panel on Climate Change, the FAO Netherlands Conference on Sustainable Agriculture, and the Dublin Conference on Water and the Environment, as well as NGO efforts such as the World Industrial Conference on Environmental Management sponsored by the International Chamber of Commerce.[33] Added to this were myriad regional endeavors such as the Mekong Committee and International Center for Integrated Mountain Development in Asia, the Southern African Development Coordination Committee and Intergovernmental Committee Against Drought in the Sahel in Africa, and the Amazon Cooperation Treaty and Andean Pact in Latin America as well as UNEP's regional seas program.[34]

In another pre-conference document, commenting on the challenge of developing an environmental regime or set of regimes that could cohere not only in terms of geographical scope but also form and content, Strong noted that "there is an increasing tendency for environment and related issues to be dealt with through legal agreements which incorporate special institutional measures. . . . In the meantime, many of the most important agreements under which practical programs are carried out are of a nontreaty, voluntary nature [such as] WHO's Environmental Health Program, FAO's Agrarian Reform Program, the Program of Action to Combat Desertification. . . . How can the institutional arrangements made pursuant to legal agreements be most effectively provided for and coordinated with

other related institutions of the UN system and the intergovernmental community more generally?"[35]

The Rio Conference proved unable to cope fully with all these
elements of environmental problem solving. Leaders of 178
countries did attend, including over 100 heads of state, while
1,500 NGOs were also represented. The results fell short of the
hopes many had harbored. A framework convention on climate
change was signed by over 150 countries, obligating them to
take measures to reduce greenhouse effect gas emissions but
failing to specify targets or timetables, mostly owing to recalci-
trance on the part of the United States. A biodiversity convention dealing with deforestation and protection of plant and
animal species was also signed, the U.S. withholding support
due to concerns about patent rights and funding arrangements.
In addition, UNCED produced a Declaration on the Environment and Development containing twenty-seven general principles relating to sustainable development, as well as a voluntary
action plan suggesting steps that could be taken locally, regionally, and globally as a follow-up to the conference, although
these documents were pale versions of the Earth Charter and
Agenda 21 plan Strong had envisioned.

The future success of such efforts in ecological and other fields
is tied to the capacity of the UN system to develop macro-level
governance arrangements that have the characteristics of the dirigible pluralism model. The specific institutional reforms
needed in support of future Earth Summits and lower-level undertakings are indicated below in the discussion of the next part
of the strategic plan for the UN.

Instruments/Strategies

The foundation for significant UN institutional reform along
the lines of the dirigible pluralism model already has been laid
by the Group of Eighteen experience. The following eleven-
point reform program contains prescriptions for political-administrative retooling whereby a more rational politics can begin to
take hold in the UN, enabling the organization to tap its poten-

tial to facilitate agreement on problems worthy of global attention and to act effectively where such agreement exists.

(1.) Starting at the bottom, the issue of the competence and independence of the human resources employed by the UN Secretariat needs to be addressed. More systematic use of competitive exams must be instituted in the hiring of professional staff at the P-1 through P-3 levels, along with special exams administered at the P-4 and P-5 levels, with the nature of the exams to be based on common elements drawn from a cross-national sampling of civil service screening procedures among UN members. A competitive salary structure (comparable to the World Bank and IMF) and reasonable promotion procedures allowing greater upward mobility must be maintained if the UN is to recruit a cadre of top-flight administrative and technical personnel seeking careers as international civil servants. The movement toward greater professionalization and depoliticization of the international civil service has been given a boost by the recent announcement of Big Five members that they would no longer insist on their nationals being appointed to the most senior positions in the UN Secretariat, thereby setting an example for others to follow, although the initial one-year appointments by Secretary-General Boutros-Ghali seem thus far to undermine the new principles.

(2.) Even with the recent cutting of USG and ASG positions and the designation of eight senior officials in seven departments reporting directly to the Secretary-General, further trimming would seem in order. There should be adoption of a plan aired by the Australians and some other delegations to create a smaller number of super-departments in the UN Secretariat, although the exact number and identity of these units need to be considered more carefully. It makes sense to have two departments covering political affairs and administration and management. However, there does not seem to be any logic to the separate portfolios given to public information, legal affairs, emergency relief, and peacekeeping, particularly the latter, which seems more properly housed within political affairs; the political affairs department should have a single head, with second-level senior officials responsible for fact-finding and mediation, peacekeeping, and arms control. A separate department devoted to human rights, as has been proposed, seems ill-conceived; continued reliance on ECOSOC's Human Rights Commission, or the possible conversion of the de facto defunct Trusteeship Council into an expanded Human Rights Council, would seem to amply cover this area without the need to create another separate bureaucracy in the Secretariat that would be a lightning rod for controversy. (The recent failure of the Conference on Security and Cooperation in Europe to reach consensus on the mandatory use of sanctions by member states against governments judged guilty of human rights abuses is ample evidence of the continuing sensitivity of human rights issues and governmental concerns about erosion of sovereignty.) A department of economic and social affairs might be too large to handle that range of issues, although the catch-all nature of the unit could be alleviated through the establishment of appropriate sectoral divisions (developmental and nondevelopmental, environmental, etc.) with DIESA and the Office of the Director-General for Development and International Economic Cooperation folded into it.

(3.) The super-departments would each be headed by a Deputy Secretary-General appointed by the Secretary-General and removable by the latter, serving as his cabinet during his tenure. Here it is true that formal-legal correctives alone cannot substitute for the willingness of member states to accept the norm that the Secretary-General must be given a high degree of independence in recruiting policy-level and professional staff judged to be meritorious in terms of their competence and integrity. The JIU and International Civil Service Commission can be relied on to provide outside expert and intergovernmental checks on possible personnel abuses within the UN bureaucracy.

(4.) The internalization of such a norm places a premium on ensuring that the Secretary-General selection process is widely perceived to be fair and responsible. Institutional reform can support norm change. The key is not the length or renewability of the term of office; it is hard to see how a single seven-year term, as some urge, will confer upon the officeholder any special legitimacy or insulation from political winds. Rather, the key is to define the role and establish appropriate selection criteria in a manner calculated to depoliticize it as much as possible. There is no questioning the importance of IGO executive heads having great leadership qualities.[36] Although the search for a dynamic individual to lead the UN cannot be wholly depoliticized, it makes sense to define the position primarily in terms of 'CEO-manager' rather than 'global statesman-crisis manager' and to stress the possession of sound administrative-managerial skills rather than diplomatic skills even if this risks undermining the stature of the office. Diplomacy can be left to others. The glamour of the office may be diminished but its moral authority and political effectiveness may be enhanced, insofar as UNO inefficiency, even if something of a red herring issue, has become an embarrassment and major political liability for the organization.

There is no reason to change the current five-year renewable term arrangement. However, the major UN donors should be able to exercise sufficient leverage over the functioning of the organization through their input into the budgetary process (discussed below) that they should be willing to relinquish the veto power a handful now have over the nomination of the UN head to a more broadly representative screening body, thereby demonstrating their commitment to a more even-handed selection process. While one must be sensitive to the need and benefit of having diversity adequately represented at the top of the international civil service—one might rightly question why there has been only one woman appointed among the 136 executive heads of UN specialized agencies and programs named since 1946[37]—the overriding ingredient must be talent in running large organizations. If it comes to be a generally accepted principle that cultural and other group characteristics should not be the basis for either choosing or excluding candidates, then talent and diversity presumably in the long run should be mutually supportive desiderata.

(5.) The process whereby the international system comes to identify problems worthy of global attention can be enhanced by a number of institutional changes, including some having to do with how international 'analytical' or 'intelligence' communities operate. Clearer lines of responsibility must be established between the Office of Research and Collection of Information in the UN Secretariat, whose focus should be on traditional conflict management concerns, and other global watch structures that have been created in UNEP, FAO, WMO and other agencies. The 'let a thousand flowers bloom' approach to developing early warning systems, manifested by UNESCO's Man and Biosphere

Program competing with the International Geosphere-Biosphere (Global Change) Program initiated in 1986, is counterproductive in that it fosters information overload. National governmental and private scientific bodies need to be drawn into a cooperative web with IGO and NGO networks sharing similar substantive concerns. The cultivation of first-rate data collection, analysis, and dissemination capabilities is not just a function of the application of sophisticated technology but also requires sophisticated organizational schemes to shorten the gap between knowledge production and consumption and utilization.

UN members should consider adoption of the Brundtland Commission's recommendation that a Global Risk Assessment Program be established, with UNEP's Earthwatch system "recognized as the center of leadership on risk assessment in the UN system" and efforts undertaken "to strengthen and focus the capacities of [various] bodies to complement and support UNEP's monitoring and assessment functions by providing timely, objective, and authoritative assessments and public reports on critical threats and risks to the world community."[38] Although its funding and staff size would have to be expanded considerably, UNEP seems well-positioned to assume such a role, given the broad-based credibility it enjoys not only in terms of the positive reputation of its scientific operations but also the quality of its leadership and the nonelitist image it projects through its relatively large governing council and headquarters location in Nairobi.[39] An alternative would be to establish a Bureau of Global Watch within the UN Secretariat, although this would seem redundant with UNEP and would seem unnecessary as long as proper channels are formed between UNEP and DIESA. UNEP assessment activities should also be integrated with those of UNDP (which produces the annual Human Development Report) and other agencies involved in analytical tasks, again in cooperation with DIESA.

UNEP should consolidate its Earthwatch arms (IRPTC, INFO-TERRA, and GEMS/GRID) in Geneva so as to facilitate better coordination of telecommunications systems worldwide. There should be a regular annual world ecological survey—a Global and Regional Environmental and Economic Narrative (GREEN) Report—issued by UNEP focusing on conditions in different geographical areas and sectors. Regional components need to be upgraded to deal with deforestation, desertification, water management and other concerns, based on the regional seas program model. Beyond UNEP's current regional offices, secretariats might be set up by region and sub-region whose responsibility would be to operate regional monitoring centers reporting on local problems, to draw up action plans for different issue-areas in consultation with states in the region, and to provide feedback to UNEP headquarters on regional successes and lessons learned that might be transferable elsewhere.[40] UNEP regional operations could be linked to counterpart, parallel operations in the specialized agencies, with ECOSOC's regional commissions performing a key liaison function. Although there has been some thought given to elevating UNEP to the status of a supranational authority or principle organ or making it a specialized agency, its current station offers certain advantages that enable it to service the entire UN system in the environmental field. While some parts of the system are more directly involved in environmentally related problem solving than others, virtually all functional agencies and programs are touched by environmental issues.

(6.) The lead agency concept is a useful one, whether as applied to UNEP in the environmental field or other entities in other fields, such as UNDP in the area of technical assistance and the Office of the UN Disaster Relief Coordinator (UNDRO) in the area of emergency relief. The UNDRO experience demonstrates that it is extremely difficult for an organization to perform the lead agency role without adequate resources. Still, the job would be made easier if there were at least better standing arrangements within the UN system and between global and regional organizations recognizing the authority of the lead unit in a given area and laying out expected procedures to be followed in relation to other agencies. As useful as it is to have an international agency leading the way in the operation of early warning systems, it is particularly critical when an immediate emergency arises in the form of a natural or man-made disaster suffered by a country seeking external assistance as in the case of earthquakes or refugee dislocations. Disaster relief (particularly of the natural variety, where political controversy is normally less present and where humanitarian impulses are especially powerful) is perhaps the single most fertile area in which the UN can promote institution-building in support of a security-community, given the strong bonds that can develop between donors and victims. Special attention should be given to reducing ad hoc-ism and improving coordination among UNDRO, UNHCR, UNICEF, the World Food Program and other UN agencies, in synch with regional IGOs as well as NGOs such as the International Red Cross, not only for the direct humanitarian benefits to be derived by aid recipients but also for the longer-term and larger institutional benefits that might materialize.[41]

(7.) The problem of various UNO units tripping over one another can be dealt with fairly readily through the formation of several operations boards for disaster relief and other specific functional areas, each headed by the chief official from the lead agency recommended by the Secretary-General and so designated by the General Assembly. UNO-specialized agencies coordination problems are harder to solve. The problems must be treated at both the headquarters and field levels. In the field the lead agency—resident representative—inter-agency team concept needs to be developed further, with its success riding on something more than serendipitous circumstances peculiar to a locale. Integrated action in the field depends ultimately on the extent to which teamwork is possible at the top. Inter-agency rivalry can be controlled and coordination forced on these bureaucracies by state actors if the latter are so inclined. The autonomy of the specialized agencies rests on the fact that they have different governance arrangements—somewhat disparate IGO memberships and disparate institutional cultures in terms of intergovernmental decision-making routines—so that there are limits to how much central direction is feasible. It should be possible, however, to improve upon the current structure which revolves around ACC.

The replacement of ACC by a Commission chaired by the UN Secretary-General, composed of the executive heads of the specialized agencies who would be chosen through common procedures in UNO organs and who would together submit a consolidated systemwide budget for approval by the UN General Assembly, has a sufficiently compelling logic to it to deserve serious consideration despite all the rehearsed arguments against such a proposal. The proposal might be workable if certain features were relaxed, particularly if executive head selection remained decentralized, and if, following upon the Group of Eighteen reforms, the inter-secretariat budget consultation process were tied more closely to a new set of UNO decision-making processes having to do with the establishment of broad programmatic priorities and funding ceilings for the UN system. The shortcomings of UN bureaucracies in implementing and executing projects are, after all, in the first instance a function of the shortcomings of the UN in involving national delegations in the issuance of directives that provide agencies with clear policy guidance.

As the basic ingredient in an enhanced planning-programming-budgeting-evaluation (PPBE) system, the Medium-Term Plan prepared by the UN Secretary-General can serve as a general policy guidance framework in support of biennial UN budgets only if it is devised in a way that makes good use of global watch data, that invites input from various UN intergovernmental and expert organs at different stages, and that engages the heads of the specialized agencies in joint planning exercises. Although regulations already stipulate that "the chapters of the proposed Medium-Term Plan shall be reviewed by the relevant sectoral, functional, and regional intergovernmental bodies, if possible during the regular cycle of their meetings prior to their review by the Committee for Program and Coordination, the Economic and Social Council and the General Assembly," Bertrand notes that "the existing calendar of preparation has never allowed interested organs to receive a draft of the relevant parts of the proposed Medium-Term Plan in timely fashion."[42] Altering the calendar so as to actively engage various elements of the UN proper in the planning process would also afford greater opportunities to engage officials from the specialized agencies.

Programming and budgeting in the UN system are best handled by a single committee charged with setting parameters in terms of both priorities and funding levels, so that ACABQ should be dissolved and its function given over to a reconstituted CPC. There needs to be a fine-tuning of the process whereby the UN Secretary-General, based on the Medium-Term Plan, in the spring of off-budget years submits to CPC an outline of the program budget for the following biennium along with resource estimates. The degree to which UN budgets can be interfaced with the individual budgets of the specialized agencies, promoting as rational an allocation of resources as possible, will depend upon how CPC is structured and how it relates to the major central political organs, including ECOSOC, the Fifth Committee, the General Assembly as a whole, and ultimately the Security Council. Administrative retooling of the UN can take one only so far in the absence of political retooling. As much as one might wish to avoid larger governance issues, they require attention. We need to put the horse before the cart.

(8.) It is fair to say that "the political crisis of the [UN] organization in the mid-1980s resulted in an informal understanding that the budget of the organization cannot be decided without the approval of those who actually pay for it."[43] Can this understanding be formalized? Resolution 41/213 that was passed by consensus in the General Assembly in December 1986 empowered CPC to set broad budgetary programmatic priorities and funding ceilings and to submit its "conclusions and recommendations" to the General Assembly Fifth Committee and plenary for the latter's approval in accordance with Articles 17 and 18 of the Charter. The size and composition of CPC, the decision-making formula to be used, and the nature of its mandate relative to the General Assembly were not completely pinned down and left room for adjustments. Questions still abound. Is twenty-one too small, or thirty-six too large a screening body? Should CPC membership, aside from including the major UN donors, be represented by region or by some other criteria? Should the persons participating in CPC deliberations be experts or governmental representatives, and, if the latter, at what level of seniority? Should CPC decisions be taken by consensus, as provided for in the resolution, or by voting? If the latter, according to a weighted or non-weighted formula, with a simple majority or two-thirds majority threshold? To what extent are CPC decisions to be viewed as guidelines subject to modification by the General Assembly, or as authoritative statements subject only to ratification or veto by the General Assembly? Is General Assembly endorsement to be obtained through consensus or voting procedures? How does CPC fit together with the Assembly committee structure and ECOSOC?

It may be possible to more fully develop and institutionalize what are now only fragile understandings about how the UN budget process is supposed to work. The 1986 resolution was sponsored primarily by a group of major donors that included all the permanent members of the Security Council, and reflected a reality that had begun to sink in among the membership at large. That reality, having to do with the correlation between budgetary reform and funding levels (particularly in support of economic development), is best expressed as follows in a report by the Nordic UN Project:

> Efforts to find an acceptable middle ground cannot be delayed much longer without risk of permanent damage. Corrective measures need to be focused on extra-constitutional solutions which give donors a greater say in determining agency budgets, management and programs without necessarily diminishing the rights of recipients or the quality of the development assistance they receive from the system. The alternative is for all technical assistance to gravitate eventually towards MDBs [multilateral development banks] in which recipients have very little real say at all.[44]

Control over the purse strings cuts to the core of the UN reform puzzle, although the problems go well beyond technical assistance and the solutions need not be limited to extra-constitutional changes.

Careful consideration has to be given to the structure of the Committee on Program and Coordination if it is to perform properly its function as a processor of the biennial budget prepared by the UN Secretary-General in consultation with deputized super-department heads and specialized agency executive heads on a new UN Commission. CPC should be reduced in size to a twenty-five-member body constituted biennially. Major donors who are assessed at least 2 percent of the UN regular budget in the current biennium would each be entitled to a seat, although the threshold for automatic representation could be increased. At present some ten states including the Group of Seven fall in this category, cumulatively accounting for over 75 percent of the total UN contributions and also dominating as sources of funding for the specialized agencies. The remaining seats would be distributed evenly across all regions, with regional representatives elected by regional groupings, and with decisions taken by consensus. Alternatively, instead of regional allocation, the remaining seats could be apportioned between mid-sized and small budget contributors, with either a two-thirds overall vote or binding triad-type voting system employed requiring endorsement by concurrent majorities of the states in the three assessment groupings. Richard Gardner has noted the drawbacks of relying on consensus procedures, warning "it is doubtful . . . if the practice of consensus decision making . . . will provide as useful a way of setting budget priorities as it will of establishing budget ceilings, since it enables small as well as large members of the committee to use their veto for bargaining purposes."[45] If CPC is relatively small, the advantages of consensus decision making (as a nonconfrontational mechanism helping to confer legitimacy) might be obtainable while minimizing the potential disadvantages (paralysis or less robust cooperation). CPC would settle on priorities and funding ceilings in the biennial budget, which would be sent to the Fifth Committee for review and ultimately to the General Assembly plenary, which would give its blanket approval or disapproval based on a two-thirds majority vote.

(9.) General Assembly approval is more likely to be forthcoming the more it can be seen that the entire process whereby budgetary matters make their way from the planning stage through CPC to the adoption stage is sensitive to the concerns of diverse constituencies. This places great importance on improving the formulation of the Medium-Term Plan that informs programmatic and funding deliberations. One is forced to come back to ECOSOC as having a pivotal role to play in bringing the programming and financing tracks closer together, meshing policy and politics and furnishing direction for the UN system in the nonsecurity field. In particular, ECOSOC's job should be to facilitate development and revision of the Medium-Term Plan by (1) taking the lead in identifying problems worthy of the international community's attention based on global watch assessments, (2) organizing in each problem area small but appropriately representative negotiating groups drawn from the UN membership as a whole meeting up to two years in an effort to formulate proposals and reach agreement on specific responses (draft treaties or other regime elements) that might then be routed through ECOSOC to the relevant General Assembly committees and plenary body for approval or taken up in Assembly special sessions or global conferences, and (3) working with the Secretary-General and the UN Commission to incorporate these organizational outputs into the planning-programming-budgeting-evaluation cycle. (Some outputs, for example those having to do with norm-setting, may entail little or no resource commitment, while others may involve operational activities requiring substantial monies.)

Aside from ECOSOC and General Assembly calendars having to become more synchronized, what would ECOSOC have to look like for it to play such a role? The UNA's Successor Vision study proposed a universalized ECOSOC energized by a twenty-five-member Ministerial Board. I propose reverting to the original conception of ECOSOC as a more straightforward way to accomplish the same purpose. That is, instead of a universal entity or the unwieldy fifty-four-member entity that now exists, ECOSOC should be an organ consisting of no more than twenty-five governments serving two-year renewable terms, with the largest developed and developing countries (as measured by population and economic size) assigned a number of seats equal to or exceeded by that held by smaller countries elected to membership on a regional basis. The composition of ECOSOC would overlap with but not necessarily duplicate that of CPC. ECOSOC members would meet at the ministerial level intermittently, involving the highest-level governmental officials from relevant departments in discussions pertaining to the formation of negotiating groups at the outset and to the final outcomes produced by the latter. As much as possible, especially when the issues are extremely complex and the costs and benefits of various responses appear highly uneven, these negotiating exercises should attempt to develop regimes that can be viewed as overarching ("mother") agreements containing flexible, variegated provisions encouraging maximum participation and compliance. ECOSOC decisions would be taken by consensus and, where agreed to, placed on the General Assembly's agenda. In addition, to reassure Third World states that their concerns would not get lost and in fact would receive upgraded attention, a Development Council could be established as an adjunct to ECOSOC that would serve both as a specialized forum for treating development issues and as a single governing body furnishing oversight of development assistance activities in place of the multiple bodies now associated with UNDP, WFP and other UN assistance agencies.

(10.) New scheduling routines would have to be developed so that ECOSOC recommendations contained in its annual report transmitted to the General Committee could be put on a fast track for General Assembly consideration, tied to the Assembly's appropriation process. Even if ECOSOC were looked to as the primary source of agenda items in the economic-social field to be addressed during the General Assembly's annual regular session, the final disposition of these matters of course would rest with the entire UN membership. The Second and Third Committees should be merged into a single body and a subcommittee structure developed to deal with the various problems falling within its jurisdiction. The membership at large would continue to have ample opportunity to shape organizational outputs through both this committee and the Fifth Committee. A word is in order about the future of UNCTAD. Although many Third World states continue to cling to UNCTAD as a preferred forum, the nexus between the Assembly and ECOSOC (featuring a Development Council) figures to become an increasingly acceptable alternative as the old postwar blocs lose their defining character, reflected in GATT and the Bretton Woods institutions becoming more globalized with the addition of erstwhile communist states as members or observers.

As global IGOs approach true universality and as their memberships include growing numbers of ministates, the workings of plenary bodies become all the more problematical. One writer may be exaggerating the trend when he states that we "are likely to see nearly 100 additional new United Nations members before many more years, most of them with only a few hundred thousand or less inhabitants. It is estimated that at that point, nearly half of the world's nations would consist of islands and archipelagos and 40 percent of the world's fully sovereign nations would have populations smaller than Norfolk, Virginia."[46] Some marginally viable ministates may well seek to join loose political and economic unions while retaining nominal sovereignty at least in domestic affairs, becoming parts of confederations or resembling protectorates of yesteryear, while others will

continue to value their independence and press for individual
representation in IGOs. Creative solutions will have to be found
which somehow permit central guidance without sacrificing
broad participation and responsiveness. Associate or consultative membership status, weighted voting formulas, and other
such devices are likely to be the wave of the future in international organization. For now, the UN General Assembly must be
content to operate primarily using the one state-one vote, majoritarian, nonbinding decision-making set of principles, although
it might be worthwhile exploring the possibility of experiment-
ing with variants of the binding triad formula on a very limited,
trial basis involving mostly housekeeping matters. Institution of
the aforementioned reforms relating to agenda-setting and policy formulation, in conjunction with tighter budgetary controls,
would go a long way in itself toward lessening the pernicious
effects of current arrangements that more often than not promote the passage of fatuous resolutions as a substitute for the
creation of regimes manifesting global policy adoption.

Most international regimes will remain limited in their scope,
either because the problem that stimulated their formation is relevant to only a few states (for example, the regime governing
the St. Lawrence Seaway) or only a few states consider themselves relevant to the problem (for example, the Antarctica regime). An improved global watch system linked to ECOSOC's
intergovernmental machinery should act as a check on whether
new regimes at the global level are called for. If ECOSOC initiatives fail to bear fruit—if proposals never make it out of negotiating groups or cannot obtain the support of the UN
membership as a whole—then the international political system
will have signalled that "likemindedness" does not exist globally and that problem-solving and regime making are best pursued through subglobal approaches. The possibility for
successful global bargaining is something to be tested rather
than dismissed out of hand. Even if global bargaining fails, the
exercise may help point the way to multilateral agreements of
lesser scope. Although the 1982 Montego Bay (UNCLOS III)
Convention on the Law of the Sea as of 1992 did not yet have the
sixty ratifications required for it to go into effect (and figured to
remain ineffective in any event without the blessing of the U.S.
and other major actors), it nonetheless crystallized issues and

provided the momentum for forging new governing arrangements regarding ocean use among different subsets of states.

For those skeptical about global agendas, global bargaining
and global governance, it is easy to forget how close the world
came in the 1970s to producing a single universally binding document governing fishing, navigation, scientific exploration, and
virtually every human activity covering 70 percent of the earth's
surface. But for the vagaries of American presidential politics
that resulted in the election of Ronald Reagan instead of Jimmy
Carter, the UNCLOS III treaty arguably would have become a
settled part of international law by now, given the fact that a
Draft Convention (Informal Text) emerged in 1980 as the product of a decade-long consensus-based negotiation process
among 157 states. The final version was approved in 1982 by
vote of 130 in favor, 4 against (U.S., Israel, Turkey, and Venezuela) and 17 abstentions, with the convention signed later that
year by 119 states. There is little doubt that the signing and ratification process would have gone far more smoothly and
quickly had American resistance not muddied the waters in
terms of the legal status of the regime.[47] In contrast, it is instructive to see how quickly bandwagoning occurred in the case of
the 1987 Montreal Protocol, which started as a minilateral exercise leading to a signing by twenty-four states, obtained the requisite eleven ratifications and an additional twenty-five by early
1989, and by 1990 (based on UN-brokered commitments by developed states to set up a $240 million technical assistance fund
to provide LDCs with CFC substitutes) had attracted the support of ninety-three countries agreeing to stop all CFC production by 2000. The law of the sea and ozone cases exemplify
different approaches to global bargaining, each suggesting the
kinds of global policy adoption processes that are possible and
that might be greased by a revamped UN.

(11.) It is important not only to test the waters to see what new
regimes might be manufactured but also to evaluate how existing regimes are working and whether they might be improved
in terms of either their scope or their content. Regimes will
never have sufficient explicitness or tangibility to allow evaluation in the manner one normally thinks of such things—a regime registry is an obvious impossibility—but this does not
mean that specific substantive elements cannot be analyzed and

refined and that regime change must be left to something other than a human hand. The UN could facilitate regime change through a variety of means, including more regularized review conferences in the case of multilateral treaties, use of zero-based budgeting and sunset provisions for scrutinizing programs, an enhanced JIU (along the lines of the General Accounting Office in the American political system), creation of units charged with sponsoring pilot demonstration projects proposed by individual states or consortia of states and disseminating through evaluation networks information on their spinoff potential for other parts of the system, in addition to global watch capabilities that can help assess institutional impacts.

To the above eleven-point platform one could add several other UN reform prescriptions, including a number that fall in the peace and security area and have been the subject of considerable discussion: the merger of the Fourth and Special Political Committees; the disbandment of the Trusteeship Council; further development of the ICJ chambers procedures; establishment of a global arms registry; creation of a special fund as well as a ready reserve of appropriately trained national military contingents to be made available to support peacekeeping missions as authorized, based on guidelines developed by the Special Peacekeeping Committee; regular annual meetings of the foreign ministers of states holding membership on the Security Council; limiting access to certain Security Council proceedings consistent with the need to hear relevant parties to a dispute in an expeditious fashion; installation of hotlines between regional security organizations and the office of the UN Secretary-General, to be used in crisis situations; and development of SOPs for carrying out economic and military sanctions should the organization authorize collective security action, as much as such activities can be routinized. More fundamental and controversial reform in the peace and security field, revolving around the composition of the Security Council, is left for discussion at the end of the chapter.

Implementation of the eleven-point reform program would require relatively little Charter revision. Article 97 would have to be amended to provide for a new mode of nominating the Secretary-General. Article 61, amended in 1965 and 1973 to accommodate the enlargement of ECOSOC, would have to be

amended again to allow its downsizing and to alter the membership term; Article 67, stipulating majority voting procedures to
be used by ECOSOC, might have to be amended to specify a
unanimity requirement, unless consensus procedures can be
implemented through understandings. The budgetary reforms
are not inconsistent with Article 17, even if it would be helpful to
clarify the competence of the General Assembly to approve the
UN budget.

While there are persuasive arguments to be made against
Charter revision of any kind, particularly given the historical
record of aversion to constitutional change in the UN and the
cumbersome nature of the amendment process, it seems rather
dogmatic to assume that the Charter is completely off the bargaining table. Such an assumption not only understates the possibilities for Charter reform but also understates the relevance of
the Charter to the functioning of the organization. As institutionalists have reminded in studies of national political systems,
"the decisions of a given level basically set the institutional rules
of the next lower level. Thus a constitution sets the basic institutional rules for a legislature, while a legislative statute sets the
basic rules governing agency permit decisions."[48] Granted comparisons between national political systems and the international political system are tenuous, the latter observation seems
to have general applicability to institutional analysis.

What the UN membership ultimately is prepared to accept in
formal-legal terms will depend on the terms offered in the bargaining process. Implementation of the kinds of reforms discussed here may require some grand bargains to be struck.

Implementation

President Bush in his address to the 46th General Assembly
called for a Pax Universalis in place of a Pax Americana or any
other such narrowly grounded peace, that is a new order "built
upon shared responsibilities and aspirations."[49] While attempts
to promote "global stability" through collective security may be
a "quixotic crusade,"[50] the prospects for peace and peaceful
change can be enhanced greatly by the collective leadership pro-

vided by a dominant coalition of states able and willing to steer the system in a manner that offers incentives for others to follow. The coalition must be broad enough to possess sufficient material resources to support the demand load and, at the symbolic level, to make a reasonable claim to the aura of legitimacy—it must combine a critical mass of military, economic, and demographic power as discussed in chapter 3—but not so broad as to be incapable of action and susceptible to breaking down.

Economic resource transfers will be especially critical. Coalition members will not only have to pay their full assessments as currently calculated but must be prepared to accept a bigger burden, both to provide necessary side-payments to the bulk of the UN membership (in the form of debt relief or some other quid pro quo) to attract initial support for reforms as well as to maintain a reformed system once it is in place. Given the magnitude of the financial requirements and the weakened state of many economies, notably the American and Russian, only a conglomerate of several states can hope to do the job.

The UN funding problem is complex. There long has been talk of creating independent revenue streams for the UN that go well beyond UN gift shop receipts and other autonomous funding mechanisms that now account for less than 5 percent of the organization's finances. These would be based on user charges involving the global commons (license fees for seabed mining, parking fees for communication satellites in geostationary orbit, etc.), service charges (for access to Weather Watch data and the like), or special taxes of the type levied by the World Intellectual Property Organization for patents and copyrights (tied to activities such as international trade in energy or other commodities). However, there remains tremendous resistance to these schemes, especially among the major donors, so that national governments no doubt will continue to be relied upon as the UN's chief revenue source.

Many proposals have been floated that call for changes in UN assessment scales. Some have suggested that no member state be assessed more than 10 percent of the UN budget[51] while others have suggested that the top assessment not exceed 15 to 20 percent,[52] the concern being that the organization does not become overly dependent upon any one state. But even if the present floor of .01 percent were raised and dozens of states could afford to pay more — a reasonable expectation — it is unrealistic to expect the membership at large to assume a significantly bigger share of the total UN budget, especially if there are pressures to expand the budget to meet growing needs in the security field and other areas. The UN is straining to meet the current demands being made upon the organization, with voluntary contributions supplied by a handful of states increasingly filling the void between expenditures and income. Peacekeeping costs alone totaled an estimated $700 million in 1991, and are expected to be four times that in 1992; UNDP has approximately a $1 billion budget based on voluntary contributions, roughly equivalent to the annual UN regular budget; UNEP in 1991 received some $40 million in voluntary payments, compared to only a $7 million allocation from the regular UN budget. Specialized agency budgets are also heavily supplemented by voluntary contributions. Major donors might be willing to convert more voluntary funding into assessed funding, thereby putting UN budgets on much more solid footing, if they could be assured of greater control over the budget process. Such a trade-off would seem to be one key element of the reform bargaining equation. The UN financial crisis remains at bottom a political crisis. While the sums of money consumed by the UN system appear staggering, they are still miniscule as a percentage of the gross national product of any one lead donor much less the aggregate GNPs of the ten largest benefactors, so that it is hardly the case that the international system has reached its limit in terms of its capacity to generate additional resources to support global organization.

Some states are better positioned than others as candidates to participate in a dominant coalition in support of UN reform, owing not just to economic clout but other attributes. It is unthinkable not to make every effort to include China, for example, in such a coalition, even if China currently pays less than 1 percent of the UN budget. Different states will bring different assets and different responsibilities to a leadership coalition. There may also be different expectations. Some will settle for a role in power steering by virtue of being accorded proper standing on CPC and/or ECOSOC, while others may insist on the ultimate leadership trophy, namely permanent membership on the Security Council. I hesitate to bring Security Council reform into the discussion since mere mention of it puts one immediately on the most treacherous constitutional terrain. However, the postwar order has now been so thoroughly changed that the concert of five permanent Council members has an inherent impermanence about it. It seems a foregone conclusion that an institutional arrangement which was increasingly a glaring anomaly in world politics as the postwar era progressed and has become even more so in the post-postwar era cannot survive much longer into the future. It may or may not be worth at this time inviting the kind of wrenching Charter debate that would ensue over Security Council reform. One can at least think out loud what the Security Council of the future might look like.

Current trends suggest that in the not-so-distant future Security Council representation will probably revolve around regional security systems anchored by national power centers, although these systems are as yet only in an embryonic stage. Earl Ravenal has painted a picture of several tiers of powers existing in the next fifteen to thirty years:

1. "hegemonic powers" (with far less latitude for action than hegemons of the past), including China, Japan, the U.S., and the USSR (Russia);

2. "rising regional countries," including Brazil, India, Indonesia, Iran, and Nigeria;

3. a "list of ponderable though doubtful contenders," including Egypt, Germany, South Africa, and Vietnam;

4. "counter-hegemonic powers," including Argentina, France, Israel, and Pakistan;

5. "perhaps a few of the less obvious or more doubtful ones," including Australia, Bangladesh, Britain, Canada, Iraq, Mexico, Saudi Arabia, South Korea, Sweden, and Syria.[53]

Although Ravenal can be criticized for dismissing too easily the possibility or desirability of a concert of powers approach, arguing that "action of states to bring about conditions in the external system that enhance their security will take the form of unilateral interventions rather than collaborative world order,"[54] his listing is richly suggestive of potential candidates to join the ranks of great powers in a world without superpowers. It overlaps with the GLOBUS listing and the set of states identified in my earlier discussion of the leadership vacuum.

The conventional wisdom presumes that any attempt to make additions to the roster of permanent members on the Security Council is doomed to defeat, or if successful could tear the organization apart in the process because of two basic facts of life. One is the difficulty of getting the present Big Five to forego their use of the veto and permit the admission of new entrants into the permanent membership club when the effect is to diminish the elite status of the charter members. The second is the difficulty of formally including certain specified countries in an expanded Council permanent membership club without alienating those who are excluded.

With respect to the first point, the U.S. and other members of the Big Five, given their own strained global organizational support capabilities, might well welcome others into the fold who would be willing to share the leadership burden, as long as they could screen potential applicants. From the perspective of the Big Five, Security Council enlargement might have to be the price paid not only in order to coopt some wealthy states to assume a bigger donor role but also to coopt into partnership some Third World states whose collaboration is critical to dealing with environmental or other issues. (For example, Brazil and India would be attractive candidates not only because of their demographic weight but also because of their strategic relevance to the forging of workable global regimes to combat greenhouse warming and to regulate arms exports.)[55] On the second point, the cost of membership in the club can be expected to be high enough that not every state would clamor to join. There have been greater acts of self-abnegation performed by states than passing up opportunities for membership on the Security Council, notably the willingness—at least up to now—on the part of over 100 non-nuclear countries (including several with nuclear weapons potential) to do without what is seemingly an unmatched badge of security and status. The same cost-benefit calculations that have led many states to avoid joining the nuclear club also figure to shape their interest or disinterest in joining other elite clubs.

An expansion of the Security Council to accommodate new permanent members will have to provide for balanced representation of nonpermanent members as well. No matter the size or composition of the Council, it is unlikely the UN membership at large will consent to grant the body any more competence than it already has to involve the organization in peace and security matters. An enlarged Council might in fact serve as a brake against excessive sovereignty-threatening intervention by the UN, while providing enhanced legitimacy where action is approved. In the immediate term there might be a transition period allowing for different categories of Security Council membership, perhaps along the lines of the Japanese proposal to add six new permanent seats without veto power.

Reforms can best be gotten off the ground not by calling for a General Conference or constitutional convention as such, which would be viewed as an invitation to rewrite the Charter and would be opposed by many states, but rather by giving the Special Committee on the Charter and on the Strengthening of the Organization a fresh mandate to undertake small group negotiations hammering out different elements of a reform package, including Charter and non-Charter changes, to be submitted to the UN membership for its approval. Although the kinds of reform prescriptions the author has presented need not be implemented all at once, and probably cannot be, the package must somehow hang together.

In considering reform implementation processes, the progress made by the European Community in its "1992" enterprise points up the utility of setting specific targets to be aimed at and concrete deadlines for their realization. Obviously, just because a date is identified is no assurance that it will be taken seriously. EEC targets and deadlines themselves have had to be relaxed, partly because of the complications stemming from German unification and other recent events and partly because of the resistance to change even among a group of states much further along the road to community-building than the UN membership. Nonetheless, the articulation of specific dates by which certain agreed upon outcomes of a reform process are to be completed is more likely to stimulate action than would be the case with more indefinite time frames.

When an organization's environment is in as much flux as the UN's, strategic planning is particularly difficult. Aside from some readers possibly taking issue with the accuracy of the author's assessment of the direction in which the international system is heading, or could be moved, the preceding analysis also no doubt for some raises certain troubling normative issues. In the final chapter I offer some concluding thoughts on a few unresolved empirical and normative questions surrounding the long-term future of global institution-building.

PART 4

Conclusion

7

Waiting for the Millennium: The Future of World Order

> The constant presence of change that is pervasive but
> somewhat indeterminate with respect to overall pattern or
> direction constitutes a fundamental aspect of the international
> milieu in which the United Nations operates at the present
> time. The resultant fluidity of the international system shapes
> the activities of the Organization in a number of significant
> ways. Under these circumstances the problems of regulating
> relationships of power, for example, are highly complex. . . .
> The role of the United Nations as a creator of norms and a
> source of collective legitimization tends to be sharply
> emphasized in a rapidly changing system in contrast to one
> that is more stable and slowly changing. And the opportunities
> thrown up by the pervasiveness of change constitute an
> invitation to various actors in the system to make an effort to
> harness the influence of the organization as an instrument for
> the accomplishment of political change.[1]

These observations were made in an article appearing in *International Organization* in 1968, when such theorizing about the UN in scholarly journals was more commonplace than today, even though they would seem far more appropriate for the 1990s. As revolutionary as the international environment might have appeared in the 1960s, few would equate that decade with the last decade of the twentieth century as a period of ferment in international relations.

The above quotation is a reminder that world politics is always in flux to some extent, albeit more changeable at some moments than at others. Previous chapters have discussed several changes over time. The convulsions in world politics since the late 1980s can be understood in retrospect as the culmination of a historical process of steady erosion of the postwar international order traceable back to its beginnings. The neat bipolar

imagery of an international system organized around two competing superpowers leading two relatively cohesive ideologi-
cally-based blocs rested on a shaky foundation from the start.
Fissures became apparent as early as the 1950s—with the beginnings of nuclear proliferation, the emergence of a third bloc, the
partial fracturing of the Western and Eastern alliances by the
twin Suez and Hungarian crises of 1956, and various other fault-
lines. Fissures widened into cracks during the 1960s and 1970s—
with the North-South axis of conflict competing for attention
with East-West issues, the Communist Chinese experiencing
mounting hostility with their Soviet brethren and Greece war-
ring against NATO ally Turkey, and American superpower credentials called into question in Vietnam (where Lyndon Johnson
wondered why "the greatest power in the world" was no match
for "a band of night-riders in black pajamas") and in the Middle
East (where a group of underdeveloped states, many of which
were "statelets" and all of which were devoid of assets traditionally associated with power, managed momentarily to bring the
Western world to its knees and, with other OPEC countries, to
quadruple the price of oil). Cracks turned into gaping holes during the 1980s, well before the end of the decade—with the international pecking order further upset by the Soviet Union's
Vietnam-style failure in Afghanistan and America's ascendancy
as the chief debtor state in the world, at the same time that West
Germany and Japan flirted with being the leading exporter and
foreign aid donor respectively, and with the alignment structure
of the international system rendered practically unintelligible by
the strange coalitions which materialized during the U.S.-led
boycott of the 1980 Moscow Olympics on the heels of the Soviet
Afghan invasion (as several American allies and even Puerto
Rico found themselves bedfellows with the USSR in joining the
games despite Jimmy Carter's call to respond to "the greatest
threat to world peace since World War II") and by a natural gas
pipeline built between Siberia and the heart of Western Europe
despite Ronald Reagan's warnings about the "evil empire."

Some scholars along the way were more perceptive than others in seeing where trends were leading. For example, Morton
Kaplan distinguished between loose and tight bipolarity, Richard Rosecrance discerned bimultipolarity, Oran Young and others pointed out discontinuities and subsystems in the global

polity, and Stanley Hoffmann found polycentrism and multiple game boards.[2] Still, there was a general sense forty years after World War II, and as late as 1988, that the postwar system was persisting in many of its essential elements and would do so into the next century. For all the volatility of the postwar system, there were certain categories one could safely rely on year after year to anchor one's analysis of world affairs, or so it seemed; the established constructs associated with a predominantly bipolar order (the "nonaligned nations," "Third World," "Cold War," etc.) continued to retain their currency over decades. That is, until the fall of the Berlin Wall and the accompanying phenomena could no longer be fitted even remotely into a bipolar (or, for that matter, bimultipolar) model. Although there had been a chipping away at the postwar order for some time, even the most prescient observers had to be stunned by the suddenness with which the old order had collapsed completely.

As East-West barriers were falling and peace was breaking out worldwide in 1989, General Colin Powell, Chairman of the U.S. Joint Chiefs of Staff, spoke for many when he remarked at the time that "the future just ain't what it used to be."[3] No sooner, though, were such comments uttered than the budding euphoria over a new, more hopeful post-Cold War world was shaken by the Iraqi invasion of Kuwait in August 1990. Although this event invited the smug observation that the more things change the more they stay the same, the experts (realists, neorealists, and virtually all other scholarly types) were generally no more prepared for the "first post-Cold War crisis" than they had been for the end of the Cold War. The crisis itself was hardly business as usual, insofar as Iraq's attempt to annex Kuwait marked the first time since World War II that one state had sought to absorb completely another sovereign entity in the international community and fellow UN member through the use of armed force. Precisely at the moment when global institution-building appeared to hold such promise, the most elemental norm of international conduct which had emerged in the postwar period and had managed to survive the Cold War intact as practically a given was being flouted.

If the future is not what it used to be, then what is it? Forecasts range from the most bullish and confident ("the twenty-first century will encompass the longest period of peace, democracy, and economic development in history")[4] to the most downbeat and skeptical ("is there hope for man?").[5] Peace, democracy, and economic well-being seem to bear upon one another in any political system: While peace may momentarily be created through a charismatic or coercive leadership, a stable order emerges through the learning of habits of compliance by the body politic based upon a widespread sense of system responsiveness and legitimacy, namely, democracy; the commitment to civility and tolerance associated with democracy cannot be nurtured and sustained without general economic prosperity; the latter cannot occur without a stable order for conducting transactions; and so on. Political systems are complex organisms, and for all these elements to be aligned properly is a difficult feat. Only a small fraction of the universe of national political systems have shown themselves capable of achieving these values up to now, and even these are showing signs of severe strain. Doing so for the planet as a whole seems a rather distant prospect. I have argued that conditions exist at present which with the proper response can set the international system on a positive course. I have tried to indicate what is needed and what is possible at this time, not what will or will not happen.

There are many unanswered questions that have systemic implications. Can the former Soviet Union, under whatever new name and form it may take, cope with its current turmoil and remain a powerful partner in international institution-building? Will China (even after its incorporation of Hong Kong after 1997) remain a communist island, and if so can it coexist with the noncommunist world? How will the European Community develop beyond 1992, when the reforms mandated by the Single European Act are scheduled for full implementation, and beyond 1993, when the EEC is slated to open its borders to the European Free Trade Area? Will the Treaty of Maastricht overcome resistance and forge a monetary and political union by 1999? Can the major Western economies avoid a collision over trade and other economic issues as they seek to refashion what remains of the Bretton Woods system? Can the Eastern European states make the difficult transition to capitalist democracies, and can the NICs maintain their own economic progress, thereby serving as exemplars for others? Given so many uncertainties in the immediate-term, it is especially hazardous to make predictions about the long-term. Even so, as the post-postwar order haltingly takes shape, certain elements are coming more clearly into focus. What reasonably can be said about the foreseeable future?

The Empirical Domain

Long observable trends in the direction of a more complex international system are becoming more pronounced and accelerated. This complexity has four main aspects:

1. *the growing diffusion and ambiguity of power,* including the decline of the United States as a hegemon, the internal and external problems of the other one-time superpower, the continued rise of Japan, the challenge presented by a reunited German state acting in combination with others within the European Community, the proliferation of ministates capable at times of frustrating the will of major actors, and shifting relationships between military, economic, and technological bases of power;

2. *the growing fluidity of alignments,* including the depolarization of the East-West conflict as former East bloc states move ideologically toward the West while West-West economic competition heats up as an axis of conflict, the North-South conflict losing its defining character also as increasing diversity among NICs, OPEC states, Fourth World countries and other LDCs makes Southern solidarity harder to sustain, and greater localization of politics related to ethnicity and other issues beneath the global level;

3. *more intricate patterns of interdependence,* associated with an expanding agenda of concerns (economics and ecology inter alia) and a broadening conception of national security beyond traditional military considerations;

4. *the growing role of nonstate actors along with increasing linkages between subnational, transnational and intergovernmental levels of activity* even as the size of national governmental budgets and state apparatuses resist shrinkage.

The question remains whether we are witnessing merely the end of the postwar era and the transformation of the international system back to the more normal historical pattern of full-blown multipolarity, in which case we can continue to rely on the state-centric paradigm and its focus on national interests, sovereignty, and international anarchy, or whether we are on the brink of a more fundamental and epic transformation, namely the unraveling of the very fabric of the Westphalian state system itself that has been the primary basis of human political organization for the past several centuries. Some seize upon the first two systemic characteristics cited above (the fragmentation of the postwar power and alignment structure) and suggest the déjà vu scenario is the correct one, that is the international system is returning to an earlier condition, particularly bearing some resemblance to the early twentieth century, complete with the absence of any hegemonic stability, mounting Balkan ethnic conflict, and other familiar features.[6] Others seize upon the other two systemic characteristics (relating to interdependence, transnationalism and intergovernmentalism) and suggest differently, namely the international system is experiencing unprecedented complexity — a "bifurcated global politics" torn between state-centrism and multi-centrism, calling for a wholly new "post-international politics" paradigm.[7]

Every generation probably views itself as living at a (perhaps *the*) pivotal point in history.[8] Temporocentrism in the late twentieth century is especially understandable, with important dramas being played out between the forces of regionalism and globalism, nationalism and transnationalism, security and welfare, and order and change. While these have been ongoing historical dramas, the curtain appears to be rising on a new act. That there is a particularly schizophrenic quality to contemporary world politics is clear, although it is hard to say how these various tensions will be resolved. Whether this is one of those special moments in time must be left for future historians to judge. It took over 200 years for historians to recognize the significance of 1648 and for the international relations discipline to be born.[9] Might historians a century or two from now look back on this era as the beginning of the end of the Westphalian state system, even if we are no more sure of what we have wrought than our seventeenth-century ancestors? Although any response to this query would be pure, idle speculation, the thought alone should at least give pause to those incapable of entertaining visions of any other world order than the present one.

There has been a change *in* the Westphalian state system, but it is premature to say there has been a change *of* the Westphalian state system. We obviously still live in a world of nation-states. Rather than the contemporary era marking the "end of history," we are likely to see societies well into the next century continuing to lurch back and forth between variants of laissez-faire capitalism and collectivism while there remains almost everywhere a generalized acceptance of the welfare state—of the expectation that governments bear some responsibility for not only the physical security but also the well-being of their national citizenry—and of the corollary notion that governments have a right to regulate the amount and type of activity in which citizens can engage outside national boundaries. Although elites will tend to be less nationalistic than the masses, especially in developed countries, nationalism and statism will persist as widespread impulses as far as the eye can see.[10]

A world of nation-states is one that still revolves around the state system. We are likely to see the state system itself lurching back and forth between what appear to be disintegrative tendencies (further fragmentation of the postwar power and bloc structure, continued proliferation of ministates as an extension of the postwar decolonialization process, and growing subnational ethnic conflict and attempts at nonwestern cultural revival such as in the Islamic world) and integrative tendencies (manifested by German reunification, the EEC, "Coca-colonization" and other forms of cultural diffusion, and the continued proliferation of IGOs and NGOs at the regional and global levels). Should nuclear proliferation prove unavoidable, multipolar trends could proceed to the point where the state system approaches a unit veto system—a faint prospect, but one given some credence recently by the reality of the Ukraine and Kazakhstan mulling the status of the strategic nuclear weapons on their soil which, were they to exercise control over those weapons, would give them more firepower than Britain, France, or China.[11] A more likely scenario, as suggested earlier, is for ministates and lesser powers to coalesce around regional security

systems headed by emergent regional powers or condomini-
ums.

The further one moves out on the time line, the murkier the
future becomes and alternative world order models not rooted
in the Westphalian state system become more thinkable—
ranging from a global system of city-states (with people oriented
primarily to smaller, more localized communities than the
present ones) to a system of region-states to world government
(in the form of either a confederation, federation, or unitary system). Nonterritorial bases of organization might also materialize
through growing networks of NGOs and alliances among multinational corporations, although a world political map defined
by corporate logos rather than geographical boundaries is even
harder to grasp mentally than the would-be territorial successors to the nation-state system. Fanciful as all these seem, they
certainly cannot be dismissed totally as possibilities for the next
millennium if not the next century. It is worth remembering that
the Europe 1992 effort was launched less than one decade after
one of the leading students of regionalism had pronounced the
"obsolescence" of regional integration theory.[12]

The nation-state of course has been written off by some as also
being obsolete, most definitively by the realist Hans Morgenthau, who toward the end of his life wrote that

> the technological revolutions of our age have rendered the
> Nation-State's principle of political organization as obsolete as
> the first modern industrial revolution of the steam engine did
> feudalism. The governments of Nation-States are no longer
> able to perform the functions for the sake of which civilized
> governments have been instituted in the first place: to defend
> and promote the life, liberty, and pursuit of happiness of its
> citizenry. Unable to perform these functions with regard to
> their own citizens, these governments are incapable of
> performing them in their relations with each other.[13]

The future of the Westphalian state system—how long it will
continue and what direction it will evolve in—will depend upon
how the states in the system are able to handle the security and
welfare functions they are counted on to perform. With respect
to the security function, if one values the state system one has to
hope that "society may have accepted killing as a legitimate in-

strument of state policy, but not, as yet, suicide"[14] and that statesmen understand how the potential costs of war in the nuclear age differ from in the past; this has been expressed as follows: "It has historically been one thing to die for your country. It is a different thing [today] to die *with* your country."[15] As regards the welfare function, one has to hope that governments can learn to manage economic and ecological interdependence better than they have demonstrated up to now.

The Normative Domain

The future is hard to predict precisely because it is subject to human action, which is only partly predictable. To the extent we have some control over what shape the future world order takes, what alternative we choose to promote will depend upon how we see the latter relating to values we hold. Definitions of interests—in particular, whether one's fate is perceived as most closely tied to that of one's clan, tribe, nation, region, or some other collectivity—change over time. Some individuals and groups are better positioned than others to give effect to their value judgments.

The nation-state system may well be the best of all possible worlds, a set of arrangements worth preserving insofar as it represents a compromise between the walled cities and the universal church of the past, neither of which proved capable of supporting peace, democracy, or other such values. However, the nation-state system has yet to prove it can do much better. As I have indicated, the future of the Westphalian system is tied to the future of international organization. This point has been lost on many who continue to look to the chimera of organization-less institutions as the salvation of the system. Like the invisible hand of the balance of power, there is an otherworldly, ethereal quality to regimes as a basis for order. Oran Young, whose 1968 comments about the role of the UN as a change agent were cited at the outset of this chapter, is typical of the new institutionalists who reflect increasing skepticism about change, especially through organizations. Compare his 1968 statement with a 1989 writing:

> I have . . . found it hard to become unduly alarmed by the
> apparent decline of the United Nations and certain other
> international organizations in recent years. . . . If one looks at
> international institutions rather than international
> organizations, I believe, there is less cause for alarm regarding
> the pursuit of international order and justice. . . . While
> recognizing the reality and importance of change, . . . we
> would do well to devote more energy to investigating the
> capacity of international society to adjust to shifting
> circumstances in institutional terms in contrast to focusing on
> strategies for transforming international society in the interests
> of pursuing some alternative vision of world order.[16]

The subtitle of this chapter and this book consciously makes reference to the future *of* world order[17] rather than the future world order, since I believe that what is at stake is not a particular vision of world order but the very existence of world order. Can one truly envisage the state system continuing to function or for that matter evolving into any other set of governing relationships among human beings in the absence of international organization? Short of the return to the politics of hunting and gathering bands that would attend the end of civilization following nuclear or environmental apocalypse, assuming the species were not completely extinct, the answer, fairly confidently stated, is no. Although some may interpret this work as being guided by a hidden agenda in support of either world federalism or great power imperium, it is meant to be simply an inquiry into the growth potential of international organization, particularly at the global level, as one component of the quest for world order in the late twentieth century.

It has been said in recent times that "the nation-state is becoming too small for the big problems of life, and too big for the small problems of life."[18] This is not a wholly new observation; Toynbee remarked earlier in the century that "what has been needed for the last 5,000 years, and has been feasible technologically, though not yet politically, for the last hundred years, is a global body politic composed of cells on the scale of the Neolithic-Age village community—a scale on which the participants would be personally acquainted with each other, while each of them would also be a citizen of the world-state."[19] There would seem to be room today for various organizational forms operating at different levels, as illustrated by the following passage from the Brundtland Commission report:

> The Law of the Sea Convention, with the establishment of the 200-mile EEZs [exclusive economic zones], has put an additional 35 percent of the ocean's surface under national control with regard to management of natural resources. It has also provided an institutional setting that could lead to better management of these areas, given that single governments may be expected to manage more rationally resources over which they have sole control. . . . [However,] where the EEZs of several states come together in semi-enclosed or regional seas, integrated management requires varying degrees of international cooperation. . . . When it comes to the high seas beyond national jurisdiction, international action is necessary.[20]

The Law of the Sea Convention did not just happen. Its creation was directly attributable to the United Nations, and its viability as international law will depend upon what agreements can be worked out among many different groupings of states found within that body. The historic and future role of global intergovernmental organization is not to create a single political space but to "contribute to the creation of a better world order so that . . . the world will be full of happy regions"[21] and, one might add, nation-states and local communities.

Of course, what is a better world, and what are big as opposed to small problems, are matters of conjecture depending upon whose values are informing the analysis. It is not surprising that American academics—viewing reality in the same terms as practitioners and laymen in the United States—have tended to treat the major problematique of the international relations field as the maintenance of order in a decentralized political system, defined as the problem of war and peace. While it is admittedly self-serving for the haves in a political system to give more attention to order than justice, it is equally self-serving for the have-nots to trumpet the ethical superiority of justice (defined as egalitarianism) over order and to reject a "morality of states" paradigm in favor of a "cosmopolitan morality" paradigm.[22] My own sense is that neither order nor justice is served by 1 million Omanis possessing the same formal power in international governance as 1 billion Chinese, although this is somewhat of a moot point as long as both peoples live under dictatorships.

Given the dynamics of interdependence, it is becoming harder to maintain these value distinctions in any case. The universal struggle for peace and dignity will go on, complicated by a reality that exists apart from any individual observer (black, brown, white, yellow, red, male or female) but that is alterable to an extent depending upon which tough normative choices are made. I have suggested how an enlightened concert of powers approach to world order might be squared with concerns about morality and might promote system stability as well as adaptability, permitting at a minimum the development of an international "society in which there will be enough justice, and in which coercion will be sufficiently nonviolent to prevent [humanity's] common enterprise from issuing into complete disaster"[23] and at a maximum the development of a true global security-community.

The Theory and Practice of International Organization in the Twenty-First Century

I began this work by offering a flippant definition of faith as "believin in what you know ain't true." Yet much of what passes for reality has some basis in faith. As Hadley Cantril wrote, there is often a fine line between theory and faith:

> We act on the basis of faith; every action is based on the assumption that probable events are relatively certain events. Our faith becomes a faith in the reliability of our whole matrix of assumptions—a faith in our reality world, a faith in ourselves. . . . In the process of creating and maintaining this faith, we support ourselves by creating and maintaining a whole variety of constancies. . . . We build up and maintain beliefs about certain social constancies concerning people and our relationships to them; we adhere to our customs, manners, loyalties, group and institutional codes. . . . Frequently the reality world we bring to an occasion proves inadequate in accounting for the new situations that have been created as we and the world move on. . . . Revisions of our reality world seem to come about only insofar as we sense the inadequacies of our assumptions. . . . It can be demonstrated . . . in the laboratory . . . that we revise our assumptions infrequently, if

at all, solely because of any factual knowledge or information
we acquire. . . . We apparently . . . incorporate into our reality
worlds only those significances that we sense are likely to be of
use to us, . . . that will make a difference. This is learning.[24]

Some theories, like some articles of faith, are more well-
founded than others. The more indisputable the empirical evidence that can be marshalled to support a body of theory, the
more likely the latter will gain wide acceptance as knowledge
rather than mere wisdom or faith. How much consensual
knowledge develops and is utilized will depend, however, not
just on how much data can be amassed but also on how much
value consensus surrounds the findings. Epistemic communities that promote learning are formed more readily in the field of
medical research than peace research.[25]

While solid scholarship that contributes to the growth of
knowledge cannot alone change—improve—the world, it has
an important role to play. The main raison d'être of the international organization field over the years has been to provide a
base of scholarship that can help inform and guide the practice
of international collaboration. The problem with much of contemporary IO scholarship is that as the field has sought to distance itself from its idealist past and to become more firmly
grounded in science and reality-testing, it has become further
removed from the real-world institutions in which practitioners
operate. The gap between international organizational phenomena studied by academics and those experienced by policymakers continues to widen as few explicit connections are made
between theory and practice.[26]

No greater challenge exists for students of international organization than that posed by the search for world order through
global institution-building, which finds its most concrete expression today in the form of the United Nations. Serious scholarship is normally defined by the degree of intellectual ferment
and hard-nosed sobriety one brings to a subject. The subject of
the UN in recent times has inspired widespread indifference
and ridicule, with scholars tending to steer clear lest they be
branded guilty of indulging in "institutionalist approaches of
yesteryear"[27] or utopian futurism and risk pariah status in the
international relations fraternity akin to some states in the inter-

national community. Excessive use of the terms "earth" and "planet" can damage one's credibility. There is the caveat that global international organization has become too large and unwieldy to be subjected to either serious scientific inquiry or social engineering. It is true that the world does not revolve around governments making "great global choices among grand alternatives."[28] Policymakers, John Ruggie notes, "do not get to choose on the future of the state system; they confront choices on exchange rates, . . . terrorist attacks on airport lobbies and embassy compounds, and garbage that floats down a river or is transported through the air. If change comes it will be the product of micro practices. Hence if we want to understand change or help to shape it, it is to these micro practices that we should look."[29] Was the creation of the UN in 1945 a micro practice? If so, are there other such practices to which we should look?

Nobody planned the national welfare state which has been the dominant political structure of the twentieth century. It was the result of historical forces pushed along by a myriad of individual decisions and accumulated learning. If a global security-community comes to pass, it will not be planned but will also emerge as a product of historical forces which likewise can be nudged along in small ways if we have the knowledge and the will to do so. There will always be an element of faith in our quest, although as John Herz said in his requiem for the territorial-state, "it is not wishful thinking that leads us on, but an ever so faint ray of hope that that which is not entirely impossible will emerge as real."[30] One can take heart in the old saw that most revolutions on their eve seem unimaginable, and on the morning after seem to have been inevitable.[31]

As the last decade of the twentieth century progresses toward the millennial mark, the quest continues. Two incidents offer a telling commentary on our time. In June of 1989, the foreign ministers of countries belonging to the non-aligned movement met in The Hague to celebrate the 90th anniversary of the 1899 Hague Peace Conference and the 50th anniversary of the start of World War II. They proceeded to produce a declaration that led to the 44th UN General Assembly officially recognizing the 1990s as "the United Nations Decade of International Law" and directing the Secretary-General to elicit from member states as well as from IGOs and NGOs suggestions for "appropriate action to be taken."[32] Almost at the same moment in another corner of the globe, reflecting another reality, a local chapter of the United Nations Association-USA was meeting in St. Louis. The head of the chapter was making an impassioned plea for expanded global thinking—the same individual who had just retired as mayor of a tiny, wealthy 15,000 person municipality after leading a fight in the name of grassroots democracy against a St. Louis metropolitan-wide reorganization plan that would have merged over 100 separate political jurisdictions each with its own police and fire departments; those in charge of the poor fiefdoms resisted almost as much as those running the rich ones.

Human beings in many places are experiencing a steady, almost inexorable interconnectedness across geographical, cultural, and other divides even as they seek to maintain the distinctiveness and separateness of their individual communities. The continued distinctiveness can be seen in the fact that not all peoples are approaching the millennium. As some observers remind, "not everyone subscribes to the calculations of the Gregorian calendar. In the year 2000 by Gregorian estimations, the Chinese will be celebrating Kang-shin in the 17th cycle, the Islamic world the 1421st year of Hegira, and the Hebrews year 5761."[33] Still, few would take issue with the wisdom embodied in the statement made by the Secretary-General of the UN Conference on Environment and Development in preparation for the 1992 Earth Summit, who cited the invocation regularly offered by leaders of the Iroquois nation as they began their council proceedings: "In our every deliberation we must consider the impact of our decisions on the next seven generations."[34] Even if we cannot think in millennial terms, at the very least we can think in terms of the next generation.

Notes

Chapter 1: The United Nations and the Global Problematique

1. *U.S. Department of State Bulletin*, 12 (April 29, 1945), p. 789.

2. *Ibid.*, 13 (July 1, 1945), p. 5.

3. Carlos Romulo, "The UN Is Dying," *Colliers* (July 23, 1954), p. 32.

4. Witness "United Nations in Crisis," a report submitted to the Committee on Foreign Affairs of the U.S. House of Representatives by congressional members of the U.S. delegation to the UN (January 28, 1964).

5. *U.S. Department of State Bulletin*, 69 (December 10, 1973), p. 708.

6. Daniel Patrick Moynihan, *A Dangerous Place* (New York: Berkley Books, 1980).

7. Kurt Waldheim, "The United Nations: The Tarnished Image," *Foreign Affairs*, 63 (Fall 1984), p. 106.

8. *New York Times*, September 24, 1990, p. 23. Likewise, a *Wall Street Journal* headline on August 30, 1990, p. 1, read "Coming of Age: UN Long Stymied by Cold War Begins to Fulfill Its Promise As World's Peacekeeper." See also George L. Sherry, *The United Nations Reborn* (New York: Council on Foreign Relations, 1990).

9. Ernst B. Haas, *Why We Still Need the United Nations: The Collective Management of International Conflict, 1945–1984*. Policy Papers in International Affairs, No. 26 (Berkeley, Calif.: Institute of International Studies, 1986), p. 20. This was in contrast to the UN's relatively successful overall record between 1945 and 1975, when the organization became involved in more than half of all international crises and was effective at crisis abatement in one-third of those cases, with effectiveness increasing as the situation became more serious and more violent. Jonathan Wilkenfeld and Michael Brecher, "International Crises 1945–1975: The UN Dimension," *International Studies Quarterly*, 28 (March 1984), pp. 45–67.

10. Paul Krugman, "Is Free Trade Passé?" *Journal of Economic Perspectives*, 1, no. 2 (1989), p. 93. See Stephen D. Krasner, *Structural Conflict: The Third World Against Global Liberalism* (Berkeley, Calif.: University of

California Press, 1985); Robert Gilpin, *The Political Economy of International Relations* (Princeton, N.J.: Princeton University Press, 1987); Jagdish Bhagwati, *The World Trading System At Risk* (Princeton, N.J.: Princeton University Press, 1991); and Miriam Camps and William Diebold, Jr., *The New Multilateralism: Can the World Trading System Be Saved?* (New York: Council on Foreign Relations, 1986).

11. Jack C. Plano and Roy Olton, *The International Relations Dictionary*, 2nd ed. (Kalamazoo: New Issues, 1979), p. 288. Since this book focuses on the phenomenon of international governmental organizations (IGOs), as opposed to international nongovernmental organizations (INGOs), I use the term "international organization" throughout the study to refer to IGOs unless otherwise noted. Technically, the distinction between IGOs and INGOs as separate classes of international organization rests on the fact that the former are ordinarily created by an agreement among governments while the latter are not. Definition and classification issues relating to international organizations are discussed in Harold K. Jacobson, *Networks of Interdependence*, 2nd ed. (New York: Knopf, 1984), chap. 1; and Clive Archer, *International Organizations* (London: Allen and Unwin, 1983), chaps. 1 and 2.

12. Friedrich Kratochwil and John Gerard Ruggie, "International Organization: A State of the Art on an Art of the State," *International Organization*, 40 (Autumn 1986), refer to the "world of actual international organizations" on p. 753. Their survey of articles published in *International Organization*, the preeminent journal in the field, found that "the formal institutional focus has declined steadily from the very beginning and now accounts for fewer than 5% of the total." *Ibid*, p. 760. An analysis I conducted of *IO* articles between 1985 and 1990 shows that 17% of the total focused on formal institutions, and only 3% on the UN. For a more general review of trends in the international organization field since World War II, see J. Martin Rochester, "The Rise and Fall of International Organization as a Field of Study," *International Organization*, 40 (Autumn 1986), pp. 777–813.

13. Kratochwil and Ruggie, *op. cit.*, p. 753. These authors see the trend away from the study of formal institutions as potentially having salutary effects on the practice of international organization.

14. John Gerard Ruggie, "International Responses to Technology: Concepts and Trends," *International Organization*, 29 (Summer 1975). See also Kratochwil and Ruggie, *op. cit.*, p. 754.

15. Oran R. Young, "International Regimes: Problems of Concept Formation," *World Politics*, 32 (April 1980), pp. 332–333.

16. Robert O. Keohane and Joseph S. Nye, *Power and Interdependence* (Boston: Little, Brown, 1977), p. 5. See also Stephen D. Krasner, ed., *International Regimes* (Ithaca, N.Y.: Cornell University Press, 1983). As

the concept is sometimes used in the literature, a regime can be just bilateral in scope and can involve a relatively narrow concern. See, for example, Joseph S. Nye, "Nuclear Learning and US-Soviet Security Regimes," *International Organization*, 41 (Summer 1987), pp. 371–402.

17. Clearly, there are many scholars who still focus their research on the UN and other international organizations, examining either the structures themselves or their performance. See, for example, Harold K. Jacobson, *Networks of Interdependence, op. cit.*; and Haas, *op. cit.*; and *When Knowledge is Power: Three Models of Change in International Organizations* (Berkeley, Calif.: University of California Press, 1990). There is also a newly created Academic Council on the United Nations System, which has issued a report on "Strengthening the Study of International Organizations" (Hanover, N.H.: Academic Council on the UN System, 1987), and publishes annual reviews of the UN, such as Donald J. Puchala and Roger A. Coate, *The Challenge of Relevance: The United Nations in A Changing World Environment* (Hanover, N.H.: Academic Council on the UN System, 1989). The point is that there has been a distinct decline in this brand of scholarship in favor of investigating more general phenomena that are relatively tangential to international organization.

18. Harold K. Jacobson, William M. Reisinger, and Todd Mathers, "National Entanglements in International Governmental Organizations," *American Political Science Review*, 80 (March 1986), p. 141. The authors note that regional IGO growth has exceeded global IGO growth since World War II, although "the absolute number [of IGOs with potentially universal membership] for the post-World War II era is impressively high" (p. 145). Even those scholars who could be labeled skeptics acknowledge that "quantitatively, . . . IGOs are still an expanding force in international affairs" despite the fact that "qualitatively . . . the world of IGOs is not in good shape." See John Gerard Ruggie, "The United States and the United Nations: Toward A New Realism," *International Organization*, 39 (Spring 1985), p. 343. Statistics on IGO growth are reported in Union of International Associations, *Yearbook of International Organizations 1989/89*, 25th ed. (1988), vol. 1, appendix 7.

19. Inis L. Claude, Jr., "The Record of International Organizations in the Twentieth Century," Tamkang Chair Lecture Series, No. 64, Tamkang University, Taiwan, January 1986 (mimeo), p. 25. Claude adds that "we cannot ignore the successful implantation of the idea of international organization. International organization may not have taken over the system, but it has certainly taken hold in the system. The twentieth century has seen the establishment of the prescription that multilateral agencies are essential to the conduct of international affairs."

20. An excellent historical treatment can be found in Inis L. Claude, Jr., *Swords Into Plowshares*, 4th ed. (New York: Random House, 1984), chaps. 2–4.

21. On this point, see David Fromkin, *The Independence of Nations* (New York: Praeger, 1981), especially chaps. 7–9.

22. These concepts were introduced by Keohane and Nye in *Power and Interdependence, op. cit.*, pp. 12–22. For more recent reflection on the concepts and ideas developed in the latter work, see Keohane and Nye, *"Power and Interdependence* Revisited," *International Organization*, 41 (Autumn 1987), pp. 725–753. To cite just one indicator of growing interdependence, world trade has grown substantially faster than world GNP in the postwar period, as documented in Maurice D. Levi, *International Finance: The Markets and Financial Management of Multinational Business* (New York: McGraw-Hill, 1990), p. 3.

23. One of the better discussions of this theme is provided by K. J. Holsti in "Change in the International System: Interdependence, Integration, and Fragmentation," in Ole R. Holsti, et al., eds., *Change in the International System* (Boulder, Colo.: Westview Press, 1980), pp. 23–53. For a less conventional treatment, see Richard Falk, "A New Paradigm for International Legal Studies: Prospects and Proposals," in Richard Falk, Friedrich Kratochwil, and Saul H. Mendlovitz, eds., *International Law: A Contemporary Perspective* (Boulder, Colo.: Westview Press, 1985), pp. 651–702.

24. Kenneth N. Waltz, *Theory of International Politics* (Reading, Mass.: Addision-Wesley, 1979), p. 109.

25. Richard Falk, Friedrich Kratochwil, and Saul H. Mendlovitz, *International Law: A Contemporary Perspective* (Boulder, Colo.: Westview Press, 1985), p. 1.

26. Fromkin, *op. cit.*, p. 6. Few writers are more cynical than Fromkin, who deplores what he sees as a continuing tendency toward idealistic thinking on the part of students of international relations. I am referring to cynicism and pessimism as it relates to the prospects for international institution-building and not human affairs. Clearly, one can find gloomy prognoses of the human condition throughout the twentieth century, including the work of Oswald Spengler and Arnold Toynbee in the early decades and of "limits to growth" thinkers in the 1970s.

27. The classic critique of interwar thinking is E. H. Carr's *The Twenty Years' Crisis, 1919–1939* (London: Macmillan, 1939), which launched the idealist-realist debate that was to color much postwar thinking about the role of international organization in world politics. For a discussion of this debate, see F. Parkinson, *The Philosophy of International Relations: A Study in the History of Thought* (London: Sage, 1977), chap. 10; John H. Herz, *Political Realism and Political Idealism* (Chicago, Ill.: University of

Chicago Press, 1951); and the series of essays in *International Studies Quarterly*, 25 (June 1981), pp. 179–241. On the evolution of the international relations field since World War II, including turns taken toward behavioralism and globalism along the way to neorealism, see William C. Olson, "The Growth of A Discipline," in B. Porter, ed., *The Aberysthwyth Papers: International Politics, 1919–1969* (London: Oxford University Press, 1972), pp. 3–29; K. J. Holsti, *The Dividing Discipline: Hegemony and Diversity in International Theory* (London: Allen and Unwin, 1985); and Rochester, *op. cit.*

28. The terms "bad idealism" and "bad realism" are taken from Giovanni Sartori, *Democratic Theory* (New York: Praeger, 1965), p. 51.

29. Stephen Haggard and Beth A. Simmons, "Theories of International Regimes," *International Organization*, 41 (Summer 1987), pp. 491–517.

30. See Duncan Snidal, "The Game Theory of International Politics," *World Politics*, 38 (October 1985), p. 25; Robert Axelrod and Robert O. Keohane, "Achieving Cooperation Under Anarchy: Strategies and Institutions," *World Politics*, 38 (October 1985), pp. 226–227 and 231–232; and other articles in the same volume. Snidal (p. 57) states that "the metaphors of 'Hobbesian anarchy' and 'international organization' . . . have divided and obscured our understanding of international politics."

31. For example, Michael Taylor, *Anarchy and Cooperation* (New York: John Wiley, 1976); Kenneth A. Oye, ed., *Cooperation Under Anarchy* (Princeton, N.J.: Princeton University Press, 1986), originally published as a symposium in *World Politics*, 38 (October 1985); Hedley Bull, *The Anarchical Society* (London: Macmillan, 1977); and Robert O. Keohane, *After Hegemony: Cooperation and Discord in the World Political Economy* (Princeton, N.J.: Princeton University Press, 1984). See also the call for papers for the 1989 Annual Meeting of the International Studies Association, featuring the convention theme of "Cooperation, Discord and the Conditions for Peace in International Society," *International Studies Newsletter*, 14 (December 1987), pp. 1 and 3.

32. The criticism that previous writers in the realist tradition gave little attention to the dynamics of cooperation while those in the idealist tradition ignored conflict seems somewhat overdone, although it is true that the earlier literature gave relatively little coverage to the welfare objectives of states, focusing overwhelmingly on security concerns. See Arnold Wolfers, *Discord and Collaboration* (Baltimore, Md.: Johns Hopkins University Press, 1962); Raymond Aron, *Peace and War*, trans. by Richard Howard and Annette Baker Fox (Garden City, N.Y.: Doubleday, 1966); Morton A. Kaplan and Nicholas DeB. Katzenbach, *The Political*

Foundations of International Law (New York: John Wiley, 1961); and Inis L. Claude, Jr., *Swords Into Plowshares* (New York: Random House, 1956).

33. "Neorealism," a term first coined by Robert Cox and sometimes referred to as "structural realism," has been defined as a body of thought which attempts to "systematize political realism into a rigorous, deductive systemic theory of international politics." Robert O. Keohane, ed., *Neorealism and Its Critics* (New York: Columbia University Press, 1986), p. 15. It is most closely associated with the work of Kenneth Waltz and Robert Gilpin. See Waltz, *op. cit.* and Gilpin, *War and Change in World Politics* (Cambridge, Eng.: Cambridge University Press, 1981). A rare use of the term "neoidealism" is "The Neoidealist Moment in International Studies?" delivered by Charles Kegley at the 1993 International Studies Association meeting.

34. The term "neoliberal" refers to those writers whose work springs from a concern about the dynamics of interdependence, following up the "globalist" thinking of the 1970s. See Joseph S. Nye, "Neorealism and Neoliberalism," *World Politics*, 40 (January 1988); Nye gives as an example of neoliberalism Richard Rosecrance's *The Rise of the Trading State* (New York: Basic Books, 1986). Richard Ashley, in "The Poverty of Neorealism," *International Organization*, 38 (Spring 1984), pp. 225–286, includes Robert Keohane in the neorealist camp, even though Keohane has denied the label, advocating a "research program [that] would pay much more attention to the roles of institutions and rules than does Structural Realism." Keohane, "Theory of World Politics: Structural Realism and Beyond," in Ada W. Finifter, ed., *Political Science: The State of the Discipline* (Washington, D.C.: APSA, 1983), p. 530. Also see Keohane, *Neorealism and Its Critics, op. cit.,* p. 25. In "Anarchy and the Limits of Cooperation: A Realist Critique of the Newest Liberal Institutionalism," *International Organization*, 42 (Summer 1988), pp. 486–507, Joseph Grieco characterizes thinkers such as Keohane as "liberal institutionalists" who, despite being far removed from the idealist tradition, are unduly optimistic about human and national behavior. That Grieco could call Keohane's heavily guarded analysis of the prospects for global institution-building excessively optimistic is itself a commentary on how much cynicism has set in.

35. This is the title of a recent special volume of *International Studies Quarterly*, 34 (September 1990). One should add here that there are some well-known scholars, such as Richard Falk and others associated with the World Order Models Project, who continue to harbor expansive, maximalist views of world order and remain close to the classical idealist tradition, although they tend to be on the fringes of the international relations field as a whole as they no doubt would be the first to admit and to lament.

36. Ruggie, for example, in his much-cited critique of Waltz, calls for a "neorealistic synthesis." See "Continuity and Transformation in the World

Polity: Toward A Neorealist Synthesis," *World Politics*, 35 (January 1983), reprinted in Keohane, *Neorealism and Its Critics, op. cit.*, pp. 131–157.

37. Keohane and Nye, *"Power and Interdependence* Revisited," *op. cit.*, p. 752. The modernist (or globalist) paradigm that they developed, based on the notion of complex interdependence, was presented not as an alternative but as a complement to the realist paradigm. Although it challenged some realist assumptions—deemphasizing the state-as-actor and relaxing the distinction between domestic and international politics—its treatment of international organizations as "clusters of intergovernmental and transgovernmental networks" was far divorced from the legal-formal roots of the idealist tradition. If anything, Keohane and Nye further distanced themselves from this tradition in the 1980s, qualifying some of their earlier suggestions about the importance of nonstate actors and particularly rejecting what, fairly or unfairly, was widely seen as an endorsement of a "cobweb" as opposed to a "billiard ball" conception of international politics. A few others, however, have reaffirmed the globalist paradigm and have attempted to expand upon it, such as Richard W. Mansbach and John A Vasquez, *In Search of Theory: A New Paradigm for Global Politics* (New York: Columbia University Press, 1981); Seyom Brown, *New Forces, Old Forces, and the Future of World Politics* (Boston: Little, Brown, 1988) and *International Relations in A Changing Global System* (Boulder: Westview, 1992); and Marvin S. Soroos, *Beyond Sovereignty: The Challenge of Global Policy* (Columbia, S.C.: University of South Carolina Press, 1986).

38. Although neorealists contend that their emphasis on the "essentially conflictual nature of international affairs" and the "primacy in all political life of power and security in human motivation" makes them true to the realist tradition, critics argue that neorealism is far more fatalistic and resigned to the status quo than is classical realism. See Robert G. Gilpin, "The Richness of the Tradition of Political Realism," *International Organization*, 38 (Spring 1984), p. 20; and Ashley, *op. cit.* Such classical realists as Morgenthau and Herz did alter their views about reality as time went on. See Hans J. Morgenthau, "The New Diplomacy of Movement," *Encounter*, 43 (August 1974), p. 57; and John H. Herz, "Political Realism Revisited," *International Studies Quarterly*, 25 (June 1981), pp. 202–203.

39. Axelrod and Keohane, *op. cit.*, p. 226. Cooperation is defined in the symposium as "conscious policy coordination" among the states having "conflicting policy preferences."

40. Among the more prominent examples are Claude, *Swords into Plowshares, op. cit.*; Ernst B. Haas, *Beyond the Nation-State* (Stanford, Calif.: Stanford University Press, 1964); Haas, "International Integration:

The European and the Universal Process," *International Organization*, 15 (Autumn 1961); Karl W. Deutsch, *et al.*, *Political Community and the North Atlantic Area* (Princeton, N.J.: Princeton University Press, 1957); Leon N. Lindberg and Stuart Scheingold, *Europe's Would Be Polity* (Englewood Cliffs, N.J.: Prentice-Hall, 1970); and Keohane and Nye, *Power and Interdependence, op. cit.*

41. Robert Jervis, "Realism, Game Theory, and Cooperation," *World Politics*, 40 (April 1988), p. 318. Jervis is specifically referring here to the latest applications of game theory to the study of cooperation, but many non-game theoretic works tend to frame the questions similarly. See Emerson M. S. Niou and Peter C. Ordeshook, "Stability in Anarchic International Systems," *American Political Science Review*, 84 (December 1990), pp. 1207–1234.

42. Robert Axelrod, *The Evolution of Cooperation* (New York: Basic Books, 1984), p. 3.

43. Keohane, *After Hegemony, op. cit.*, p. 183.

44. James N. Rosenau, "Before Cooperation: Hegemons, Regimes, and Habit-Driven Actors in World Politics," *International Organization*, 40 (Autumn 1986), pp. 870–871.

45. Jervis, *op. cit.*, p. 317.

46. On policy implications, see Axelrod, *The Evolution of Cooperation, op. cit.*, pp. 136–139 and 190–191.

47. See, for example, Harold Guetzkow, "Isolation and Collaboration," *Journal of Conflict Resolution*, 1 (March 1957), pp. 48–68; or John Gerard Ruggie, "Collective Goods and Future International Collaboration," *American Political Science Review*, 66, (September 1972), pp. 874–893. Students of international law have long noted the utilitarian basis for cooperative acceptance of rules in international affairs, and how actors will subject themselves to binding agreements even in the absence of a central constraint system in the Austinian sense. William D. Coplin, *The Functions of International Law* (Chicago, Ill.: Rand McNally, 1966).

48. Compare the tit-for-tat reciprocity strategies recommended by Axelrod in *The Evolution of Cooperation, op. cit.*, with the strategies found in Thomas Schelling, *The Strategy of Conflict* (Cambridge, Mass.: Harvard University Press, 1960) and Charles E. Osgood, *An Alternative to War or Surrender* (Urbana, Ill.: University of Illinois Press, 1962).

49. Kenneth A. Oye, "Explaining Cooperation Under Anarchy: Hypotheses and Strategies," *World Politics*, 38 (October 1985), pp. 2 and 12–18. As Joanne Gowa points out, many of the "strategies" suggested by game theorists may have questionable practical relevance not only for institution-building but also for ad hoc cooperation, given the state-centric rationality and other assumptions governing this mode of anal-

ysis. See Gowa, "Anarchy, Egoism, and Third Images: *The Evolution of Cooperation* and International Regimes," *International Organization*, 40 (Winter 1986), pp. 167–186.

50. Oye, *op. cit.*, pp. 4 and 18–22. On the problems of cooperation among large numbers of actors, also see Michael Taylor, *The Possibility of Cooperation* (Cambridge: Cambridge University Press, 1987). The argument that the larger a group is, the less likely are its members to cooperate voluntarily in providing collective goods (due to "free rider" and other problems) originated with Mancur Olson's *The Logic of Collective Action* (Cambridge, Mass.: Harvard University Press, 1965); the size problem is stated on p. 36. The view that global institution-building is not only unlikely but undesirable in many cases is forcefully presented in John Conybeare, "International Organization and the Theory of Property Rights," *International Organization*, 34 (Summer 1980), pp. 307–334.

51. Oye, *op. cit.*, p. 1.

52. Keohane and Nye, "*Power and Interdependence* Revisited," *op. cit.*, p. 740.

53. Oye, "Explaining Cooperation Under Anarchy," *op. cit.*, p. 24; and Axelrod and Keohane, *op. cit.*, pp. 248–254. Kratochwil and Ruggie, *op. cit.*, p. 767, state that "what distinguishes international regimes from other international phenomena—from strategic interaction, let us say—is a specifically normative element."

54. The failure of scholars to think in broader terms beyond strategic cooperation is noted in Alexander Wendt and Raymond Duvall, "Institutions and International Order," in Ernst Otto Czempiel and James N. Rosenau, eds., *Global Changes and Theoretical Challenges* (Lexington: Lexington Books, 1989), p. 59. Even hegemony theory has been criticized for not fully treating international relations in a systemic context, for example ignoring noncapitalist states and glossing over bipolar features of the international system in analyzing the postwar economic order. The theory has been criticized not only for lacking accurate empirical referents and lacking predictive power but on other grounds as well, including the fact that it deals as much with instability as stability, that it confuses cooperation with coercion, that it excludes other possibly superior bases for cooperation, and that it offers little advice to policymakers concerned about the requirements of world order other than to allow a single state to become and remain a hegemon. See Duncan Snidal, "The Limits of Hegemonic Stability Theory," *International Organization*, 39 (Autumn 1985), pp. 579–614; Haggard and Simmons, *op. cit.*, pp. 500–504; Isabelle Grunberg, "Exploring the 'Myth' of Hegemonic Stability," *International Organization*, 44 (Autumn 1990), pp. 431–477; and K. Edward Spiezo, "British Hegemony and Major Power War,

1815–1939: An Empirical Test of Gilpin's Model of Hegemonic Governance," *International Studies Quarterly*, 34 (June 1990), pp. 165–181.

55. Haggard and Simmons, *op. cit.*, p. 508. These authors distinguish between the functional, structural, game-theoretic, and cognitive strains of the regime literature.

56. Keohane and Nye, *"Power and Interdependence Revisited," op. cit.*, p. 747.

57. Robert O. Keohane and Joseph S. Nye, "Two Cheers for Multilateralism," *Foreign Policy*, 60 (Fall 1985), p. 159. Of course, one does not have to rely on game theory or collective goods theory to observe that the greater the number of actors, the more likely there is to be diversity and, hence, difficulty in reconciling differences.

58. *Ibid.*, p. 155. They equate institution-building through the UN with an ill-advised "grand design" approach to world order.

59. *Ibid.*, pp. 158–159.

60. At least one critic dismisses the study of regimes as "a fad, one of those shifts of fashion not too difficult to explain as a temporary reaction to events in the real world." Susan Strange, *"Cave! Hic Dragones:* A Critique of Regime Analysis," *International Organization*, 36 (Spring 1982), p. 479.

61. Rochester, *op. cit.*, p. 803.

62. The term is Arnold Wolfers's, referring to the overuse and misuse of the concept of "national security." "National Security As An Ambiguous Symbol," in Wolfers, *op. cit.*, p. 147.

63. Robert O. Keohane, "Reciprocity in International Relations," *International Organization*, 40 (Winter 1986), p. 2.

64. Inis L. Claude, Jr., *Power and International Relations* (New York: Random House, 1962), p. 12; cited in *ibid.*

65. James G. March and Johan P. Olsen, "The New Institutionalism: Organizational Factors in Political Life," *American Political Science Review*, 78 (September 1984); and *Rediscovering Institutions* (New York: Free Press, 1989).

66. Oran R. Young, "International Regimes: Toward a New Theory of Institutions," *World Politics*, 39 (October 1986), pp. 104–122.

67. *Ibid.*, pp. 121–122.

68. Kratochwil and Ruggie, *op. cit.*, pp. 771–772. Among the few recent attempts to pursue this link are Gayl D. Ness and Steven R. Brechin, "Bridging the Gap: International Organizations as Organizations," *International Organization*, 42 (Spring 1988), pp. 245–273; and Christer Jonsson, "Interorganization Theory and International Organization, *International Studies Quarterly*, 30 (March 1986), pp. 39–57.

69. Ruggie, "The United States and the United Nations," *op. cit.*, p. 345.

70. *Ibid.*, p. 356. Stirrings of renewed interest in the study of international organization can be seen lately in "The Political Economy of International Change" series published by Columbia University Press and edited by Ruggie; the new Ford Foundation program on International Organizations and Law; and Harvard University's pre- and post-doctoral fellowship program in the area of international institutions including the UN. However, in a 1992 symposium on "Multilateralism" in *International Organization*, Ruggie still hedges on the subject of global organization. Although he speaks of "generalized organizing principles," he states that "the generic institutional form of multilateralism must not be confused with formal multilateral organizations, a relatively recent arrival, and still of only relatively modest importance." See "Multilateralism: The Anatomy of an Institution," *International Organization*, 46 (Summer 1992), p. 567. In the same volume, James Caporaso, "International Relations Theory and Multilateralism: The Search for Foundations," pp. 599–632, adopts a tone similar to Ruggie, while Miles Kahler, "Multilateralism with Small and Large Numbers," pp. 681–708, is more supportive of formal and universal approaches to multilateralism.

71. Puchala and Coate, *op. cit.*, pp. 102 and 108. Also see Coate and Puchala, "Global Policies and the United Nations System: A Current Assessment," *Journal of Peace Research*, 27 (May 1990), pp. 127–140. Likewise, Inis Claude, in "The Balance of Power Revisited," *Review of International Studies*, 15 (April 1989), pp. 77–86, suggests that universal approaches to problem solving have seen their day come and go and that they no longer can be given the credence they enjoyed earlier in the twentieth century. For an especially cynical view on "the limits of IO," see Guilio Gallarotti, "The Limits of International Organization: Systematic Failure in the Management of International Relations," *International Organization*, 45 (Spring 1991), pp. 183–220.

72. Robert W. Cox, "Social Forces, States, and World Order: Beyond International Relations Theory," in R.B.J. Walker, ed., *Culture, Ideology, and World Order* (Boulder, Colo.: Westview Press, 1984), p. 263.

73. Herz, "Political Realism Revisited," *op. cit.*, p. 202.

74. Charles A. McClelland, "International Relations: Wisdom or Science?," in James N. Rosenau, ed., *International Politics and Foreign Policy*, rev. ed. (New York: Free Press, 1969), p. 4.

75. Robert Cox, among others, has pointed to the way in which changing economic production and exchange processes may be altering centuries-old patterns of relations within and between nation-states. See *Production, Power and World Order* (New York: Columbia University Press, 1987).

76. Francis Fukuyama, "The End of History," *The National Interest*, 16 (Summer 1989), pp. 3–16.

77. George F. Will, "Europe's Second Reformation," essay in *Newsweek*, November 20, 1989, p. 90.

78. This view is exemplified by John J. Mearsheimer, "Why We Will Soon Miss the Cold War," *The Atlantic*, 266 (August 1990), pp. 35–50.

79. See Yosef Lapid, "The Third Debate: On the Prospects of International Theory in A Post-Positivist Era," *International Studies Quarterly*, 33 (September 1989), pp. 235–254; and a special volume of *International Studies Quarterly*, 34 (September 1990).

80. Robert Keohane, "*International Organization* and the Crisis of Interdependence," *International Organization*, 29 (Spring 1975), p. 360.

81. John Maynard Keynes, *The General Theory of Employment, Interest and Money* (London: Macmillan, 1957), p. 383. Joseph Nye, in "Nuclear Learning and U.S.-Soviet Security Regimes," *op. cit.*, p. 376, points out that the Soviet leadership in the 1980s started increasingly to utilize the language of "regimes," referring to the nuclear non-proliferation regime and other such institutional developments.

82. In *Global Problems and World Order* (Madison, Wisc.: University of Wisconsin Press, 1986), R. D. McKinlay and R. Little note the difficulties surrounding the concept of world order and how one's definition may be in the eyes of the beholder. They discuss three competing world order models—realism, liberalism, and socialism—and argue that there is little room for "compromise and constructive debate" among these models, which "pass like ships in the night" (p. 273). However, there are other ways of looking at world order than through these perceptual lenses. Interestingly, despite the title of the book, the authors do not think in clearly global terms, stating at the outset that "throughout this book, 'global,' 'world,' and 'international' are used interchangeably," implying "in each case . . . relations across state boundaries" (p. 6).

83. Cox, *Production, Power and World Order, op. cit.*, p. 395.

Chapter 2: The Logic of Global Institution-Building

1. A more expansive definition is provided by the Consortium on World Order Studies, which defines world order as the "study and appraisal of efforts of creating a more dependable international environment which would lead to a significant reduction of violence and the improvement of the quality of life throughout the globe." Consortium on World Order Studies (mimeo), p. 1; cited in Friedrich Kratochwil, "Of Law and Human Action: A Jurisprudential Plea for a World Order

Perspective in International Legal Studies," in Richard Falk, Friedrich Kratochwil, and Saul H. Mendlovitz, eds., *International Law: A Contemporary Perspective* (Boulder, Colo.: Westview Press, 1985), p. 646.

2. Kenneth N. Waltz, *Theory of International Politics* (Reading, Mass: Addison-Wesley, 1979), p. 162. Waltz's latest writings recognize that in the 1990s the international system seems to be returning to a multipolar condition.

3. Richard N. Rosecrance, *Action and Reaction in World Politics* (Boston: Little, Brown, 1963). Among others, K. J. Holsti identifies distinct international systems in the periods from the early eighteenth century until 1789, 1789 to 1939, and 1945 to the present. Evan Luard cites 1789 and 1914 as watershed dates. Seyom Brown speaks of five historical systems since 1648. See K. J. Holsti, *International Politics: A Framework for Analysis*, 4th ed. (Englewood Cliffs, N.J.: Prentice-Hall, 1983); Evan Luard, *Types of International Society* (New York: Free Press, 1976); and Seyom Brown, *New Forces, Old Forces, and The Future of World Politics* (Boston: Little, Brown, 1988), p. 14.

4. The term "bimultipolarity" was coined by Richard Rosecrance in 1966 to describe a hypothetical system that he felt might exist in the future but did not yet exist at the time. Others, like Stanley Hoffmann, suggested that, by the late 1960s, such a system had materialized. See Rosecrance, "Bipolarity, Multipolarity, and the Future," *Journal of Conflict Resolution*, 10 (September 1966), pp. 314–327; and Hoffmann, *Gulliver's Troubles, or the Setting of American Foreign Policy* (New York: McGraw-Hill, 1968), pp. 21–46. These writers foresaw the movement of the international system away from bipolarity that was to accelerate in the late 1980s.

5. Brown, *op. cit.*, chap. 12. Also see James N. Rosenau, "Global Changes and Theoretical Challenges: Toward a Postinternational Politics for the 1990s," in Ernst-Otto Czempiel and Rosenau, eds., *Global Changes and Theoretical Challenges* (Lexington, Mass.: Lexington Books, 1989), p. 8.

6. Morton A. Kaplan, *System and Process in International Politics* (New York: John Wiley, 1957).

7. Some observers have suggested that recent disintegrative trends in the form of the breakup of colonial empires and increased subnational conflict in both established and young states, combined with the erosion of state sovereignty associated with multinational corporations and transnationalism, threaten to move the international system toward a "new feudalism" or "new medievalism." See, for example, Hedley Bull, *The Anarchical Society* (London: Macmillan, 1977), pp. 254–256 and 264–276, and James A. Nathan, "The New Feudalism," *Foreign Policy* (Spring 1981), pp. 156–166, as well as the discussion of polyarchy

in Brown, *op. cit.* The trend away from politics based upon well-defined territoriality is discussed in John G. Ruggie, "Territoriality and Beyond," *International Organization*, 47 (Winter 1993), pp. 139–174.

8. Barry Buzan, *People, States, and Fear* (Chapel Hill, N.C.: University of North Carolina Press, 1983), p. 97.

9. World order values have been most extensively discussed in the World Order Models Project literature, such as Richard Falk, *A Study of Future Worlds* (New York: Free Press, 1975). Also, see Robert C. Johansen, *The National Interest and the Human Interest* (Princeton, N.J.: Princeton University Press, 1980).

10. For a concise review of the Waltz, Singer, and related controversies on this question, see Buzan, *op. cit.*, chap. 4. In "Why We Will Soon Miss the Cold War," *The Atlantic* (August 1990), John Mearsheimer discusses the concern that the end of the Cold War and bipolarity might well produce a more unstable, violent international system.

11. Kenneth A. Oye, "Explaining Cooperation Under Anarchy: Hypotheses and Strategies," *World Politics*, 38 (October 1985), p. 1.

12. In their article on "Achieving Cooperation Under Anarchy: Strategies and Institutions," *World Politics*, 38 (October 1985), pp. 226–228, Axelrod and Keohane stress that except for the fact that "anarchy remains a constant," the "context" in which games occur in international relations is "malleable." They might have taken this point further and examined cooperation in a larger context. Interestingly, in an article focusing on institutions, they manage never once to use the term "international organization."

13. Robert O. Keohane and Joseph S. Nye, *Power and Interdependence*, 2nd ed. (Boston: Scott, Foresman, 1989), p. 3.

14. On some dimensions of interdependence, some parts of the world may be less interdependent today than in the past. This does not contradict my statement which refers to the overall condition of the international system. A large array of data showing growing interdependence in economic and other spheres is presented by Mark W. Zacher in "The Decaying Pillars of the Westphalian Temple: Implications for International Order and Governance," paper presented at annual meeting of International Studies Association, Vancouver, March 22, 1991. Even Waltz's well-known caveat about the myth of interdependence does not deny that empirically one can demonstrate growing interdependence. As he says, his quarrel is a conceptual one, in that he confines interdependence to a "relationship among equals" and focuses on interdependence between certain parts of the system, namely the "great powers." Waltz, *op. cit.*, pp. 144–145. See also Richard N. Rosecrance and Arthur Stein, "Interdependence: Myth or Reality?" *World Pol-*

itics, 26 (October 1973), pp. 1–27; and Alex Inkeles, "The Emerging Social Structure of the World," *World Politics*, 27 (July 1975), pp. 467–495.

15. Robert North and Nazli Choucri, "Global Environmental Change: Toward a Framework for Decision and Policy," paper presented at annual meeting of International Studies Association, Washington, D.C., April 13, 1990, p. 14. In *War, Peace, Survival* (Boulder, Colo.: Westview Press, 1990), North stresses the importance of adding a "fourth image" (that of the global system) to Waltz's three images (the individual, nation-state, and international levels of analysis) in attempting to understand world affairs.

16. Janice E. Thompson and Stephen D. Krasner, "Global Transactions and the Consolidation of Sovereignty," in Ernst-Otto Czempiel and James N. Rosenau, eds., *Global Changes and Theoretical Challenges* (Lexington, Mass.: Lexington Books, 1989), pp. 203–204.

17. Shahrokh Fardoust and Ashok Dhareshwar, *A Long-Term Outlook for the World Economy: Issues and Perspectives for the 1990s* (Washington, D.C.: World Bank, 1990), pp. 5–6. See also Mark Amen, "The Impact of the U.S. Economy on International Economic Security," paper presented at annual meeting of the International Studies Association, Washington, D.C., April 13, 1990.

18. North, *op. cit.*, p. 192.

19. Joan E. Spero, *The Politics of International Economic Relations*, 4th ed. (New York: St. Martin's Press, 1990), p. 237.

20. Richard S. Newfarmer, "Multinationals and Marketplace Magic in the 1980s," in Jeffrey A. Frieden and David A. Lake, eds., *International Political Economy*, 2nd ed. (New York: St. Martin's Press, 1991), p. 199.

21. Earl H. Fry, "Foreign Direct Investment in the U.S.: Public Options," paper presented at annual meeting of International Studies Association, Washington, D.C., April 13, 1990, pp. 1–2.

22. *Ibid.*, p. 7.

23. Harold D. Lasswell, *Politics: Who Gets What, When, How?* (Cleveland, Ohio: World Publishing, 1958); David Easton, *A Systems Analysis of Political Life* (New York: John Wiley, 1965).

24. Richard W. Mansbach and John A. Vasquez, in *In Search of Theory: A New Paradigm for Global Politics* (New York: Columbia University Press, 1981), develop a "global politics" paradigm which includes a discussion of "allocation mechanisms." Although they rely on Easton's definition of politics ("the authoritative allocation of valued things") as the starting point for their paradigm, it is questionable whether such a definition is appropriate to international politics even if his systems framework seems quite applicable. Among the numerous articles comparing the international political system with national political systems,

see Fred W. Riggs, "International Relations as a Prismatic System," *World Politics*, 14 (October 1961), pp. 144–181.

25. Sounding somewhat like regimes, a policy has been defined in a national context as "a general principle concerning the pattern of activity, or a general commitment to the pattern of activity, developed or adopted for use in making particular decisions about programs or actions." David V. Edwards, *The American Political Experience*, 4th ed. (Englewood Cliffs, N.J.: Prentice-Hall, 1988), p. 481.

26. Commenting on the proscription against armed aggression written into the UN Charter, Louis Henkin contends that "the norm against the unilateral national use of force has survived. Indeed, . . . the norm has been largely observed . . . and the kinds of international wars which it sought to prevent have been infrequent." Henkin, *How Nations Behave*, 2nd ed. (New York: Columbia University Press, 1979), p. 146. While the incidence of traditional interstate wars seems to have decreased over time, there was considerable internationalization of civil wars in the post-World War II era along with growing security anxiety and war preparation as manifested by enormously increased global military expenditures. Trends are reported in *World Military Expenditures and Arms Transfers, 1987* (Washington, D.C.: U.S. Arms Control and Disarmament Agency, 1988), p. 1; and Melvin Small and J. David Singer, "Conflict in the International System, 1816–1977: Historical Trends and Policy Futures," in Charles W. Kegley, Jr. and Patrick J. McGowan, eds., *Challenges to America: United States Foreign Policy in the 1980s* (Beverly Hills, Calif.: Sage, 1979), pp. 89–115. However, the momentum of global military expenditures and arms races started slowing somewhat in the late 1980s, as reported in Ruth Sivard, *World Military and Social Expenditures, 1987–1988* (Washington, D.C.: World Priorities, 1987), p. 8, and *World Military Expenditures and Arms Transfers, 1989* (Washington, D.C.: U.S. Arms Control and Disarmament Agency, 1989), p. 1. Trends in warfare are discussed further below.

27. George Modelski, "Is World Politics Evolutionary Learning?" *International Organization*, 44 (Winter 1990), p. 11.

28. Bull, *op. cit.*

29. Cultural diffusion is occurring at such an accelerated pace that distinctive cultures can find it difficult to resist the forces of "coca-colonization." Richard Peet, in "The Destruction of Regional Cultures," in R. J. Johnson and Peter J. Taylor, eds., *A World in Crisis: Georgraphical Perspectives* (Oxford, Eng.: Basil Blackwell, 1986), pp. 151 and 169, cites empirical evidence to support the conclusion that "cultural imperialism by the capitalist centre" is resulting in the "destruction of regional cultures" and the tendency "towards the production of one world mind [and] one world culture." Also see Theodore Van Laue, *The World Rev-*

olution of Westernization (New York: Oxford University Press, 1987); R. B. J. Walker, *Culture, Ideology, and World Order* (Boulder, Colo.: Westview Press, 1984); and Zacher, *op. cit.*, pp. 16–17.

30. The evolution of the nation-state in Western Europe from a national security state to a welfare state is traced in Charles Tilly, ed. *The Formation of National States in Western Europe* (Princeton, N.J.: Princeton University Press, 1975) and Tilly, *Coercion, Capital, and European States, A.D. 90–1990* (Cambridge, Eng.: Basil Blackwell, 1990).

31. Although there has been some rethinking of the welfare state recently in the U.S. and elsewhere, an examination of trends in the postwar era shows social, nondefense expenditures by government rising as a percentage of GDP in most states. On trends in OECD countries, in particular, see OECD, *Social Expenditure, 1960–1990* (Paris: OECD, 1985). Wagner's law, "that the share of the economy taxed and spent by government was on a steady upward curve," has yet to be repealed since it was first posited in 1890. Stuart A. Bremer and Barry B. Hughes, *Disarmament and Development: A Design for the Future?* (Englewood Cliffs, N.J.: Prentice-Hall, 1990), p. 180.

32. The term originated with Keohane and Nye, *op. cit.*

33. Wolfram Hanrieder, "Dissolving International Politics: Reflections on the Nation-State," *American Political Science Review*, 72 (December 1978), p. 1279.

34. Tilly, *The Formation of National States*, p. 638. Earlier, John Herz in *International Politics in the Atomic Age* (New York: Columbia University Press, 1959) had noted that the growing military and economic permeability of nation-state boundaries threatened to result in the "demise of the territorial state."

35. It is commonly noted, for example, that almost half of the 100 largest economic units in the world are MNCs rather than countries (measuring country size by GNP and MNC size by gross annual sales); see Charles W. Kegley and Eugene R. Wittkopf, *World Politics: Trend and Transformation*, 3rd ed. (New York: St. Martin's Press, 1989), pp. 164–165; and *Fortune*, July 30, 1990, pp. 269–270. One study which attempted to map empirically the impact of nonstate actors in the global system is Richard W. Mansbach, *et al.*, *The Web of World Politics* (Englewood Cliffs, N.J.: Prentice-Hall, 1976).

36. Thompson and Krasner, *op. cit.*, p. 198.

37. The "loss of control" theme was first discussed in a special issue of *International Organization*, 25 (Summer 1971), subsequently published in a volume edited by Robert Keohane and Joseph Nye, entitled *Transnational Relations and World Politics* (Cambridge, Mass.: Harvard University Press, 1971). See especially pp. 392–395.

38. Rosenau, *op. cit.*, p. 6.

39. Richard Rosecrance, *The Rise of the Trading State* (New York: Basic Books, 1986), p. 14.

40. Charles Kindleberger, *American Business Abroad* (New Haven, Conn.: Yale University Press, 1969), p. 207.

41. James N. Rosenau, "Patterned Chaos in Global Life: Structure and Process in Two Worlds of World Politics," mimeo, Institute for Transnational Studies, University of Southern California, April 1987, pp. 3 and 6.

42. Oran R. Young, "Regime Dynamics: The Rise and Fall of International Regimes," *International Organization*, 36 (Spring 1982), p. 277, reminds that "the members of international regimes are always sovereign states, though the parties carrying out the actions governed by international regimes are often private entities (for example, fishing companies, banks, or private airlines). It follows that implementing the terms of international regimes will frequently involve a two-step procedure."

43. Robert Cox makes this point, arguing that "previous historical systems referred to more limited areas, more or less sealed off from external influences, which were the relevant 'worlds' for the people in them" See "On Thinking About Future World Order," *World Politics*, 28 (January 1976), p. 195.

44. President Truman's address to the UN Conference on International Organization, cited in *U.S. Department of State Bulletin*, 13 (July 1, 1945), p. 4. The original UN membership consisted of 51 countries.

45. Although an increase in the number of actors in the international system increases the "transaction costs" of reaching agreements, it need not in itself cause an increase in interstate violence; the incidence of militarized disputes has been found to depend more on the manner in which new states are created and enter the international system than on the size of the system. See Zeev Moaz, "Joining the Club of Nations: Political Development and International Conflict, 1816–1976," *International Studies Quarterly*, 33 (June 1989), pp. 199–231. Miles Kahler, in "Multilateralism with Small and Large Numbers," *International Organization*, 46 (Summer 1992), pp. 681–708, discusses how large numbers need not pose insurmountable obstacles to international institution-building.

46. An overview of "political development" as a field of study, including some of the biases and criticisms surrounding the concept, can be found in Gabriel A. Almond, "The Development of Political Development," in Myron Weiner and Samuel P. Huntington, eds., *Understanding Political Development* (Boston: Little Brown, 1987), pp. 437–478.

47. Alfred Diamant, "The Nature of Political Development," in Jason

L. Finkle and Richard W. Gable, eds., *Political Development and Social Change* (New York: John Wiley, 1966), p. 92.

48. Lucian W. Pye, "The Concept of Political Development," in Finkle and Gable, *op. cit.*, p. 90.

49. Lucian W. Pye, *Aspects of Political Development* (Boston: Little, Brown, 1966); and Gabriel A. Almond and G. Bingham Powell, *Comparative Politics: A Developmental Approach* (Boston: Little, Brown, 1966). On the Western experience, in particular, see Tilly, *The Formation of National States*, chap. 9.

50. For a good discussion of the relationship between political stability, or peace, on the one hand and political democracy and economic equality, or justice, on the other, see Samuel P. Huntington, "The Goals of Development," in Weiner and Huntington, *op. cit.*, pp. 3–32. Huntington states that although the "assumptions that 'all good things go together' is generally wrong and easy to criticize," "it would be wrong to dismiss it entirely" (p. 7). He notes that, following the predominance of the "conflict" literature in the political development field in the 1970s, which suggested that such values as stability and equality or democracy might be incompatible in developing societies, the "reconciliation" literature in the 1980s attempted to explore how they might all be increasingly realized over time, with political scientists urging "the temporal priority of order over democracy" (p. 19).

51. In addition to Huntington's article cited in the previous note, writings which examine the empirical link between political violence and inequality in a comparative politics context are Manus I. Midlarsky, "Rulers and the Ruled: Patterned Inequality and the Onset of Mass Political Violence," *American Political Science Review*, 82 (June 1988); Edward N. Muller, "Income Inequality, Regime Repressiveness, and Political Violence," *American Sociological Review*, 50 (June 1985); and Ted R. Gurr, *Why Men Rebel* (Princeton, N.J.: Princeton University Press, 1970). The general view is that increased political and economic equality in the long run tends to lessen violence but in the short run may aggravate instability and lead to greater violence insofar as it produces a revolution of rising expectations that cannot be fulfilled. In an international politics context, an article which looks at whether peace and prosperity "go together" is Bruce Russett's "Prosperity and Peace," *International Studies Quarterly*, 27 (December 1983), pp. 381–387.

52. Stanley Hoffmann, *Primacy or World Order* (New York: McGraw Hill, 1978), p. 108.

53. *Ibid.*, p. 184.

54. *Ibid.*, pp. 185–186. Hoffmann calls for "gradual economic and social progress," as opposed to "the utopia of global welfare-and-justice." For another view that questions whether the distribution of wealth is

something that can or ought to be placed on the global agenda, see Robert W. Tucker, *The Inequality of Nations* (New York: Basic Books, 1977). See also Bull, *op. cit.*

55. Hoffmann, *Primacy or World Order, op. cit.*, p. 101.

56. Buzan maintains that "only when the weaker members [of the international system] have become more firmly established as states" and "can project a basic solidity into the system" will "the system as a whole be able to advance in maturity." Buzan *op. cit.*, p. 118. For an argument that international institution-building must be centered around not only states but nonstate actors, given the polyarchical structure of world politics, see Brown, *op. cit.*, chaps. 12 and 13.

57. It is hard to quarrel with Hedley Bull's caution that "[although] the system of a plurality of sovereign states gives rise to classic dangers, . . . these have to be reckoned against the dangers inherent in the attempt to contain disparate communities within the framework of a single government" and his conclusion that "world order at the present time . . . [may be] best served by living with the former dangers rather than by attempting to face the latter." Bull, *op. cit.*, p. 287.

58. Karl W. Deutsch, et al., "Political Community and the North Atlantic Area," in *International Political Communities* (Garden City, N.Y.: Doubleday, 1966), p. 2. Mansbach and Vasquez, *op. cit.*, p. 292, associate political development of the international system with "increasing institutionalization, legitimacy, and hierarchy in games among actors," which in their scheme of things can include acceptance of war as an allocation mechanism.

59. Deutsch, *et al.*, "Political Community and the North Atlantic Area," *op. cit.*, p. 45.

60. *Ibid.*, p. 89.

61. See n. 26. For evidence that the international system over time has been moving in the direction of war avoidance, edging toward the foundations of a global security-community, and that the reduction in interstate violence is correlated with IGO growth, see Harold K. Jacobson, William M. Reisinger, and Todd Mathers, "National Entanglements in International Governmental Organizations," *American Political Science Review*, 80 (March 1986), p. 156; and Jacobson, *Networks of Interdependence*, 2nd ed. (New York: Knopf, 1984), pp. 190–192 and 198–199.

62. Jack Levy, *War in the Modern Great Power System, 1495–1975* (Lexington, Ky.: University of Kentucky Press, 1983).

63. Kenneth N. Waltz, "Nuclear Myths and Political Realities," *American Political Science Review*, 84 (September 1990), p. 744. On the possible obsolescence of war, especially among modern industrial powers (and especially among democracies), see John Mueller, *Retreat from Doomsday* (New York: Basic Books, 1989); James Lee Ray, "The Aboli-

tion of Slavery and the End of International War," *International Organization*, 43 (Summer 1989), pp. 405–440; Rosecrance, *op. cit.*; and Carl Kaysen, "Is War Obsolete? A Review Essay," *International Security*, 14 (Spring 1990), pp. 42–64.

64. The strategy of building international cooperation through "decomposition," as game theorists have stressed, has also been reflected in recent practitioner thinking. See, for example, the Atlantic Council Working Group on the United Nations, *The Future of the UN: A Strategy for Like-Minded Nations* (Boulder: Westview Press, 1977); and the United Nations Association of the USA, *A Successor Vision: The United Nations of Tomorrow* (New York: UNA-USA, 1987). Also, see North, *op. cit.*, pp. 260–261; although adopting a global perspective, North is cautious about the possibilities for global governance and argues along the lines of Keohane that "nestings and networks of specialized international regimes" among "small groups of nations" may be a necessary "interim stage" through which "center and periphery nations could deal with each other." The problems encountered in determining the optimal size of regimes are discussed in Oran R. Young, *Resource Regimes* (Berkeley, Calif.: University of California Press, 1982), chap. 3. Kahler, *op. cit.*, p. 683, addresses "cooperation with large numbers" and criticizes the "misplaced pessimism of the neoliberals."

65. Ernst B. Haas, "On Systems and International Regimes," *World Politics*, 27 (January 1975), p. 148.

66. Robert W. Cox, "Social Forces, States and World Orders: Beyond International Relations Theory," in Robert O. Keohane, ed., *Neorealism and Its Critics* (New York: Columbia University Press, 1986), p. 206.

67. Jacobson, *Networks of Interdependence, op. cit., p. 391.*

68. Hoffmann, *Primacy or World Order, op. cit.*, p. 189. I use the term "central guidance" more loosely than Richard Falk. See his *A Study of Future Worlds, op. cit.*, chap. 4.

69. Samuel P. Huntington, *Political Order in Changing Societies* (New Haven, Conn.: Yale University Press, 1968), pp. 8–9.

70. See William D. Coplin, *The Functions of International Law* (Chicago, Ill.: Rand McNally, 1966), and Richard Falk, "The Relevance of Political Context to the Nature and Functioning of International Law: An Intermediate View," in Karl W. Deutsch and Stanley Hoffmann, eds., *The Relevance of International Law* (Cambridge, Eng.: Schenkman, 1968).

71. I am referring to functions here in a broader sense than does Jacobson in *Networks of Interdependence, op. cit.*, chap. 5. Earlier works that take a functional approach to the study of international organizations are Paul Tharp, ed., *Regional International Organizations/Structures and Functions* (New York: St. Martin's Press, 1971); and Wolfram Hanrieder,

"International Organizations and International Systems," *Journal of Conflict Resolution*, 10 (September 1966), pp. 297–313. See also Clive Archer, *International Organizations* (London: Unwin and Allen, 1983), chap. 4.

72. Cited in Richard Gardner, "To Make the World Safe for Interdependence," *UN 30* (New York: UNA-USA, 1975), p. 16.

73. Gayl D. Ness and Steven R. Brechin, "Bridging the Gap: International Organizations as Organizations," *International Organization*, 42 (Spring 1988), p. 247.

74. Deutsch, *et al.*, "Political Community and the North Atlantic Area," *op. cit.*, p. 3.

75. See Richard Bilder, *Managing the Risks of International Agreement* (Madison, Wisc.: University of Wisconsin Press, 1981), p. 232, citing Peter Rohn's University of Washington Treaty Research Center findings. Rohn's treaty data can be found in *World Treaty Index: Volume 1* (Santa Barbara, Calif.: ABC-Clio, 1984). One writer notes that the "official published version of treaties entered into by the United Kingdom in 1892 . . . filled 190 pages; the treaties entered into by the United Kingdom in 1960 filled 2,500 pages in the same series." Michael Akehurst, *A Modern Introduction to International Law*, 6th ed. (London: Unwin and Allen, 1987), p. 25.

76. Jacobson, *et al.*, "National Entanglements in International Governmental Organizations," *op. cit.*, p. 144.

77. *Ibid.*

78. Union of International Associations, *Yearbook of International Organizations, 1988/89*, 25th ed. (New York: K. G. Sauer Munchen, 1988), vol. 1, appendix 7.

79. John G. Ruggie, "Multilateralism: The Anatomy of An Institution," *International Organization*, 46 (Summer 1992), p. 584. Ruggie is responding here to questions posed by David Kennedy's examination of IGO growth in the twentieth century in "The Move to Institutions," *Cardozo Law Review*, 8 (April 1987), pp. 841–988.

80. Jacobson, *et al.*, "National Entanglements in International Governmental Organizations," p. 142.

81. Inis L. Claude, "The Record of International Organizations in the Twentieth Century," Tamkang Chair Lecture Series, No. 64, Tamkang University, Taiwan, January 1986 (mimeo), pp. 4–5.

82. *Ibid.*, p. 48.

83. An overwhelming majority of the more than 15,000 treaties in force as of 1980 were bilateral agreements. For example, of some 7,000 international agreements the U.S. was party to, over 6,000 were bilateral. See Bilder, *op. cit.*, pp. 6 and 233.

84. The twentieth century has witnessed much more multilateralism than previous eras, as noted in Mark W. Janis, *An Introduction to International Law* (Boston: Little Brown, 1988), p. 20. For data on the growth of multilateral treaty making in this century, see John King Gamble, "Reservations to Multilateral Treaties: A Macroscopic View of State Practice," *American Journal of International Law*, 74 (April 1980), pp. 377–378. Also, M. J. Bowman and J. J. Harris, *Multilateral Treaties: Index and Current Status* (London: Butterworth's, 1984).

85. Jacobson, *Networks of Interdependence, op. cit.*, p. 81.

86. James M. McCormick and Young W. Kihl, "Intergovernmental Organizations and Foreign Policy Behavior: Some Empirical Findings," *American Political Science Review*, 73 (June 1979), p. 502.

87. Friedrich Kratochwill and John Gerard Ruggie, "International Organization: A State of the Art or an Art of the State," *International Organization*, 40 (Autumn 1986), p. 773. Inis Claude was among the first to comment on the "collective legitimization" function of international organizations, in "Collective Legitimization As A Political Function of the United Nations," *International Organization*, 20 (Summer 1966), pp. 367–379.

88. On the circumstances that give rise to the need for explicit organizations to accompany regimes, see Young, *Resource Regimes, op. cit.*, pp. 58–61; and Young, "International Resource Regimes," in Clifford S. Russell, ed. *Collective Decision Making: Applications from Public Choice Theory* (Baltimore, Md.: Johns Hopkins University Press, 1979). In *Resource Regimes*, pp. 62–63, discussing social institutions generally, Young notes "it is apparent that the prominence of regulations [i.e. directives specifying certain behaviors and emanating from administrative agencies] will increase as a function of the complexity of the activity to be managed as well as the heterogeneity of the . . . actors," although he takes the view that this generalization does not apply as much in highly decentralized systems. Also see Lisa Martin, "Interests, Power, and Multilateralism," *International Organization*, 46 (Autumn 1992), pp. 765–792, on the role of formal organizations in facilitating "coordination and collaboration games" among states; Martin distinguishes between multilateral institutions or organizations (MO) and the institution of multilateralism (IM).

89. For example, one author notes: "In an analysis of compliance with 2,475 treaties during the period 1918–1957, it was calculated that the Soviet infidelity ratio was 11.5 per thousand, less than 1.2%. This is to say that the Soviet Union fails to honor a political promise, on the average, in only about one month out of every 120 (10 years) over which it is bound." Lloyd Jensen, *Explaining Foreign Policy* (Englewood Cliffs, N.J.: Prentice-Hall, 1982), pp. 251–252.

90. Based on the work of Abraham Maslow, Gerald and Patricia Miche in *Toward A Human World Order* (New York: Paulist Press, 1977), p. 28, infer a "natural human genetic propensity for bonding and unification" which contends with more parochial, centrifugal tendencies. As simplistic as this notion appears in light of the Westphalian state system, the evolution of the state itself may lend some credence to it, since as Roger Masters points out "contemporary nation-states are so much larger than the groups observed in other mammals." See "The Biological Nature of the State," *World Politics*, 35 (January 1983), p. 161. Also see Miriam Steiner, "Human Nature and Truth as World Order Issues," *International Organization*, 34 (Summer 1980). The UN remains a powerful symbol. During the 1980s, even in the United States, where anti-UN sentiment was among the highest in the world, Gallup and other public opinion polls consistently showed overwhelming support for remaining in the organization despite widespread dissatisfaction with UN performance. A Gallup poll taken in the Fall of 1983, when U.S. agreement with the UN General Assembly reached its lowest percentage level in the postwar era, revealed that 80% of the American public felt the UN remained a "worthwhile" organization even though only 36% felt it was doing a good job.

91. Jacobson, *et al.*, "National Entanglements in International Governmental Organizations," *op. cit.*, p. 157.

92. Seyom Brown and Larry Fabian, "Toward Mutual Accountability in the Nonterrestrial Realms," *International Organization*, 29 (Summer 1975), pp. 877–892. Ernst Haas has referred to global politics as "a turbulent field," suggesting that "the search for world order is nothing but an attempt to conquer turbulence." He has questioned how much "aggregation of institutions" is possible, whether at the regional level or higher level. See "Turbulent Fields and the Theory of Regional Integration," *International Organization*, 30 (Spring 1976), pp. 179–195.

93. Stanley J. Michalak, "The League of Nations and the United Nations in World Politics: A Plea for Comparative Research on Universal International Organizations," *International Studies Quarterly*, 15 (December 1971), p. 387. A few works at the time explored the relationship between international organizations and international systems, such as Oran R. Young, "The United Nations and the International System," *International Organization*, 22 (Autumn 1968), pp. 902–922; Stanley Hoffmann, "International Organization and the International System," *International Organization*, 24 (Summer 1970), pp. 389–413; and Ernst B. Haas, *Collective Security and the International System* (Denver, Colo.: University of Denver, 1968). An important work which attempted to examine how changes in the international system (relating to power stratification, alignment patterns, and economic and political character-

istics of states) impacted on the operation of specific UN specialized agencies was Robert W. Cox and Harold K. Jacobson, *The Anatomy of Influence: Decision Making in International Organization* (New Haven, Conn.: Yale University Press, 1973).

94. American Assembly, Final Report, "U.S. Interests in the 1990s" (New York: Columbia University, 1989), p. 5.

95. The Stockholm International Peace Research Institute documented a significant decline in the number and size of wars fought after 1987. See *SIPRI Yearbook of World Armaments and Disarmament, 1989* (New York: Oxford University Press, 1989). SIPRI includes not only interstate but also internal wars (with at least 1,000 deaths) in its inventory of wars. See also William Eckhardt, "Wars Started in the 1980s," St. Louis Lentz Peace Research Laboratory (1990).

96. Young, "The United Nations and the International System," *op. cit.*, p. 903.

Chapter 3: The Contemporary International System

1. Dennis Pirages, *Global Technopolitics* (Pacific Grove, Calif.: Brooks/ Cole, 1989), p. 202. Also representative of this view is Harry Clay Blaney III, *Global Challenges: A World At Risk* (New York: Franklin Watts, 1979).

2. Stanley Hoffmann, *Primacy or World Order* (New York: McGraw-Hill, 1978), p. 193.

3. Crisis is typically defined in the international relations literature as "a situation deriving from change in a state's internal or external environment which gives rise to decision makers' perceptions of *threat to basic values, finite time for response,* and the *likelihood of involvement in military hostilities.*" Michael Brecher and Jonathan Wilkenfeld, "Crisis in World Politics," *World Politics,* 34 (April 1982), p. 383. As employed here, the term refers to a disturbance in a state's environment that is of a magnitude as to heighten perceptions of threat to basic values, although it need not entail finite response time or the likelihood of military hostilities.

4. Michael J. Brenner, "The Problem of Innovation and the Nixon-Kissinger Foreign Policy," *International Studies Quarterly,* 17 (September 1973), pp. 267–268. An early discussion of the role of images in structuring reality, and of their resistance to change, is Kenneth Boulding's *The Image* (Ann Arbor, Mich.: University of Michigan Press, 1956).

5. Richard Falk and his associates speak of the "Grotian moment" as a "time of transition between world order systems," akin to the time

of Hugo Grotius and the creation of the Westphalian state system in the seventeenth century. See Richard Falk, Friedrich Kratochwil, and Saul H. Mendlovitz, eds., *International Law: A Contemporary Perspective* (Boulder, Colo.: Westview Press, 1985), p. 7.

6. John H. Herz, *International Politics in the Atomic Age* (New York: Columbia University Press, 1959), p. 304. Donella H. Meadows, *et al.*, *The Limits to Growth* (New York: Universe Books, 1972), pp. 9–10. Two more recent reports of the Club of Rome are Meadows, *et al.*, *Beyond the Limits* (Post Mills, Vt.: Chelsea Green, 1992); and Alexander King and Bertrand Schneider, *The First Global Revolution* (New York: Pantheon, 1991).

7. *The Global 2000 Report to the President* (Washington, D.C.: U.S. Government Printing Office, 1980), p. 1.

8. Brandt Commission, *North-South: A Programme for Survival* (Cambridge, Mass.: MIT Press, 1980), p. 30.

9. Brundtland Commission, *Our Common Future* (Oxford, Eng.: Oxford University Press, 1987). The report was presented to the UN General Assembly in October 1987.

10. Julian L. Simon, "Life on Earth Is Getting Better, Not Worse," *The Futurist* (August 1983), p. 7. Also see *The Ultimate Resource* (Princeton, N.J.: Princeton University Press, 1981).

11. Herman Kahn, William Brown, and Leon Martel, *The Next 200 Years* (New York: Morrow, 1976), p. 1. Also see Herman Kahn and Ernest Schneider, "Globaloney 2000," *Policy Review*, 16 (Spring 1981), pp. 129–147; and Simon and Kahn, eds., *The Resourceful Earth* (Oxford, Eng.: Basil Blackwell, 1984).

12. Pirages, *op. cit.*, p. 28. In the U.S. there has been a decline in "happiness" among the general public over the course of the post-World War II era and an increasing tendency for individuals to view the nation and its institutions as in a state of deterioration even if they are hopeful about their personal lives. See Angus Campbell, Philip E. Converse, and Willard L. Rogers, *The Quality of American Life* (New York: Russell Sage Foundation, 1976), pp. 26–30 and 269–275; Campbell, *The Sense of Well-Being in America* (New York: McGraw-Hill, 1981), pp. 164–174; and *Gallup Report*, no. 266 (November 1987), p. 25. Although comparative data are hard to find, similar trends in public mood can be discerned in other nations. See *Index to International Public Opinion*. Ronald Inglehart, examining Euro-Barometer surveys since 1973, found relatively stable public attitudes in regard to personal life satisfaction in nine European Community countries, although in only one— Denmark—did a majority of the population indicate they were "very satisfied." Ronald Inglehart, "The Renaissance of Political Culture," *American Political Science Review*, 82 (December 1988), pp. 1205–1206.

13. Kenneth Boulding has explained how national images deeply rooted in historical experience, however durable, persist intact only as long as they are not jarred by strong stimuli—"reorganizing events"—which call them into question. See "National Images and International Systems," *Journal of Conflict Resolution*, 3 (June 1959), pp. 120–131.

14. J. Martin Rochester, "The Contemporary International System: Is There a Growing Crisis?," Center for International Studies Occasional Paper Series, University of Missouri-St. Louis, 1992.

15. Mark W. Zacher, "The Decaying Pillars of the Westphalian Temple: Implications for International Order and Governance," paper delivered at the annual meeting of the International Studies Association, Vancouver, March 22, 1991, speaks of the erosion of six pillars of the Westphalian system (including state autonomy, the rationality of war, and other conditions) and argues much like this author that states will not disappear but will have to adjust to new circumstances.

16. See World Bank, *World Development Report, 1989* (New York: Oxford University Press, 1989), pp. 20–21; UN Department of International Economic and Social Affairs, *World Economic Survey, 1987* (New York: UN, 1987), p. 8; and International Monetary Fund, *World Economic Outlook* (Washington, D.C.: IMF, 1991). A somewhat more upbeat projection can be found in Shahrokh Fardorst and Ashok Dhareshwar, *A Long-Term Outlook for the World Economy: Issues and Projections for the 1990s* (Washington, D.C.: World Bank, 1990).

17. Blaney, *op. cit.*, p. viii.

18. See. for example, Richard Falk, "The Global Promise of Social Movements: Explorations At the Edge of Time," *Alternatives*, 12 (1987), pp. 173–196.

19. Oran R. Young, "Regime Dynamics: The Rise and Fall of International Regimes," *International Organization*, 36 (Spring 1982), p. 283. Although Young is concerned with the creation and transformation of regimes covering specific activities, such as fishing or mining, his classification scheme can be applied as well to the manner in which more general institutional arrangements evolve. Young discusses the three modes of regime creation and transformation on pp. 282–285.

20. Charles P. Kindleberger, "Hierarchy versus Inertial Cooperation," *International Organization*, 40 (Autumn 1986), p. 841. Kindleberger's major work on the role of hegemony in forging order in international economic relations is *The World in Depression, 1929–1939* (Berkeley, Calif.: University of California Press, 1973). Young, *op. cit.*, p. 284, also acknowledges that "overt hegemony," which he defines as raw coercion, has become a less prevalent form of imposed order than "de facto imposition," which involves a more subtle and complicated exercise of power. Joseph S. Nye, in *Bound to Lead: The Changing Nature*

of American Power (New York: Basic Books, 1990), speaks of "soft" or "co-optive" power, while G. John Ikenberry and Charles A. Kupchan, in "Socialization and Hegemonic Power," *International Organization*, 44 (Summer 1990), p. 284, speak of "the projection by the hegemon of a set of norms and their embrace by leaders in other nations." For critiques of the theory of hegemonic stability, see the works cited in n. 54 in chap. 1.

21. Leonard Kohr, *The Breakdown of Nations* (Swansea: Christopher Davies, 1957), p. 54. This is the opposite of the theory of hegemonic stability, which states that "power inequality [preponderance] leads to stability and power inequality leads to conflict." See Jacek Kugler and A.F.K. Organski, "The End of Hegemony?", *International Interactions*, 15, no. 2 (1989), p. 126. It is also in opposition to the notion advanced by Karl Deutsch and his associates, in the context of nation-building, that the formation of a security-community benefits from the presence of key actors with sufficient resources to carry an expanding "demand load." See n. 58–60 in chap. 2.

22. Robert Gilpin, *War and Change in World Politics* (New York: Cambridge University Press, 1981), p. 29.

23. Thomas A. Bailey, "America's Emergence as a World Power: The Myth and the Verity," *Pacific Historical Review*, 30 (February 1961), p. 15. Bailey (pp. 1–2) argues that, if one defines a "world power" as "a nation with sufficient power in being, or capable of being mobilized, to affect world politics positively and over a period of time," then the U.S. was such a power at birth, as of 1776.

24. Kindleberger, "Hierarchy versus Inertial Cooperation," *op. cit.*, p. 841.

25. C. Fred Bergsten, "Interdependence and the Reform of International Institutions," *International Organization*, 30 (Spring 1976), p. 364.

26. A fundamental assumption of Robert Keohane's *After Hegemony: Cooperation and Discord in the World Political Economy* (Princeton, N.J.: Princeton University Press, 1984) is that it is highly unlikely any single state will emerge in the foreseeable future as a hegemon. See p. 244.

27. William D. Coplin and Michael K. O'Leary, in *Everyman's Prince* (North Scituate, Mass: Duxbury Press, 1972), discuss the interaction of such variables as actor issue-positions, salience, and power in shaping outcomes among any group of political actors.

28. For general conceptual treatments of power, see Peter Bacharach and Morton Baratz, "The Two Faces of Power," *American Political Science Review*, 56 (December 1962), pp. 947–952; and Kenneth Boulding, *The Three Faces of Power* (Beverly Hills, Calif.: Sage, 1989). For attempts at measuring trends in the distribution of power capabilities in the international system, see J. David Singer, Stuart Bremer, and John

Stuckey, "Capability Distribution, Uncertainty, and Major Power War," in Bruce Russett, ed., *Peace, War and Numbers* (Beverly Hills, Calif.: Sage 1972), pp. 19–48; John Stuckey and J. David Singer, "The Powerful and the War Prone: Ranking the Nations by Relative Capability and War Experience, 1820–1964," paper presented at Conference on Social Power, Mexico City, 1973; Charles F. Doran and Wes Parsons, "War and the Cycle of Relative Power," *American Political Science Review*, 74 (December 1980), pp. 947–965; and Ray Cline, *World Power Assessment* (Boulder, Colo.: Westview, 1975).

29. On the decline of the United States, see for example Paul Kennedy, *The Rise and Fall of the Great Powers* (New York: Random House, 1987); Kenneth A. Oye, "International Systems Structure and American Foreign Policy," in Oye, Robert J. Lieber and Donald Rothchild, eds., *Eagle Defiant: United States Foreign Policy in the 1980s* (Boston: Little, Brown, 1983); Charles Maynes and Richard Ullman, "Ten Years of Foreign Policy," *Foreign Policy*, 40 (Fall 1980), pp. 3–17; and Richard Rosecrance, ed., *America as an Ordinary Country* (Ithaca, N.Y.: Cornell University Press, 1976). On the decline of the Soviet Union, see also Kennedy, *op. cit.*; Valerie Bunce, "The Empire Strikes Back: The Evolution of Eastern Europe from a Soviet Asset to a Soviet Liability," *International Organization*, 39 (Winter 1985), pp. 3–42; Robert G. Kaiser, "The USSR in Decline," *Foreign Affairs*, 67 (Winter 1988/89), pp. 97–113; and the series of articles on "Soviet Backsliding" in *Foreign Policy*, 82 (Spring 1991), pp. 97–158.

30. On the emergence of five power centers, see Henry A. Kissinger, *American Foreign Policy*, 3rd ed. (New York: W. W. Norton, 1977), p. 416. In Kennedy, *op. cit.*, chap. 8, the author speculates about the U.S., USSR, the EEC, China and Japan assuming leadership roles in the next century.

31. On the matter of fungibility and how it complicates power assessment in international relations, see David A. Baldwin, "Power Analysis and World Politics: New Trends Versus Old Tendencies," *World Politics*, 31 (January 1979), pp. 161–194; Baldwin, *Paradoxes of Power* (New York: Basil Blackwell, 1989), especially chap. 2; and Robert O. Keohane, "Theory of World Politics: Structural Realism and Beyond," in Ada W. Finifter, ed., *Political Science: The State of the Discipline* (Washington, D.C.: American Political Science Association, 1983), pp. 522–526.

32. The U.S. reference is from David P. Calleo, *Beyond American Hegemony* (New York: Basic Books, 1987), p. 220. The Soviet reference is from Kaiser, *op. cit.*, p. 97.

33. These correspond roughly to the "three faces of power" —

"threat power," "economic power," and "integrative power" — discussed in Boulding, *op. cit.*

34. Klaus Knorr, *On the Uses of Military Power in the Nuclear Age* (Princeton, N.J.: Princeton University Press, 1966), presents a cogent analysis of the changed environment in which military power functions in the atomic era. In this work and even more so in "Is International Coercion Waning or Rising?," *International Security*, 1 (Spring 1977), pp. 92–110, as well as *Power and Wealth: The Political Economy of International Power* (New York: Basic Books, 1973), he still sees a role for military power. One of the few analysts who argues nuclear weapons have little or no effect on risk-taking and war is A.F.K. Organski. See his *World Politics* (New York: Knopf, 1968), esp. chaps. 12–14; and Organski and Jacek Kugler, *The War Ledger* (Chicago, Ill.: University of Chicago Press, 1980). John Mueller, in "The Essential Irrelevance of Nuclear Weapons," *International Security*, 13 (Fall 1988), argues that the destructive nature of conventional weapons has grown to the point that warfare among major powers would be unlikely even in the absence of nuclear weapons. For a counterpoint to this, see Robert Jervis's article in the same volume, stressing "The Political Effects of Nuclear Weapons." On war avoidance, see the works cited in n. 26 and 61–63 in chap. 2.

35. Jonathan Schell, *The Fate of the Earth* (New York: Knopf, 1982).

36. Some states, such as Israel and South Africa, are already considered at least unofficial members of the club, or capable of joining whenever they choose to demonstrate their capacity to explode a nuclear bomb. On the problem of nuclear proliferation, see Leonard S. Spector, *Nuclear Proliferation Today* (New York: Random House, 1984); and Spector, "Proliferation: The Silent Spread," *Foreign Policy*, 58 (Spring 1985), pp. 53–78.

37. Ruth L. Sivard, *World Military and Social Expenditures, 1987–88* (Washington, D.C.: World Priorities, 1987), pp. 9 and 16. As the Soviet Union was giving way to the Commonwealth in December 1991, it was still in possession of nearly 30,000 nuclear weapons. Les Aspin, "The Bush Foreign Policy: Winning the War But Losing the Peace," White Paper, December 19, 1991, p. 2.

38. U.S. Arms Control and Disarmament Agency, *World Military Expenditures and Arms Transfers 1988* (Washington, D.C.: USACDA, 1989), table 1; and *World Military Expenditures and Arms Transfers 1989* (Washington, D.C.: USACDA, 1990), fig. 3 and pp. 3–4.

39. *Ibid.; World Military Expenditures and Arms Transfers 1988, op. cit.*, table 1. One can only speculate about how the current political and economic turmoil in the commonwealth will impact upon its future military standing, but it seems reasonable to assume that even a Soviet state reduced to and coterminous with the Russian Federation will sup-

port a sizable defense establishment positioned toward the top of national rankings.

40. *World Military Expenditures and Arms Transfers 1989, op. cit.* The 1,000,000 man armies of Vietnam and Iraq have undergone some changes related to conflicts the two countries have been engaged in recently.

41. Bruce M. Russett, "The Mysterious Case of Vanishing Hegemony; Or Is Mark Twain Really Dead?" *International Organization*, 39 (Spring 1985), p. 211.

42. Kennedy, *op. cit.*, p. 436; and Oye, *op. cit.*, p. 8. I am using data here that are based on CIA analyses, although Oye notes that the U.S. decline appears less severe if one accepts other estimates such as those found in the Council on International Economics Policy series.

43. On the "Phoenix factor" and the tendency for "great power" losers of systemic wars to revive themselves over time relative to the victors, see A.F.K. Organski and Jacek Kugler, "The Costs of Major War: The Phoenix Factor," *American Political Science Review*, 71 (December 1977), pp. 1347–1366; and Kugler and Marina Arbetman, "Exploring the 'Phoenix Factor' with the Collective Goods Perspective," *Journal of Conflict Resolution*, 33 (March 1989), pp. 84–112.

44. On the three deficits, see Pirages, *op. cit.*, pp. 204–209; and Earl Fry, *et al.*, *America the Vincible* (forthcoming).

45. Russett, *op. cit.*, p. 211. Another who strongly questions the validity of "declinist" theories as applied to the U.S. is Samuel Huntington, as seen in "The U.S. —Decline or Renewal?", *Foreign Affairs*, 67 (Winter 1988/89), pp. 76–96. Also see Nye, *op. cit.*; Susan Strange, "Toward a Theory of Transnational Empire," in Ernst-Otto Czempiel and James N. Rosenau, eds., *Global Changes and Theoretical Challenges* (Lexington, Mass.: Lexington Books, 1989), pp. 161–176; and Henry R. Nau, *The Myth of America's Decline: Leading the World Economy into the 1990s* (New York: Oxford University Press, 1990).

46. U.S. Central Intelligence Agency, *Handbook of Economic Statistics 1989* (Washington, D.C.: CIA, 1989), p. 12.

47. In the early 1990s, the U.S. still accounted for half of all grain sales on the world market, remained the leader in high technology exports, and with Japan accounted for half of all sales of such products in the areas of computers, telecommunications, aerospace, and machine tools. As for lost American control over world financial reserves, the U.S. dollar remained a preferred currency, accounting for some three-quarters of the reserves held by central banks globally. *Ibid.*, p. 18, and Pirages, *op. cit.*, pp. 89–94.

48. C. Fred Bergsten, *America in the World Economy: A Strategy for the*

1990s (Washington, D.C.: Institute for International Economics, 1988), p. 65.

49. GNP data are found in *Handbook of Economic Statistics 1989, op. cit.*, p. 12; also see *World Bank Atlas 1989* (Washington, D.C.: World Bank, 1989), pp. 6–9; and U.S. Central Intelligence Agency, *Handbook of Economic Statistics 1990* (Washington, D.C.: CIA, 1990), p. 15.

50. Dimitri Simes, "Russia Reborn," *Foreign Policy*, 85 (Winter 1991–1992), p. 42. See also *The Republics of the Former Soviet Union* (Washington, D.C.: CIA, 1992), p. 1.

51. Karl W. Deutsch, *The Analysis of International Relations* (Englewood Cliffs, N.J.: Prentice-Hall, 1968), pp. 17–19. Deutsch acknowledges the importance of coercion—the "credible probability of enforcement"—as a foundation for social order but suggests that habits of compliance ultimately stem from more than the fear of retaliation. Others as well have argued that the most stable societies rely less on coercion than on other bases of compliance in maintaining order. A particularly strong case for this view is presented by Oran Young in *Compliance and Public Authority: A Theory with International Applications* (Baltimore, Md.: Johns Hopkins University Press, 1979).

52. The classic realist position is that morality has no place in international society, since the latter is marked by moral relativism rather than any single moral compass, and that any states basing foreign policy decisions on moral considerations may be guilty of either naive sentimentalism or reckless messianism. However, this caveat overlooks the reality of an ethical dimension to international politics. See Dorothy V. Jones, *Code of Peace: Ethics and Security in the World of the Warlord States* (Chicago, Ill.: University of Chicago Press, 1991); Stanley Hoffmann, *Duties Beyond Borders: On the Limits and Possibilities of Ethical International Politics* (Syracuse, N.Y.: Syracuse University Press, 1981); and Thomas Franck, *The Power of Legitimacy Among Nations* (New York: Oxford University Press, 1990).

53. Robert North, in *War, Peace, Survival* (Boulder, Colo.: Westview Press, 1990), p. 218, notes that "of 114 countries categorized in the . . . 1980s as developing, 56 . . . were under military control." A 1985 study found only 53 countries that could be called free, compared with 59 that were partly free and 55 labeled not free, and noted that "since the first survey [of freedom] published in . . . 1973, . . . worldwide the percentage of people living in freedom or the percentage of free nations has not changed noticeably." Raymond G. Gastil, *Freedom in the World: Political Rights and Civil Liberties* (Westport, Conn.: Greenwood Press, 1985), pp. 11 and 25. However, according to a subsequent survey, the events of the late 1980s and early 1990s have set in motion a process whereby free nations are soon likely to outnumber not free nations. See *Comparative*

Survey of Freedom (New York: Freedom House, 1990). Also see Lucian W. Pye, "Political Science and the Crisis of Authoritarianism," *American Political Science Review*, 84 (March 1990), pp. 3–20.

54. The point here is simply that virtually all states at the very least outwardly associate themselves with the norm of democracy, granted a large number of states in actual practice are non-democratic while those that conform in some fashion to the democratic model differ in their adherence to liberal and non-liberal interpretations. For differing interpretations of human rights among various cultures and political systems, see Rhoda E. Howard and Jack Donnelly, "Human Dignity, Human Rights, and Political Regimes," *American Political Science Review*, 80 (September 1986), pp. 801–817. Although I previously noted that the weak compatibility of political values held by the members of the international system is a problem which complicates efforts to build a security-community at the global level, there may be more commonality than one might think. At least one prominent scholar has observed that "there is a much broader consensus than there ever has been on the normative goals of international public policy and on the characteristics of a desirable world order. This consensus extends to goals with respect to the status of individuals and includes agreement on the essential elements of human dignity and justice." Harold K. Jacobson, "The Global System and the Realization of Human Dignity and Justice," *International Studies Quarterly*, 26 (September 1982), p. 320. On the trend toward democratization, see Larry Diamond, Juan Linz, and Seymour Martin Lipset, *Democracy in Developing Countries*, vol. 1 (Boulder, Colo.: Lynne Reiner, 1989), pp. ix and x.

55. Murray Edelman, "Political Language and Political Reality," *PS* 18 (Winter 1985), p. 10, based on a paper presented as a part of the Lasswell Symposium lectures at the annual meeting of the American Political Science Association, Washington, D.C., 1984.

56. Thirty-four of these states are identified in World Bank, *World Development Report 1988* (Washington, D.C.: World Bank, 1988), p. 289. Four others recently admitted to the UN are Micronesia, Pacific Islands, Liechtenstein, and San Marino.

57. A classic analysis of the problems encountered in attempting to institute majoritarianism in international organizations is offered by Inis L. Claude in *Swords Into Plowshares*, 4th ed. (New York: Random House, 1984), pp. 120–140.

58. A discussion of population trends globally and regionally can be found in Brundtland Commission, *op. cit.*, pp. 98–103.

59. Pirages, *op. cit.*, p. 37.

60. World Resources Institute and International Institute for Environment and Development, *World Resources 1986* (New York: Basic

Books, 1986), p. 11. Also see *Handbook of Economic Statistics 1990, op. cit.*, p. 15; and *World Bank Atlas 1989, op. cit.*

61. Brundtland Commission, *op. cit.*, p. 101.

62. Based on data in Charles L. Taylor and David Jodice, *World Handbook of Political and Social Indicators*, 3rd ed. (New Haven, Conn.: Yale University Press, 1983), p. 91; and *Handbook of Economic Statistics 1989, op. cit.*, p. 12.

63. Simes, *op. cit.*, p. 60, notes that "Russia—with 150 million people, a well-educated labor force, and a great culture—[can still claim] a major part in world affairs." Likewise, see Edward Luttwak, "The Shape of Things to Come," *Commentary*, 89 (June 1990), p. 24. In the late 1980s, the *Atlas of the Soviet Union* (Washington, D.C.: U.S. Department of State, 1987), p. 2, reported statistics on "the Soviet Union as a world power" and listed the USSR as occupying the top rank in six out of eight categories. On most of the indicators used, the Russian Federation would still rank high.

64. On the current milieu of the UN, particularly the potential for conciliation among countries across different blocs and for an enhanced role for mid-sized and large powers other than the former superpowers, see Donald J. Puchala and Roger A. Coate, *The Challenge of Relevance: The United Nations in a Changing World Environment* (Hanover, N.H.: Academic Council on the United Nations System, 1989), especially pp. 2–8 and chap. 3; Richard A. Higgott and Andrew Fenton Cooper, "Middle Power Leadership and Coalition Building: Australia, The Cairns Group, and the Uruguay Round of Trade Negotiations," *International Organization*, 44 (Autumn 1990), pp. 589–632; and Higgott and Cooper, "Middle Power Leadership in the International Order: Towards a Reformulated Theory for the 1990s," paper delivered at the annual meeting of the International Studies Association, Vancouver, March 22, 1991.

65. Karl W. Deutsch, "A Path Among the Social Sciences," in Joseph Kruzel and James N. Rosenau, eds., *Journeys Through World Politics* (Lexington, Mass.: Lexington Books, 1989), pp. 22–23. The GLOBUS project is discussed at length in Stuart A. Bremer, ed., *The GLOBUS Model* (Boulder, Colo.: Westview, 1987). The original GLOBUS model included East Germany as a separate state, prior to the merger of the two Germanys. North, *op. cit.*, provides another grouping of states (having "alpha"-"zeta" profiles) based on population growth, access to resources, and technological development. While not based on power considerations per se, this classification scheme might suggest other coalition-building possibilities.

66. Bergsten, "Interdependence and the Reform of International Institutions" *op. cit.*, p. 364.

67. Robert W. Cox and Harold K. Jacobson, *The Anatomy of Influence: Decision Making in International Organization* (New Haven, Conn.: Yale University Press, 1973), p. 435.

68. *Ibid.*

69. *Ibid.*, p. 436.

70. Keohane, *After Hegemony, op. cit.*, and William H. Riker, *The Theory of Political Coalitions* (New Haven, Conn.: Yale University Press, 1962).

71. The term is borrowed from Donald J. Puchala and Roger A. Coate, *The State of the United Nations, 1988* (Hanover, N.H.: Academic Council on the United Nations System, 1988), p. 46.

72. Hart, *op. cit.*, p. 293. Hart's observation is based on the work of John Harsanyi, "The Measurement of Social Power, Opportunity Costs, and the Theory of Two-Person Bargaining Games," *Behavioral Science*, 7 (January 1962), pp. 67–80. Although Harsanyi deals here with two-person games, much of his analysis can be applied to n-person games involving multiple players, such as UN reform and multilateral institution-building.

73. Keohane, "Theory of World Politics, *op. cit.*, p. 517.

74. For a discussion of the relative merits of viewing states from inside-out as opposed to outside-in perspectives, see Kenneth N. Waltz, *Theory of International Politics* (Reading, Mass.: Addison-Wesley, 1979), especially chap. 4; and Michael Mastanduno, David A. Lake, and G. John Ikenberry, "Toward A Realistic Theory of State Action," *International Studies Quarterly*, 33 (December 1989), pp. 457–474. On "domestic-international entanglements" and "the inevitability of domestic conflict about what the 'national interest' requires," see Robert D. Putnam, "Diplomacy and Domestic Politics: The Logic of Two-Level Games," *International Organization*, 42 (Summer 1988), p. 432.

75. Cox and Jacobson, *op. cit.*, p. 19, challenge the rational actor model in noting the role of "country subsystems" in "defining the national interests concerning the international organization and in placing demands upon the national political system for resources to influence decisions in the international organization." See also Jacobson, *Networks of Interdependence*, 2nd ed. (New York: Knopf, 1984), chap. 6. Country subsystems are more likely to form around functionally specific IGOs than multipurpose ones like the UN, and are more likely to be operative when discrete, narrow concerns are at stake than when larger governance matters are at issue.

76. Cited in Susan Strange, "Protectionism and World Politics," in *International Organization*, 39 (Spring 1985), p. 256. Nye, *op. cit.*, makes a similar argument.

77. The U.S., USSR, and Great Britain were particularly insistent on the veto privilege. Inis Claude, *op. cit.*, p. 62, in his discussion of the origins of the UN system, characterized France and China as belonging in the second rank of powers.

78. *Ibid.*, p. 62.

79. *Ibid.*, pp. 63–64.

80. *Ibid.*, p. 62.

81. For discussions of the declining role of the United Nations in U.S. foreign policy, see Chadwick F. Alger, "The United States in the United Nations," *International Organization*, 27 (Winter 1973), pp. 1–23; H. W. Barber, "The United States vs. The United Nations," *International Organization*, 27 (Spring 1973), pp. 139–163; Lawrence S. Finkelstein, ed., "The United States and International Organization: The Changing Setting," *International Organization*, 23 (Summer 1969); and Seymour Maxwell Finger, "United States Policy Toward International Institutions," *International Organization*, 30 (Spring 1976), pp. 347–360.

82. General Assembly voting statistics (excluding decisions taken by consensus) are reported in Robert E. Riggs and Jack C. Plano, *The United Nations: International Organization and World Politics* (Chicago, Ill.: Dorsey Press, 1988), pp. 85–86. The "Zionism is racism" language was contained in Resolution 3379 passed by the General Assembly in 1975. In 1974 the General Assembly adopted Resolution 3201 and Resolution 3281, a "Declaration on the Establishment of a New International Economic Order" and a "Charter of Economic Rights and Duties of States." The "tyranny of the majority" phrase was uttered by John Scali in a speech he gave as U.S. Ambassador to the UN in 1974, as reported in *The New York Times*, December 7, 1964, p. 1. Scali's successor, Daniel Moynihan, was the author of *A Dangerous Place* (New York: Berkley Books, 1980).

83. These remarks were contained in a speech given by President Jimmy Carter at Notre Dame University's commencement exercises on May 22, 1977; found in *U.S. Department of State Bulletin*, 76 (June 13, 1977), p. 622.

84. Charles W. Maynes, "The U.S. Approach to the United Nations: New Directions," address before the United Nations Association of Chicago on July 13, 1977, *U.S. Department of State Bulletin*, 77 (August 29, 1977), pp. 285–286.

85. The fate of the Baker-McGovern exercise, as well as the general evolution of American attitudes toward UN reform in the postwar era, is discussed in Frederic S. Pearson and J. Martin Rochester, "The Carter Foreign Policy and the Use of International Organization: The Limits of Policy Innovation," *World Affairs*, 142 (Fall 1979), pp. 75–97.

86. Riggs and Plano, *op. cit.*, p. 86.

87. The remarks of Charles Lichtenstein were reported in *New York Times*, September 20, 1983.

88. See "The United Nations As a Political System: A Practicing Political Scientist's Insights Into U.N. Politics," *World Affairs*, 146 (Spring 1984), pp. 358–359; and "The U.N. Versus the U.S.," interviews in *New York Times Magazine* (January 22, 1984), p. 18.

89. "The U.N. Versus the U.S.," *op. cit.*, p. 68.

90. Jeanne Kirkpatrick's statement before the Subcommittee on Foreign Operations of the Senate Appropriations Committee on March 2, 1984, *U.S. Department of State Bulletin*, 84 (April 1984), pp. 68–70.

91. U.S. Department of State, *Report to Congress on Voting Practices in the United Nations During 1985* (1986).

92. *Official Records of the General Assembly, Forty-second Session*, Supplement No. 49 (A/42/49). The fact that the majority of resolutions passed by the General Assembly were approved by consensus admittedly skewed the record of U.S. success in siding with the majority. The degree of American isolation from the majority over the years, however, has been distorted by the fact that a high percentage of votes have tended to be on a handful of issues relating to South African apartheid or the Middle East. Even so, in the words of the U.S. Ambassador to the UN, "the increased cooperation, reduced rhetoric, and behind-the-scenes help which characterized the 42nd General Assembly are difficult to capture in statistics." Vernon A. Walters, comments before the House Foreign Affairs Committee on February 25, 1988, published as "US Interests in the United Nations," U.S. Department of State, Bureau of Public Affairs, Current Policy No. 1053, p. 2. A statistical analysis that finds little linkage between the allocation of U.S. foreign aid and recipient voting behavior in the UN General Assembly is provided by Charles W. Kegley and Steven W. Hook in "U.S. Foreign Aid and U.N. Voting: Did Reagan's Linkage Strategy Buy Deference or Defiance?" *International Studies Quarterly*, 35 (September 1991), pp. 295–312.

93. Dennis C. Goodman, Acting Assistant Secretary of State for International Organization Affairs, "US Assessments for the United Nations," *U.S. Department of State Bulletin*, 88 (October 1988), p. 70. Goodman noted that the General Assembly "after making some adjustments to the recommendations, adopted significant reforms through UN General Assembly Resolution 41/213." The Report of the Group of High-Level Intergovernmental Experts to Review the Efficiency of the Administrative and Financial Functioning of the UN was contained in UN Doc. A/41/49 (1986).

94. These conditions are discussed in Goodman, *op. cit.*, p. 71. The Kassebaum-Solomon Amendment was modified to include this threefold presidential certification process.

95. Walters, *op. cit.*, p. 3.

96. Speech before the UN General Assembly on September 16, 1988. *U.S. Department of State Bulletin*, 88 (November 1988), p. 1

97. Margaret E. Galey, "The Changing International Regime for Financing International Organization: Regime Change vs. Reform," paper delivered at the annual meeting of the International Studies Association, St. Louis, March 29, 1988, p. 24; a variation of this paper appears in *Howard Law Review*, 31, No. 4 (1988), pp. 557–574. The budget figures cited here are taken from Galey. See also Annual Report, *United States Contributions to International Organizations*, published by the U.S. Department of State, for the years discussed.

98. Goodman, *op. cit.*, p. 71. Earlier, in April of 1988, Assistant Secretary Richard S. Williamson when testifying before the House Foreign Affairs Committee had outlined "a disciplined set of criteria [that had been established] for use in assigning funding priorities" to 46 different IGOs funded by the U.S. These criteria included such "rational" desiderata as "the level of direct benefit or substantive importance of the agency's work to the United States," "the extent to which the agency has achieved program budget reform or an effective budget process," and "the possible negative impact on U.S. interests and on the organization, should there be shortages in U.S. funding." Williamson confessed that, despite "my generally favorable attitude toward the UN's technical agencies and my concern that they may be damaged by the shortfall in overall appropriations," the Gramm-Rudman ceilings dictated that overall FY 1989 requests would be no more than 2% over the FY 1988 levels. *U.S. Department of State Bulletin*, 88 (April 1988), pp. 84–85.

99. Witness, for example, President Bush's address before the 44th session of the UN General Assembly on September 25, 1989, when he opened his remarks by alluding to his earlier experience as UN Ambassador: "This is a homecoming for Barbara and me. The memories of my time here in 1971 and 1972 are still with me today." Bush added, "[The UN] is a vital forum where the nations of the world seek to replace conflict with consensus, and it must remain a forum for peace. The United Nations is moving closer to that ideal. And it has the support of the United States of America. In recent years—certainly since my time here—the war of words that has often echoed in this chamber is giving way to a new mood." He concluded by recalling "beyond the frantic pace and sometimes frustrating experiences of daily life here . . . the quiet conviction that we could make the world more peaceful, more free." "Outlines of A New World of Freedom," U.S. Department of State, Bureau of Public Affairs, Current Policy No. 1207. While the president's remarks could well be interpreted as both a ritualized obser-

vance of diplomatic niceties at the UN and a not-so-subtle jab at communist regimes reeling under the pressure of democratic reform movements, one might also read between the lines the socialization effects Bush's UN experience had in leaving him with a sympathetic orientation toward the organization.

100. Congressional views of the UN are discussed by Robert W. Gregg in an insightful essay on "The Politics of Financing the UN," presented at the Annual Meeting of the International Studies Association, St. Louis, March 29, 1988, pp. 26–37.

101. Testifying before the Senate Foreign Relations Committee on February 1, 1990, Baker had noted that "the President has emphasized the urgency of restoring financial viability to the United Nations" and called for "a carefully structured [phased in] arrears initiative" as "essential to maintaining U.S. leadership in . . . multilateral organizations." U.S. Department of State, Bureau of Public Affairs, Current Policy No. 1245, pp. 8 and 10. Secretary of State Baker characterized the UN funding request as one of four funding initiatives "intergral to our ability to protect American values and interests into the next decade." See *The Interdependent*, 16 (Spring 1990), p.4.

102. Decreasing UN salience in American governmental and media circles can be traced to the 1970s, as measured by the media attention the UN warranted. By 1976, the number of full-time correspondents representing U.S. news organizations at the UN had fallen to an all-time low, with the *New York Times* being the only major U.S. daily paper maintaining a year-round UN reporter. Associated Press and United Press International had reduced their UN staff to three reporters compared to double that ten years earlier. *The Interdependent*, 5 (November 1978), p. 7. In contrast, Third World news coverage has increased over time. The relationship between the UN and news media is also discussed in *The Interdependent*, 5 (Fall 1989), p. 3.

103. Thomas Hughes, "The Twilight of Internationalism," *Foreign Policy*, 61 (Winter 1985–1986), p. 26.

104. The 1989 poll results are summarized in Jeffrey Laurenti, "The U.N. at a Watershed in U.S. Opinion," mimeo published by the United Nations Association-USA, May 1989. The 1991 data are in *The Emerging World Order*, Americans Talk Issues, No. 16 (Washington, D.C.: Americans Talk Issues Foundation, August 1991). Also see a 1992 poll reported in *The Interdependent*, 18 (Summer 1992), showing only 35% of the American public viewing the UN unfavorably.

105. William Watts and Lloyd A. Free, "Nationalism, Not Isolationism," *Foreign Policy*, 24 (Fall 1976), pp. 16–18. Also see n. 90 in chap. 2. On the role of public opinion and domestic politics in shaping U.S. attitudes toward the UN, see Margaret P. Karns and Karen A. Mingst,

eds., *The United States and Multilateral Institutions* (Boston: Unwin Hyman, 1990).

106. As of 1990, according to *The Defense Monitor*, 19 (1990) published by the Center for Defense Information, the B-2 Stealth bomber was priced at almost $870 million per plane.

107. See Williamson, *op. cit.*, and *The Interdependent* 16, no. 2 (1990), p. 2.

108. Data can be found in U.S. Department of State, *U.S. Contributions to International Organizations*, Report to Congress for FY 1988, and subsequent reports.

109. See Mancur Olson, *The Logic of Collective Action* (Cambridge, Mass.: Harvard University Press, 1965); and Bruce M. Russett and John D. Sullivan, "Collective Goods and International Organization," *International Organization*, 25 (Autumn 1971), pp. 845–865.

110. The U.S. has the most extensive network of overseas diplomatic and trade missions, is home to the most MNCs, is the top host country for foreign investment, is the biggest foreign aid donor, is first in international tourism receipts and passenger-miles flown internationally by scheduled airlines, has the most troops stationed abroad, and leads in numerous other indicators of systemic involvement. For indicators of systemic involvement, see *Atlas of United States Foreign Relations* (Washington, D.C.: U.S. Department of State, 1989); *United Nations Statistical Yearbook* (New York: UN 1985–1986 and 1988); *Travel Industry World Yearbook* (1988); UN Centre on Transnational Corporations, *Foreign Direct Investment, the Service Sector, and International Banking* (New York: UN, 1987); and UN Centre on Transnational Corporations, "Trends and Issues in Foreign Direct Investment and Related Flows: A Technical Paper," UN Doc. ST/CTC/59 (1985).

111. See especially the writings of scholars associated with the CATO Institute, such as Earl C. Ravenal's *Never Again: Learning from America's Foreign Policy Failures* (Philadelphia: Temple University Press, 1980) and *Foreign Policy in An Uncontrollable World* (Washington, D.C.: Cato Institute, 1986).

112. North, *op. cit.*, p. 223, notes that "in the early 1980s the United States had 360 major military bases . . . and 1,600 installations in thirty-six nations—the largest . . . system of military, naval, and air bases in history." In the 1990s, immediately prior to the Gulf War buildup, 435,000 American troops were stationed at 395 major military bases in thirty-five foreign countries. See *Defense Monitor*, 20 (1991). Charles Kegley, in "The Bush Administration and the Future of American Foreign Policy: Pragmatism, or Procrastination?" *Presidential Studies Quarterly*, 19 (Fall 1989), p. 719, discusses the Bush administration's continued commitment to globalism, reflected in the president's state-

ment that "You see, I don't believe any other country can pick up the mantle [of world leadership]."

113. On the inherent contradiction in the U.S. pursuing a foreign policy based on global military reach amidst structural federal budgetary constraints, see Earl C. Ravenal, *Defining Defense: The 1985 Military Budget* (Washington, D.C.: Cato Institute, 1984). Ravenal does not call for global multilateralism but for "disengagement," a term he prefers to "isolationism."

114. Williamson, *op. cit.*, p. 12

115. *Ibid.*, p. 5.

116. Remarks by John R. Bolton, Assistant Secretary of State for International Organization Affairs, before the Geneva Group consultative-level meeting, June 29, 1989, reported in "The Concept of the 'Unitary UN,' " U.S. Department of State, Bureau of Public Affairs, Current Policy No. 1191, p. 1.

117. On this point, see Pearson and Rochester, *op. cit.*

118. The proposal, contained in General Assembly Resolution 42/93 (1987), will be discussed below under "The View from Moscow." The proposal "urges states to focus efforts on ensuring a universal security through peaceful political means in accordance with the UN Charter, reaffirms the need for strict adherence to international law, calls for a halt to the arms race, a peaceful settlement of disputes, an equitable world economic environment, including a new international economic order, respect for human rights and a strengthened role of the UN system in the maintenance of international peace." See U.S. Department of State, *Report to Congress on Voting Practices in the United Nations* (March 14, 1988), p.III-4, for the above language and the vote on the resolution, which was adopted by majority vote by the First Committee of the 42nd General Assembly not counting 70 member states that abstained or were absent. The proposal was resubmitted in General Assembly sessions after 1987, with a substantial number of states continuing to withhold their endorsement.

119. Bolton, *op. cit.*, pp. 1–2. Bush's concept of a "new world order" was articulated in his address to the 45th UN General Assembly on October 2, 1990.

120. *Ibid.* In "The US and the UN," U.S. Department of State Bureau of Public Affairs (September 1989), p. 2, the administration stated that "the UN must be approached in systematic fashion, what the U.S. is calling a 'unitary United Nations' concept. A primary objective . . . is to rationalize the UN system to eliminate the proliferation of committees, conferences and meetings that cover essentially the same issues."

121. For example, U.S. demands are spelled out in Williamson, *op. cit.*, p. 4.

122. John de Gara, *Administrative and Financial Reform of the United Nations: A Documentary Essay* (Hanover, N.H.: Academic Council on the United Nations System, 1989), p. 9.

123. *The President's Report on the Reform and Restructuring of the United Nations System*, p. 1; the report was a condensation of the 64-page *Report of the Secretary of State to the President on the Reform and Restructuring of the United Nations System* (Washington, D.C.: U.S. State Department, 1978).

124. *Ibid.*, p. 2.

125. Jonathan Haslam, "The UN and the Soviet Union: New Thinking?" *International Affairs*, 65 (Autumn 1989), p. 678.

126. C. Osakwe, *Participation of the Soviet Union in Universal International Organizations* (Leiden: A. W. Sijthoff, 1972), p. 23.

127. *Ibid.*, pp. 28–29. A general discussion of Marxist views on international organization is furnished by Clive Archer in *International Organizations* (London: Allen and Unwin, 1983), pp. 102–117.

128. Osakwe, *op. cit.*, p. 33.

129. The early Soviet view on the UN is discussed in Alexander Dallin, *The Soviet Union and the United Nations* (New York: Praeger, 1962).

130. On the adoption and operation of the veto provision, see *ibid.*, chap. 1; and Claude, *Swords Into Plowshares, op. cit.*, chap. 8. Statistics on the use of the veto can be found in Sydney D. Bailey, *Voting in the Security Council* (Bloomington, Ind.: Indiana University Press, 1969); and Riggs and Plano, *op. cit.*, pp. 76–77.

131. Riggs and Plano, *op. cit.*, p. 86.

132. The Soviets were not alone in such behavior during the early life of the UN. The U.S. circumvented the UN Charter in pushing through the 1950 Uniting for Peace Resolution enabling the General Assembly to authorize enforcement action in threatening situations when the Security Council might fail to act; the French joined the Soviets in refusing to pay peace-keeping expenses; and the U.S., particularly during the McCarthy era in the 1950s, required that any of its nationals being considered for a Secretariat appointment first take a loyalty oath and undergo screening by the FBI. Still, Western dominance in the organization made for a greater institutional commitment originally. Commenting on early Soviet aloofness from the UN, Alvin Z. Rubenstein, *Soviet Foreign Policy Since World War II*, 3rd ed. (Boston: Little, Brown, 1989), p. 326, notes "until 1960, Moscow assigned few Soviet nationals to the secretariats of international organizations, a reflection of its general depreciation and lack of understanding of the value of such groups in shaping the implementation of policy and gathering intelligence." The Soviet discovery that the UN could be a useful place to conduct intelligence activities in the U.S. is documented in Arkady Shevehenko, *Breaking with Moscow* (New York: Knopf, 1987).

133. John Stoessinger, *The United Nations and The Superpowers: China, Russia, and America*, 4th ed. (New York: Random House, 1977), p. 212.

134. According to Riggs and Plano, *op. cit.*, p. 86, the Soviet Union's percent agreement with the majority in the General Assembly climbed in the 1960s to the point where it registered a score of 54.7 for the 1961–65 period compared to 54.5 for the U.S.

135. *Ibid.*, pp. 77 and 86.

136. Political Report of the CPSU Central Committee to the 17th Congress of the Communist Party of the Soviet Union. *Current Soviet Policies IX: The Documentary Record of the 27th Congress of the Communist Party of the Soviet Union* (Columbus, Ohio: Current Digest of the Soviet Press, 1968). p. 17.

137. Quoted in Haslam, *op. cit.*, p. 677.

138. *Ibid.*, p. 678.

139. Reported in *Pravda* (September 28, 1988).

140. Reported in *Pravda* (December 8, 1988).

141. Haslam, *op. cit.*, p. 678.

142. The Soviet view of the UN under Gorbachev is discussed in *ibid*; Thomas G. Weiss and Meryl A. Kessler, "Moscow's UN Policy," *Foreign Policy*, 79 (Summer 1990), pp. 94–112; Puchala and Coate, *The State of the United Nations, op. cit.*; Puchala and Coate, *The Challenge of Relevance, op. cit.*; and Brian Urquhart, "The United Nations System and the Future," *International Affairs*, 65 (Spring 1989), pp. 225–231.

143. Mikhail Gorbachev, *Realities and Guarantees for a Secure World* (Moscow: Novosti Press, 1987), p. 3. The article was published in *Pravda* and *Izvestia* on September 17, 1987, and also distributed as a press release by the Soviet Mission to the UN (No. 119).

144. Remarks by Radomir Bogdanov made on Soviet television on August 14, 1988; quoted in Haslam, *op. cit.*, p. 679.

145. Puchala and Coate, *State of the United Nations, op. cit.*, p. 45. The Soviet Deputy Minister of Foreign Affairs was quoted in 1988 as saying "We have told our embassies: No more Mr. Nyet." Cited in Johan Kaufmann and Nico Schrijver, *Changing Global Needs: Expanding Roles for the UN System* (Hanover, N.H.: Academic Council on the UN System, 1990), p. 89.

146. On the Soviet expression of interest and the motives behind it, see U.S. Congress, Joint Economic Committee, *Gorbachev's Economic Plans*, 1 (November 23, 1987), pp. 110–111.

147. *The Interdependent*, (Fall 1989), p. 4.

148. Gorbachev, *Realities and Guarantees, op. cit.*, p. 12.

149. Urquhart, *op. cit.*, p. 226. On Soviet deeds matching words, also see Weiss and Kessler, *op. cit.*

150. *Pravda* (April 9, 1986). Quoted in Timothy J. Colton, *The Dilemma of Reform in the Soviet Union*, revised ed. (New York: Council on Foreign Relations, 1986), p. 200.

151. The explanation of Soviet foreign policy moderation as a rational response to declining Soviet capabilities is offered by Kenneth Waltz, in "On the Nature of States and Their Recourse to Violence," *U.S. Institute of Peace Journal 3*, no. 2 (June 1990), pp. 6–7. On the relationship between the politics of Soviet internal reform and Soviet foreign policy behavior, see Colton, *op. cit.*; Jerry F. Hough, *Russia and The West: Gorbachev and the Politics of Reform*, 2nd ed. (New York: Simon and Shuster, 1990); and Jack Snyder, "International Leverage on Soviet Domestic Change," *World Politics*, 42 (October 1989), pp. 1–30. An alternative explanation of changed Soviet foreign policy behavior, focusing on the operation of transnational coalitions, was provided by Matthew Evangelista, in "Transnational Coalitions and the Moderation of Soviet Security Policy," paper presented at annual meeting of the International Studies Association, Vancouver, March 20–23, 1991.

152. This point about Soviet UN experience was made to me by John Washburn, Special Assistant to the UN Secretary-General and a former U.S. State Department official, in an interview on October 25, 1989. Regarding the specialized agencies, in a letter to the Secretary-General dated October 13, 1989, the Deputy head of the Soviet delegation to the UN stated that "such international organizations as the International Monetary Fund, the World Bank and the Food and Agriculture Organization . . . have accumulated extensive experience in their various key areas of world economic relations" and that "the USSR favors close contacts with such institutions, with a view to its becoming part of them." UN Doc. A/44/645 (October 17, 1989), p. 6.

153. See n. 140 and 143.

154. See n. 118. In 1986, when the Soviets first aired their proposal, 82 countries voted in favor of a General Assembly resolution (41/92) recommending adoption of the Soviet plan, whereas in 1987 the proposal suffered a setback as a smaller majority of only 76 countries voted for the resolution (42/93), 12 opposed it, 63 abstained, and 7 were absent. The proposal, recast in "severely watered down" form (according to U.S. characterizations), recovered some support in 1988, with 97 votes in favor of the resolution (43/89), 3 against, and 59 abstaining or absent. U.S. Department of State. *Report to Congress on Voting Practices in the United Nations* (April 20, 1989), pp. I–7 and III–60. The full text of the resolutions can be found in *Resolutions and Decisions Adopted by the General Assembly during Its 41st Session* and the respective publications for the 42nd and 43rd sessions.

155. Haslam, *op. cit.*, p. 680.

156. Letter of October 13, 1989 from V. Petrovsky, Deputy Head of Soviet Delegation, to the Secretary-General. UN Doc. A.44/645 (October 17, 1989).

157. *Ibid.*

158. Statement by Anatoly Lukianov, made on October 9, 1989 at the 32nd Session of the Plenary Assembly of the World Federation of United Nations Associations.

159. Quoted in *New York Times*, September 24, 1990, p. 3.

160. Urquhart, *op. cit.*, p. 226.

161. Jerry F. Hough, "Gorbachev's Politics," *Foreign Affairs*, 68 (Winter 1989/90), p. 27.

162. Robert Legvold, "The Revolution in Soviet Foreign Policy," *Foreign Affairs*, 68 (1989), pp. 82–98. Also see Edward N. Luttwak, "The Shape of Things to Come," *Commentary*, 89 (June 1990), pp. 17–25. On Gorbachev's importance, see Allen Lynch, "Does Gorbachev Matter Anymore?," *Foreign Affairs*, 69 (1990), pp. 19–29.

163. Urquhart, *op. cit.*, p. 226.

164. Petrovsky, *op. cit.*

165. One study which questioned American dominance even during the UN's first two decades was Catherine Senf Manno, "Majority Decisions and Minority Responses in the UN General Assembly," *Journal of Conflict Resolution*, 10 (March 1966), pp. 1–20. Manno, examining General Assembly roll-call voting in three sessions (1954, 1959, and 1962), found that the U.S. sided with the majority less often than 80% of the UN membership. Edward T. Rowe, in "Changing Patterns in the Voting Success of Member States in the United Nations General Assembly: 1945–1966," *International Organization*, 23 (Spring 1969), pp. 231–253, concluded from a study of all roll-call votes during the first two decades that the U.S. was regularly on the winning side before 1960 but much less so after 1960.

166. Robert E. Riggs, *Politics in the United Nations* (Urbana, Ill.: University of Illinois Press, 1958), p. 163.

167. Robert E. Riggs, *US/UN Foreign Policy and International Organization* (New York: Appleton-Century-Crofts, 1971), p. 10.

168. On 174 roll-call votes during the 42nd UN General Assembly in 1987, the NATO allies voted with the U.S. 62.4% of the time, by far the highest of any other single group of states; the score for Japan was 60%. The average voting coincidence of all UN members with the U.S. on roll-call votes was 18.6%. See *Report to Congress on Voting Practices in the United Nations* (1988), *op. cit.*, pp. I–7, I–8, and II–8. These statistical patterns were almost identical for the 43rd UN General Assembly in 1988. See Report to *Congress on Voting Practices in the United Nations* (1989), *op. cit.*, pp. I–4, II–5, and II–11.

169. On early voting patterns see Thomas Hovet, *Bloc Politics in the United Nations* (Cambridge, Mass.: Harvard University Press, 1960), especially pp. 47–55. On the evolution of Soviet bloc voting in support of the General Assembly majority, see Miguel Martin-Bosch, "How Nations Vote in the General Assembly of the United Nations," *International Organization*, 41 (Autumn 1987), pp. 705–724.

170. See *ibid.*, p. 708 for evidence of increased efforts at compromise on General Assembly resolutions, resulting in "General Assembly resolutions [being] accepted by an increasing majority of its members." "By 1986, resolutions were adopted by an average of 127 votes in favor and 5.2 against, with 25.7 abstentions or absences." During the 1987, 1988, and 1989 sessions, over 60% of the resolutions were adopted through consensus procedures. As a specific illustration of the tendency toward reduced confrontation on issues that are especially threatening to the functioning of the organization, there has been a decline in recent years in the number of states voting in favor of removing Israel from participating in the General Assembly.

171. On the same day, Soviet Foreign Minister Shevardnadze signed the USSR's first commercial accord with the European Community, uttering these comments, and embarked on the first visit to NATO headquarters by a Warsaw Pact Minister. *New York Times*, December 19, 1989, p. 31.

172. Interview in *Newsweek*, December 4, 1989, p. 51.

173. Harold K. Jacobson, William M. Reisinger, and Todd Mathers, "National Entanglements in International Governmental Organizations," *American Political Science Review*, 90 (March 1986), pp. 148–149.

174. Treaty data are from Gerhard von Glahn, *Law Among Nations*, 4th ed. (New York: Macmillan, 1981), p. 54. On the Chinese "image of world order," the traditional Chinese aversion to multilateralism, and the record of China's early involvement in the UN, see Samuel S. Kim, *China, the United Nations and World Order* (Princeton, N.J.: Princeton University Press, 1979).

175. Kim, *op. cit.*, pp. 159–161.

176. On China's growing internationalism in the post-Mao era, see Samuel S. Kim, *China and the World Order: Chinese Foreign Policy in the Post-Mao Era* (Boulder, Colo.: Westview Press, 1984); John Gittings, *China Faces Change: The Road from Revolution, 1949–1989* (New York: Oxford University Press, 1989), especially chaps. 11 and 12; and Kim, "Thinking Globally in Post-Mao China," *Journal of Peace Research*, 27 (May 1990), pp. 191–209. In *ibid.*, pp. 192–193, Kim furnishes data on increased Chinese participation in IGOs and NGOs and notes (p. 192) that although "the concept of global interdependence . . . runs counter to centuries of civilizational autonomy and self-sufficiency," for the first

time in modern history, China has become an active, if somewhat still elusive, member of the global system."

177. Kim, *China, the United Nations, and World Order, op. cit.*, p. 439. Puchala and Coate, *The Challenge of Relevance, op. cit.*, p. 23 cites recent signs that China is becoming more inclined to join in "great power" consensus even if it means distancing itself somewhat from the Third World.

178. Puchala and Coate, *State of the United Nations, op. cit.*, pp. 41–42. See also *The Challenge of Relevance, op. cit.*, pp. 40–44. Japan's early view of the UN is expressed in Japanese International Law Association, *Japan and The United Nations* (New York: Manhattan Publishing Co., 1958).

179. Samuel P. Huntington, "The U.S. — Decline or Renewal?" *Foreign Affairs*, 67 (Winter 1988/89), p. 92.

180. Sadako Ogata, "The Changing Role of Japan in the United Nations," *Journal of International Affairs*, 37 (Summer 1983), p. 36. Also see Masaru Tamamoto, "Japan's Search for a World Role," *World Policy Journal*, 7 (Summer 1990), pp. 493–520.

181. Huntington, *op. cit.*, pp. 93–94. On European Community efforts to pressure the U.S. to pay its UN arrearages, see *New York Times*, June 15, 1988, p. 5. Puchala and Coate, *The Challenge of Relevance, op. cit.*, pp. 32–40, discusses growing Western European influence in the UN and the increased efforts by members of the European Community to coordinate their policies. EEC voting cohesion is discussed in Kaufmann and Schrijver, *op. cit.*, p. 8. Also see Beverly Crawford and Peter W. Schulze, eds., *The New Europe Asserts Itself* (Berkeley, Calif.: University of California International and Area Studies Series, 1990), no. 77.

182. Puchala and Coate, *State of the United Nations, op. cit.*, p. 47. In *Challenge of Relevance, op. cit.*, Puchala and Coate discuss "new diplomatic space" for middle powers.

183. The 25 states in the GLOBUS model include 7 OECD countries, 5 OPEC members, 4 East European countries, and 9 non-OPEC LDCs. See n. 65.

184. Jacobson, *Networks of Interdependence, op. cit.*, p. 118. Jacobson discusses the nature of the influence exercised by IGO executive heads and secretariats in chap. 6. On the role of "multilateral players" in helping to shape regimes in various issue-areas, see John G. Ruggie, "Multilateralism: The Anatomy of An Institution," *International Organization*, 46 (Summer 1992), pp. 596–597, esp. the works cited in his note 124.

185. Claude, "The Record of International Organizations in the Twentieth Century," *op. cit.*, pp. 52–53.

186. Roughly two-thirds of the countries in the world maintain diplomatic missions in fewer than 60 countries. See Elmer Plishke, *Microstates in World Affairs* (Washington, D.C.: American Enterprise Institute,

1977), chap. 4. For a survey of studies supporting the general proposition that "international organizations are by far the most common method of diplomatic contact for most nations." see Patrick J. McGowan and Howard B. Shapiro, *The Comparative Study of Foreign Affairs: A Survey of Scientific Findings* (Beverly Hills, Calif.: Sage, 1973), p. 140.

187. James McCormick and Young W. Kihl, "Intergovernmental Organizations and Foreign Policy Behavior: Some Empirical Findings," *American Political Science Review*, 73 (June 1979), p. 501. Their findings are viewed as consistent with those in another study showing that "small states tend to act more selectively in conducting foreign policy than do large states and tend to seek maximum impact with their actions." Maurice A. East, "Size and Foreign Policy Behavior: A Test of Two Models," *World Politics*, 25 (July 1973), pp. 556–576.

188. Lynn H. Miller, *Global Order*, 2nd ed. (Boulder, Colo.: Westview, 1990), p. 29.

189. More typical is the view expressed by Zbigniew Brezezinski, that the industrialized democracies of the world, led by the U.S., will continue to have global interests requiring attention. He argues "in the years ahead, three regions other than the far western and far eastern extremities of Eurasia are likely to become the central foci of America's concerns"—Eastern Europe, the Persian Gulf and Middle East, and Latin America. "America's New Geostrategy," *Foreign Affairs*, 66 (Spring 1988), p. 686.

190. The term "prominent solution" was coined by Thomas C. Schelling. See *The Strategy of Conflict* (Cambridge, Mass.: Harvard University Press, 1960).

191. Bremer and Hughes, *op. cit.*, p. 188, shows that "savings from even a moderate arms spending reduction scenario would be more than adequate to financially allow donors to meet the NIEO aid target of 0.7% of GDP," although the authors acknowledge this would take "an act of substantial political will." The authors also caution that reduced arms spending in the North combined with increased aid and growth promoting reforms in the South may in time narrow military and economic gaps between certain states and possibly aggravate "West-South" tensions. In the end, though, they say (p. 174) "we remain convinced that there exists a package of policies that will ameliorate many (but not all) long-term global conflicts." Their work focuses on the linkages between disarmament and development and gives little attention to international organization.

192. Puchala and Coate, *State of the United Nations, op. cit.*, p. 42, notes that "UN insiders suggest that Tokyo has a definite strategy for moving Japan to permanent member status [on the Security Council] during the next ten to fifteen years." Other major states likely will have

to be accommodated in some fashion as well if they are to attach greater salience to the organization and not get "bent out of shape" over status concerns. Puchala and Coate, *The Challenge of Relevance, op. cit.*, p. 27.

193. Richard Gardner, "Practical Internationalism," *Foreign Affairs* 66 (Spring 1988), pp. 830–831.

194. *Ibid.*, p. 830. A call for "practical internationalism" can be found also in Peter Fromuth's *The U.N. at 40: The Problems and the Opportunities* (New York: United Nations Association-USA, 1986), p. 7.

195. Young, *op. cit*, pp. 280–281.

Chapter 4: An Overview of the United Nations System

1. Yves Beigbeder, in *Management Problems in United Nations Organizations: Reform or Decline?* (New York: St. Martin's Press, 1987), p. 22, cites a 1985 poll of 900 UN staff members showing that less than half (45%) found the organization performing a useful mission, and an overwhelming number (80%) felt some reform was necessary, particularly in the Secretariat.

2. Cited in Richard Gardner, "To Make the World Safe for Interdependence," *UN 30* (New York: United Nations Association, 1975), p. 16.

3. Trygve Lie, *In The Cause of Peace* (New York: Macmillan, 1954), p. 423.

4. Seymour Finger, "U.S. Policy Toward International Institutions," *International Organization*, 30 (Spring 1976), p. 356.

5. Group of Experts on the Structure of the United Nations System, *A New United Nations Structure for Global Economic Cooperation* (New York: UN, 1975), p.2.

6. Inis Claude referred to the establishment of the League of Nations as "the first time a conscious effort had been made to create a systematic structural pattern for the organization of international relations . . . [as] the multistate system had been equipped with a central institutional instrument." *Swords Into Plowshares*, 4th ed. (New York: Random House, 1984), p. 55.

7. *Ibid.*, p. 60.

8. Cited in Roger A. Coate and Donald J. Puchala, "Global Policies and the United Nations System: A Current Assessment," *Journal of Peace Research*, 27 (May 1990), p. 129.

9. On this point, see Kjell Skjelsbaek, *Peaceful Settlement of Disputes by the United Nations and Other Intergovernmental Organizations* (Oslo: Norwegian Institute of International Affairs, 1984).

10. Oran R. Young, *The Politics of Force: Bargaining During International Crisis* (Princeton, N.J.: Princeton University Press, 1968), p. 169.

11. Ernst B. Haas, *Why We Still Need the United Nations: The Collective Management of International Conflict, 1945–1984*. Policy Papers in International Affairs, No. 26 (Berkeley, Calif.: Institute of International Studies, 1986); and "Regime Decay: Conflict Management and International Organizations, 1945–1981," *International Organization* 37 (Spring 1983), pp. 189–256.

12. The investigators found that the UN was active in 29 out of 32 cases involving "full-scale war" and was effective in 13 of these cases. Jonathan Wilkenfeld and Michael Brecher, "International Crises 1945–1975: The UN Dimension," *International Studies Quarterly*, 28 (March 1984), pp. 45–67.

13. William D. Coplin and J. Martin Rochester, "The Permanent Court of International Justice, the International Court of Justice, the League of Nations, and the United Nations: A Comparative Empirical Survey," *American Political Science Review*, 66 (June 1972), pp. 529–550. Also see Mark W. Zacher, *International Conflicts and Collective Security* (New York: Praeger, 1979).

14. On the functioning of the Security Council, including trends in voting and use of the veto, see Sydney D. Bailey, *Voting in the Security Council* (Bloomington, Ind.: Indiana University Press, 1969); Leland M. Goodrich, "The UN Security Council," in James Barros, ed., *The United Nations: Past, Present and Future* (New York: Free Press, 1972), pp. 16–63; and Robert E. Riggs and Jack C. Plano, *The United Nations: International Organization and World Politics* (Chicago, Ill.: Dorsey Press, 1988), chaps. 3, 5, and 6.

15. *The Blue Helmets*, 2nd ed. (New York: United Nations, 1991) is a compendium reviewing all UN peacekeeping operations between 1945 and 1990. Among the many works dealing with UN peacekeeping, see Larry L. Fabian, *Soldiers Without Enemies* (Washington, D.C.: Brookings Institution, 1971); Rosalyn Higgins, *United Nations Peacekeeping*, 4 vols. (London: Oxford University Press, 1969–1981); Indar Jit Rikhye, *The Theory and Practice of Peacekeeping* (London: Christopher Hurst, 1984); and Alan James, *Peacekeeping in International Politics* (London: Macmillan, 1990).

16. *Ibid.*

17. The Soviet Union cast 105 vetoes in the UN prior to 1971, although 77 of these were in the first decade alone, and half of the total dealt with membership admission questions rather than security matters. While the Soviets drastically reduced their use of the veto after 1970, the U.S. in that year exercised its veto power for the first time and proceeded to resort to its use over fifty times in the next two decades.

See Riggs and Plano, *op. cit.*; and U.S. Department of State, *Report to Congress on Voting Practices in the United Nations During 1988* (1989).

18. Haas, *op. cit.*, did find that "energetic management makes a difference" and that in the postwar era "strong decisions [involving military operations] were associated with relatively effective management except for the 1975–1980 era." See pp. 26–27.

19. Raimo Vayrynen, "Is There a Role for the United Nations in Conflict Resolution?" *Journal of Peace Research*, 22 (1985), pp. 189–196.

20. Final Panel Report of the United Nations Management and Decision-Making Project, *A Successor Vision: The United Nations of Tomorrow* (New York: United Nations Association-USA, September 1987), pp. i and 6.

21. *Ibid.*, p. 8.

22. Speech before the UN General Assembly on September 26, 1988. *U.S. Department of State Bulletin*, 88 (November 1988), p. 1. In the same month, the foreign ministers of the five permanent members of the Security Council issued a communique which "stressed their continuing confidence in the United Nations" and in the "increasingly significant part it had to play in the achievement of international peace and security." " 'Big Five' Believe in UN," *UN Chronicle*, 25 (December 1988), p. 4.

23. Typical was George L. Sherry, *The United Nations Reborn: Conflict Control in the Post-Cold War World* (New York: Council on Foreign Relations, 1990).

24. Johan Kaufmann and Nico Schrijver, *Changing Global Needs: Expanding Roles for the United Nations System* (Hanover, N.H.: Academic Council on the UN System, 1990), p. 70.

25. *Ibid.*, p. 69.

26. Haas, *op. cit.*, p. 31. On recent global approaches to regional conflict settlement, see G. R. Berridge, *Return to the UN: UN Diplomacy in Regional Conflicts* (New York: St. Martin's Press, 1990).

27. Even the World Court's most charitable apologists must confess that the ICJ has been among the most grossly underutilized international institutions, even when compared with the League's Permanent Court of International Justice. For a comparison of the PCIJ and ICJ, and how they have been used relative to the "political" institutions of the League and UN, see Coplin and Rochester, *op. cit.*

28. J. Alan Beesley, *New Frontiers of Multilateralism* (Hanover, N.H.: Academic Council on the UN System, 1989), p. 9. Data on ICJ caseloads can be found in Coplin and Rochester, *op. cit.*; A. Leroy Bennett, *International Organizations*, 5th ed. (Englewood Cliffs, N.J.: Prentice-Hall, 1991), pp. 172–177; and *UN Chronicle* 20, no. 11 (1983), pp. 47–53. On the impacts contributed by the ICJ even in those disputes where the

Court does not render a judgment, see Dana D. Fischer, "Decisions to Use the International Court of Justice," *International Studies Quarterly*, 26 (June 1982), pp. 251–277.

29. These are the words of Benjamin Civiletti, former U.S. Attorney-General, in his oral argument presented before the ICJ on December 10, 1979, during the proceedings of the *U.S Diplomatic and Consular Staff in Tehran* case; cited in U.S. Department of State, Bureau of Public Affairs, Current Policy No. 118 (December 1979), p. 1.

30. The eleven peacekeeping missions in 1992 were expected to exceed $3 billion. See Indar Jit Rikhye, *The Future of Peacekeeping* (New York: International Peace Academy, 1989); and *United Nations Peace-Keeping Operations: Information Notes* (New York: UN Department of Public Information, January 1992).

31. This relates to the observation made by one writer that in seeking "to hold together a wide-ranging coalition," the UN is critical since "it creates the opportunity for international consensus-building which, by its very nature, helps in most Western states with domestic consensus-building." Lawrence Freedman, "Escalators and Quagmires: Expectations and the Use of Force," *International Affairs*, 67 (January 1991), p. 30.

32. Financing, troop command structure, intelligence coordination, and other such issues stemming from the Gulf War experience are discussed in Bruce M. Russett and James S. Sutterlin, "The UN in A New World Order," *Foreign Affairs*, 70 (Spring 1991), pp. 69–83.

33. Kaufmann and Schrijver, *op. cit.*, p. 77.

34. *Ibid.*, p. 69. The authors discuss this new role for the UN in chaps. 4 and 5. It needs to be added that concerns about UN institutional capabilities in the monitoring of elections are not completely new. See *General Assembly Official Records, 4th Session, Supplement No. 11, A/966*, and *General Assembly Official Records, 22nd Session, Annexes*, agenda item 45.

35. Evidence can be cited in the form of the 1991 *UN Human Development Report*, which listed Western countries as clearly allowing the greatest freedom (although ranking the U.S. only thirteenth), and identified the countries with the worst "freedom index" as Iraq, Libya, Romania, Ethiopia, China, South Africa, the Soviet Union, Bulgaria, Zaire and Pakistan.

36. The reference to the "other UN" is found in Robert W. Gregg, "UN Economic, Social, and Technical Activities," in James Barros, ed., *The United Nations: Past, Present, and Future* (New York: Macmillan, 1972), p. 221. Recent works that examine UN economic, social, and technical activities and the problems that have been experienced include Kaufmann and Schrijver, *op. cit.*, and Maurice Bertrand, *The Role*

of the UN in the Economic and Social Fields (New York: United Nations Association-USA, 1987).

37. Maurice Bertrand, *The UN in Profile: How Its Resources Are Distributed* (New York: United Nations Association-USA, 1986), p. 10.

38. *Ibid.*

39. Donald J. Puchala and Roger A. Coate, *The Challenge of Relevance: The United Nations in A Changing World Environment* (Hanover, N.H.: Academic Council on the UN System, 1989), p. 45.

40. Richard C. Snyder, Charles F. Hermann, and Harold D. Lasswell, "A Global Monitoring System: Appraising the Effects of Government on Human Dignity," *International Studies Quarterly*, 20 (June 1976), p. 221.

41. See Morris Morris, *Measuring the Condition of the World's Poor: The Physical Quality of Life Index* (New York: Pergamon Press, 1979) and the work of the Overseas Development Council; Harold K. Jacobson, *Networks of Interdependence*, 2nd ed. (New York: Knopf, 1984); Jacobson, "The Global System and the Realization of Human Dignity and Justice," *International Studies Quarterly*, 26 (September 1982); and Michael J. Sullivan III, *Measuring Global Values: The Ranking of 162 Countries* (Westport, Conn.: Greenwood Press, 1991). At another level, Eugene Meehan and Hans Michelman are currently at work on a research project entitled "Government and the Human Condition: Four Cases from Contemporary Industrial Society."

42. *The United Nations*, 7th ed. in Worldmark Series (New York: John Wiley, 1988), p. 149.

43. *Ibid.* Although there is concern over the possibility of another outbreak of the disease, the general view is that smallpox has been conquered.

44. Gayl D. Ness and Steven R. Brechin, "Bridging the Gap: International Organizations as Organizations," *International Organization*, 42 (Spring 1988), p. 257, argue that it was a technological innovation ("the new non-coitally specific contraceptive technology") which "gave established governments and international organizations something they could actually do to affect population growth rates" and that "it might even be reasonable to propose that without this technology, there would be no UNFPA." They add that "the lack of an effective technique has obstructed concerted . . . action" by governments and IGOs in the field of "social forestry" (p. 258).

45. Marvin S. Soroos, *Beyond Sovereignty: The Challenge of Global Policy* (Columbia, S.C.: University of South Carolina Press, 1986), p. 20. See also the articles on the theme of "The Challenge of Global Policy" in a special issue of *The Journal of Peace Research*, 27 (May 1990). Some of the

discussion in this section of chap. 6 draws on the author's article in the latter volume entitled "Global Policy and the Future of the UN."

46. For definitions of policy along these lines as found in the public policy literature, see James E. Anderson, *Public Policy-Making: Decisions and their Implementation* (New York: Praeger, 1975), p. 3; Duncan MacRae and James E. Wilde, *Policy Analysis for Public Decisions* (North Scituate, Mass.: Duxbury, 1979), p. 3; Charles O. Jones, *An Introduction to the Study of Public Policy* (Monterey, Calif.: Brooks Cole, 1984), pp. 24–26; and B. Guy Peters, *American Public Policy: Promise and Performance*, 2nd ed. (Chatham, N.J.: Chatham House, 1986).

47. Eugene Bardach, *The Implementation Game* (Cambridge, Mass.: MIT Press, 1977), p. 3.

48. Roger Hilsman, *The Politics of Policy Making in Defense and Foreign Affairs* (New York: Harper and Row, 1971), p. 5.

49. Eugene Meehan, "Policy: Constructing A Definition," *Policy Sciences*, 18, no. 4 (1985), p. 295.

50. These categories, taken from Jones, *op. cit.* are commonly discussed in one manner or another in the policy literature.

51. Soroos, *op. cit.*, p. 82.

52. Claude, *op. cit.*, p. 175.

53. Roger H. Davidson, "Subcommittee Government New Channels for Policy Making," in Thomas E. Mann and Norman J. Ornstein, eds., *The New Congress* (Washington, D.C.: American Enterprise Institute, 1981), chap. 4.

54. Meehan, *op. cit.*, p. 310.

55. H. G. Nicholas, *The United Nations As A Political Institution*, 5th ed. (New York: Oxford University Press, 1975), p. 104. A fuller description of the workings of the General Assembly is provided in M. J. Peterson, *The General Assembly in World Politics* (Boston: Unwin and Allen, 1986).

56. Bertrand, *The Role of the UN in the Economic and Social Fields, op. cit.*, p. 23.

57. Jacobson, *Networks of Interdependence, op. cit.*, p. 86.

58. Discussions of the structural features of the specialized agencies are discussed in *ibid*; and Robert Cox and Harold K. Jacobson, eds., *Anatomy of Influence: Decisionmaking in International Organizations* (New Haven, Conn.: Yale University Press, 1972).

59. Frederick K. Lister, *Fairness and Accountability in UN Financial Decision-Making* (New York: United Nations Association-USA, 1987), pp. 22–23.

60. Peter Fromuth, *The UN at 40* (New York: United Nations Association-USA, 1986), p. 23.

61. On the failure of CPC and other entities to facilitate the establishment of priorities, see Bertrand, *op. cit.*; Lister, *op. cit.*; and Maurce Bertrand, *Planning, Programming, Budgeting, and Evaluation in the United Nations* (New York: United Nations Association-USA, March 1987). Current efforts to deal with these problems are discussed in Kaufmann and Schrijver, *op. cit.*, pp. 10–11.

62. Coate and Puchala, "Global Policies and the United Nations System," *op. cit.*, p. 132.

63. Problems having to do with inter-agency coordination are discussed in Douglas Williams, *The Specialized Agencies and the United Nations: The System in Crisis* (London: Hurst, 1987); and David Steele, *The Reform of the United Nations* (London: Croom Helm, 1987), chap. 4. Relationships between the Bretton Woods institutions and the rest of the UN system are discussed in Kaufmann and Schrijver, *op. cit.*, pp. 12–17; and The Nordic UN Project, *The United Nations in Development* (Stockholm: Almgvist and Wiksell, 1991), pp. 68–73.

64. The ILO Constitution stipulates that amendments take effect only when ratified or accepted by two-thirds of the member states, including five of chief industrial importance. As of 1991, only 78 countries in the 149 member body had ratified, including 3 states of chief industrial importance.

65. Christer Jonsson, "Interorganization Theory and International Organization," *International Studies Quarterly*, 30 (March 1986), p. 44.

66. The quasi-legislative nature of rule-making in the specialized agencies is treated in Robert E. Riggs, "The UN System and the Politics of Law," mimeo, March 1985.

67. Jeffrey Laurenti and Francesca Lyman, *One Earth, Many Nations* (New York: United Nations Association-USA, 1990), p. 48.

68. Historical trends are discussed by Miguel Marin Bosch in "How Nations Vote in the General Assembly of the United Nations," *International Organization*, 41 (Autumn 1987), pp. 705–724. More recent data were obtained from the official records of Resolutions and Decisions Adopted by the General Assembly.

69. *Ibid.*

70. Bosch, *op. cit.*, p. 708.

71. Weighted voting schemes themselves pose obvious and no-so-obvious problems, as pointed out by William J. Dixon in "The Evaluation of Weighted Voting Schemes for the United Nations General Assembly," *International Studies Quarterly*, 27 (September 1983), pp. 295–314.

72. The notion that American and other leaders betrayed the original design of the UN by later demanding that senior positions be filled with persons belonging to and approved by certain governments seems an

idealized account of the intentions and expectations harbored by the founders. For such a view, see Shirley Hazzard's two-part critique of the UN in *The New Yorker*, September 25, 1989 and October 2, 1989.

73. Fixed-term appointments as a percentage of all appointments to UN posts subject to geographical distribution increased from roughly 10% in 1955 to 25% in 1965 to over 35% in 1986, although this trend may be reversed as communist states become more permissive with their nationals and as developing states are able to free up skilled manpower. Riggs and Plano, *op. cit.*, p. 106. On personnel problems, see Peter Fromuth and Ruth Raymond, *UN Personnel Policy Issues* (New York: United Nations Association-USA, January 1987). Broad issues surrounding international administration are discussed in Thomas Weiss, *International Bureaucracy* (Lexington, Mass.: Lexington Books, 1975).

74. These figures are cited in Jacques Fomerand, *Strengthening the UN Economic and Social Programs: A Documentary Essay* (Hanover, N.H.: Academic Council on the UN System, 1990), p. 1.

75. In addition to the works cited in n. 63, management problems in the UN system are discussed in Beigbeder, *op. cit.*

76. See "U.S. Proposal for Improving UN Institutional Involvement in Environmental Affairs: Enhancing Central Coordination and the Role of UNEP," submitted to the Preparatory Committee of the UN Conference on the Environment and Development, 1991. The Environment Coordinating Board actually originated in the 1970s.

77. Such was the recommendation of the 1969 Jackson Report.

78. Coate and Puchala, "Global Policies and the United Nations System," *op. cit.*, p. 136.

79. Cox and Jacobson, *op. cit.*, p. 19; also see Jacobson, *op. cit.*, chap. 6.

80. *Ibid.*

81. This point is made by Coate and Puchala in both "Global Policies and the United Nations System," *op. cit.*, p. 137, and *The Challenge of Relevance, op. cit.*, p. 98. In the latter writing, they give as an example of cooperation in lieu of coordination the use of special representatives by the UN Secretary-General to achieve collaboration and a division of labor among various agencies in coping with crises and threatening situations, such as the recovery of Afghanistan following the withdrawal of Soviet troops.

Chapter 5: The Problem of United Nations Reform

1. Ronald I. Meltzer, "Restructuring the United Nations System: In-

stitutional Reform Efforts in the Context of North-South Relations," *International Organization*, 32 (Autumn 1978), p. 1009.

2. Johan Kaufmann and Nico Schrijver, *Changing Global Needs: Expanding Roles for the United Nations System* (Hanover, N.H.: Academic Council on the United Nations System, 1990), p. 55.

3. The first quote is from George Santayana, *Life of Reason*, I (New York: Scribner's, 1954), p. 12; the statement attributed to Crane Brinton is cited in Jagdish Bhagwati, "Economics and World Order from the 1970s to the 1990s: The Key Issues," in *Economics and World Order*, ed. by Bhagwati (London: Macmillan, 1972), p. 4.

4. Annotated bibliographies listing various UN resolutions and reports relating to structural reform generally and particularly in the economic-social field can be found in Jacques Fomerand, *Strengthening the United Nations Economic and Social Programs: A Documentary Essay* (Hanover, N.H.: Academic Council on the UN System, 1990); and John de Gara, *Administrative and Financial Reform of the United Nations: A Documentary Essay* (Hanover, N.H.: Academic Council on the UN System, 1989). See also John Renninger, "Survey and Analysis of Evaluations of the United Nations Intergovernmental Structure and Functions in the Economic and Social Fields," UNITAR Informal Paper No. 15 (1987).

5. M. Leigh, *U.S. Department of State Bulletin*, 74 (February 1976), p. 118. A good discussion of the positions the permanent members of the Security Council have taken toward Charter reform is provided by Samuel Kim in *China, The United Nations, and World Order* (Princeton, N.J.: Princeton University Press, 1979), chap. 8.

6. Resolution 3/268D (1949). The work of the Interim Committee as well as other early efforts at reform in the peace and security field are discussed in Sydney D. Bailey, *Peaceful Settlement of Disputes* (New York: UNITAR, 1970). Annex I contains a listing of selected proposals transmitted to UN organizations between 1945 and 1970.

7. Created by General Assembly resolutions 19/2006 (1964) and 20/2053 A (1965).

8. UN Doc. A/27/152 (1972) and UN Doc. A/28/9144 (1973).

9. UN Doc. A/24/7659 (1969).

10. The Ad Hoc Committee was created by resolution 29/3349 (1974) and the Group of Experts by resolution 29/3343 (1974).

11. The Romanian resolution was contained in UN Doc. A/27/8792 (1972). The Special Committee was created by resolution 30/3499 (1975).

12. The report was published under the title *Common Security: A Programme for Disarmament* (London: Pan, 1982).

13. United Nations, "Secretary-General Announces Changes in the Secretariat," press release SG/A/479, February 7, 1992. The Secretary-

General on June 17, 1992 issued his full recommendations in a report entitled "An Agenda for Peace," A/47/277 and S/24111 (1992).

14. See Report of the Commission on International Development (Pearson Commission), *Partners in Development* (New York: Praeger, 1969); Report of the Independent Commission on International Development Issues (Brandt Commission), *North-South: A Programme for Survival* (Cambridge, Mass.: MIT Press, 1980); and the World Commission on Environment and Development (Brundtland Commission), *Our Common Future* (New York: Oxford University Press, 1987).

15. The Committee of Eight submitted its report in 1961 (UN Doc. A/4667); the Committee on the Reorganization of the Secretariat, in 1968 (UN Doc. A/7359).

16. UN Doc. DP/5 (1969).

17. See n. 10. Resolution 29/3343 (1974) called for the creation of the Group of 25 in connection with a General Assembly Special Session on Development and International Economic Cooperation.

18. Isabel Gruhn, "The UN Maze Confounds African Development," *International Organization*, 32 (Spring 1978), p. 548.

19. UN Doc. A/31/34, Addendum 2 (1975).

20. *A New United Nations Structure for Global Economic Cooperation.* UN Doc. E/AC.62/9 (1975).

21. The actual drafting group numbered ten, six of whom were from developing countries. Richard Gardner of Columbia University played a lead role as general rapporteur.

22. *Concluding Report on The Implementation of General Assembly Resolution 32/197 Concerning The Restructuring of the Economic and Social Sector of the UN System.* UN Doc. JIU/REP 89/7 (1989). The implementation process is discussed in Fomerand, *op. cit.*, pp. 6–10 and 18–23; and Kaufmann and Schrijver, *op. cit.*, pp. 42–44.

23. Maurce Bertrand, "Some Reflections on Reform of The United Nations," UN Doc. JIU/REP/85/9 (1985) and A/40/988.

24. Resolution 40/237 (1985).

25. The committee was established by General Assembly resolution 20/2049 (1965). Two reports were authored, UN Doc. A/6289 (1966) and A/6343 (1966), the latter of which Maurice Bertrand calls "a fundamental document insofar as it established the basis of the system of planning, programming, budgeting, and evaluation that has been progressively developed." Maurice Bertrand, *Planning, Programming, Budgeting, and Evaluation in the United Nations System* (New York: United Nations Association-USA, March 1987), p. 5.

26. Committee reports were contained in UN Doc. A/36/44 (1981) and A/37/44 (1982).

27. For a discussion of reports urging managerial reform in personnel and other areas, see Bertrand, *Planning, Programming, Budgeting, op. cit.*; and Yves Beigbeder, *Management Problems in United Nations Organizations: Reform or Decline?* (New York: St. Martin's Press, 1987), especially chap. 5.

28. UN Doc. A/24/7822 (1969). The implementation of medium-term planning is discussed by Bertrand, *Planning, Programming, Budgeting, op. cit.*, pp. 7–10.

29. The characterization is Beigbeder's, *op. cit.*, p. 154. He writes (p. 155): "For the first time in the history of the UN, an expert body is proposing reductions in staffing and in staff entitlements."

30. UN Doc. A/41/49 (1986).

31. Resolution 41/213 (1986).

32. Implementation of the Group of Eighteen recommendations and resolution 41/213 is treated with extensive documentation in de Gara, *op. cit.*, 6–17 and Fomerand, *op. cit.*, pp. 12–14 and 24–25. Also see Donald J. Puchala and Roger A. Coate, *The Challenge of Relevance: The United Nations in A Changing World Environment* (Hanover, N.H.: Academic Council on the UN System, 1989), pp. 74–76.

33. The progress made in meeting the three-year timetable for Secretariat reforms mandated by resolution 41/213 was outlined in the Secretary-General's Report of April 1989, UN Doc. A/44/222.

34. The November 1991 *UN Secretariat News* reported UN "morale is at its lowest ebb ever."

35. See n. 13. As Boutros-Ghali came into office, over thirty units of the Secretariat were supposed to report directly to the Secretary-General.

36. The Report of the Special Commission of the Economic and Social Council on the In-Depth Study of the United Nations Intergovernmental Structure and Functions in the Economic and Social Fields, UN Doc. E/1988/75.

37. Kaufmann and Schrijver, *op. cit.*, p. 30.

38. As part of this effort, see *Secretariat Reform: Background Memorandum*, issued by the Australian Mission to the UN on November 29, 1991.

39. A general bibliography on UN reform is provided in Joseph P. Baratta, *Strengthening the United Nations: A Bibliography on U.N. Reform and World Federalism* (Westport, Conn.: Greenwood Press, 1987).

40. President Carter's report was submitted on March 2, 1978, to the Speaker of the U.S. House of Representatives and the Chairman of the Committee on Foreign Relations of the U.S. Senate, pursuant to section 503 (the Baker-McGovern Amendment) of the Foreign Relations Authorization Act Fiscal Year 1978.

41. The studies were undertaken by the United Nations Association-USA under the heading of the United Nations Management and Decision-Making Project. The core set of recommendations were contained in *A Successor Vision: The United Nations of Tomorrow*, Final Panel Report (New York: UNA-USA, September 1987). The panel consisted of 23 prominent individuals drawn internationally from both the private and public sectors, including several former UN officials or delegates.

42. The "radical" school, tending toward sweeping structural reform involving the main political arrangements in the organization, is best exemplified by the early study of Grenville Clark and Louis Sohn, *World Peace Through World Law: Two Alternative Plans*, 3rd ed. (Cambridge, Mass.: Harvard University Press, 1966), and by writings of the World Federalists, such as the "14-Point Program" advanced in response to the Carter Report; see *Fourteen-Point Program of the Campaign for UN Reform* (Wayne, N.J.: Campaign for UN Reform, 1978). At the opposite end of the reform spectrum, several reports issued as part of the UNA-USA project in the 1980s dealt with relatively limited, highly specialized matters, such as Peter Fromuth and Ruth Raymond, *UN Personnel Policy Issues* (New York: UNA-USA, January 1987), although granted some significant and even "spectacular" changes can occur in these areas.

43. Report of the President's Commission for the Observance of the Twentieth Anniversary of the UN.

44. Congress authorized the president to appoint 4 members and the House and Senate majority party and minority party leadership to name the other 12. The congressional selections included an unusual mix of views, ranging from Walter Hoffmann, long-time executive director of the World Federalist Association, to former UN ambassador Jeanne Kirkpatrick and her deputy Charles Lichtenstein (currently with the conservative Heritage Foundation). The president did not make his selections until 1992, delaying the work of the commission. The delay in activating the commission also had to do with funding problems, preoccupation with the Gulf War, disagreement over its proper mandate, and lukewarm State Department support.

45. See Paul Lewis' article in the *New York Times*, August 12, 1990, p. E-3.

46. See, for example, Richard Hudson, "Give UN the Power to Make Peace," *St. Louis Post-Dispatch*, July 20, 1990.

47. Brian Urquhart, *Peacemaking, Peacekeeping and the Future* (Toronto: York University, 1990); "Learning from the Gulf," *New York Review of Books*, March 7, 1991; and Urquhart and Erskine Childers, "A World in Need of Leadership: Tomorrow's United Nations," *Development Dialogue*, 1–2 (1990). Also see Robert C. Johansen and Saul H. Mendlovitz, "The Role of Enforcement of Just Law in the Establishment of a New

International Order: A Proposal for a Transnational Police Force," in Richard Falk, *et al.*, eds., *International Law: A Contemporary Perspective* (Boulder, Colo.: Westview, 1985), pp. 346–364; Paul F. Diehl, "A Permanent UN Peacekeeping Force: An Evaluation," in *Bulletin of Peace Proposals*, 20, no. 1 (1989), pp. 27–36; Indar Jit Rikhye, *The Future of Peacekeeping* (New York: International Peace Academy, 1989), pp. 14–29, and "Roles for the United Nations After the Gulf War," UNA-USA Occasional Paper No. 3, February 1991; and William J. Durch and Barry M. Blechman, *Keeping the Peace: The United Nations in the Emerging World Order* (Washington, D.C.: Henry L. Stimson Center, 1992).

48. World Institute for Development Economics Research, *World Economic Summits: The Role of Representative Groups in the Governance of the World Economy*, Study Group Series No. 4, Helsinki, 1989; cited in Kaufmann and Schrijver, *op. cit.*, p. 44.

49. Hegel Henderson, "G-15: A Different Economic Summit," *Christian Science Monitor*, July 9, 1990, p. 19.

50. The UNA-USA's *Successor Vision, op. cit.*, p. 102, recommends a single seven-year term. Urquhart and Childers, "A World in Need of Leadership," *op. cit.*, likewise urge a single seven-year term. In "Towards A More Effective United Nations," *Development Dialogue*, 1 (1991), Urquhart and Childers advocate a cabinet consisting of four Deputy Secretaries-General.

51. Those who argue that the present institutional arrangements embodied in the UN Charter already provide the foundation needed for the effective functioning of the organization, if states would only abide by the Charter tenets, might be accused more of idealism than cynicism. However one wishes to characterize such a position, it reflects a negative view of reform. See, for example, Pierre de Senarclens, "*La Crise des Nations Unies* (Paris: Presses Universitaries de France, 1988).

52. Beigbeder, *op. cit.* He discusses broader structural reform very briefly in chap. 10.

53. *Ibid.*, p. 145.

54. *Ibid.*, pp. 164–165.

55. The tendency for the U.S. to use politicization and mismanagement charges against the specialized agencies as a cover for its own ideological disagreements with UNESCO and other agencies is discussed in Roger A. Coate, *Unilateralism, Ideology and U.S. Foreign Policy: The United States In and Out of UNESCO* (Boulder, Colo.: Lynne Reiner, 1989); and Mark F. Imber, *The USA, ILO, UNESCO, and IAEA: Politicization and Withdrawal in the Specialized Agencies* (London: Macmillan, 1990).

56. Marc Nerfin, "The Future of the UN System—Some Questions on the Occasion of an Anniversary," *Development Dialogue* 1 (1985), p.

21. This is in the tradition of Clark-Sohn and the World Federalists (cited in n. 42), although the scale of change envisioned by Nerfin is even greater than that contemplated by these writers.

57. See n. 41 in chap. 2. Among those scholars who, along the lines of Nerfin, have focused on nonterritorial and grassroots bases of world politics, see Richard Falk, "A New Paradigm for International Legal Studies: Prospects and Proposals," in Falk, *et al.*, *International Law: A Contemporary Perspective* (Boulder, Colo.: Westview Press, 1985), pp. 651–702; Falk, *A Study of Future Worlds* (New York: Free Press, 1975), especially chap. 4; and Chadwick F. Alger, "Grass-roots Perspectives on Global Policies for Development," *Journal of Peace Research*, 27 (May 1990), pp. 155–168.

58. Remarks of a UN official, cited in Puchala and Coate, *op. cit.*, p. 95.

59. Richard Hudson, executive director of the Center for War/Peace Studies in New York City, has authored several publications discussing the binding triad concept, one of which is cited in n. 46.

60. Inis L. Claude, *Swords Into Plowshares*, 4th ed. (New York: Random House, 1971), p. 120. Claude's classic analysis of "the problem of voting" is found in chap. 7.

61. Hanna Newcombe's statistical analysis (done up to the 28th General Assembly session) showed that, had weighted voting based on population been in effect, it would not have altered significantly the adoption of resolutions, although voting based on budget assessments would have. See Newcombe, *et al.*, *Nations on Record: UN General Assembly Roll Call Votes 1946–1973* (Dundas, Ontario: Peace Research Institute, 1975), and Newcombe and Terry Mahoney, *Alternative Pasts: How General Assembly Roll Call Votes Would Have Fared Under Twenty-Five Different Weighted Voting Formulas 1946–1973* (Dundas, Ontario: Peace Research Institute, 1983); also, Newcombe, "Revamping the UN Voting Structure," in *Solutions for a Troubled World*, ed. by Mark Macy (Boulder, Colo.: Earthview Press, 1987). More recent analyses are not as revealing, given the growing reliance on consensus and the lopsided majorities recorded when votes are taken.

62. Claude, *op. cit.*, p. 125.

63. *Ibid.*, p. 126.

64. Maurice Bertrand, *The Role of the United Nations in The Economic and Social Fields* (New York: UNA-USA, May 1987).

65. See n. 23.

66. Bertrand, *The Role of the United Nations, op. cit.*, p. ii.

67. *Ibid.*, p. 24.

68. *Ibid.*, p. 38.

69. *Ibid.*, p. 34.

70. *Ibid.*, p. 41.

71. *Ibid.*, p. 44. On the global watch function, see Peter Brecke, "Taking the Global Vital Signs: A Computerized Early Warning System for the UN," paper presented at annual meeting of the International Studies Association, Vancouver, March 20, 1991; and John Renninger, *Early Warning: What Role for the UN* (New York: UNITAR, 1989).

72. *Ibid.*, p. 43.

73. See, for example, Harry Clay Blaney III, *Global Challenges: A World at Risk* (New York: Franklin Watts, 1979), p. 239. Blaney, in chap. 8, discusses the "global watch" concept at some length, calling for "global indicators and analysis centers."

74. Kaufmann and Schrijver, *op. cit.*, p. 43. The presence of heads of state at the "Earth Summit" meeting in Rio de Janeiro in 1992 offered a partial test of the capacity of high-level representation to produce results that might not otherwise be attainable, with the jury still out on the impact of the conference.

75. The hostile reaction of the ILO's Director-General and other executive heads to Bertrand's prescriptions, first issued in his 1985 JIU report, is discussed by Beigbeder, *op. cit.*, p. 144.

76. Bertrand, *The Role of the United Nations, op. cit.*, p. 46.

77. See n. 41.

78. *Successor Vision, op. cit.*, p. 94.

79. *Ibid.*, p. 95.

80. *Ibid.*, p. 106.

81. In subsequent publications, coinciding with improvements in East-West relations and revitalization of the UN in the peace and security field since the late 1980s, the UNA-USA has developed further proposals for revamping the operation of the Security Council. See, for example, *Pulling Together* (New York: UNA-USA, 1988); and the 1990–1991 proposals of UNA's Multilateral Issues Committee on US/UN Relations.

82. The report contains many additional recommendations pertaining to Secretariat staff recruitment, PPBE routines, and assorted other subjects. The Nordic UN Project, *The United Nations in Development* (Stockholm: Almgvist and Wiksell, 1991), sponsored by the governments of Sweden, Norway, Denmark, and Finland, also calls attention to the need for improved global watch capabilities and DIESA reorganization (pp. 13 and 46–49), an International Development Council like the Development Assistance Board (pp. 53–60), and a longer tenure for the Secretary-General assisted by 3–4 key deputies (pp. 43–44), although it is less enthusiastic about the Ministerial Board and Commission concepts. See also the writings by Urquhart and Childers cited in n. 50 earlier in this chapter.

83. *Successor Vision, op. cit.,* p. 89.

84. *Ibid.,* pp. 11, 75, 21 and 50.

85. The UNA report also advocates merging the Special Political Committee into the Fourth Committee. See p. 107.

86. *Ibid.,* p. 72.

87. Consensual knowledge has been defined as "the sum of technical information and theories about that information which commands sufficient consensus at a given time among interested actors to serve as a guide to public policy designed to achieve some social goal." Ernst B. Haas, "Why Collaborate?: Issue-Linkage and International Regimes," *World Politics,* 32 (April 1980), pp. 367–368.

88. David Steele, *The Reform of the United Nations* (London: Croom Helm, 1987). Steele has worked in various capacities in several agencies in the UN system. In the book he looks at UN reform in terms of three discrete problem-areas (global economic management, rural development, and collective security and disarmament), which he uses as case studies to elucidate insights into "common institutional solutions" that transcend the specific issue-area.

89. *Ibid.,* see chap. 5.

90. *Ibid.,* p. 154.

91. *Ibid.,* pp. 141–142.

92. *Ibid.,* p. 136.

93. *Ibid.,* p. 138.

94. *Ibid.,* p. 152.

95. Fomerand, *op. cit.,* p. 10.

96. Criticizing the realist theory developed by Kenneth Waltz, John Ruggie notes that his thesis "provides no means by which to account for, or even to describe, the most important contextual change in international politics in this *millennium*: the shift from the medieval to the modern international system." "Continuity and Transformation in the World Polity: Toward A Neorealist Synthesis," *World Politics,* 35 (January 1983), p. 273.

97. Oran R. Young, "Political Leadership and Regime Formation: On the Development of Institutions in International Society," *International Organization,* 45 (Summer 1991), p. 282.

Chapter 6: Prescriptions

1. "The New World Disorder" is the title of an article by Ted Galen Carpenter in *Foreign Policy,* 84 (Fall 1991), pp. 24–39.

2. Harold K. Jacobson, *Networks of Interdependence*, 2nd ed. (New York: Knopf, 1984), p. 212.

3. Inis L. Claude, "The Record of International Organizations in the Twentieth Century," Tamkang Chair Lecture Series, #64, Tamkang University, Taiwan, January 1986 (mimeo), p. 2.

4. Inis L. Claude, *Swords Into Plowshares*, 4th ed. (New York: Random House, 1984), p. 448.

5. *Collective Security and the United Nations: An Old Promise In A New Era* (Muscatine, Iowa: Stanley Foundation, 1991), p. 35.

6. Roger A. Coate and Donald J. Puchala, "Global Policies and The United Nations System: A Current Assessment," *Journal of Peace Research*, 27 (May 1990), p. 127.

7. John C. Whitehead and Jeffrey Laurenti, "The Hydra-Headed UN," *Christian Science Monitor*, May 29, 1991, p. 18. Also, see Donald J. Puchala and Roger A. Coate, *The Challenge of Relevance: The United Nations in a Changing World Environment* (Hanover, N.H.: Academic Council on the UN System, 1989), p. 45.

8. See, for example, Jessica Tuchman Matthews, "The Environment and International Security," *Foreign Affairs*, 68 (Spring 1989), pp. 162–177.

9. Claude, *op. cit.*, p. 399.

10. Wolfram Hanrieder, "International Organizations and International Systems," *Journal of Conflict Resolution*, 10 (1966), pp. 297–301.

11. Oran R. Young, "The United Nations and the International System," *International Organization*, 22 (Autumn 1968), p. 903.

12. Jacobson, *op. cit.*, p. 83.

13. Peter Fromuth, *The UN at 40: The Problems and the Opportunities* (New York: United Nations Association-USA, 1986), Part III.

14. C. Fred Bergsten, "Interdependence and the Reform of International Institutions," *International Organization*, 30 (Spring 1976) pp. 362–363.

15. John G. Ruggie, "Proposal for a Study of the Crisis of Multilateralism" (mimeo) (April 1985).

16. Bergsten, *op. cit.*, p. 366.

17. Robert O. Keohane and Joseph S. Nye, *Power and Interdependence*, 2nd ed. (Boston: Little, Brown, 1989), pp. 240 and 256.

18. Gayl D. Ness and Steven R. Brechin, "Bridging the Gap: International Organizations as Organizations," *International Organization*, 42 (Spring 1988), p. 253.

19. Christer Jonsson, "Interorganization Theory and International Organization," *International Studies Quarterly*, 30 (March 1986), p. 43.

20. Eugene J. Meehan, "Policy: Constructing A Definition," *Policy Sciences*, 18, no. 4 (1985), pp. 291–294.

21. *Ibid.*, pp. 291, 293.

22. See the discussion in chap. 2 and chap. 4. Throughout this section of chap. 6, I draw on my earlier article "Global Policy and the Future of the UN," *Journal of Peace Research*, 27 (May 1990), pp. 141–154.

23. The ECE example is taken from Johan Kaufmann and Nico Schrijver, *Changing Global Needs: Expanding Roles for The United Nations System* (Hanover, N.H.: Academic Council on the UN System, 1990), p. 50. Kaufmann and Schrijver, on p. 26–28, also point to the role of the UN in contributing to the negotiation of over 300 bilateral investment treaties, regional treaties such as the Inter-Arab Investment Protection Treaty and ASEAN Investment Treaty, and inter-regional agreements such as provisions in the Lome Conventions, as well as establishment of the World Bank's International Center for Settlement of Investment Disputes. As the authors state (p. 28), "even if a comprehensive UN Code of Conduct is never adopted, the discussion and information generated by the [UN Commission] negotiations have had a positive impact in identifying the issues and the problems and, in so doing, have facilitated negotiations in other forums."

24. See J. Chin and Jonathan Mann, "Global Surveillance and Forecasting of AIDS," *Bulletin of the World Health Organization*, 67 (1989), pp. 1–7; and Peter M. Haas, "Ozone Alone, No CFCs: Ecological Epistemic Communities and the Stratospheric Ozone Depletion," *International Organization*, forthcoming. Clearly, there is more consensual knowledge in some technical areas than others. Kaufmann and Schrijver, *op. cit.*, pp. 121–122, point out that while "there is no single UN agency for energy which can provide generally accepted statistics and estimates . . . by and large, balance of payments statistics developed by the International Monetary Fund have acquired undisputed acceptance."

25. The concept of epistemic communities is developed by Peter Haas in *op. cit.* and *Saving the Mediterranean: The Politics of International Environmental Cooperation* (New York: Columbia University Press, 1990). The processes whereby public policy problems and solutions are identified and then acted upon by political systems are discussed in John Kingdon, *Agendas, Alternatives, and Public Policies* (Boston: Little, Brown, 1984). While Kingdon is interested in national policy making, his analysis is relevant to the international political system.

26. Peter H. Sand, *Lessons Learned in Global Environmental Governance* (New York: World Resources Institute, 1990).

27. Richard E. Benedick, "Ozone Diplomacy," *Issues in Science and Technology* (Fall 1989), p. 43. His longer work is *Ozone Diplomacy* (New York: World Wildlife Fund, 1990).

28. Benedick, "Ozone Diplomacy," *op. cit.*, p. 43.

29. *Ibid.* A total of 24 countries signed the Protocol initially. By 1990, over 50 states had become parties, although China and India were notable exceptions. For data on Chinese and Indian shares of CFC consumption, CO_2 emissions, and the implications for global environment policy, see Nazli Choucri and Robert C. North, "Global Environmental Change: Toward A Framework for Decision and Policy," paper presented at International Studies Association annual meeting, Washington, D.C., April 1990.

30. Kaufmann and Schrijver, *op. cit.*, pp. 38–39.

31. *Ibid.*, pp. 52–55 and 118–119.

32. Maurice Strong, Statement to Second Session of Preparatory Committee for UN Conference on Environment and Development, April 2, 1991 (A/Conf. 151/PC/36), pp. 4–7.

33. *Ibid.*, pp. 8–9.

34. These are mentioned in Maurice Strong, Report of the Secretary-General of the UN Conference on Environment and Development to the Preparatory Committee, January 31, 1991 (A/Conf. 151/PC/36), p. 7.

35. *Ibid.*, pp. 4–5.

36. Oran Young has noted the critical role played by individual leaders in regime formation, in "Political Leadership and Regime Formation: On the Development of Institutions in International Society," *International Organization*, 45 (Summer 1991); also see Benedick, *op. cit.*, on the role played by Mostafa Tolba, UNEP's executive director, in the conclusion of the Montreal Protocol.

37. This observation is made by Brian Urquhart in an op-ed piece in *New York Times*, September 24, 1990.

38. Brundtland Commission, *Our Common Future* (Oxford, Eng.: Oxford University Press, 1987), pp. 324–325.

39. There are concerns over the departure of many senior staff members in 1992, including the heads of all major program offices and the Deputy Executive Director due to mandatory retirement regulations. While the Nairobi site of UNEP's secretariat has great symbolic importance to the developing world, it poses a handicap in attracting and retaining world-class expertise.

40. Recommendations along these lines were offered in a "Draft U.S. Proposal for Improving UN Institutional Involvement in Environmental Affairs: Enhancing Central Coordination and the Role of UNEP," a 1991 working paper in preparation for the Rio Conference. Also, see Lee A. Kimball, *Forging International Agreement: Strengthening Intergovernmental Institutions for Environment and Development* (Washington, D.C.: World Resources Institute, April 1992), p.6.

41. Useful proposals for "strengthening international response to humanitarian emergencies" are offered in Urquhart and Childers, "To-

wards A More Effective United Nations," *Development Dialogue*, 2 (1991). The back of the volume contains recommendations issued by the UN General Assembly in 1991.

42. Maurice Bertrand, *Planning, Programming, Budgeting, and Evaluation in the United Nations* (New York: United Nations Association-USA, 1989), p. 35.

43. Göran Ohlin, *The United Nations Contribution to the Improvement of the Human Condition*, mimeo, January 30, 1991, cited in Nordic UN Project, *The United Nations in Development* (Stockholm: Almquist and Wiksell, 1991), p. 29.

44. *Financing the Multilateral System*, Nordic UN Project report no. 13 (1990), cited in *ibid.*, p. 89.

45. Richard Gardner, "Practical Internationalism," *Foreign Affairs*, 66 (Spring 1988), p. 835.

46. Harry Clay Blaney III, *Global Challenges: A World At Risk* (New York: Franklin Watts, 1979), p. 236.

47. On signature and ratification trends, see David L. Larson, "Will There Be an UNCLOS IV?," paper delivered at annual meeting of the International Studies Association, Washington, D.C., April 10–14, 1990.

48. Paul A. Sabatier, "Toward Better Theories of the Policy Process," *PS* 24 (June 1991), p. 147. See also Larry Kiser and Elinor Ostrom, "The Three Worlds of Action," in *Strategies of Political Inquiry*. ed. by Ostrom (Beverly Hills, Calif.: Sage, 1982), pp. 179–222; Ostrom, "An Agenda for the Study of Institutions," *Public Choice*, 48 (1986), pp. 3–25; and Ostrom, *Governing the Commons* (Cambridge, Eng.: Cambridge University Press, 1990).

49. *New York Times*, September 23, 1991, A6.

50. The wording is from Carpenter, *op. cit.*, pp. 37 and 39. Carpenter can be accused of being equally quixotic in his assumptions that states such as the United States can afford to ignore what happens outside their borders and region.

51. Maurice Strong and Aga Khan have suggested the 10% figure. See *International Herald Tribune*, October 9, 1985.

52. Proponents have included Javier Perez de Cuellar and Olaf Palme. See *International Herald Tribune*, April 30, 1986; *UN Chronicle*, 9 (1985), p. 57; and Frederick K. Lister, *Fairness and Accountability in UN Financial Decision Making* (New York: United Nations Association-USA, 1987).

53. Earl C. Ravenal, "The Case for Adjustment," *Foreign Policy*, 81 (Winter 1990–91), pp. 3–19. His analysis and methodology are given larger treatment in *Beyond the Balance of Power: The Future of International Order* (Washington, D.C.: CATO Institute, forthcoming).

54. "The Case for Adjustment," *op. cit.*, pp. 12–13.

55. With regard to greenhouse warming, many observers have noted how the United States and other industrialized countries, even should they develop their own strict environmental safeguards, are essentially hostage to decisions taken on energy policy and other matters by the likes of Brazil and India. See, for example, the comments by Richard Gardner made on a Council of Foreign Relations panel discussion on C-SPAN on July 6, 1991. On arms exports, the agreement reached by the Big Five in 1991 to develop new guidelines for cooperating in limiting arms transfers covered essentially 85% of the world's arm trade. The addition of Brazil and India, growing arms producers and exporters, would have added substantially to the coverage of the regime.

Chapter 7: Waiting for the Millennium

1. Oran R. Young, "The United Nations and the International System," *International Organization*, 20 (Autumn 1968), p. 906.

2. Morton A. Kaplan, *System and Process in International Politics* (New York: John Wiley, 1957); Richard N. Rosecrance, "Bipolarity, Multipolarity, and the Future," *Journal of Conflict Resolution*, 10 (September 1966), pp. 314–327; Oran R. Young, "Political Discontinuities in the International System," *World Politics*, 20 (April 1968), pp. 369–392; Stanley Hoffmann, *Gulliver's Troubles, or The Setting of American Foreign Policy* (New York: McGraw-Hill, 1968); and Hoffmann, "Choices," *Foreign Policy* (Fall 1973), pp. 3–42.

3. Remarks delivered in Landon lectures, Kansas State University, November 8, 1989; cited in "Is the Future What It Used to Be?" *Defense '90* (January-February 1990), p. 2.

4. Allan E. Goodman, "A Brief History of the Future," paper prepared for the Sixth Alumni Conference, Georgetown Leadership Seminar, Berlin, June 23–26, 1991, p.1.

5. Robert Heilbroner first raised this question in *An Inquiry Into the Human Prospect* (New York: W. W. Norton, 1975), p. 13. He reexamines the question in a second edition published in 1991.

6. Representative of this view is John J. Mearsheimer, "Why We Will Soon Miss The Cold War," *The Atlantic*, 266 (August 1990), pp. 35–50.

7. James N. Rosenau, *Turbulence in World Politics* (Princeton, N.J.: Princeton University Press, 1990). Rosenau states that "postinternational politics is an appropriate designation because it clearly suggests the decline of long-standing systemic patterns without at the same time in-

dicating where the changes may be leading." "Global Changes and Theoretical Challenges: Toward A Postinternational Politics for the 1990s," in Ernst-Otto Czempiel and James N. Rosenau, eds., *Global Changes and Theoretical Challenges* (Lexington, Mass.: Lexington Books, 1989), p. 3. In an essay entitled *The United Nations in a Turbulent World* (Boulder, Colo.: Lynne Rienner, 1992), Rosenau attempts to draw out the implications of his analysis for the UN and generally sees the latter benefitting from the "turbulence."

8. For example, note H. J. Mackinder's hypothesizing about the pivotal place of the early twentieth century in the history of the world, particularly as marking the globalization of human relations, in "The Geographical Pivot of History," *Geographic Journal*, 23 (1904).

9. Jeremy Bentham, the nineteenth-century British theorist, is credited with inventing the term "international," while international relations as a distinct field of study traceable to the Peace of Westphalia emerged only in the early twentieth century. Lynn Miller, in *Global Order*, 2nd ed. (Boulder, Colo.: Westview Press, 1990), points out very persuasively that we do not have sufficient perspective to render judgments about the importance of recent developments in the overall scheme of things.

10. Lucian Pye makes the interesting observation that "it is true that in some respects we live in a more nation-bound world than did the Europeans of the nineteenth century. It is, for example, astonishing that it was not considered odd for the tsarist government to raise the funds for fighting the Crimean War by floating bonds on the London market, the same market that the British government was using to cover its own expenses in the same war." "Political Science and the Crisis of Authoritarianism," *American Political Science Review*, 84 (March 1990), p. 6.

11. "A New Kind of Threat: Nuclear Weapons in An Uncertain Soviet Union," U.S. House Armed Services Committee White Paper (September 12, 1991), p. 4.

12. Ernst Haas wrote in 1976 that "theorizing about regional integration as such is no longer profitable as a distinct . . . intellectual pursuit. In that sense . . . regional integration theory is obsolescent." "Turbulent Fields and the Theory of Regional Integration," *International Organization*, 30 (Spring 1976), p. 174.

13. Hans J. Morgenthau, "The New Diplomacy of Movement," *Encounter*, 43 (August 1974), p. 57.

14. Michael Howard, *The Causes of War and Other Essays* (Cambridge, Mass.: Harvard University Press, 1983), p. 22.

15. Remark by Governor Richard Lamm of Colorado, cited in *Christian Science Monitor*, April 24, 1985, p. 5.

16. Oran R. Young, "Odysseus Twenty-five Years On: Reflections on The Study of International Relations," in Joseph R. Kruzel and James N. Rosenau, eds., *Journeys Through World Politics* (Lexington, Mass.: Lexington Books, 1989), p. 76.

17. The phrase is borrowed from the title of the last section of Inis Claude's *Swords Into Plowshares.*

18. Daniel Bell, "The World in 2013," *New Society* (December 8, 1987), p. 35.

19. Cited in Lynn Miller, *Global Order*, 1st ed. (Boulder, Colo.: Westview Press, 1985), p. 215.

20. World Commission on Environment and Development, *Our Common Future* (New York: Oxford University Press, 1987), pp. 264–265.

21. R. J. Johnston and Peter J. Taylor, "Introduction: A World In Crisis?," in Johnston and Taylor, eds., *A World in Crisis? Geographical Perspectives* (Oxford, Eng.: Basil Blackwell, 1986), p. 10.

22. These terms are employed by Robert Keohane in *After Hegemony: Cooperation and Discord in the World Political Economy* (Princeton, N.J.: Princeton University Press, 1984), pp. 245–255. The problem of justice is discussed in Edward Weisband, ed., *Poverty Amidst Plenty* (Boulder, Colo.: Westview Press, 1989); Terry Nardin, *Law, Morality, and the Relations of States* (Princeton, N.J.: Princeton University Press, 1983); and Charles Beitz, *Political Theory and International Relations* (Princeton, N.J.: Princeton University Press, 1979). The "morality of states" view is perhaps most forcefully argued in Robert Tucker's *The Inequality of Nations* (New York: Basic Books, 1977).

23. Reinhold Niebuhr, *Moral Man and Immoral Society: A Study in Ethics and Politics* (New York: Charles Scribner's Sons, 1936), p. 22.

24. Hadley Cantril, *The Politics of Despair* (New York: Basic Books, 1958), pp. 39–42.

25. On learning that occurs in international organizations, see Ernst B. Haas, *When Knowledge Is Power: Three Models of Change in International Organization* (Berkeley, Calif.: University of California Press, 1990).

26. Leon Gordenker, *Thinking About the United Nations System* (Hanover, N.H.: Academic Council on the United Nations System, 1990).

27. Friedrich Kratochwil and John G. Ruggie, "International Organization: A State of the Art on An Art of the State," *International Organization*, 40 (Autumn 1986), p. 772.

28. Robert A. Dahl, *Research Frontiers in Politics and Government* (Washington, D.C.: Brookings Institute, 1955), p. 46.

29. John G. Ruggie, "International Structure and International Transformation: Space, Time and Method," in Czempiel and Rosenau, *op. cit.*, p. 32.

30. John Herz, *International Politics in the Atomic Age* (New York: Columbia University Press, 1959), p. 305.

31. One is also reminded of Winston Churchill's 1936 comments regarding the "spacious conception" of the League of Nations: "You must not underrate the force which these ideals exert. . . . One does not know how these seeds are planted by the winds of the centuries in the hearts of the working people." Cited in Shirley Hazzard, "Breaking Faith," *The New Yorker*, September 25, 1989, p. 76.

32. This is referred to in Johan Kaufmann and Nico Schrijver, *Changing Global Needs: Expanding Roles for the United Nations System* (Hanover, N.H.: Academic Council on the United Nations System, 1990), p. 111.

33. Earl Fry, *et al.*, *America the Vincible* (Englewood Cliffs, N.J.: Prentice-Hall, forthcoming).

34. Maurice Strong, Statement to Second Session of Preparatory Committee for UN Conference on Environment and Development, April 2, 1991, p. 13.

Select Bibliography

Alger, Chadwick F. "Grass-roots Perspectives on Global Policies for Development," *Journal of Peace Research*, 27 (May 1990), pp. 155–168.

Archer, Clive. *International Organizations*. London: Allen and Unwin, 1983.

Atlantic Council Working Group on the United Nations. *The Future of the UN: A Strategy for Like-Minded Nations*. Boulder, Colo.: Westview Press, 1977.

Axelrod, Robert and Robert O. Keohane. "Achieving Cooperation Under Anarchy: Strategies and Institutions," *World Politics*, 38 (October 1985), pp. 226–254.

Baratta, Joseph P. *Strengthening the United Nations: A Bibliography on UN Reform and World Federalism*. Westport, Conn.: Greenwood Press, 1987.

Beigbeder, Yves. *Management Problems in United Nations Organizations: Reform or Decline?* New York: St. Martin's Press, 1987.

Benedick, Richard E. *Ozone Diplomacy*. New York: World Wildlife Fund, 1990.

Bergsten, C. Fred. "Interdependence and the Reform of International Institutions," *International Organization*, 30 (Spring 1976), pp. 361–372.

Berridge, G. R. *Return to the UN: UN Diplomacy in Regional Conflicts*. New York: St. Martin's Press, 1990.

Bertrand, Maurice. "Some Reflections on Reform of the United Nations," UN Doc. JIU/REP/85/9, 1985.

Bertrand, Maurice. *Planning, Programming, Budgeting, and Evaluation*. New York: UNA-USA, 1987.

Bertrand, Maurice. *The Role of the UN in the Economic and Social Fields*. New York: UNA-USA, 1987.

Bilder, Richard. *Managing the Risks of International Agreement*. Madison, Wisc.: University of Wisconsin Press, 1981.

Blaney, Harry Clay III. *Global Challenges: A World At Risk*. New York: Franklin Watts, 1979.

Boulding, Kenneth. *The Three Faces of Power*. Beverly Hills, Calif.: Sage, 1989.

Boutros-Ghali, Boutros. "An Agenda for Peace," UN Doc. A/47/277 and S/24111, 1992.

Bremer, Stuart A. *The GLOBUS Model*. Boulder, Colo.: Westview Press, 1987.

Bremer, Stuart A. and Barry B. Hughes. *Disarmament and Development: A Design for the Future?* Engelwood Cliffs, N.J.: Prentice-Hall, 1990.

Brown, Seyom and Larry Fabian. "Toward Mutual Accountability in the Nonterrestrial Realm," *International Organization*, 29 (Summer 1975), pp. 877–892.

Brown, Seyom. *New Forces, Old Forces, and the Future Of World Politics*. Boston: Little, Brown, 1988.

Brundtland Commission. *Our Common Future*. Oxford, Eng.: Oxford University Press, 1987.

Bull, Hedley. *The Anarchical Society*. London: Macmillan, 1977.

Buzan, Barry. *People, States, and Fear*. Chapel Hill: University of North Carolina Press, 1983.

Calleo, David P. *Beyond American Hegemony*. New York: Basic Books, 1987.

Caporaso, James A. "International Relations Theory and Multilateralism: The Search for Foundations," *International Organization*, 46 (Summer 1992), pp. 599–632.

Carpenter, Ted Galen. "The New World Disorder," *Foreign Policy*, 84 (Fall 1991), pp. 24–39.

Carr, E. H. *The Twenty Years' Crisis, 1919–1939*. London: Macmillan, 1939.

Childers, Erskine and Brian Urquhart. *A World in Need of Leadership: Tomorrow's United Nations*. New York: Ford Foundation, 1990.

Claude, Inis, Jr. "Collective Legitimization As A Political Function of the United Nations," *International Organization*, 20 (Summer 1966), pp. 367–379.

Claude, Inis, Jr. "The Record of International Organizations in the Twentieth Century," Tamkang Chair Lecture Series, No. 64, Tamkang University, Taiwan (mimeo), 1986.

Claude, Inis, Jr. *Swords into Plowshares*, 4th ed. New York: Random House, 1984.

Coate, Roger A. *Unilateralism, Ideology, and US Foreign Policy: The United States In and Out of UNESCO*. Boulder, Colo.: Lynne Rienner, 1989.

Coate, Roger A. and Donald J. Puchala. "Global Policies and the United Nations System: A Current Assessment," *Journal of Peace Research*, 27 (May 1990), pp. 127–140.

Conybeare, John. "International Organization and the Theory of Property Rights," *International Organization*, 34 (Summer 1980), pp. 307–334.

Cox, Robert W. and Harold K. Jacobson. *The Anatomy of Influence: Decision-Making in International Organization*. New Haven, Conn.: Yale University Press, 1973.

Cox, Robert W. "On Thinking About Future World Order," *World Politics*, 28 (January 1976), pp. 175–196.

Cox, Robert W. *Production, Power and World Order*. New York: Columbia University Press, 1987.

Cox, Robert W. "Social Forces, States, and World Order," in Robert O. Keohane, ed., *Neorealism and Its Critics*. New York: Columbia University Press, 1986.

DeGara, John. *Administrative and Financial Reform of the United Nations: A Documentary Essay*. Hanover, N.H.: Academic Council on the UN System, 1989.

Deutsch, Karl W., et. al. *Political Community and the North Atlantic Area*. Princeton, N.J.: Princeton University Press, 1957.

Diehl, Paul F. "A Permanent UN Peacekeeping Force: An Evaluation," *Bulletin of Peace Proposals*, 20, no. 1, (1989), pp. 27–36.

Dixon, William J. "The Evaluation of Weighted Voting Schemes for the United Nations General Assembly," *International Studies Quarterly*, 27 (September 1983), pp. 295–314.

Durch, William J. and Barry M. Blechman. *Keeping the Peace: The United Nations in the Emerging World Order*. Washington, D.C.: Henry L. Stimson Center, 1992.

Falk, Richard. "The Global Promise of Social Movements: Explorations at the Edge of Time," *Alternatives*, 12, (1987), pp. 173–196.

Falk, Richard, Friedrich Kratochwil, and Saul H. Mendlovitz. *International Law: A Contemporary Perspective*. Boulder, Colo.: Westview Press, 1985.

Falk, Richard. "A New Paradigm for International Legal Studies: Prospects and Proposals," in Falk, Friedrich Kratochwil, and Saul H.

Mendlovitz (ed.), *International Law: A Contemporary Perspective*. Boulder, Colo.: Westview Press, 1985.

Fardoust, Shahrokh and Ashok Dhareshwar. *A Long-Term Outlook for the World Economy: Issues and Perspectives for the 1990s*. Washington, D.C.: World Bank, 1990.

Fomerand, Jacques. *Strengthening the UN Economic and Social Programs: A Documentary Essay*. Hanover, N.H.: Academic Council on UN System, 1990.

Fromuth, Peter. *The UN at 40: The Problems and the Opportunities*. New York: UNA-USA, 1986.

Fromuth, Peter and Ruth Raymond. *UN Personnel Policy Issues*. New York: UNA-USA, 1987.

Fukuyama, Francis. "The End of History?," *The National Interest*, 16 (Summer 1989), pp. 3-16.

Galey, Margaret. "The Changing International Regime for Financing International Organization: Regime Change vs. Reform," paper presented at International Studies Association annual meeting, St. Louis, March 29, 1988.

Gallarotti, Guilio. "The Limits of International Organization: Systematic Failure in the Management of International Relations," *International Organization*, 45 (Spring 1991), pp. 183–220.

Gamble, John King. "Reservations to Multilateral Treaties: A Macroscopic View of State Practice," *American Journal of International Law*, 74 (April 1980), pp. 372–394.

Gardner, Richard. "The Case for Practical Internationalism," *Foreign Affairs*, 66 (Spring 1988), pp. 827–845.

Gilpin, Robert G. "The Richness of the Tradition of Political Realism," *International Organization*, 38 (Spring 1984), pp. 287–304.

Gilpin, Robert G. *War and Change in World Politics*. Cambridge, Eng.: Cambridge University Press, 1981.

Gorbachev, Mikhail. *Realities and Guarantees for A Secure World*. Moscow: Novosti Press, 1987.

Gowa, Joanne. "Anarchy, Egoism, and Third Images: *The Evolution of Cooperation* and International Regimes," *International Organization*, 40 (Winter 1986), pp. 167–186.

Gregg, Robert W. "The Politics of Financing the UN," paper presented at International Studies Association annual meeting, St. Louis, March 29, 1988.

Grieco, Joseph. "Anarchy and the Limits of Cooperation: A Realist Critique of the Newest Liberal Institutionalism," *International Organization*, 42 (Summer 1988), pp. 486–507.

Group of Experts on the Structure of the United Nations System. *A New United Nations Structure for Global Economic Cooperation.* New York: United Nations, 1975.

Grunberg, Isabelle. "Exploring the 'Myth' of Hegemonic Stability," *International Organization*, 44 (Autumn 1990), pp. 431–477.

Haas, Ernst B. "Turbulent Fields and the Theory of Regional Integration," *International Organization*, 30 (Spring 1976), pp. 173–212.

Haas, Ernst B. *When Knowledge Is Power: Three Models of Change in International Organizations.* Berkeley, Calif.: University of California Press, 1990.

Haas, Ernst B. "Why Collaborate? Issue Linkage and International Regimes," *World Politics*, 32 (April 1980), pp. 357–405.

Haas, Ernst B. *Why We Still Need the United Nations: The Collective Management of International Conflict, 1945–1984.* Berkeley, Calif.: Institute of International Studies, 1986.

Haas, Peter M. *Saving the Mediterranean: The Politics of International Environmental Cooperation.* New York: Columbia University Press, 1990.

Haggard, Stephen and Beth Simmons. "Theories of International Regimes," *International Organization*, 41 (Summer 1987), pp. 491–517.

Hanrieder, Wolfram. "International Organizations and International Systems," *Journal of Conflict Resolution*, 10 (September 1966), pp. 297–313.

Hanrieder, Wolfram. "Dissolving International Politics: Reflections on the Nation-State," *American Political Science Review*, 72 (December 1978), pp. 1276–1287.

Haslam, Jonathan. "The UN and the Soviet Union: New Thinking?," *International Affairs*, 65 (Autumn 1989), pp. 678–688.

Herz, John H. *Political Realism and Political Idealism.* Chicago, Ill.: University of Chicago Press, 1951.

Herz, John H. *International Politics in the Atomic Age.* New York: Columbia University Press, 1959.

Herz, John H. "Political Realism Revisited," *International Studies Quarterly*, 25 (June 1981), pp. 182–197.

Higgot, Richard A. and Andrew Fenton Cooper. "Middle Power Leadership and Coalition Building: Australia, The Cairns Group, and the

Uruguay Round of Trade Negotiations," *International Organization*, 44 (Autumn 1990), pp. 589–632.

Hoffmann, Stanley. "International Organization and the International System," *International Organization*, 24 (Summer 1970), pp. 389–413.

Hoffmann, Stanley. *Primacy or World Order*. New York: McGraw-Hill, 1978.

Hough, Jerry. *Russia and the West: Gorbachev and the Politics of Reform*, 2nd ed., New York: Simon and Shuster, 1990.

Howard, Rhoda E. and Jack Donnelly. "Human Dignity, Human Rights and Political Regimes," *American Political Science Review*, 80 (September 1986), pp. 801–817.

Hughes, Thomas. "The Twilight of Internationalism," *Foreign Policy*, 61 (Winter 1985–86), pp. 25–48.

Huntington, Samuel P. *Political Order in Changing Societies*. New Haven, Conn.: Yale University Press, 1968.

Huntington, Samuel P. "The Goals of Development," in Myron Weiner and Huntington, eds., *Understanding Political Development*. Boston: Little, Brown, 1987.

Huntington, Samuel P. "The U.S.—Decline or Renewal?," *Foreign Affairs*, 67 (Winter 1989), pp. 79–96.

Ikenberry, G. John and Charles A. Kupchan. "Socialization and Hegemonic Power," *International Organization*, 44 (Summer 1990), pp. 283–316.

Jacobson, Harold K. "The Global System and the Realization of Human Dignity and Justice," *International Studies Quarterly*, 26 (September 1982), pp. 315–331.

Jacobson, Harold K., William M. Reisinger, and Todd Mathers. "National Entanglements in International Governmental Organizations," *American Political Science Review*, 80 (March 1986), pp. 141–159.

James, Alan. *Peacekeeping in International Politics*. London: Macmillan, 1990.

Jervis, Robert. "Realism, Game Theory, and Cooperation," *World Politics*, 40 (April 1988), pp. 317–349.

Jones, Dorothy V. *Code of Peace: Ethics and Security in the Warlord States*. Chicago, Ill.: University of Chicago Press, 1991.

Jonsson, Christer. "Interorganization Theory and International Organization," *International Studies Quarterly*, 30 (March 1986), pp. 39–57.

Kahler, Miles. "Multilateralism with Small and Large Numbers," *International Organization*, 46 (Summer 1992), pp. 681–708.

Karns, Margaret and Karen A. Mingst, eds. *The United States and Multilateral Institutions*. Boston: Unwin Hyman, 1990.

Kaufmann, Johan and Nico Schrijver. *Changing Global Needs: Expanding Roles for the UN System*. Hanover, N.H.: Academic Council on the UN System, 1990.

Kaysen, Carl. "Is War Obsolete? A Review Essay," *International Security*, 14 (Spring 1990), pp. 42–64.

Kegley, Charles W. "The Bush Administration and the Future of American Foreign Policy: Pragmatism or Procrastination?," *Presidential Studies Quarterly*, 19 (Fall 1989), pp. 719–729.

Kegley, Charles W. "The Neoidealist Moment in International Studies?" paper presented at International Studies Association annual meeting, Acapulco, March 25, 1993.

Kegley, Charles W. and Steven W. Hook. "US Foreign Aid and UN Voting: Did Reagan's Linkage Strategy Buy Deference or Defiance?," *International Studies Quarterly*, 35 (September 1991), pp. 295–312.

Kennedy, David. "The Move to Institutions," *Cardozo Law Review*, 8 (April 1987), pp. 841–888.

Kennedy, Paul. *The Rise and Fall of the Great Powers*. New York: Random House, 1987.

Keohane, Robert O. *After Hegemony: Cooperation and Discord in the World Political Economy*. Princeton, N.J.: Princeton University Press, 1984.

Keohane, Robert O., ed. *Neorealism and Its Critics*. New York: Columbia University Press, 1986.

Keohane, Robert O. and Joseph S. Nye. *Power and Interdependence*, 2nd ed. Glenview, Ill.: Scott, Foresman, 1989.

Keohane, Robert O. and Joseph S. Nye. *Transnational Relations and World Politics*. Cambridge, Mass.: Harvard University Press, 1971.

Keohane, Robert O. and Joseph S. Nye. "Two Cheers for Multilateralism," *Foreign Policy*, 60 (Fall 1985), pp. 148–167.

Kim, Samuel S. *China, the United Nations, and World Order*. Princeton, N.J.: Princeton University Press, 1979.

Kim, Samuel S. "Thinking Globally in Post-Mao China," *Journal of Peace Research*, 27 (May 1990), pp. 191–209.

Kimball, Lee A. *Forging International Agreement: Strengthening Intergovernmental Institutions for Environment and Development*. Washington, D.C.: World Resources Institute, 1992.

Kindleberger, Charles P. *The World in Depression, 1929–1938*. Berkeley, Calif.: University of California Press, 1973.

Kindleberger, Charles P. "Hierarchy Versus Inertial Cooperation," *International Organization*, 40 (Autumn 1986), pp. 841–847.

King, Alexander and Bertrand Schneider. *The First Global Revolution.* New York: Pantheon, 1991.

Kirkpatrick, Jeanne. "The United Nations as a Political System: A Practicing Political Scientist's Insights into UN Policy," *World Affairs*, 146 (Spring 1984), pp. 358–364.

Krasner, Stephen D., ed. *International Regimes.* Ithaca, N.Y.: Cornell University Press, 1983.

Krasner, Stephen D. *Structural Conflict: The Third World Against Global Liberalism.* Berkeley, Calif.: University of California Press, 1985.

Kratochwil, Friedrich and John G. Ruggie. "International Organization: A State of the Art on an Art of the State," *International Organization*, 40 (Autumn 1986), pp. 753–776.

Kugler, Jacek and A.F.K. Organski. "The End of Hegemony?," *International Interactions*, 15, no. 2 (1989), pp. 102–119.

Legvold, Robert. "The Revolution in Soviet Foreign Policy," *Foreign Affairs*, 68, (1989), pp. 82–98.

Levy, Jack. *War in the Modern Great Power System, 1495–1975.* Lexington: University of Kentucky Press, 1983.

Lister, Frederick K. *Fairness and Accountability in UN Financial Decision-Making.* New York: UNA-USA, 1987.

Mansbach, Richard W. and John A. Vasquez. *In Search of Theory: A New Paradigm for Global Politics.* New York: Columbia University Press, 1981.

March, James G. and Johan P. Olsen. *Rediscovering Institutions.* New York: Free Press, 1989.

Martin, Lisa. "Interest, Power, and Multilateralism," *International Organization*, 46 (Autumn 1992), pp. 765–792.

Martin-Bosch, Miguel. "How Nations Vote in the General Assembly of the United Nations," *International Organization*, 41 (Autumn 1987), pp. 705–724.

Masters, Roger. "The Biological Nature of the State." *World Politics*, 35 (January 1983), pp. 161–193.

McKinlay, R. D. and R. Little. *Global Problems and World Order.* Madison: University of Wisconsin Press, 1986.

Meadows, Donella H. *Beyond the Limits.* Post Mills, Vt: Chelsea Green, 1992.

Meehan, Eugene. "Policy: Constructing A Definition," *Policy Sciences*, 18, no. 4, (1985), pp. 295–305.

Meltzer, Ronald I. "Restructuring the United Nations System: Institutional Reform Efforts in the Context of North-South Relations," *International Organization*, 32 (Autumn 1978), pp. 993–1018.

Michalak, Stanley J. "The League of Nations and the United Nations in World Politics: A Plea for Comparative Research on Universal International Organizations," *International Studies Quarterly*, 15 (December 1971), pp. 387–441.

Miller, Lynn H. *Global Order*, 2nd ed. Boulder, Colo.: Westview Press, 1990.

Modelski, George. "Is World Politics Evolutionary Learning?," *International Organization*, 44 (Winter 1990), pp. 1–24.

Morgenthau, Hans J. "The New Diplomacy of Movement," *Encounter*, 43 (August 1974), pp. 57–68.

Moynihan, Daniel P. *A Dangerous Place*. New York: Berkeley Books, 1980.

Mueller, John. *Retreat from Doomsday*. New York: Basic Books, 1989.

Nardin, Terry. *Law, Morality, and the Relations of States*. Princeton, N.J.: Princeton University Press, 1983.

Nau, Henry R. *The Myth of America's Decline: Leading the World Economy into the 1990s*. New York: Oxford University Press, 1990.

Nerfin, Mark. "The Future of the UN System—Some Questions on the Occasion of an Anniversary," *Development Dialogue*, 1 (1985).

Ness, Gayle D. and Stevin R. Brechin. "Bridging the Gap: International Organizations As Organizations," *International Organization*, 42 (Spring 1988), pp. 245–273.

Newcombe, Hanna. "Revamping the UN Voting Structure," in *Solutions for A Troubled World*, Mark Macy, ed. Boulder, Colo.: Earthview Press, 1987.

Niou, Emerson and Peter C. Ordeshook. "Stability in Anarchic International Systems," *American Political Science Review*, 84 (December 1990), pp. 1207–1234.

North, Robert. *War, Peace, Survival*. Boulder, Colo.: Westview Press, 1990.

Nordic UN Project. *The United Nations in Development*. Stockholm: Almgvist and Wiksell, 1991.

Nye, Joseph S. *Bound to Lead: The Changing Nature of American Power*. New York: Basic Books, 1990.

Nye, Joseph S. "Neorealism and Neoliberalism," *World Politics*, 40 (January 1988), pp. 235–251.

Ogata, Sadako. "The Changing Role of Japan in the United Nations," *Journal of International Affairs*, 37 (Summer 1983), pp. 36–46.

Oye, Kenneth, ed. *Cooperation Under Anarchy*. Princeton, N.J.: Princeton University Press, 1986.

Palme Commission. *Common Security: A Programme for Disarmament*. London: Pan, 1982.

Pearson, Frederic S. and J. Martin Rochester. "The Carter Foreign Policy and the Use of International Organization: The Limits of Policy Innovation," *World Affairs*, 142 (Fall 1979), pp. 75–97.

Peterson, M. J. *The General Assembly in World Politics*. Boston: Unwin and Allen, 1986.

Pirages, Dennis. *Global Technopolitics*. Pacific Grove, Calif.: Brooks/Cole, 1989.

Puchala, Donald J. and Roger A. Coate. *The Challenge of Relevance: The United Nations in a Changing World Environment*. Hanover, N.H.: Academic Council on the UN System, 1989.

Puchala, Donald J. and Roger A. Coate. *The State of the United Nations, 1988*. Hanover, N.H.: Academic Council on the UN System, 1988.

Pye, Lucian. "Political Science and the Crisis of Authoritarianism," *American Political Science Review*, 84 (March 1990), pp. 3–19.

Ravenal, Earl C. "The Case for Adjustment," *Foreign Policy*, 81 (Winter 1991), pp. 3–19.

Ravenal, Earl C. *Beyond the Balance of Power: The Future of International Order*. Washington, D.C.: CATO Institute, 1992.

Ray, James Lee. "The Abolition of Slavery and the End of International War," *International Organization*, 43 (Summer 1989), pp. 405–440.

Renninger, John. *Early Warning: What Role for the UN*. New York: UNITAR, 1989.

Riggs, Robert E. and Jack C. Plano. *The United Nations: International Organization and World Politics*. Chicago, Ill.: Dorsey Press, 1988.

Rikhye, Indar Jit. *The Future of Peacekeeping*. New York: International Peace Academy, 1989.

Rochester, J. Martin. "The Rise and Fall of International Organization as a Field of Study," *International Organization*, 40 (Autumn 1986), pp. 777-813.

Rosecrance, Richard. *The Rise of the Trading State*. New York: Basic Books, 1986.

Rosenau, James N. "Before Cooperation: Hegemons, Regimes, and Habit-Driven Actors in World Politics," *International Organization,* 40 (Autumn 1986), pp. 849–894.

Rosenau, James N. "Global Changes and Theoretical Challenges: Toward A Postinternational Politics for the 1990s," in Ernst-Otto Czempiel and Rosenau, eds., *Global Changes and Theoretical Challenges.* Lexington, Mass.: Lexington Books, 1989.

Rosenau, James N. *Turbulence in World Politics.* Princeton, N.J.: Princeton University Press, 1990.

Rosenau, James N. *The United Nations In A Turbulent World.* Boulder, Colo.: Lynne Rienner, 1992.

Ruggie, John G. "The United States and the United Nations: Toward a New Realism," *International Organization,* 39 (Spring 1985), pp. 343–356.

Ruggie, John G. "Multilateralism: The Anatomy of An Institution," *International Organization,* 46 (Summer 1992), pp. 561–598.

Ruggie, John G. "Territoriality and Beyond," *International Organization,* 47 (Winter 1993), pp. 139–174.

Russett, Bruce M. "The Mysterious Case of Vanishing Hegemony: Or Is Mark Twain Really Dead?," *International Organization,* 39 (Spring 1985), pp. 207–232.

Russett, Bruce M. and James S. Sutterlin. "The UN In A New World Order," *Foreign Affairs,* 70 (Spring 1991), pp. 69–83.

Sand, Peter H. *Lessons Learned in Global Environmental Governance.* New York: World Resources Institute, 1990.

Sherry, George L. *The United Nations Reborn.* New York: Council on Foreign Relations, 1990.

Simes, Dimitri. "Russia Reborn," *Foreign Policy,* 85 (Winter 1991–92), pp. 41–62.

Snidal, Duncan. "The Game Theory of International Politics," *World Politics,* 38 (October 1985), pp. 25–57.

Snidal, Duncan. "The Limits of Hegemonic Stability Theory," *International Organization,* 39 (Autumn 1985), pp. 579–614.

Soroos, Marvin S. *Beyond Sovereignty: The Challenge of Global Policy.* Columbia, S.C.: University of South Carolina Press, 1986.

Spiezo, K. Edward. "British Hegemony and Major Power War, 1815–1939: An Empirical Test of Gilpin's Model of Hegemonic Governance," *International Studies Quarterly,* 34 (June 1990), pp. 165–181.

Steele, David. *The Reform of the United Nations.* London: Croom Helm, 1987.

Steiner, Miriam. "Human Nature and Truth as World Order Issues," *International Organization,* 34 (Summer 1980), pp. 335–354.

Sullivan, Michael J. III. *Measuring Global Values: The Ranking of 162 Countries.* Westport, Conn.: Greenwood Press, 1991.

Tamamoto, Masaru. "Japan's Search for A World Role," *World Policy Journal,* 7 (Summer 1990), pp. 493–520.

Thompson, Janice E. and Stephen D. Krasner. "Global Transactions and the Consolidation of Sovereignty," in Ernst-Otto Czempiel and James N. Rosenau, eds., *Global Changes and Theoretical Challenges.* Lexington, Mass.: Lexington Books, 1980.

Tilly, Charles, ed., *The Formation of National States in Western Europe.* Princeton, N.J.: Princeton University Press, 1975.

Tilly, Charles. *Coercion, Capital, and European States, A.D. 90–1990.* Cambridge, Eng.: Basil Blackwell, 1990.

Tucker, Robert. *The Inequality of Nations.* New York: Basic Books, 1977.

United Nations Association - USA. *A Successor Vision: The United Nations of Tomorrow.* New York: UNA-USA, 1987.

United Nations. *The Blue Helmets,* 2nd ed. New York: United Nations, 1991.

Urquhart, Brian. "The United Nations System and the Future," *International Affairs,* 65 (Spring 1989), pp. 225–231.

Urquhart, Brian and Erskine Childers. "A World In Need of Leadership: Tomorrow's United Nations," *Development Dialogue,* 1–2 (1990).

Urquhart, Brian and Erskine Childers. "Towards A More Effective United Nations," *Development Dialogue,* 1–2 (1991).

Vayrynen, Raimo. "Is There a Role for the United Nations in Conflict Resolution?," *Journal of Peace Research,* 22 (1985), pp. 189–196.

Waldheim, Kurt. "The United Nations: The Tarnished Image," *Foreign Affairs,* 63 (Fall 1984), pp. 93–107.

Walker, R. B. J. *Culture, Ideology, and World Order.* Boulder, Colo.: Westview Press, 1984.

Waltz, Kenneth N. "Nuclear Myths and Political Realities," *American Political Science Review,* 84 (September 1990), pp. 732–745.

Waltz, Kenneth N. *Theory of International Politics.* Reading, Mass.: Addison-Wesley, 1979.

Weiss, Thomas and Meryl A. Kessler. "Moscow's UN Policy," *Foreign Policy*, 79 (Summer 1990), pp. 94–112.

Wilkenfeld, Jonathan and Michael Brecher. "International Crises 1945–1975: The UN Dimension," *International Studies Quarterly*, 28 (March 1984), pp. 45–67.

Williams, Douglas. *The Specialized Agencies and the United Nations: The System in Crisis*. London: Hurst, 1987.

Young, Oran R. "The United Nations and the International System," *International Organization*, 22 (Autumn 1968), pp. 902–922.

Young, Oran R. "International Regimes: Problems of Concept Formation," *World Politics*, 32 (April 1980), pp. 331–356.

Young, Oran R. "International Regimes: Toward a New Theory of Institutions," *World Politics*, 39 (October 1986), pp. 104–122.

Young, Oran R. "Political Leadership and Regime Formation: On the Development of Institutions in International Society," *International Organization*, 45 (Summer 1991), pp. 281–308.

Young, Oran R. "Regime Dynamics: The Rise and Fall Of International Regimes," *International Organization*, 36 (Spring 1982), pp. 277–298.

Zacher, Mark W. "The Decaying Pillars of the Westphalian Temple: Implications for International Order and Governance," paper presented at International Studies Association annual meeting, Vancouver, March 22, 1991.

Index